"Jack Kornfield offers a friendly, warm and eminently useful guide to the meditator's path, brimming with clarity. *A Path with Heart* is an ideal companion for anyone exploring the life of the spirit."   —Daniel Goleman

"Reading *A Path with Heart* is a rich and satisfying experience. God bless Jack Kornfield! He is always deep, always honest, always cuts to the bone of the matter."
    —Sherry Ruth Anderson, co-author of *The Feminine Face of God*

"Once again Jack Kornfield demonstrates his breadth of knowledge and experience of the mindscape and heart rhythm of the spiritual, and particularly the meditative, journey. With an open-hearted expertise rare in a Westerner, Jack offers a benevolent travelogue along the Way."
    —Stephen Levine

"It's the mixture that makes Jack's book work so wonderfully well. Humor, ordinary stories, exact advice for critical moments, huge learning of his discipline, and a happy heart—what a pleasant path into the depths."
    —James Hillman

"Our psychological and spiritual processes are too often treated as discrete. *A Path with Heart* happily shows how Humpty Dumpty can be put back together again!"   —Ram Dass

"Kornfield shows that what happens in meditation is a paradigm for life. Through wonderful stories and personal anecdotes, Kornfield shows both the depths and simplicity of Buddhist practice in everyday life."
    —Linda Leonard

"Jack Kornfield, drawing on his combined background as a Buddhist monk and teacher as well as an academically trained psychologist, has succeeded in presenting the most profound Buddhist philosophy and psychology in an easy-to-read, heartful and humorous style. Wonderful. This unique blend of spiritual teaching, poetry, psychological insight and simple life wisdom is by far the most significant book of American Buddhism."
    —Stanislav Grof

Other Books by Jack Kornfield

Living Buddhist Masters
A Still Forest Pool (with Paul Breiter)
Seeking the Heart of Wisdom (with Joseph Goldstein)
Stories of the Spirit, Stories of the Heart (with Christina Feldman)
Sayings of the Buddha

For Information About Insight Meditation Write to:

Spirit Rock Center
P.O. Box 909-B
Woodacre, California 94973

For Tapes of Lectures and Guided Meditations Write to:

Dharma Seed Tape Library
P.O. Box 66-B
Wendell Depot, Massachusetts 01380

A PATH WITH HEART

A Guide Through the Perils
and Promises of Spiritual Life

JACK KORNFIELD

BANTAM BOOKS

NEW YORK · TORONTO · LONDON · SYDNEY · AUCKLAND

A PATH WITH HEART

A Bantam Book / July 1993

All rights reserved.
Copyright © 1993 by Jack Kornfield.

BOOK DESIGN BY DONNA SINISGALLI

Library of Congress Cataloging-in-Publication Data

Kornfield, Jack, 1945–
A path with heart : a guide through the perils and promises of spiritual life /
Jack Kornfield.
p.   cm.
Includes bibliographical references.
ISBN 0-553-37211-4 (alk. paper)
1. Spiritual life—Buddhism.   I. Title.
BQ5660.K67   1993   92-42894
294.3′444—dc20   CIP

Published simultaneously in the United States and Canada

Bantam Books are published by Bantam Books, a division of Bantam
Doubleday Dell Publishing Group, Inc. Its trademark, consisting of the
words "Bantam Books" and the portrayal of a rooster, is Registered in
U.S. Patent and Trademark Office and in other countries. Marca
Registrada. Bantam Books, 1540 Broadway, New York, New York 10036.

PRINTED IN THE UNITED STATES OF AMERICA

BVG   0 9

To my wife, Liana,
from whom I've learned so much,
for her love, wisdom,
deep questioning, and heartfelt support,
and for the blessings of our marriage together.

To Hameed Ali, A. H. Almaas,
for his teachings
that so profoundly integrate life, love, and the sacred.

To the spirit of innovation
of Achaan Chah, the Dalai Lama, Mahasi Sayadaw,
Buddhadasa Bhikkhu,
Chogyam Trungpa, Maha Ghosananda, U Ba Khin,
and
so many other courageous modern masters.

CONTENTS

PART III

Widening Our Circle   169

ACKNOWLEDGMENTS

Without Evelyn Sweeney this book would not have been possible. A senior student, editor, friend, and assistant, Evelyn has helped in all aspects of the creation of this manuscript. She is a tireless worker who at seventy-three is a pillar of support to our community and a wellspring of energy for this book and the books of several other vipassana teachers as well. Thank you, Evelyn. May the dharma you have offered bring blessings and happiness to you again and again.

I would like to express my gratitude for the crystal clarity and deep dharma wisdom of Jane Hirshfield. She is a poet, a writer, and a clear-eyed student of the dharma whose help has been invaluable. The structure and content of this book has benefited in every chapter by having her as my key editor and adviser.

Barbara Gates, writer, editor, and friend in the dharma, has also helped this manuscript greatly by bushwhacking through several of the early chapters, creating a clear and orderly garden out of the thickets of my dharma talks. I offer her my thanks.

This book began as talks given to the Spiritual Emergency Network in 1986. The Spiritual Emergency Network is a group of psychologists and spiritual counselors who offer support to those going through the powerful spiritual transitions that are poorly understood in our culture and often confused with mental illness. For this work, I express my respect.

It is important to acknowledge that over the years much of my dharma has been learned from teaching colleagues. In particular, I owe a great deal to my good friends Joseph Goldstein, Sharon Salzberg, and Stephen Levine, as well as to Stan and Christina Grof, and honor them as the source of certain important themes of this book.

Beyond this I have had the blessings of many great teachers in Asia, Europe, and North America. To them I am grateful beyond measure.

I thank all of the many students and colleagues I've had the privilege of learning from over these years. Their stories used in this book are true. However, names and particulars have been changed to respect individual privacy.

Finally, I wish to honor Leslie Meredith of Bantam Books, who has been a splendid editor, knowledgeable reader, and supportive friend through the whole development of this book.

Jack Kornfield
Spirit Rock Center
Woodacre, California
1992

PART 1

A PATH WITH HEART: THE FUNDAMENTALS

A BEGINNING

*In beginning this book I have emphasized my
own personal journey, because the greatest lesson I have learned is that the universal must be
wedded to the personal to be fulfilled in our
spiritual life.*

In the summer of 1972 I returned to the home of my parents in
Washington, D.C., head shaved and robed as a Buddhist monk, after
my first five-year study in Asia. No Theravada Buddhist monasteries had
been established in America at that time, but I wanted to see how it
would be to live as a monk in America, even if for only a short while.
After several weeks with my parents, I decided to visit my twin brother
and his wife on Long Island. With my robes and bowl I boarded a train
en route from Washington to New York's Grand Central Station, carrying
a ticket my mother had purchased for me—as a renunciate, I was not
using or handling money myself.

I arrived that afternoon and began to walk up Fifth Avenue to meet
my sister-in-law. I was still very calm after so many years of practice. I
walked as if I were meditating, letting shops such as Tiffany's and the
crowds of passersby be the same in my mind as the wind and the trees

of my forest monastery. I was to meet my sister-in-law in front of Elizabeth Arden's. She had been given a birthday certificate for a full day of care in that establishment, including facial, hairdo, massage, manicure, and more. I arrived at Elizabeth Arden's at four o'clock as promised, but she did not appear. After some period of waiting, I went inside. "May I help you?" exclaimed the shocked receptionist as I entered. "Yes, I'm looking for Tori Kornfield." "Oh," she replied. "She's not finished yet. There's a waiting lounge on the fourth floor." So I took the elevator to the fourth floor. Coming out of the door, I met the waiting lounge receptionist, who also inquired in a slightly incredulous tone, "May I help you?" I told her I was waiting for my sister-in-law and was instructed to take a seat.

I sat on a comfortable couch, and after waiting a few minutes, I decided to cross my legs, close my eyes, and meditate. I was a monk after all, and what else was there to do? After ten minutes I began to hear laughter and noises. I continued to meditate, but finally I heard a group of voices and a loud exclamation of "Is he for real?" from the hall across the room, which caused me to open my eyes. I saw eight or ten women dressed in Elizabeth Arden "nighties" (the gowns given them for the day) staring at me. Many had their hair in rollers or in other multiple fishing-reel-shaped contraptions. Several had what looked like green avocado smeared on their faces. Others were covered with mud. I looked back at them and wondered what realm I had been born into and heard myself say, "Are they for real?"

From that moment, it became clear that I would have to find a way to reconcile the ancient and wonderful teachings I had received at the Buddhist monastery with the ways of our modern world. Over the years, this reconciliation has become one of the most interesting and compelling inquiries for me and for many other people seeking to live a genuine spiritual life as we enter the twenty-first century. Most Americans do not wish to live as traditional priests or monks or nuns, yet many of us wish to bring a genuine spiritual practice to life in our own world. This book will speak to this possibility.

My own spiritual life was triggered at age fourteen by the gift of T. Lobsang Rampa's book *The Third Eye*, a semifictional account of mystical adventures in Tibet. It was exciting and thought-provoking and offered a world to escape to that seemed far better than the one I inhabited. I grew up on the East Coast in a scientific and intellectual household. My father was a biophysicist who developed artificial hearts and artificial lungs, worked in space medicine for the space program, and taught in medical schools. I had a "good education" and went to an

Ivy League college. I was surrounded by many bright and creative people. In spite of their success and their intellectual attainments, however, many of them were unhappy. It became clear to me that intelligence and worldly position had little to do with happiness or healthy human relationships. This was most painfully evident in my own family. Even in my loneliness and confusion I knew that I would have to seek happiness somewhere else. So I turned to the East.

At Dartmouth College in 1963, I was blessed with a wise old professor, Dr. Wing Tsit Chan, who sat cross-legged on a desk while lecturing on the Buddha and the Chinese classics. Inspired by him, I majored in Asian studies and, after graduating, immediately went to Asia (with the help of the Peace Corps) seeking teachings and ordination in a Buddhist monastery. I began practice and when I was finally ordained and retreated to the Thai forest monastery at Wat Ba Pong, led by the young but later quite famous master Achaan Chah, I was surprised. While I hadn't necessarily expected the monks to levitate as they did in T. Lobsang Rampa's stories, I had hoped for special effects from the meditation—happiness, special states of rapture, extraordinary experiences. But that was not primarily what my teacher offered. He offered a way of life, a lifelong path of awakening, attention, surrender, and commitment. He offered a happiness that was not dependent on any of the changing conditions of the world but came out of one's own difficult and conscious inner transformation. In joining the monastery, I had hoped to leave behind the pain of my family life and the difficulties of the world, but of course they followed me. It took many years for me to realize that these difficulties were part of my practice.

I was fortunate enough to find wise instruction and to undergo the traditional ancient trainings that are still offered in the best monasteries. This entailed living with great simplicity, possessing little more than a robe and bowl, and walking five miles each day to collect food for the single midday meal. I spent long periods of meditation in traditional practices, such as sitting in the forest all night watching bodies burn on the charnel grounds, and I undertook a year-long silent retreat in one room, sitting and walking for twenty hours a day. I was offered excellent teachings in great monasteries led by Mahasi Sayadaw, Asabha Sayadaw, and Achaan Buddhadasa. I learned wonderful things in these periods of practice and am perennially grateful to these teachers. Yet, intensive meditation in these exotic settings turned out to be just the beginning of my practice. Since then I have had equally compelling meditations in quite ordinary places, arising simply as a result of committed systematic training. I did not know what lay ahead at the time of my early training and left Asia still very idealistic, expecting that the special meditation experiences I had found would solve all my problems.

Over subsequent years, I returned for further training in monasteries of Thailand, India, and Sri Lanka and then studied with several renowned Tibetan lamas, Zen masters, and Hindu gurus. In nineteen years of teaching I've had the privilege of collaborating with many other Western Buddhist teachers to establish Insight Meditation, the Buddhist practice of mindfulness, in America. I have led retreats of one day's to three months' duration and worked in conjunction with many centers, Christian, Buddhist, transpersonal, and others. In 1976 I completed a Ph.D. in clinical psychology and have worked ever since as a psychotherapist as well as a Buddhist teacher. And mostly, as I've gone through these years, I have been trying to answer the question: How can I live my spiritual practice, how can I bring it to flower in every day of my life?

Since beginning to teach, I've seen how many other students misunderstand spiritual practice, how many have hoped to use it to escape from their lives, how many have used its ideals and language as a way to avoid the pains and difficulties of human existence as I tried to do, how many have entered temples, churches, and monasteries looking for the special effects.

My own practice has been a journey downward, in contrast to the way we usually think of our spiritual experiences. Over these years I've found myself working my way *down* the chakras (the spiritual energy centers of the body) rather than up. My first ten years of systematic spiritual practice were primarily conducted through my mind. I studied, read, and then meditated and lived as a monk, always using the power of my mind to gain understanding. I developed concentration and samadhi (deep levels of mental absorption), and many kinds of insights came. I had visions, revelations, and a variety of deep awakenings. The whole way I understood myself in the world was turned upside down as my practice developed and I saw things in a new and wiser way. I thought that this insight was the point of practice and felt satisfied with my new understandings.

But alas, when I returned to the U.S. as a monk, all of that fell apart. In the weeks after Elizabeth Arden's, I disrobed, enrolled in graduate school, got a job driving a taxi, and worked nights at a mental hospital in Boston. I also became involved in an intimate relationship. Although I had arrived back from the monastery clear, spacious, and high, in short order I discovered, through my relationship, in the communal household where I lived, and in my graduate work, that my meditation had helped me very little with my human relationships. I was still emotionally immature, acting out the same painful patterns of blame and fear, acceptance and rejection that I had before my Buddhist training; only the horror now was that I was beginning to see these patterns more clearly. I could do loving-kindness meditations for a thousand beings elsewhere but had terrible trouble relating intimately to one person here and now. I had used the strength of my mind in meditation to suppress painful feelings, and all too often I didn't even recognize that I was angry, sad, grieving, or frustrated until a long time later. The roots of my unhappiness in relationships had not been examined. I had very few skills for dealing with my feelings or for engaging on an emotional level or for living wisely with my friends and loved ones.

I was forced to shift my whole practice down the chakras from the mind to the heart. I began a long and difficult process of reclaiming my emotions, of bringing awareness and understanding to my patterns of relationship, of learning how to feel my feelings, and what to do with the powerful forces of human connection. I did this through group and individual therapy, through heart-centered meditations, through transpersonal psychology, and through a series of both successful and disastrous relationships. I did it through examining my family of origin and early history, bringing this understanding into my relationships in the present. Eventually this led me to an initially difficult relationship that is now a happy marriage with my wife, Liana, and to a beautiful daughter, Caroline. Gradually I have come to understand this work of the heart as a fully integrated part of my spiritual practice.

After ten years of focusing on emotional work and the development of the heart, I realized I had neglected my body. Like my emotions, my body had been included in my early spiritual practice in only a superficial way. I learned to be quite aware of my breathing and work with the pains and sensations in my body, but mostly I had used my body as an athlete might. I had been blessed with sufficient health and strength that I could climb mountains or sit like a yogi on the bank of the Ganges River through the fiery pain for ten or twenty hours without moving, I could eat one meal a day as a monk and walk long distances barefoot, but I discovered that I had *used* my body rather than inhabiting it. It had been a vehicle to feed and move and fulfill my mental, emotional, and spiritual life.

As I had come to reinhabit my emotions more fully, I noticed that my body also required its own loving attention and that it was not enough to see and understand or even to feel with love and compassion—I had to move further down the chakras. I learned that if I am to live a spiritual life, I must be able to embody it in every action: in the way I stand and walk, in the way I breathe, in the care with which I eat. All my activities must be included. To live in this precious animal body on this earth is as great a part of spiritual life as anything else. In beginning to reinhabit my body, I discovered new areas of fear and pain that kept me away from my true self, just as I had discovered new areas of fear and pain in opening my mind and opening my heart.

As my practice has proceeded down the chakras, it has become more intimate and more personal. It has required more honesty and care each step of the way. It has also become more integrated. The way I treat my body is not disconnected from the way I treat my family or the commitment I have to peace on our earth. So that as I have been working my way down, the vision of my practice has expanded to include, not just my own body or heart, but all of life, the relationships we hold, and the environment that sustains us.

In this process of deepening and expanding my commitment to spiritual life, I have seen both my effort and motivation change greatly. At first I practiced and taught from a place of great striving and effort. I had used strong effort of mind to hold my body still, to concentrate and marshal mental power in my meditation, to overcome pains, feelings, and distractions. I used spiritual practice to strive for states of clarity and light, for understanding and vision, and I initially taught this way. Gradually, though, it became clear that for most of us this very striving itself increased our problems. Where we tended to be judgmental, we became more judgmental of ourselves in our spiritual practice. Where we had been cut off from ourselves, denying our feelings, our bodies, and our humanity, the striving toward enlightenment or some spiritual goal only increased this separation. Whenever a sense of unworthiness or self-hatred had a foothold—in fear of our feelings or judgment of our thoughts—it was strengthened by spiritual striving. Yet I knew that spiritual practice is impossible without great dedication, energy, and commitment. If not from striving and idealism, from where was this to come?

What I discovered was wonderful news for me. To open deeply, as genuine spiritual life requires, we need tremendous courage and strength, a kind of warrior spirit. But the place for this warrior strength is in the heart. We need energy, commitment, and courage not to run from our life nor to cover it over with any philosophy—material or spiritual. We need a warrior's heart that lets us face our lives directly, our pains and limitations, our joys and possibilities. This courage allows us to include every aspect of life in our spiritual practice: our bodies, our families, our society, politics, the earth's ecology, art, education. Only then can spirituality be truly integrated into our lives.

When I began working at a state mental hospital while studying for my Ph.D., I naively thought I might teach meditation to some of the patients. It quickly became obvious that meditation was not what they needed. These people had little ability to bring a balanced attention to their lives, and most of them were already lost in their minds. If any meditation was useful to them, it would have to be one that was earthy and grounded: yoga, gardening, tai chi, active practices that could connect them to their bodies.

But then I discovered a whole large population at this hospital who desperately needed meditation: the psychiatrists, psychologists, social workers, psychiatric nurses, mental health aides, and others. This group cared for and often controlled the patients through antipsychotic drugs and out of fear, fear of the energies in the patients and fear of these energies in themselves. Not many among these caregivers seemed to know firsthand in their own psyches the powerful forces that the patients were encountering, yet this is a very basic lesson in meditation: facing our own greed, unworthiness, rage, paranoia, and grandiosity, and the opening of wisdom and fearlessness beyond these forces. The staff could all have greatly benefited from meditation as a way of facing within themselves the psychic forces that were unleashed in their patients. From this they would have brought a new understanding and compassion to their work and their patients.

The need to include spiritual life in treatment and therapy is beginning to be recognized by the mental health profession. An awareness of the necessity of integrating a spiritual vision has spread to such fields as politics, economics, and ecology as well. Yet to be beneficial, this spirituality must be grounded in personal experience. For the reader who wants to learn firsthand, chapters throughout this book offer a series of traditional practices and contemporary meditations. These exercises are ways to directly work with the teachings presented here, to enter more deeply into your own body and heart as a vehicle for spiritual practice. The core of the meditations presented here comes from the Theravada Buddhist tradition of Southeast Asia. These are the mindfulness practices of Insight Meditation (vipassana), also called the heart of Buddhist meditation, which offer a systematic training and awakening of body, heart, and mind that is integrated with the world around us. It is this tradition that I have followed and taught for many years, and it is this central teaching that forms the basis of almost all Buddhist practice worldwide.

While this book will draw upon my experience in the Buddhist traditions, I believe the principles of spiritual practice it touches on are universal. The first half introduces the ground of an integrated spiritual life: ways of practice, common perils, techniques for dealing with our wounds and difficulties, and some Buddhist maps of spiritual states of human consciousness and how these extraordinary experiences can be grounded in common sense. The second half of the book will speak more directly to the integration of this practice into our contemporary lives, addressing topics such as codependence and compassion, compartmentalization, psychotherapy and meditation, and the benefits and difficulties encountered with spiritual teachers. We will conclude by looking at spiritual maturity: the ripening of wisdom and compassion, and the ease and joy it brings to our life.

In beginning this book, I have emphasized my own personal journey, because the greatest lesson I have learned is that the universal must be wedded to the personal to be fulfilled in our spiritual life. We are human beings, and the human gate to the sacred is our own body, heart, and mind, the history from which we've come, and the closest relationships and circumstances of our life. If not here, where else could we bring alive compassion, justice, and liberation?

An integrated sense of spirituality understands that if we are to bring light or wisdom or compassion into the world, we must first begin with ourselves. The universal truths of spiritual life can come alive only in each particular and personal circumstance. This personal approach to practice honors both the uniqueness and the commonality of our life, respecting the timeless quality of the great dance between birth and death, yet also honoring our particular body, our particular family and community, the personal history and the joys and sorrows that have been given to us. In this way, our awakening is a very personal matter that also affects all other creatures on earth.

I

DID I LOVE WELL?

Even the most exalted states and the most exceptional spiritual accomplishments are unimportant if we cannot be happy in the most basic and ordinary ways, if we cannot touch one another and the life we have been given with our hearts.

In undertaking a spiritual life, what matters is simple: *We must make certain that our path is connected with our heart.* Many other visions are offered to us in the modern spiritual marketplace. Great spiritual traditions offer stories of enlightenment, bliss, knowledge, divine ecstasy, and the highest possibilities of the human spirit. Out of the broad range of teachings available to us in the West, often we are first attracted to these glamorous and most extraordinary aspects. While the promise of attaining such states can come true, and while these states do represent the teachings, in one sense, they are also one of the advertising techniques of the spiritual trade. They are not the goal of spiritual life. In the end, spiritual life is not a process of seeking or gaining some extraordinary condition or special powers. In fact, such seeking can take us away from ourselves. If we are not careful, we can easily find the great failures of our modern society—its ambition, materialism, and individual isolation—repeated in our spiritual life.

In beginning a genuine spiritual journey, we have to stay much closer to home, to focus directly on what is right here in front of us, to make sure that our path is connected with our deepest love. Don Juan, in his teachings to Carlos Castaneda, put it this way:

> Look at every path closely and deliberately. Try it as many times as you think necessary. Then ask yourself and yourself alone one question. This question is one that only a very old man asks. My benefactor told me about it once when I was young and my blood was too vigorous for me to understand it. Now I do understand it. I will tell you what it is: Does this path have a heart? If it does, the path is good. If it doesn't, it is of no use.

The teachings in this book are about finding such a path with heart, about undertaking a path that transforms and touches us in the center of our being. To do so is to find a way of practice that allows us to live in the world wholly and fully from our heart.

When we ask, "Am I following a path with heart?" we discover that no one can define for us exactly what our path should be. Instead, we must allow the mystery and beauty of this question to resonate within our being. Then somewhere within us an answer will come and understanding will arise. If we are still and listen deeply, even for a moment, we will know if we are following a path with heart.

It is possible to speak with our heart directly. Most ancient cultures know this. We can actually converse with our heart as if it were a good friend. In modern life we have become so busy with our daily affairs and thoughts that we have forgotten this essential art of taking time to converse with our heart. When we ask it about our current path, we must look at the values we have chosen to live by. Where do we put our time, our strength, our creativity, our love? We must look at our life without sentimentality, exaggeration, or idealism. Does what we are choosing reflect what we most deeply value?

Buddhist tradition teaches its followers to regard all life as precious. The astronauts who leave the earth have also rediscovered this truth. One set of Russian cosmonauts described it in this way: "We brought up small fish to the space station for certain investigations. We were to be there three months. After about three weeks the fish began to die. How sorry we felt for them! What we didn't do to try to save them! On earth we take great pleasure in fishing, but when you are alone and far away from anything terrestrial, any appearance of life is especially welcome. You see just how precious life is." In this same spirit, one astronaut, when his capsule landed, opened the hatch to smell the moist air of earth. "I actually got down and put it to my cheek. I got down and kissed the earth."

To see the preciousness of all things, we must bring our full attention to life. Spiritual practice can bring us to this awareness without the aid of a trip into space. As the qualities of presence and simplicity begin to permeate more and more of our life, our inner love for the earth and all beings begins to express itself and brings our path alive.

To understand more deeply what evokes this sense of preciousness and how it gives meaning to a path with heart, let us work with the following meditation. In Buddhist practice, one is urged to consider how to live well by reflecting on one's death. The traditional meditation for this purpose is to sit quietly and sense the tentativeness of life. After reading this paragraph, close your eyes and feel the mortality of this human body that you have been given. Death is certain for us—only the time of death is yet to be discovered. Imagine yourself to be at the end of your life—next week or next year or next decade, some time in the future. Now cast your memory back across your whole life and bring to mind two good deeds that you have done, two things that you did that were good. They need not be grandiose; let whatever wants to arise show itself. In picturing and remembering these good deeds, also become aware of how these memories affect your consciousness, how they transform the feelings and state of the heart and mind, as you see them.

When you have completed this reflection, look very carefully at the quality of these situations, at what is comprised in a moment of goodness picked out of a lifetime of words and actions. Almost everyone who is able to remember such deeds in this meditation discovers them to be remarkably simple. They are rarely the deeds one would put on a résumé. For some people a moment of goodness was simply the one when they told their father before he died that they loved him, or when they flew across country in the midst of their busy life to care for their sister's children as she was healing from a car accident. One elementary school teacher had the simple vision of those mornings when she held the children who were crying and having a hard day. In response to this meditation someone once raised her hand, smiled, and said, "On crowded streets when we get to parking spaces at the same time, I always give the parking space to the other person." That was the good deed in her life.

Another woman, a nurse in her sixties who had raised children and grandchildren and had lived a very full life, came up with this memory: She was six years old when a car broke down in front of her house, steam spouting from under the hood. Two elderly people got out and looked at it, and one went off to the corner pay phone to call a garage. They returned to sit in the car and wait for much of the morning for a tow. As a curious six-year-old, she went out to speak to them, and after seeing them wait for a long time in a hot car, she went inside. Without even asking them, she prepared a tray of iced tea and sandwiches and carried the tray out to them on the curb.

The things that matter most in our lives are not fantastic or grand. They are the moments when we touch one another, when we are there in the most attentive or caring way. This simple and profound intimacy is the love that we all long for. These moments of touching and being touched can become a foundation for a path with heart, and they take place in the most immediate and direct way. Mother Teresa put it like this: "In this life we cannot do great things. We can only do small things with great love."

Some people find this exercise very difficult. No good deeds will come to their mind, or a few may arise only to be rejected immediately because they are judged superficial or small or impure or imperfect. Does this mean that there are not even two good moments in a lifetime of one hundred thousand deeds? Hardly! We all have had many. It has another more profound meaning. It is a reflection of how hard we are on ourselves. We judge ourselves so harshly, only an Idi Amin or a Stalin would hire us to preside over their courts. Many of us discover we have little mercy for ourselves. We can hardly acknowledge that genuine love and goodness can shine freely from our hearts. Yet it does.

To live a path with heart means to live in the way shown us in this meditation, to allow the flavor of goodness to permeate our life. When we bring full attention to our acts, when we express our love and see the preciousness of life, the quality of goodness in us grows. A simple caring presence can begin to permeate more moments of our life. And so we should continually ask our own heart, What would it mean to live like this? Is the path, the way we have chosen to live our life, leading to this?

In the stress and complexity of our lives, we may forget our deepest intentions. But when people come to the end of their life and look back, the questions that they most often ask are not usually, "How much is in my bank account?" or "How many books did I write?" or "What did I build?" or the like. If you have the privilege of being with a person who is aware at the time of his or her death, you find the questions such a person asks are very simple: "Did I love well?" "Did I live fully?" "Did I learn to let go?"

These simple questions go to the very center of spiritual life. When we consider loving well and living fully, we can see the ways our attachments and fears have limited us, and we can see the many opportunities for our hearts to open. Have we let ourselves love the people around us, our family, our community, the earth upon which we live? And, did we also learn to let go? Did we learn to live through the changes of life with grace, wisdom, and compassion? Have we learned to forgive and live from the spirit of the heart instead of the spirit of judgment?

Letting go is a central theme in spiritual practice, as we see the preciousness and brevity of life. When letting go is called for, if we have not learned to do so, we suffer greatly, and when we get to the end of our life, we may have what is called a crash course. Sooner or later we have to learn to let go and allow the changing mystery of life to move through us without our fearing it, without holding and grasping.

I knew a young woman who sat with her mother during an extended bout of cancer. Part of this time her mother was in the hospital hooked up to dozens of tubes and machines. Mother and daughter agreed that the mother did not want to die this way, and when the illness progressed, she was finally removed from all of the medical paraphernalia and allowed to go home. Her cancer progressed further. Still the mother had a hard time accepting her illness. She tried to run the household from her bed, to pay bills and oversee all the usual affairs of her life. She struggled with her physical pain, but she struggled more with her inability to let go. One day in the midst of this struggle, much sicker now and a bit confused, she called her daughter to her and said, "Daughter, dear, please now pull the plug," and her daughter gently pointed out, "Mother, you are not plugged in." Some of us have a lot to learn about letting go.

Letting go and moving through life from one change to another brings the maturing of our spiritual being. In the end we discover that to love and let go can be the same thing. Both ways do not seek to possess. Both allow us to touch each moment of this changing life and allow us to be there fully for whatever arises next.

There is an old story about a famous rabbi living in Europe who was visited one day by a man who had traveled by ship from New York to see him. The man came to the great rabbi's dwelling, a large house on a street in a European city, and was directed to the rabbi's room, which was in the attic. He entered to find the master living in a room with a bed, a chair, and a few books. The man had expected much more. After greetings, he asked, "Rabbi, where are your things?" The rabbi asked in return, "Well, where are yours?" His visitor replied, "But, Rabbi, I'm only passing through," and the master answered, "So am I, so am I."

To love fully and live well requires us to recognize finally that we do not possess or own anything—our homes, our cars, our loved ones, not even our own body. Spiritual joy and wisdom do not come through possession but rather through our capacity to open, to love more fully, and to move and be free in life.

This is not a lesson to be put off. One great teacher explained it this way: "The trouble with you is that you think you have time." We don't know how much time we have. What would it be like to live with the knowledge that this may be our last year, our last week, our last day? In light of this question, we can choose a path with heart.

Sometimes it takes a shock to awaken us, to connect us with our path. Several years ago I was called to visit a man in a San Francisco hospital by his sister. He was in his late thirties and already rich. He had a construction company, a sailboat, a ranch, a town house, the works. One day when driving along in his BMW, he blacked out. Tests showed that he had a brain tumor, a melanoma, a rapid-growing kind of cancer. The doctor said, "We want to operate on you, but I must warn you that the tumor is in the speech and comprehension center. If we remove the tumor, you may lose all your ability to read, to write, to speak, to understand any language. If we don't operate, you probably have six more weeks to live. Please consider this. We want to operate in the morning. Let us know by then."

I visited this man that evening. He had become very quiet and reflective. As you can imagine, he was in an extraordinary state of consciousness. Such an awakening will sometimes come from our spiritual practice, but for him it came through these exceptional circumstances. When we spoke, this man did not talk about his ranch or sailboat or his money. Where he was headed, they don't take the currency of bankbooks and BMWs. All that is of value in times of great change is the currency of our heart—the ability and understandings of the heart that have grown in us.

Twenty years before, in the late 1960s, this man had done a little Zen meditation, had read a bit of Alan Watts, and when he faced this moment, that is what he drew on and what he wanted to talk about: his spiritual life and understanding of birth and death. After a most heartfelt conversation, he stopped to be silent for a time and reflect. Then he turned to me and said, "I've had enough of talking. Maybe I've said too many words. This evening it seems so precious just to have a drink of tap water or to watch the pigeons on the windowsill of the medical center fly off in the air. They seem so beautiful to me. It's magic to see a bird go through the air. I'm not finished with this life. Maybe I'll just live it more silently." So he asked to have the operation. After fourteen hours of surgery by a very fine surgeon, his sister visited him in the recovery room. He looked up at her and said, "Good morning." They had been able to remove the tumor without his losing his speech.

When he left the hospital and recovered from his cancer, his entire life changed. He still responsibly completed his business obligations, but he was no longer a workaholic. He spent more time with his family, and he became a counselor for others diagnosed with cancer and grave illnesses. He spent much of his time in nature and much of his time touching the people around him with love.

Had I met him before that evening, I might have considered him a spiritual failure because he had done a little spiritual practice and then quit completely to become a businessman. He seemed to have forgotten all of those spiritual values. But when it came down to it, when he stopped to reflect in these moments between his life and death, even the little spiritual practice he had touched became very important to him. We never know what others are learning, and we cannot judge someone's spiritual practice quickly or easily. All we can do is look into our own hearts and ask what matters in the way that we are living. What might lead me to greater openness, honesty, and a deeper capacity to love?

A path with heart will also include our unique gifts and creativity. The outer expression of our heart may be to write books, to build buildings, to create ways for people to serve one another. It may be to teach or to garden, to serve food or play music. Whatever we choose, the creations of our life must be grounded in our hearts. Our love is the source of all energy to create and connect. If we act without a connection to the heart, even the greatest things in our life can become dried up, meaningless, or barren.

You may remember that some years ago a series of articles ran in the newspapers about plans to start a sperm bank for Nobel Prize winners. At this time a concerned feminist wrote to the *Boston Globe* pointing out that if there were sperm banks there should also be egg banks. The *Boston Globe* printed a letter of reply to her from George Wald, himself a Nobel Prize–winning biologist from Harvard University, a gentleman and a man of wisdom at that. George Wald wrote to her:

You're absolutely right. It takes an egg as well as a sperm to start a Nobel laureate. Every one of them has had a mother as well as a father. You can say all you want of fathers, but their contribution to conception is really rather small.

But I hope you weren't seriously proposing an egg bank. Nobel laureates aside, there isn't much in the way of starting one technically. There are some problems, but nothing as hard as involved in the other kinds of breeder reactors. . . .

But think of a man so vain as to insist on getting a superior egg from an egg bank. Then he has to fertilize it. When it's fertilized where does he go with it? To his wife? "Here, dear," you can hear him saying, "I just got this superior egg from an egg bank and just fertilized it myself. Will you take care of it?" "I've got eggs of my own to worry about," she answers. "You know what you can do with your superior egg. Go rent a womb. While you're at it, you'd better rent a room too."

You see, it just won't work. The truth is what one really needs is not Nobel laureates but love. How do you think one gets to be a Nobel laureate? Wanting love, that's how. Wanting it so bad one works all the time and ends up a Nobel laureate. It's a consolation prize.

What matters is love. Forget sperm banks and egg banks. Banks and love are incompatible. If you don't know that, you haven't been to your bank lately.

So just practice loving. Love a Russian. You'd be surprised how easy it is and how it will brighten your morning. Love an Iranian, a Vietnamese, people not just here but everywhere. Then when you've gotten really good at it, try something hard like loving the politicians in our nation's capital.

The longing for love and the movement of love is underneath all of our activities. The happiness we discover in life is not about possessing or owning or even understanding. Instead, it is the discovery of this capacity to love, to have a loving, free, and wise relationship with all of life. Such love is not possessive but arises out of a sense of our own well-being and connection with everything. Therefore, it is generous and wakeful, and it loves the freedom of all things. Out of love, our path can lead us to learn to use our gifts to heal and serve, to create peace around us, to honor the sacred in life, to bless whatever we encounter, and to wish all beings well.

Spiritual life may seem complicated, but in essence it is not. We can find a clarity and simplicity even in the midst of this complex world when we discover that the quality of heart we bring to life is what matters most. The beloved Zen poet Ryokan summed this up when he said:

The rain has stopped, the clouds have drifted away,
and the weather is clear again.
If your heart is pure, then all things in your world are
pure. . . .
Then the moon and flowers will guide you along the
Way.

All other spiritual teachings are in vain if we cannot love. Even the most exalted states and the most exceptional spiritual accomplishments are unimportant if we cannot be happy in the most basic and ordinary ways, if, with our hearts, we cannot touch one another and the life we have been given. What matters is how we live. This is why it is so difficult and so important to ask this question of ourselves: "Am I living my path fully, do I live without regret?" so that we can say on whatever day is the end of our life, "Yes, I have lived my path with heart."

A MEDITATION ON LOVING-KINDNESS

The quality of *loving-kindness* is the fertile soil out of which an integrated spiritual life can grow. With a loving heart as the background, all that we attempt, all that we encounter, will open and flow more easily. While loving-kindness can arise naturally in us in many circumstances, it can also be cultivated.

The following meditation is a 2,500-year-old practice that uses repeated phrases, images, and feelings to evoke loving-kindness and friendliness toward oneself and others. You can experiment with this practice to see if it is useful for you. It is best to begin by repeating it over and over for fifteen or twenty minutes once or twice daily in a quiet place for several months. At first this meditation may feel mechanical or awkward or even bring up its opposite, feelings of irritation and anger. If this happens, it is especially important to be patient and kind toward yourself, allowing whatever arises to be received in a spirit of friendliness and kind affection.

In its own time, even in the face of inner difficulties, loving-kindness will develop.

Sit in a comfortable fashion. Let your body relax and be at rest. As best you can, let your mind be quiet, letting go of plans and preoccupations. Then begin to recite inwardly the following phrases directed to yourself. You begin with yourself because without loving yourself it is almost impossible to love others.

May I be filled with loving-kindness.
May I be well.
May I be peaceful and at ease.
May I be happy.

As you say the phrases, you may also wish to use the image from the Buddha's instructions: picture yourself as a young and beloved child, or sense yourself as you are now, held in a heart of loving-kindness. Let the feelings arise with the words. Adjust the words and images so that you find the exact phrases that best open your heart of kindness. Repeat the phrases again and again, letting the feelings permeate your body and mind.

Practice this meditation repeatedly for a number of weeks until the sense of loving-kindness for yourself grows.

When you feel ready, in the same meditation period you can gradually expand the focus of your loving-kindness to include others. After yourself, choose a benefactor, someone in your life who has truly cared for you. Picture them and carefully recite the same phrases, *May he/she be filled with loving-kindness,* and so forth. When loving-kindness for your benefactor has developed, begin to include other people you love in the meditation, picturing them and reciting the same phrases, evoking a sense of loving-kindness for them.

After this you can gradually begin to include others: friends, community members, neighbors, people everywhere, animals, the whole earth, and all beings. Then you can even experiment with including the most difficult people in your life, wishing that they, too, be filled with loving-kindness and peace. With some practice a steady sense of loving-kindness can develop and in the course of fifteen or twenty minutes you will be able to include many beings in your meditation, moving from yourself, to a benefactor and loved ones, to all beings everywhere.

Then you can learn to practice it anywhere. You can use this meditation in traffic jams, in buses and airplanes, in doctors' waiting rooms, and in a thousand other circumstances. As you silently practice this loving-kindness meditation among people, you will immediately feel a wonderful connection with them—the power of loving-kindness. It will calm your life and keep you connected to your heart.

2

STOPPING
THE WAR

*When we step out of the battles, we see anew,
as the* Tao te Ching *says, "with eyes unclouded
by longing."*

The unawakened mind tends to make war against the way things are. To follow a path with heart, we must understand the whole process of making war, within ourselves and without, how it begins and how it ends. War's roots are in ignorance. Without understanding, we can easily become frightened by life's fleeting changes, the inevitable losses, disappointments, the insecurity of our aging and death. Misunderstanding leads us to fight against life, running from pain or grasping at security and pleasures that by their nature can never be truly satisfying.

Our war against life is expressed in every dimension of our experience, inner and outer. Our children see, on average, eighteen thousand murders and violent acts on TV before they finish high school. The leading cause of injury for American women is beatings by the men they live with. We carry on wars within ourselves, with our families and communities, among races and nations worldwide. The wars between peoples are a reflection of our own inner conflict and fear.

My teacher Achaan Chah described this ongoing battle:

> We human beings are constantly in combat, at war to escape the fact of being so limited, limited by so many circumstances we cannot control. But instead of escaping, we continue to create suffering, waging war with good, waging war with evil, waging war with what is too small, waging war with what is too big, waging war with what is too short or too long, or right or wrong, courageously carrying on the battle.

Contemporary society fosters our mental tendency to deny or suppress our awareness of reality. Ours is a society of denial that conditions us to protect ourselves from any direct difficulty and discomfort. We expend enormous energy denying our insecurity, fighting pain, death, and loss, and hiding from the basic truths of the natural world and of our own nature.

To insulate ourselves from the natural world, we have air conditioners, heated cars, and clothes that protect us from every season. To insulate ourselves from the specter of aging and infirmity, we put smiling young people in our advertisements, while we relegate our old people to nursing homes and old-age establishments. We hide our mental patients in mental hospitals. We relegate our poor to ghettos. And we construct freeways around these ghettos so that those fortunate enough not to live in them will not see the suffering they house.

We deny death to the extent that even a ninety-six-year-old woman, newly admitted to a hospice, complained to the director, "Why me?" We almost pretend that our dead aren't dead, dressing up corpses in fancy clothes and makeup to attend their own funerals, as if they were going to parties. In our charade with ourselves we pretend that our war is not really war. We have changed the name of the War Department to the Defense Department and call a whole class of nuclear missiles Peace Keepers!

How do we manage so consistently to close ourselves off from the truths of our existence? We use denial to turn away from the pains and difficulties of life. We use addictions to support our denial. Ours has been called the Addicted Society, with over twenty million alcoholics, ten million drug addicts, and millions addicted to gambling, food, sexuality, unhealthy relationships, or the speed and busyness of work. Our addictions are the compulsively repetitive attachments we use to avoid feeling and to deny the difficulties of our lives. Advertising urges us to keep pace, to keep consuming, smoking, drinking, and craving food, money, and sex. Our addictions serve to numb us to what is, to help us avoid our own experience, and with great fanfare our society encourages these addictions.

Anne Wilson Schaef, author of *When Society Becomes an Addict,* has described it this way:

> The best-adjusted person in our society is the person who is not dead and not alive, just numb, a zombie. When you are dead you're not able to do the work of the society. When you are fully alive you are constantly saying "No" to many of the processes of society, the racism, the polluted environment, the nuclear threat, the arms race, drinking unsafe water and eating carcinogenic foods. Thus it is in the interests of our society to promote those things that take the edge off, keep us busy with our fixes, and keep us slightly numbed out and zombie-like. In this way our modern consumer society itself functions as an addict.

One of our most pervasive addictions is to speed. Technological society pushes us to increase the pace of our productivity and the pace of our lives. Panasonic recently introduced a new VHS tape recorder that was advertised as playing voice tapes at double the normal speed while lowering the tone to the normal speaking range. "Thus," the advertiser said, "you can listen to one of the great speeches by Winston Churchill or President Kennedy or a literary classic in half the time!" I wonder if they would recommend double-speed tapes for Mozart and Beethoven as well. Woody Allen commented on this obsession, saying he took a course in speed reading and was able to read *War and Peace* in twenty minutes. "It's about Russia," he concluded.

In a society that almost demands life at double time, speed and addictions numb us to our own experience. In such a society it is almost impossible to settle into our bodies or stay connected with our hearts, let alone connect with one another or the earth where we live. Instead, we find ourselves increasingly isolated and lonely, cut off from one another and the natural web of life. One person in a car, big houses, cellular phones, Walkman radios clamped to our ears, and a deep loneliness and sense of inner poverty. That is the most pervasive sorrow in our modern society.

Not only have individuals lost the sense of their interconnection, this isolation is the sorrow of nations as well. The forces of separation and denial breed international misunderstanding, ecological disaster, and an endless series of conflicts between nation states.

On this earth, as I write today, more than forty wars and violent revolutions are killing thousands of men, women, and children. We have had 115 wars since World War II, and there are only 165 countries in the entire world. Not a good track record for the human species. Yet what are we to do?

Genuine spiritual practice requires us to learn how to *stop the war*. This is a first step, but actually it must be practiced over and over until it becomes our way of being. The inner stillness of a person who truly "is peace" brings peace to the whole interconnected web of life, both inner and outer. To stop the war, we need to begin with ourselves. Mahatma Gandhi understood this when he said:

I have only three enemies. My favorite enemy, the one most easily influenced for the better, is the British Empire. My second enemy, the Indian people, is far more difficult. But my most formidable opponent is a man named Mohandas K. Gandhi. With him I seem to have very little influence.

Like Gandhi, we cannot easily change ourselves for the better through an act of will. This is like wanting the mind to get rid of itself or pulling ourselves up by our own bootstraps. Remember how short-lived are most New Year's resolutions? When we struggle to change ourselves, we, in fact, only continue the patterns of self-judgment and aggression. We keep the war against ourselves alive. Such acts of will usually backfire, and in the end often strengthen the addiction or denial we intend to change.

One young man came to meditation with a deep distrust for authority. He had rebelled in his family, understandably, for he had quite an abusive mother. He had rebelled in school and dropped out to join the counterculture. He had fought with a girlfriend who, he said, wanted to control him. Then he went to India and Thailand to find his freedom. After an initial positive experience in meditation, he signed up for a period of practice in a monastery. He decided to practice very strictly and make himself clear and pure and peaceful. However, after a short time he found himself in conflict again. The daily chores didn't leave him enough time to meditate nonstop. The sound of visitors and an occasional car were disturbing his meditation. The teacher, he felt, wasn't giving enough guidance, and due to this, his meditation was weak and his mind wouldn't stop. He struggled to quiet himself and resolved to do it his own way but ended up fighting himself.

Finally, the teacher called him to task at the end of a group meditation. "You are struggling with everything. How is it that the food bothers you, the sounds bother you, the chores bother you, even your mind bothers you? Doesn't it seem odd? What I want to know is when you hear a car come by, does it really come in and bother you, or are you going out to bother it? Who is bothering whom?" Even this young man had to laugh, and that moment was the beginning of his learning to stop the war.

The purpose of a spiritual discipline is to give us a way to stop the war, not by our force of will, but organically, through understanding and gradual training. Ongoing spiritual practice can help us cultivate a new way of relating to life in which we let go of our battles.

When we step out of the battle, we see anew, as the *Tao te Ching* says, "with eyes unclouded by longing." We see how each of us creates conflict. We see our constant likes and dislikes, the fight to resist all that frightens us. We see our own prejudice, greed, and territoriality. All this is hard for us to look at, but it is really there. Then underneath these ongoing battles, we see pervasive feelings of incompleteness and fear. We see how much our struggle with life has kept our heart closed.

When we let go of our battles and open our heart to things as they are, then we come to rest in the present moment. This is the beginning and the end of spiritual practice. Only in this moment can we discover that which is timeless. Only here can we find the love that we seek. Love in the past is simply memory, and love in the future is fantasy. Only in the reality of the present can we love, can we awaken, can we find peace and understanding and connection with ourselves and the world.

A sign in a Las Vegas casino aptly says, "You Must Be Present to Win." Stopping the war and becoming present are two sides of the same activity. To come into the present is to stop the war. To come into the present means to experience whatever is here and now. Most of us have spent our lives caught up in plans, expectations, ambitions for the future, in regrets, guilt, or shame about the past. When we come into the present, we begin to feel the life around us again, but we also encounter whatever we have been avoiding. We must have the courage to face whatever is present—our pain, our desires, our grief, our loss, our secret hopes, our love—everything that moves us most deeply. As we stop the war, each of us will find something from which we have been running—

our loneliness, our unworthiness, our boredom, our shame, our unful-filled desires. We must face these parts of ourselves as well.

You may have heard of "out-of-the-body experiences," full of lights and visions. A true spiritual path demands something more challenging, what could be called an "in-the-body experience." We must connect to our body, to our feelings, to our life just now, if we are to awaken.

To live in the present demands an ongoing and unwavering commitment. As we follow a spiritual path, we are required to stop the war not once but many times. Over and over we feel the familiar tug of thoughts and reactions that take us away from the present moment. When we stop and listen, we can feel how each thing that we fear or crave (really two sides of the same dissatisfaction) propels us out of our hearts into a false idea of how we would like life to be. If we listen even more closely, we can feel how we have learned to sense ourselves as limited by that fear and identified with that craving. From this *small* sense of ourselves, we often believe that our own happiness can come only from possessing something or can be only at someone else's expense.

To stop the war and come into the present is to discover a greatness of our own heart that can include the happiness of all beings as inseparable from our own. When we let ourselves feel the fear, the discontent, the difficulties we have always avoided, our heart softens. Just as it is a courageous act to face all the difficulties from which we have always run, it is also an act of compassion. According to Buddhist scriptures, compassion is the "quivering of the pure heart" when we have allowed ourselves to be touched by the pain of life. The knowledge that we can do this and survive helps us to awaken the greatness of our heart. With greatness of heart, we can sustain a presence in the midst of life's suffering, in the midst of life's fleeting impermanence. We can open to the world—its ten thousand joys and ten thousand sorrows.

As we allow the world to touch us deeply, we recognize that just as there is pain in our own lives, so there is pain in everyone else's life. This is the birth of wise understanding. Wise understanding sees that suffering is inevitable, that all things that are born die. Wise understanding sees and accepts life as a whole. With wise understanding we allow ourselves to contain all things, both dark and light, and we come to a sense of peace. This is not the peace of denial or running away, but the peace we find in the heart that has rejected nothing, that touches all things with compassion.

Through stopping the war, we can embrace our own personal griefs and sorrows, joys and triumphs. With greatness of heart we can open to the people around us, to our family, to our community, to the social problems of the world, to our collective history. With wise understanding we can live in harmony with our life, with the universal law called the Tao or dharma, the truth of life.

A Buddhist student who is a Vietnam veteran tells a story about a meditation retreat where he experienced for the first time the terrible atrocities he had witnessed as a soldier. For many years he had carried the Vietnam War inside himself because he hadn't had a way to face the memories of what he had been through. Finally, he stopped.

I had served as a field medical corpsman with the Marine Corps ground forces in the early days of the war in the mountainous provinces on the border of what was then North and South Vietnam. Our casualty rates were high, as were those of the villagers we treated when circumstances permitted.

It had been eight years since my return when I attended my first meditation retreat. At least twice a week for all those years I had sustained the same recurring nightmares common to many combat veterans: dreaming that I was back there facing the same dangers, witnessing the same incalculable suffering, waking suddenly alert, sweating, scared. At the retreat, the nightmares did not occur during sleep, they filled the mind's eye during the day, at sittings, during walking meditations, at meals. Horrific wartime flashbacks were superimposed over a quiet redwood grove at the retreat center. Sleepy students in the dormitory became body parts strewn about a makeshift morgue on the DMZ. What I gradually came to see was that as I relived these memories as a thirty-year-old spiritual seeker, I was also enduring for the first time the full emotional impact of experiences that as a twenty-year-old medic I was simply unprepared to withstand.

I began to realize that my mind was gradually yielding up memories so terrifying, so life-denying, and so spiritually eroding that I had ceased to be consciously aware that I was still carrying them around. I was, in short, beginning to undergo a profound catharsis by openly facing that which I had most feared and therefore most strongly suppressed.

At the retreat I was also plagued by a more current fear, that having released the inner demons of war I would be unable to control them, that they would now rule my days as well as my nights, but what I experienced instead was just the opposite. The visions of slain friends and dismembered children gradually gave way to other half-remembered scenes from that time and place: the entrancing, intense beauty of a jungle forest, a thousand different shades of green, a fragrant breeze blowing over beaches so white and dazzling they seemed carpeted by diamonds.

What also arose at the retreat for the first time was a deep sense of compassion for my past and present self: compassion for the idealistic, young would-be physician forced to witness the unspeakable obscenities of which humankind is capable, and for the haunted veteran who could not let go of memories he could not acknowledge he carried.

Since the first retreat the compassion has stayed with me. Through practice and continued inner relaxation, it has grown to sometimes encompass those around me as well, when I'm not too self-conscious to let it do so. While the memories have also stayed with me, the nightmares have not. The last of the sweating screams happened in silence, fully awake, somewhere in Northern California over a decade ago.

Lloyd Burton, now a father and a teacher, stopped the war in himself through an uncompromising courage to be present. And in that process a healing compassion arose for himself and those around him.

This is a task for all of us. Individually and as a society, we must move from the pain of our speed, our addictions, and our denial to stop the war. The greatest of transformations can come from this simple act. Even Napoleon Bonaparte understood this when, at the end of his life, he stated, "Do you know what astonished me most in the world? The inability of force to create anything. In the long run, the sword is always beaten by the spirit."

Compassion and a greatness of heart arise whenever we stop the war. The deepest desire we have for our human heart is to discover how to do this. We all share a longing to go beyond the confines of our own fear or anger or addiction, to connect with something greater than "I," "me," and "mine," greater than our small story and our small self. It is possible to stop the war and come into the timeless present—to touch a great ground of being that contains all things. This is the purpose of a spiritual discipline and of choosing a path with heart—to discover peace and connectedness in ourselves and to stop the war in us and around us.

A MEDITATION ON STOPPING
THE WAR WITHIN

Sit comfortably for a few minutes, letting your body be at rest. Let your breathing be easy and natural. Bring your attention into the present, sit quietly, and notice whatever sensations are present in your body. In particular, be aware of any sensations, tensions, or pains you may have been fighting. Do not try to change them, simply notice them with an interested and kind attention. In each area of struggle you discover, let your body relax and your heart soften. Open to whatever you experience without fighting. Let go of the battle. Breathe quietly and let it be.

Then, after a time, shift your attention to your heart and mind. Now notice what feelings and thoughts are present. In particular, be aware of any feelings or thoughts you are now struggling with, fighting, denying, or avoiding. Notice them with an interested and kind attention. Let your heart be soft. Open to whatever you experience without fighting. Let go of the battle. Breathe quietly and let it be.

Continue to sit quietly. Then cast your attention over all the battles that still exist in your life. Sense them inside yourself. If you have an ongoing struggle with your body, be aware of that. If you have been fighting inner wars with your feelings, been in conflict with your own loneliness, fear, confusion, grief, anger, or addiction, sense the struggle you have been waging. Notice the struggles in your thoughts as well. Be aware of how you have carried on the inner battles. Notice the inner armies, the inner dictators, the inner fortifications. Be aware of all that you have fought within yourself, of how long you have perpetuated the conflict.

Gently, with openness, allow each of these experiences to be present. Simply notice each of them in turn with interest and kind attention. In each area of struggle, let your body, heart, and mind be soft. Open to whatever you experience without fighting. Let it be present just as it is. Let go of the battle. Breathe quietly and let yourself be at rest. Invite all parts of yourself to join you at the peace table in your heart.

3

TAKE THE ONE SEAT

When we take the one seat on our meditation cushion we become our own monastery. We create the compassionate space that allows for the arising of all things: sorrows, loneliness, shame, desire, regret, frustration, happiness.

Spiritual transformation is a profound process that doesn't happen by accident. We need a repeated discipline, a genuine training, in order to let go of our old habits of mind and to find and sustain a new way of seeing. To mature on the spiritual path we need to commit ourselves in a systematic way. My teacher Achaan Chah described this commitment as "taking the one seat." He said, "Just go into the room and put one chair in the center. Take the one seat in the center of the room, open the doors and windows, and see who comes to visit. You will witness all kinds of scenes and actors, all kinds of temptations and stories, everything imaginable. Your only job is to stay in your seat. You will see it all arise and pass, and out of this, wisdom and understanding will come."

Achaan Chah's description is both literal and metaphorical, and his image of taking the one seat describes two related aspects of spiritual work. Outwardly, it means selecting one practice and teacher among all of the possibilities, and inwardly, it means having the determination to stick with that practice through whatever difficulties and doubts arise until you have come to true clarity and understanding.

Great spiritual traditions in every age offer many vehicles for awakening. These include body disciplines, prayer, meditation, selfless service, ceremonial and devotional practices, even certain forms of modern therapy. All of these are used as means to ripen us, to bring us face to face with our life, and to help us to see in a new way by developing a stillness of mind and a strength of heart. Undertaking any of these practices requires a deep commitment to stopping the war, to stopping running away from life. Each practice brings us into the present with a clearer, more receptive, more honest state of consciousness, but we must choose.

While choosing among practices, we will often encounter others who will try to convert us to their way. There are born-again Buddhists, Christians, and Sufis. There are missionaries of every faith who insist that they have found the only true vehicle to God, to awakening, to love. Yet it is crucial to understand that there are many ways up the mountain—that there is never just one true way.

Two disciples of a master got into an argument about the right way to practice. As they could not resolve their conflict, they went to their master, who was sitting among a group of other students. Each of the two disciples put across his point of view. The first talked about the path of effort. He said, "Master, is it not true that we must make a full effort to abandon our old habits and unconscious ways? We must make great effort to speak honestly, be mindful and present. Spiritual life does not happen by accident," he said, "but only by giving our wholehearted effort to it." The master replied, "You're right."

The second student was upset and said, "But master, isn't the true spiritual path one of letting go, of surrender, of allowing the Tao, the divine to show itself?" He continued, "It is not through our effort that we progress, our effort is only based on our grasping and ego. The essence of the true spiritual path is to live from the phrase, 'Not my will but thine.' Is this not the way?" Again the master replied, "You're right."

A third student listening said, "But master, they can't both be right." The master smiled and said, "And you're right too."

There are many ways up the mountain and each of us must choose a practice that feels true to our heart. It is not necessary for you to evaluate the practices chosen by others. Remember, the practices themselves are only vehicles for you to develop awareness, loving-kindness, and compassion on the path toward freedom. That is all.

As the Buddha said, "One need not carry the raft on one's head after crossing the stream." We need to learn how to honor and use a practice for as long as it serves us—which in most cases is a very long time—but to look at it as just that, a vehicle, a raft to help us cross through the waters of doubt, confusion, desire, and fear. We can be thankful for the raft that supports our journey, and still realize that though we benefit, not everyone will take the same raft.

The poet Rumi describes the many vehicles for awakening:

Some people work and become wealthy.
Others do the same and remain poor.
Marriage fills one with energy,
Another it drains.
Don't trust ways, they change.
A means flails about like a donkey's tail.
Always add the gratitude clause
To any sentence, if God wills,
then go . . .

We can discover the power of the great traditions of practice without losing our perspective that each is a raft, a means for awakening. Then while keeping this perspective we need to make a definite choice—select a meditation or devotional practice, a prayer or mantra—and commit to it with our heart, enter it fully as a way of practice.

Many experienced students have come to the Insight Meditation retreats I teach without having made a commitment to any practice. Instead they have sampled the numerous traditions that are now available in the West. They have been initiated by lamas, done Sufi dancing in the mountains, sat a Zen retreat or two, and participated in shamanic rituals, and yet they ask: Why am I still unhappy? Why am I caught in the same old struggles? Why haven't my years of practice changed any-thing? Why hasn't my spiritual practice progressed? And I ask them: What is your spiritual practice? Do you have a committed relationship of trust with your teacher and a specific form of practice? They often answer that they practice many ways, or that they have not chosen yet. Until a person chooses one discipline and commits to it, how can a deep understanding of themselves and the world be revealed to them? Spiritual work requires sustained practice and a commitment to look very deeply into ourselves and the world around us to discover what has created human suffering and what will free us from any manner of conflict. We must look at ourselves over and over again in order to learn to love, to discover what has kept our hearts closed, and what it means to allow our hearts to open.

If we do a little of one kind of practice and a little of another, the work we have done in one often doesn't continue to build as we change to the next. It is as if we were to dig many shallow wells instead of one deep one. In continually moving from one approach to another, we are never forced to face our own boredom, impatience, and fears. We are never brought face to face with ourselves. So we need to choose a way of practice that is deep and ancient and connected with our hearts, and then make a commitment to follow it as long as it takes to transform ourselves. This is the outward aspect of taking the one seat.

Once we have made the outward choice among the many paths available and have begun a systematic practice, we often find ourselves assailed from within by doubts and fears, by all the feelings that we have never dared experience. Eventually all of the dammed-up pain of a lifetime will arise. Once we have chosen a practice, we must have the courage and the determination to stick with it and use it in the face of all our difficulties. This is the inward aspect of taking the one seat.

There are stories about how the Buddha practiced when he was assailed by doubts and temptations. The teaching about his commitment in the face of his challenges is called "The Lion's Roar." On the night of his enlightenment, the Buddha had vowed to sit on his one seat and not get up until he had awakened, until he found a freedom and a joy in the midst of all things in the world. He was then attacked by Mara, the god who personifies all of the forces of aggression, delusion, and temptation in the mind. After flinging every force of temptation and difficulty at the Buddha to no avail, Mara then challenged the Buddha's right to sit on that spot. The Buddha responded with a lion's roar and called upon the Goddess of the Earth to bear witness to his right to sit there, based on the thousands of lifetimes of patience, earnestness, compassion, virtue, and discipline he had cultivated. At this, the armies of Mara were washed away.

Later, as the Buddha taught, he was challenged by other yogis and ascetics for having given up austerity: "You eat beautiful food that your followers put in your bowl each morning and wear a robe in which you cover yourself from the cold, while we eat a few grains of rice a day and lie without robes on beds of nails. What kind of a teacher and yogi are you? You are soft, weak, indulgent." The Buddha answered these challenges, too, with a lion's roar. "I, too, have slept on nails; I've stood with my eyes open to the sun in the hot sands of the Ganges; I've eaten so little food that you couldn't fill one fingernail with the amount I ate each day. Whatever ascetic practices under the sun human beings have done, I, too, have done! Through them all I've learned that fighting against oneself through such practices is not the way."

Instead, the Buddha discovered what he called the Middle Way, a way not based on an aversion to the world, nor on attachment, but a way based on inclusion and compassion. The Middle Way rests at the center of all things, the one great seat in the center of the world. On this seat the Buddha opened his eyes to see clearly and opened his heart to embrace all. Through this he completed the process of his enlightenment. He declared, "I have seen what there is to be seen and known what there is to be known in order to free myself completely from all illusion and suffering." This, too, was his lion's roar.

We each need to make our lion's roar—to persevere with unshakable courage when faced with all manner of doubts and sorrows and fears— to declare our right to awaken. We need to take the one seat, as the Buddha did, and completely face what is true about this life. Make no mistake about this, it is not easy. It can take the courage of a lion or a lioness, especially when we are asked to sit with the depth of our pain or fear.

At one meditation retreat, I encountered a man whose only child, a four-year-old girl, had died in an accident just a few months before. Because she died in a car he was driving, he was filled with guilt as well as grief. He had stopped working and turned to full-time spiritual practice for solace. When he came to this retreat, he had already been to other retreats, he had been blessed by a great swami, and he had taken vows with a holy nun from South India. At the retreat his meditation cushion looked like a nest. It was surrounded by crystals, feathers, rosaries, and pictures of various great gurus. Each time he sat he would pray to each of the gurus and chant and recite sacred mantras. All of this to heal himself, he said. But perhaps all of this was to ward off his grief. After a few days I asked him if he would be willing simply to sit, without all his sacred objects, without prayer or chanting or any other practice. The next time he came in he just sat. In five minutes he was crying. In ten minutes he was sobbing and wailing. He had finally let himself take the seat in the midst of his sorrow; he had finally, truly begun to grieve. We all exercise this courage when we take the one seat.

In Buddhist practice, the outward and inward aspects of taking the one seat meet on our meditation cushion. In sitting on the meditation cushion and assuming the meditation posture, we connect ourselves with the present moment in this body and on this earth. We sit in this physical body halfway between heaven and earth, and we sit erect and straight. We possess a regal strength and dignity in this act. At the same time, we must also have a sense of relaxation, an openness, a gracious receptivity to life. The body is present, the heart is soft and open, the mind is attentive. To sit in this posture is to be like the Buddha. We can sense the universal human capacity to open, to awaken.

When we take the one seat on our meditation cushion we become our own monastery. We create the compassionate space that allows for the arising of all things: sorrows, loneliness, shame, desire, regret, frustration, happiness. In a monastery, monks and nuns take robes and shave their heads as part of the process of letting go. In the monastery of our own sitting meditation, each of us experiences whatever arises again and again as we let go, saying, "Ah, this too." The simple phrase, "This too, this too," was the main meditation instruction of one great woman yogi and master with whom I studied. Through these few words we were encouraged to soften and open to see whatever we encountered, accepting the truth with a wise and understanding heart.

In the same spirit, a zealous young student went to practice with one of the abbots of the Christian Desert Fathers. After some days he asked, "Tell us, master, when we see our brothers dozing during the sacred services, should we pinch them so they stay awake?" The old master replied with great kindness, "When I see a brother sleeping, I put his head on my lap and let him rest." After the heart has rested, it will naturally practice with renewed energy.

To take the one seat requires trust. We learn to trust that what needs to open within us will do so, in just the right fashion. In fact, our body, heart, and spirit know how to give birth, to open naturally, like the petals of a flower. We need not tear at the petals nor force the flower. We must simply stay planted and present.

Whatever practice we have chosen we must use in this fashion. As we take the one seat we discover our capacity to be unafraid and awake in the midst of all life. We may fear that our heart is not capable of weathering the storms of anger or grief or terror that have been stored up for so long. We may have a fear of accepting all of life, what Zorba the Greek called, "the Whole Catastrophe." But to take the one seat is to discover that we are unshakable. We discover that we can face life fully, with all its suffering and joy, that our heart is great enough to encompass it all.

Martin Luther King, Jr., understood this spirit and brought it alive in the darkest period of the civil rights marches. His church had been bombed and a number of people killed. He called upon the power of the heart to face this suffering and through this come to freedom. He said:

> We will match your capacity to inflict suffering with our capacity to endure suffering. We will meet your physical force with Soul Force. We will not hate you, but we cannot in all good conscience obey your unjust laws. But we will soon wear you down with our capacity to suffer. And in winning our freedom we will so appeal to your heart and conscience that we will win yours in the process.

Martin Luther King, Jr., understood that underneath all of the struggle and sorrow there is a force of life that is unstoppable. In taking the one seat, each of us awakens this force. It is through our own strength of being, our own integrity, the discovery of our own greatness of heart that we bring freedom to our lives and bring it to those around us as well. I have seen this over and over in working with students in meditation. Some great difficulty or insurmountable loss from the past will arise that seems impossible to face, impossible to resolve. Yet, given enough time and courage, it unravels itself, and out of the darkness inevitably comes a renewed vitality, a new spirit of life itself.

When we take the one seat on this earth, the great force of life will begin to move through us. I saw this force of life in the midst of tremendous desolation some years ago in the dry and barren land of the Cambodian refugee camps that I had visited to assist. After the Cambodian holocaust only parts of families had survived—a mother and three children, an old uncle and two nephews—and each was given a little bamboo hut about four feet wide, six feet long, and five feet high. In front of each hut was a little patch of land perhaps no bigger than one square yard. After only a few months of camp life, next to most of the huts in their little squares of ground, people had planted gardens. They would have a squash plant with two or three small squash on it, or a bean plant, or some other vegetable. The plants were very carefully tended, with little bamboo stakes for support. The tendrils of a bean plant would wind around the stake and up over the roof of the house.

Every day each refugee family would walk a mile and stand for half an hour in a long line at the pit well at the far end of the camp and carry back a bucket of water for their plants. It was a beautiful, beautiful thing to see these gardens in the middle of this camp in the dry season, when you could barely believe that anything would grow on such a hot barren field.

As these war-shattered families planted and watered their tiny gardens, they awakened the unstoppable force of life. So can we! No matter what inner difficulty or suffering we may experience, in taking the one seat and in tending to all that arises with compassionate awareness, we will discover this same unstoppable life force.

To commit ourselves to a spiritual practice is to awaken this force and to learn that we can trust it absolutely. We discover that we can face not only personal difficulties but even "heaven and hell," as the Buddha put it, and survive. We discover the capacity of our heart to open and encompass all. We discover our birthright as human beings.

From taking the one seat, a tremendous sense of wholeness and abundance arises within us. This is because we are open to everything, we reject nothing. Thomas Merton described the power of such openness in his *Asian Journals*. He visited the ancient monastery of Polonarua, where several enormous statues of the Buddha are carved in the face of a marble cliff. He described them as almost alive, the most wonderful works of art he had ever seen. Looking at the Buddhas, peaceful and empty, he saw "the silence of the extraordinary faces, the great smiles, huge, and yet subtle, filled with every possibility, questioning nothing, rejecting nothing. The great smiles of peace, not of emotional resignation but a peace that has seen through every question without trying to discredit anyone or anything—without refutation." For the Buddha the whole world arises in emptiness and everything in it is connected in compassion. In this awakened and compassionate consciousness, the whole world becomes our seat.

A MEDITATION ON
TAKING THE ONE SEAT

Let your body be seated comfortably in your chair or on your cushion. Take a posture that is stable, erect, and connected with the earth. Sit as the Buddha did on his night of enlightenment, with great dignity and centeredness, sensing your capacity to face anything that arises. Let your eyes close and let your attention turn to your breathing. Let your breath move freely through your body. Let each breath bring a calmness and an ease. As you breathe, sense your capacity to open in body, heart, and mind.

Open your senses, your feelings, your thoughts. Become aware of what feels closed in your body, closed in your heart, closed in your mind. Breathe and make space. Let the space open so that anything may arise. Let the windows of your senses open. Be aware of whatever feelings, images, sounds, and stories show themselves. Notice with interest and ease all that presents itself to you.

Continue to feel your steadiness and connectedness to the earth, as if you had taken the one seat in the center of life and opened yourself to an awareness of its dance. As you sit, reflect on the benefit of balance and peace in your life. Sense your capacity to rest unshakably as the seasons of life change. All that arises will pass away. Reflect on how joys and sorrows, pleasant events and unpleasant events, individuals, nations, even civilizations, arise and pass away. Take the one seat of a Buddha and rest with a heart of equanimity and compassion in the center of it all.

Sit this way, dignified and present, for as long as you wish. After some time, still feeling centered and steady, open your eyes. Then let yourself stand up and take some steps, walking with the same centeredness and dignity. Practice sitting and walking in this fashion, sensing your ability to be open, alive, and present with all that arises on this earth.

4

NECESSARY HEALING

True maturation on the spiritual path requires that we discover the depth of our wounds. As Achaan Chah put it, "If you haven't cried a number of times, your meditation hasn't really begun."

Almost everyone who undertakes a true spiritual path will discover that a profound personal healing is a necessary part of his or her spiritual process. When this need is acknowledged, spiritual practice can be directed to bring such healing to body, heart, and mind. This is not a new notion. Since ancient times, spiritual practice has been described as a process of healing. The Buddha and Jesus were both known as healers of the body, as well as great physicians of the spirit.

I encountered a powerful image of the connection of these two teachers in Vietnam, during the war years. In spite of active fighting in the area, I was drawn to visit a temple built by a famous master known as the Coconut Monk on an island in the Mekong Delta. When our boat arrived, the monks greeted us and showed us around. They explained to us their teachings of peace and nonviolence. Then they took us to one end of the island where on top of a hill was an enormous sixty-foot-tall statue of a standing Buddha. Just next to Buddha stood an equally tall statue of Jesus. They had their arms around each other's shoulders, smiling. While helicopter gunships flew by and war raged around them, Buddha and Jesus stood there like brothers expressing compassion and healing for all who would follow their way.

Wise spiritual practice requires that we actively address the pain and conflict of our life in order to come to inner integration and harmony. Through the guidance of a skillful teacher, meditation can help bring this healing. Without including the essential step of healing, students will find that they are blocked from deeper levels of meditation or are unable to integrate them into their lives.

Many people first come to spiritual practice hoping to skip over their sorrows and wounds, the difficult areas of their lives. They hope to rise above them and enter a spiritual realm full of divine grace, free from all conflict. Some spiritual practices actually do encourage this and teach ways of accomplishing this through intense concentration and ardor that bring about states of rapture and peace. Some powerful yogic practices can transform the mind. While such practices have their value, an inevitable disappointment occurs when they end, for as soon as practitioners relax in their discipline, they again encounter all the unfinished business of the body and heart that they had hoped to leave behind.

One man I knew practiced as a yogi in India for ten years. He had come to India after a divorce, and when he left his home in England, he was depressed and unhappy in his work as well. As a yogi he did years of deep and strict breath practices that led to long periods of peace and light in his mind. These were healing in a certain way. But, later, his loneliness returned, and he found himself drawn back home, only to discover that the unfinished issues that had ended his marriage, made him unhappy in his work, and, worst of all, contributed to his depression, all arose again as strong as before he had left. After some time, he saw that a deep healing of his heart was necessary. He realized he could not run from himself and began to seek a healing in the midst of his life. So he found a teacher who wisely guided him to include his depression and loneliness in his meditation. He sought a reconciliation (though not remarriage) with his former wife. He joined support groups that could help him to understand his childhood; he found communal work with people he liked. Each of these became part of the long process of healing his heart that had only begun in India.

True maturation on the spiritual path requires that we discover the depth of our wounds: our grief from the past, unfulfilled longing, the sorrow that we have stored up during the course of our lives. As Achaan

Chah put it, "If you haven't cried deeply a number of times, your meditation hasn't really begun."

This healing is necessary if we are to embody spiritual life lovingly and wisely. Unhealed pain and rage, unhealed traumas from childhood abuse or abandonment, become powerful unconscious forces in our lives. Until we are able to bring awareness and understanding to our old wounds, we will find ourselves repeating their patterns of unfulfilled desire, anger, and confusion over and over again. While many kinds of healing can come through spiritual life in the form of grace, charismatic revivals, prayer, or ritual, two of the most significant kinds develop naturally through a systematic spiritual practice.

The first area of healing comes when we develop a relationship of trust with a teacher. The image of the statues of Jesus and Buddha in the midst of the Vietnam War reminds us that even in great difficulties healing is possible. It also reminds us that healing cannot come from ourselves alone. The process of inner healing inevitably requires developing a committed relationship with a teacher or guide. Because many of our greatest pains come from past relationships, it is through our experience of a wise and conscious relationship that these pains are healed. This relationship itself becomes the ground for our opening to compassion and freedom of the spirit. Where the pain and disappointment of the past have left us isolated and closed, with a wise teacher we can learn to trust again. When we allow our darkest fears and worst dimensions to be witnessed and compassionately accepted by another, we learn to accept them ourselves.

A healthy relationship with a teacher serves as a model for trust in others, in ourselves, in our bodies, in our intuitions, our own direct experience. It gives us a trust in life itself. Teachings and teacher become a sacred container to support our awakening. (We will say more later in this book about relationships with teachers.)

Another kind of healing takes place when we begin to bring the power of awareness and loving attention to each area of our life with the systematic practice of mindfulness. The Buddha spoke of cultivating awareness in four fundamental aspects of life that he called the Four Foundations of Mindfulness. These areas of mindfulness are: awareness of the body and senses, awareness of the heart and feelings, awareness of the mind and thoughts, and awareness of the principles that govern life. (In Sanskrit these principles are called *the dharma*, or the *universal laws*.)

The development of awareness in these four areas is the basis for all of the Buddhist practices of insight and awakening. The power of sustained awareness is always healing and opening, and the ways to extend it to every area of life are taught throughout this book. Here is how healing is brought about by directing a meditative attention to each of the four aspects of life:

HEALING THE BODY

Meditation practice often begins with techniques for bringing us to an awareness of our bodies. This is especially important in a culture such as ours, which has neglected physical and instinctual life. James Joyce wrote of one character, "Mr. Duffy lived a short distance from his body." So many of us do. In meditation, we can slow down and sit quietly, truly staying with whatever arises. With awareness, we can cultivate a willingness to open to physical experiences without struggling against them, to actually live in our bodies. As we do so, we feel more clearly its pleasures and its pains. Because our acculturation teaches us to avoid or run from pain, we do not know much about it. To heal the body we must study pain. When we bring close attention to our physical pains, we will notice several kinds. We see that sometimes pain arises as we adjust to an unaccustomed sitting posture. Other times, pains arise as signals that we're sick or have a genuine physical problem. These pains call for a direct response and healing action from us.

However, most often the kinds of pains we encounter in meditative attention are not indications of physical problems. They are the painful, physical manifestations of our emotional, psychological, and spiritual holdings and contractions. Reich called these pains our muscular armor, the areas of our body that we have tightened over and over in painful situations as a way to protect ourselves from life's inevitable difficulties. Even a healthy person who sits somewhat comfortably to meditate will probably become aware of pains in his or her body. As we sit still, our shoulders, our backs, our jaws, or our necks may hurt. Accumulated knots in the fabric of our body, previously undetected, begin to reveal themselves as we open. As we become conscious of the pain they have held, we may also notice feelings, memories, or images connected specifically to each area of tension.

As we gradually include in our awareness all that we have previously shut out and neglected, our body heals. Learning to work with this opening is part of the art of meditation. We can bring an open and respectful attention to the sensations that make up our bodily experience. In this process, we must work to develop a feeling awareness of what is actually going on in the body. We can direct our attention to notice the patterns of our breathing, our posture, the way we hold our back, our chest, our belly, our pelvis. In all these areas we can carefully sense the free movement of energy or the contraction and holding that prevents it.

When you meditate, try to allow whatever arises to move through you as it will. Let your attention be very kind. Layers of tension will gradually release, and energy will begin to move. Places in your body where you have held the patterns of old illness and trauma will open. Then a deeper physical purification and opening of the energy channels will occur as the knots release and dissolve. Sometimes with this opening we will experience a powerful movement of the breath, sometimes a spontaneous vibration and other physical sensations.

Let your attention drop beneath the superficial level that just notices "pleasure," "tension," or "pain." Examine the pain and unpleasant sensations you usually block out. With careful mindfulness, you will allow "pain" to show itself to have many layers. As a first step, we can learn to be aware of pain without creating further tension, to experience and observe pain physically as pressure, tightness, pinpricks, needles, throbbing, or burning. Then we can notice all the layers around the "pain." Inside are the strong elements of fire, vibration, and pressure. Outside is often a layer of physical tightness and contraction. Beyond this may be an emotional layer of aversion, anger, or fear and a layer of thoughts and attitudes such as, "I hope this will go away soon," or "If I feel pain, I must be doing something wrong," or "Life is always painful." To heal, we must become aware of all these layers.

Everyone works with physical pain at some time in their spiritual practice. For some people it is a perennial theme. In my own practice, I have had periods of deep physical release that have been organic and very peaceful, and other times have felt like painful and powerful purifications, where my body would shake, my breathing was labored, sensations of heat and fire would move through my body, and strong feelings and images would arise. I would feel as if I were being wrung out. Staying with this process inevitably led to a great opening in my body, often accompanied by tremendous feelings of rapture and well-being. Such physical openings, both gentle and intense, are a common part of prolonged meditation. As you deepen your practice of the body, honor what arises, stay present with an open and loving awareness so that the body itself can unfold in its own way.

Other attitudes toward the body can be found in meditation: ascetic practices, warrior training, and inner yogas to conquer the body. Sometimes healers will recommend consciously aggressive meditation for healing certain illnesses. For instance, in one such practice cancer patients picture their white blood cells as little white knights who spear and destroy the cancer. For certain people this has been helpful, but for myself and others such as Stephen Levine, who has worked so extensively with healing meditation, we have found that a deeper kind of healing takes place when instead of sending aversion and aggression to wounds and illness, we bring loving-kindness. Too often we have met our pain and disease, whether a simple backache or a grave illness, by hating it, hating the whole afflicted area of our body. In mindful healing we direct a compassionate and loving attention to touch the innermost part of our wounds, and healing occurs. As Oscar Wilde put it, "It's not the perfect but the imperfect that is in need of our love."

One woman student came to her first meditation retreat with cancer throughout her body. Although she had been told she would die within weeks, she was determined to heal herself using meditation as a tool. She undertook a regimen of excellent Chinese medicine, acupuncture, and daily healing meditations. Though her belly was hot and distended with the cancer the whole time, she so bolstered her immune system that she lived well for ten more years. She credited her healing attention as a key to keeping her cancer in check.

Bringing systematic attention to our body can change our whole relationship to our physical life. We can notice more clearly the rhythms and needs of our bodies. Without mindfully attending to our bodies, we may become so busy in our daily lives that we lose touch with a sense of appropriate diet, movement, and physical enjoyment. Meditation can help us find out in what ways we are neglecting the physical aspects of our lives and what our body asks of us.

A mistaken disregard for the body is illustrated in a story of Mullah Nasrudin, the Sufi wise and holy fool. Nasrudin had bought a donkey, but it was costing him a lot to keep it fed, so he hatched a plan. As the weeks went on, he gradually fed the donkey less and less. Finally, he was only feeding it one small cupful of grain throughout the day. The plan seemed to be succeeding, and Nasrudin was saving a lot of money. Then, unfortunately, the donkey died. Nasrudin went to see his friends in the tea shop and told them about his experiment. "It's such a shame. If that donkey had been around a little longer, maybe I could have gotten him used to eating nothing!"

To ignore or abuse the body is mistaken spirituality. When we honor the body with our attention, we begin to reclaim our feelings, our instincts, our life. Out of this developing attention we can then experience a healing of the senses. The eyes, the tongue, the ears, and the sense of touch are rejuvenated. Many people experience this after some period of meditation. Colors are pure, flavors fresh, we can feel our feet on the earth as if we were children again. This cleansing of the senses allows us to experience the joy of being alive and a growing intimacy with life here and now.

HEALING THE HEART

Just as we open and heal the body by sensing its rhythms and touching it with a deep and kind attention, so we can open and heal other dimensions of our being. The heart and the feelings go through a similar process of healing through the offering of our attention to their rhythms, nature, and needs. Most often, opening the heart begins by opening to a lifetime's accumulation of unacknowledged sorrow, both our personal sorrows and the universal sorrows of warfare, hunger, old age, illness, and death. At times we may experience this sorrow physically, as contractions and barriers around our heart, but more often we feel the depth of our wounds, our abandonment, our pain, as unshed tears. The Buddhists describe this as an ocean of human tears larger than the four great oceans.

As we take the one seat and develop a meditative attention, the heart presents itself naturally for healing. The grief we have carried for so long, from pains and dashed expectations and hopes, arises. We grieve for our past traumas and present fears, for all of the feelings we never dared experience consciously. Whatever shame or unworthiness we have within us arises—much of our early childhood and family pain, the mother and father wounds we hold, the isolation, any past abuse, physical or sexual, are all stored in the heart. Jack Engler, a Buddhist teacher and psychologist at Harvard University, has described meditation practice as primarily a practice of grieving and of letting go. At most of the spiritual retreats I have been a part of, nearly half of the students are working with some level of grief: denial, anger, loss, or sorrow. Out of this grief work comes a deep renewal.

Many of us are taught that we shouldn't be affected by grief and loss, but no one is exempt. One of the most experienced hospice directors in the country was surprised when he came to a retreat and grieved for his mother who had died the year before. "This grief," he said, "is different from all the others I work with. It's *my* mother."

Oscar Wilde wrote, "Hearts are meant to be broken." As we heal through meditation, our hearts break open to feel fully. Powerful feelings, deep unspoken parts of ourselves arise, and our task in meditation is first to let them move through us, then to recognize them and allow them to sing their songs. A poem by Wendell Berry illustrates this beautifully.

I go among trees and sit still.
All my stirring becomes quiet
around me like circles on water.
My tasks lie in their places
Where I left them, asleep like cattle . . .

Then what I am afraid of comes.
I live for a while in its sight.
What I fear in it leaves it,
And the fear of it leaves me.
It sings, and I hear its song.

What we find as we listen to the songs of our rage or fear, loneliness or longing, is that they do not stay forever. Rage turns into sorrow; sorrow turns into tears; tears may fall for a long time, but then the sun comes out. A memory of old loss sings to us; our body shakes and relives the moment of loss; then the armoring around that loss gradually softens; and in the midst of the song of tremendous grieving, the pain of that loss finally finds release.

In truly listening to our most painful songs, we can learn the divine art of forgiveness. While there is a whole systematic practice of forgiveness that can be cultivated (see Chapter 19), both forgiveness and compassion arise spontaneously with the opening of the heart. Somehow, in feeling our own pain and sorrow, our own ocean of tears, we come to know that ours is a shared pain and that the mystery and beauty and pain of life cannot be separated. This universal pain, too, is part of our connection with one another, and in the face of it we cannot withhold our love any longer.

We can learn to forgive others, ourselves, and life for its physical pain. We can learn to open our heart to all of it, to the pain, to the pleasures we have feared. In this, we discover a remarkable truth: Much of spiritual life is self-acceptance, maybe all of it. Indeed, in accepting the songs of our life, we can begin to create for ourselves a much deeper and greater identity in which our heart holds all within a space of boundless compassion.

Most often this healing work is so difficult we need another person as an ally, a guide to hold our hand and inspire our courage as we go through it. Then miracles happen.

Naomi Remen, a physician who uses art, meditation, and other spiritual practices in the healing of cancer patients, told me a moving story that illustrates the process of healing the heart, which accompanies a healing of the body. She described a young man who was twenty-four years old when he came to her after one of his legs had been amputated at the hip in order to save his life from bone cancer. When she began her work with him, he had a great sense of injustice and a hatred for all "healthy" people. It seemed bitterly unfair to him that he had suffered this terrible loss so early in his life. His grief and rage were so great that it took several years of continuous work for him to begin to come out of himself and to heal. He had to heal not simply his body, but also his broken heart and wounded spirit.

He worked hard and deeply, telling his story, painting it, meditating, bringing his entire life into awareness. As he slowly healed, he developed a profound compassion for others in similar situations. He began to visit people in the hospital who had also suffered severe physical losses. On one occasion, he told his physician, he visited a young singer who was so depressed about the loss of her breasts that she would not even look at him. The nurses had the radio playing, probably hoping to cheer her up. It was a hot day, and the young man had come in running shorts. Finally, desperate to get her attention, he unstrapped his artificial leg and began dancing around the room on his one leg, snapping his fingers to the music. She looked at him in amazement, and then she burst out laughing and said, "Man, if you can dance, I can sing."

When this young man first began working with drawing, he made a crayon sketch of his own body in the form of a vase with a deep black crack running through it. He redrew the crack over and over and over, grinding his teeth with rage. Several years later, to encourage him to complete his process, my friend showed him his early pictures again. He saw the vase and said, "Oh, this one isn't finished." When she suggested that he finish it then, he did. He ran his finger along the crack, saying, "You see here, this is where the light comes through." With a yellow crayon, he drew light streaming through the crack into the body of the vase and said, "Our hearts can grow strong at the broken places."

This young man's story profoundly illustrates the way in which sorrow or a wound can heal, allowing us to grow into our fullest, most compassionate identity, our greatness of heart. When we truly come to terms with sorrow, a great and unshakable joy is born in our heart.

HEALING THE MIND

Just as we heal the body and the heart through awareness, so can we heal the mind. Just as we learn about the nature and rhythm of sensations and feelings, so can we learn about the nature of thoughts. As we notice our thoughts in meditation, we discover that they are not in our control—we swim in an uninvited constant stream of memories, plans, expectations, judgments, regrets. The mind begins to show how it contains all possibilities, often in conflict with one another—the beautiful qualities of a saint and the dark forces of a dictator and murderer. Out of these, the mind plans and imagines, creating endless struggles and scenarios for changing the world.

Yet the very root of these movements of mind is dissatisfaction. We seem to want both endless excitement and perfect peace. Instead of being served by our thinking, we are driven by it in many unconscious and unexamined ways. While thoughts can be enormously useful and creative, most often they dominate our experience with ideas of likes versus dislikes, higher versus lower, self versus other. They tell stories about our successes and failures, plan our security, habitually remind us of who and what we think we are.

This dualistic nature of thought is a root of our suffering. Whenever we think of ourselves as separate, fear and attachment arise and we grow constricted, defensive, ambitious, and territorial. To protect the separate self, we push certain things away, while to bolster it we hold on to other things and identify with them.

A psychiatrist from the Stanford University School of Medicine discovered these truths when he attended his first ten-day intensive retreat. While he had studied psychoanalysis and been in therapy, he had never actually encountered his own mind in the nonstop fashion of fifteen hours a day of sitting and walking meditation. He later wrote an article on this experience in which he described how a professor of psychiatry felt sitting and watching himself go crazy. The nonstop flood of thought astounded him, as did the wild variety of stories it told. Especially repetitious were thoughts of self-aggrandizement, of becoming a great teacher or famous writer or even world savior. He knew enough to look at the source of these thoughts, and he discovered they were all rooted in fear: during the retreat he was feeling insecure about himself and what he knew. These grand thoughts were the mind's compensation so he would not have to feel the fear of not knowing. Over the many years since, this professor has become a very skillful meditator, but he first had to make peace with the busy and fearful patterns of an untrained mind. He has also learned, since that time, not to take his own thoughts too seriously.

Healing the mind takes place in two ways: In the first, we bring attention to the content of our thoughts and learn to redirect them more skillfully through practices of wise reflection. Through mindfulness, we can come to know and reduce the patterns of unhelpful worry and obsession, we can clarify our confusion and release destructive views and opinions. We can use conscious thought to reflect more deeply on what we value. Asking the question, Do I love well? from the first chapter is an example of this, and we can also direct our thought into the skillful avenues of loving-kindness, respect, and ease of mind. Many Buddhist practices use the repetition of certain phrases in order to break through old, destructively repetitious patterns of thought to effect change.

However, even though we work to reeducate the mind, we can never be completely successful. The mind seems to have a will of its own no matter how much we wish to direct it. So, for a deeper healing of the conflicts of the mind, we need to let go of our identification with them. To heal, we must learn to step back from all the stories of the mind, for the conflicts and opinions of our thoughts never end. As the Buddha said, "People with opinions just go around bothering one another." When we see that the mind's very nature is to think, to divide, to plan, we can release ourselves from its iron grip of separatism and come to rest in the body and heart. In this way, we step out of our identification, out of our expectations, opinions, and judgments and the conflicts to which they give rise. The mind thinks of the self as separate, the heart knows better. As one great Indian master, Sri Nisargadatta, put it, "The mind creates the abyss, and the heart crosses it."

Many of the great sorrows of the world arise when the mind is disconnected from the heart. In meditation we can reconnect with our heart and discover an inner sense of spaciousness, unity, and compassion underneath all the conflicts of thought. The heart allows for the stories and ideas, the fantasies and fears of the mind without believing in them, without having to follow them or having to fulfill them. When we touch beneath all the busyness of thought, we discover a sweet, healing silence, an inherent peacefulness in each of us, a goodness of heart, strength, and wholeness that is our birthright. This basic goodness is sometimes called our original nature, or Buddha nature. When we return to our original nature, when we see all the ways of the mind and yet rest in this peace and goodness, we discover the healing of the mind.

HEALING THROUGH EMPTINESS

The last aspect of mindful healing is awareness of the universal laws that govern life. Central to it is an understanding of emptiness. This is most difficult to describe in words. In fact, while I can try to describe it here, the understanding of openness and emptiness will need to come directly through the experience of your own spiritual practice.

In Buddhist teaching, "emptiness" refers to a basic openness and nonseparation that we experience when all small and fixed notions of our self are seen through or dissolved. We experience it when we see that our existence is transitory, that our body, heart, and mind arise out of the changing web of life, where nothing is disconnected or separate. The deepest experiences in meditation lead us to an intimate awareness of life's essential openness and emptiness, of its everchanging and unpossessable nature, of its nature as an unstoppable process.

The Buddha described human life as comprising a series of everchanging processes: a physical process, a feeling process, a memory and recognition process, a thought and reaction process, and a consciousness process. These processes are dynamic and continuous, without a single element we can call our unchanging self. We ourselves are a process, woven together with life, without separateness. We arise like a wave out of the ocean of life, our tentative forms still one with the ocean. Some traditions call this ocean the Tao, the divine, the fertile void, the unborn. Out of it, our lives appear as reflections of the divine, as a movement or dance of consciousness. The most profound healing comes when we sense this process, this life-giving emptiness.

As our meditation practice deepens, we are able to see the movement of our experience. We note feelings and find that they last for only a few seconds. We pay attention to thoughts and find that they are ephemeral, that they come and go, uninvited, like clouds. We bring our awareness to the body and find that its boundaries are porous. In this practice, our sense of the solidity of a separate body or a separate mind starts to dissolve, and suddenly, unexpectedly, we find out how much at ease we are. As our meditation deepens still further, we experience expansiveness, delight, and the freedom of our interconnectedness with all things, with the great mystery of our life.

One hospice director experienced this interconnectedness as he sat with the children of a dying sixty-five-year-old man outside his room. They had just received news that their father's younger brother had been killed in a car accident and were struggling with whether or not to tell him. Their father was close to death and, fearing it would upset him, they decided not to speak of it. As they entered the room he looked up and said, "Don't you have something to tell me?" They wondered what he could mean. "Why didn't you tell me that my brother died?" Astonished, they asked how he had found out. "I've been talking with him for the past half hour," said their father, who then called them to his bedside. He spoke some last words to each child and in ten minutes rested his head back and died.

The Tibetan teacher Kalu Rinpoche puts it this way:

> You live in illusion and the appearance of things. There is a reality, but you do not know this. When you understand this, you will see that you are nothing, and being nothing you are everything. That is all.

Healing comes in touching this realm of nonseparation. We discover that our fears and desires, our attempts to enhance and defend ourselves, are based on delusion, on a sense of separateness that is fundamentally untrue.

In discovering the healing power of emptiness, we sense that everything is intertwined in a continuous movement, arising in certain forms that we call bodies or thoughts or feelings, and then dissolving or changing into new forms. With this wisdom we can open to one moment after another and live in the everchanging Tao. We discover we can let go and trust, we can let the breath breathe itself and the natural movement of life carry us with ease.

Each dimension of our being, the body, the heart, and the mind, is healed through the same loving attention and care. Our attention can honor the body and discover the blessings of the physical life that has been given us. Attention can bring us fully into the heart to honor the whole range of our human feelings. It can heal the mind and help us to honor thought without being trapped by it. And it can open us to the great mystery of life, to the discovery of the emptiness and wholeness that we are and our fundamental unity with all things.

DEVELOPING A
HEALING ATTENTION

Sit comfortably and quietly. Let your body rest easily. Breathe gently. Let go of your thoughts, past and future, memories and plans. Just be present. Begin to let your own precious body reveal the places that most need healing. Allow the physical pains, tensions, diseases, or wounds to show themselves. Bring a careful and kind attention to these painful places. Slowly and carefully feel their physical energy. Notice what is deep inside them, the pulsations, throbbing, tension, needles, heat, contraction, aching, that make up what we call pain. Allow these all to be felt fully, to be held in a receptive and kind attention. Then be aware of the surrounding area of your body. If there is contraction and holding, notice this gently. Breathe softly and let it open. Then, in the same way, be aware of any aversion or resistance in your mind. Notice this, too, with a soft attention, without resisting, allowing it to be as it is, allowing it to open in its own time. Now notice the thoughts and fears that accompany the pain you are exploring: "It will never go away." "I can't stand it." "I don't deserve this." "It is too hard, too much trouble, too deep," etc.

Let these thoughts rest in your kind attention for a time. Then gently return to your physical body. Let your awareness be deeper and more allowing now. Again, feel the layers of the place of pain, and allow each layer that opens to move, to intensify or dissolve in its own time. Bring your attention to the pain as if you were gently comforting a child, holding it all in a loving and soothing attention. Breathe softly into it, accepting all that is present with a healing kindness. Continue this meditation until you feel reconnected with whatever part of your body calls you, until you feel at peace.

As your healing attention develops, you can direct it regularly to significant areas of illness or pain in your body. You can then scan your body for additional areas that call for your caring attention. In the same way, you can direct a healing attention to deep emotional wounds you carry. Grief, longing, rage, loneliness, and sorrow can all first be felt in your body. With careful and kind attention, you can feel deep inside them. Stay with them. After some time you can breathe softly and open your attention to each of the layers of contraction, emotions, and thoughts that are carried with them. Finally, you can let these, too, rest, as if you were gently comforting a child, accepting all that is present, until you feel at peace. You can work with the heart in this way as often as you wish. Remember, the healing of our body and heart is always here. It simply awaits our compassionate attention.

A MEDITATIVE VISIT TO THE HEALING TEMPLE

Sit comfortably, let your eyes close. Bring your attention to your breath. Feel your breath and your body as you sit, without trying to change them. Notice what's comfortable and what's uncomfortable. Notice if you're sleepy or wide awake. Notice if there's a lot of clutter in the mind or if it is quiet. Just be aware of what is. Notice the state of your heart. Does it feel contracted? Does it feel soft and open? Or is it somewhere in the middle? Is it tired, is it joyful? Notice and receive what is present.

Then imagine you are magically transported to a beautiful healing temple or power spot, a place of great wisdom and love. Take as much time as you need to sense it, feel it, picture it, in any way that feels good to you. Sense yourself sitting there, restfully and attentively meditating in this place. As you sit at this temple, this place of great wisdom, begin to reflect on your own spiritual journey more deeply. Gradually let yourself be aware of the wounds you carry that will require healing in the course of your journey. Breathe softly, and gently feel whatever arises.

As you sit, a wonderful and wise being from this healing temple will gently approach you. When this being comes quite near, you can picture or imagine or sense who or what they are. They will bow lightly and then come over and put the gentlest hand on a part of your body where you are deeply wounded. With their most loving care, let them touch the part of your body that holds one of your sorrows. Let them teach you their healing touch. If you can't feel their touch, then take your own hand as you sit at that temple and imagine that you bring it to the place of your deepest wound, the place of sorrow or difficulty, touching it with your hand as if you yourself were that beautiful being. Know that no matter how many times you have buried or resisted your sorrow, no matter how many times you have greeted it with your hatred, you can finally open to it.

Let your own attention become like the hand of this wonderful wise being. Touch this place of sorrow with softness and tenderness. As you touch it, explore what is there. Is it warm or cool there? Is it hard, tight, or is it soft? Is it vibrating or moving, or is it still? Let your awareness be like the loving touch of the Buddha or the Goddess of Compassion, of Mother Mary or Jesus. What is the temperature and texture of this sorrow? What color is there to be felt? What feelings are there to be felt? Let yourself become aware of all your feelings with a very loving and receptive heart. Let them be anything they need to be. Then very gently and softly, as if you were the Goddess of Compassion herself, touch it with pure sweetness. Open yourself to the pain. What is the core of this place that has been wrapped up and held inside you for so long? As you look at it, let yourself see how much you've closed off to it, how much you've suppressed or rejected it, wished that it would go away, wished that you didn't have to feel it, and treated it with fear and aversion. Let yourself sit peacefully, opening your heart to this pain at last.

Rest in this temple, allowing your healing and compassionate attention to suffuse every part of it. Stay as long as you wish. When you are ready to leave, imagine yourself bowing with gratitude. As you leave, remember this temple is inside you. You can always go there.

5

TRAINING THE PUPPY:
MINDFULNESS OF BREATHING

Concentration is never a matter of force or coercion. You simply pick up the puppy again and return to reconnect with the here and now.

A story is told of the Buddha when he was wandering in India shortly after his enlightenment. He was encountered by several men who recognized something quite extraordinary about this handsome prince now robed as a monk. Stopping to inquire, they asked, "Are you a god?" "No," he answered. "Well, are you a deva or an angel?" "No," he replied. "Well, are you some kind of wizard or magician?" "No." "Are you a man?" "No." They were perplexed. Finally they asked, "Then what are you?" He replied simply, "I am awake." The word *Buddha* means to awaken. How to awaken is all he taught.

Meditation can be thought of as the art of awakening. Through the mastering of this art we can learn new ways to approach our difficulties and bring wisdom and joy alive in our life. Through developing meditation's tools and practices, we can awaken the best of our spiritual, human capacities. The key to this art is the steadiness of our attention.

When the fullness of our attention is cultivated together with a grateful and tender heart, our spiritual life will naturally grow.

As we have seen, some healing of mind and body must take place for many of us before we can sit quietly and concentrate. Yet even to begin our healing, to begin understanding ourselves, we must have some basic level of attention. To deepen our practice further, we must choose a way to develop our attention systematically and give ourselves to it quite fully. Otherwise we will drift like a boat without a rudder. To learn to concentrate we must choose a prayer or meditation and follow this path with commitment and steadiness, a willingness to work with our practice day after day, no matter what arises. This is not easy for most people. They would like their spiritual life to show immediate and cosmic results. But what great art is ever learned quickly? Any deep training opens in direct proportion to how much we give ourselves to it.

Consider the other arts. Music, for example. How long would it take to learn to play the piano well? Suppose we take months or years of lessons once a week, practicing diligently every day. Initially, almost everyone struggles to learn which fingers go for which notes and how to read basic lines of music. After some weeks or months, we could play simple tunes, and perhaps after a year or two we could play a chosen type of music. However, to master the art so that we could play music well, alone or in a group, or join a band or an orchestra, we would have to give ourselves to this discipline over and over, time and again. If we wanted to learn computer programming, oil painting, tennis, architecture, any of the thousand arts, we would have to give ourselves to it fully and wholeheartedly over a long period of time—a training, an apprenticeship, a cultivation.

Nothing less is required in the spiritual arts. Perhaps even more is asked. Yet through this mastery we master ourselves and our lives. We learn the most human art, how to connect with our truest self.

Trungpa Rinpoche called spiritual practice manual labor. It is a labor of love in which we bring a wholehearted attention to our own situation over and over again. In all sorts of weather, we steady and deepen our prayer, meditation, and discipline, learning how to see with honesty and compassion, how to let go, how to love more deeply.

However, this is not how we begin. Suppose we begin with a period of solitude in the midst of our daily life. What happens when we actually try to meditate? The most frequent first experience—whether in prayer or chanting, meditation or visualization—is that we encounter the disconnected and scattered mind. Buddhist psychology likens the untrained mind to a crazed monkey that dashes from thought to memory, from sight to sound, from plan to regret without ceasing. If we were able to sit quietly for an hour and fully observe all the places our mind went, what a script would be revealed.

When we first undertake the art of meditation, it is indeed frustrating. Inevitably, as our mind wanders and our body feels the tension it has accumulated and the speed to which it is addicted, we often see how little inner discipline, patience, or compassion we actually have. It doesn't take much time with a spiritual task to see how scattered and unsteady our attention remains even when we try to direct and focus it. While we usually think of it as "our mind," if we look honestly, we see that the mind follows its own nature, conditions, and laws. Seeing this, we also see that we must gradually discover a wise relationship to the mind that connects it to the body and heart, and steadies and calms our inner life.

The essence of this connecting is the bringing back of our attention again and again to the practice we have chosen. Prayer, meditation, repeating sacred phrases, or visualization gives us a systematic way to focus and steady our concentration. All the traditional realms and states of consciousness described in mystical and spiritual literature worldwide are arrived at through the art of concentration. These arts of concentration, of returning to the task at hand, also bring the clarity, strength of mind, peacefulness, and profound connectedness that we seek. This steadiness and connection in turn gives rise to even deeper levels of understanding and insight.

Whether a practice calls for visualization, question, prayer, sacred words, or simple meditation on feelings or breath, it always involves the steadying and conscious return, again and again, to some focus. As we learn to do this with a deeper and fuller attention, it is like learning to steady a canoe in waters that have waves. Repeating our meditation, we relax and sink into the moment, deeply connecting with what is present. We let ourselves settle into a spiritual ground; we train ourselves to come back to this moment. This is a patient process. St. Francis de Sales said, "What we need is a cup of understanding, a barrel of love, and an ocean of patience."

For some, this task of coming back a thousand or ten thousand times in meditation may seem boring or even of questionable importance. But how many times have we gone away from the reality of our life?—perhaps a million or ten million times! If we wish to awaken, we have to find our way back here with our full being, our full attention.

St. Francis de Sales continued by saying:

Bring yourself back to the point quite gently. And even if you do nothing during the whole of your hour but bring your heart back a thousand times, though it went away every time you brought it back, your hour would be very well employed.

In this way, meditation is very much like training a puppy. You put the puppy down and say, "Stay." Does the puppy listen? It gets up and it runs away. You sit the puppy back down again. "Stay." And the puppy runs away over and over again. Sometimes the puppy jumps up, runs over, and pees in the corner or makes some other mess. Our minds are much the same as the puppy, only they create even bigger messes. In training the mind, or the puppy, we have to start over and over again.

When you undertake a spiritual discipline, frustration comes with the territory. Nothing in our culture or our schooling has taught us to steady and calm our attention. One psychologist has called us a society of attentional spastics. Finding it difficult to concentrate, many people respond by forcing their attention on their breath or mantra or prayer with tense irritation and self-judgment, or worse. Is this the way you would train a puppy? Does it really help to beat it? Concentration is never a matter of force or coercion. You simply pick up the puppy again and return to reconnect with the here and now.

Developing a deep quality of interest in your spiritual practice is one of the keys to the whole art of concentration. Steadiness is nourished by the degree of interest with which we focus our meditation. Yet, to the beginning student, many meditation subjects appear plain and uninteresting. There is a traditional story about a Zen student who complained to his master that following the breath was boring. The Zen master grabbed this student and held his head under water for quite a long time while the student struggled to come up. When he finally let the student up, the Zen master asked him whether he had found breath boring in those moments under water.

Concentration combines full interest with delicacy of attention. This attention should not be confused with being removed or detached. Awareness does not mean separating ourselves from experience; it means allowing it and sensing it fully. Awareness can vary like a zoom lens. Sometimes we are in the middle of our experience. Sometimes it is as if we sit on our own shoulder and notice what is present, and sometimes we can be aware with a great spacious distance. All of these are useful aspects of awareness. They each can help us sense and touch and see our life more clearly from moment to moment. As we learn to steady the quality of our attention, it is accompanied by a deeper and deeper sense of stillness—poised, exquisite, and subtle.

The art of subtle attention was learned by one meditation student while she and her husband lived in a remote community in the mountains of British Columbia. She had studied yoga in India, and some years later she, with the help of her husband, gave birth to a baby boy, alone, without doctor or midwife. Unfortunately, it was a long and complicated breech delivery, with the baby delivered feetfirst and the umbilical cord wrapped around his neck. The baby was born quite blue, and he could not start to breathe on his own. His parents gave him infant artificial respiration as best they could. Then they would pause for a moment between their breathing into his lungs to see if he would begin to breathe by himself. During these excruciating moments, they watched for the tiniest movement of his breath to see if he would live or die. Finally, he started to breathe on his own. His mother smiled at me when she told this story, and said, "It was at that time that I learned what it meant to be truly aware of the breath. And it wasn't even my own breath!"

The focusing of attention on the breath is perhaps the most universal of the many hundreds of meditation subjects used worldwide. Steadying attention on the movement of the life-breath is central to yoga, to Buddhist and Hindu practices, to Sufi, Christian, and Jewish traditions. While other meditation subjects are also beneficial, and each has its unique qualities, we will continue to elaborate on the practice of breath meditation as an illustration for developing any of these practices. Breathing meditation can quiet the mind, open the body, and develop a great power of concentration. The breath is available to us at any time of day and in any circumstance. When we have learned to use it, the breath becomes a support for awareness throughout our life.

But awareness of breathing does not come right away. At first we must sit quietly, letting our body be relaxed and alert, and simply practice finding the breath in the body. Where do we actually feel it—as a coolness in the nose, a tingling in the back of the throat, as a movement in the chest, as a rise and fall of the belly? The place of strongest feeling is the first place to establish our attention. If the breath is apparent in several places, we can feel its whole movement of the body. If the breath is too soft and difficult to find, we can place our palm on our belly and feel the expansion and contraction in our hand. We must learn to focus our attention carefully. As we feel each breath we can sense how it moves in our body. Do not try to control the breath, only notice its natural movement, as a gatekeeper notices what passes by. What are its rhythms? Is it shallow or long and deep? Does it become fast or slow? Is there a temperature to the breath? The breath can become a great teacher because it is always moving and changing. In this simple breathing, we can learn about contraction and resistance, about opening and letting go. Here we can feel what it means to live gracefully, to sense the truth of the river of energy and change that we are.

Yet even with interest and a strong desire to steady our attention, distractions will arise. Distractions are the natural movement of mind. Distractions arise because our mind and heart are not initially clear or pure. Mind is more like muddy or turbulent water. Each time an enticing image or an interesting memory floats by, it is our habit to react, to get entangled, or to get lost. When painful images or feelings arise, it is our habit to avoid them and unknowingly distract ourselves. We can feel the power of these habits of desire, of distracting ourselves, of fear and reaction. In many of us these forces are so great that after a few unfamiliar moments of calm, our mind rebels. Again and again restlessness, busyness, plans, unfelt feelings, all interrupt our focus. Working with these distractions, steadying the canoe, letting the waves pass by, and coming back again and again in a quiet and collected way, is at the heart of meditation.

After your initial trial, you will begin to recognize that certain external conditions are particularly helpful in developing concentration. Finding or creating a quiet and undistracting place for your practice is necessary. Select regular and suitable times that best fit your temperament and schedule; experiment to discover whether morning or evening meditations best support the silent aspects of your inner life. You may wish to begin with a short period of inspiring reading before sitting, or do some stretching or yoga first. Some people find it extremely helpful to sit in a regular group with others or to go off to periodic retreats. Experiment with these external factors until you discover which are most helpful for your own inner peace. Then make them a regular part of your life. Creating suitable conditions means living wisely, providing the best soil for our spiritual hearts to be nourished and to grow.

As we give ourselves to the art of concentration over the weeks and months, we discover that our concentration slowly begins to settle by itself. Initially we may have struggled to focus, trying to hold on to the subject of our meditation. Then gradually the mind and the heart become eased from distractions, and periodically we sense them as purer, more workable and malleable. We feel our breath more often and more clearly, or we recite our prayers or mantra with greater wholeness. This is like beginning to read a book. When we start, we will often be interrupted by many distractions around us. But if it is a good book, perhaps a mystery novel, by the last chapter we will be so absorbed in the plot that people can walk right by us and we will not notice them. In meditation at first, thoughts carry us away and we think them for a long time. Then, as concentration grows we remember our breath in the middle of a thought. Later we can notice thoughts just as they arise or allow them to pass in the background, so focused on the breath that we are undisturbed by their movement.

As we continue, the development of concentration brings us closer to life, like the focusing of a lens. When we look at pond water in a cup, it appears clear and still. But under the simplest microscope it shows itself to be alive with creatures and movement. In the same way, the more deeply we pay attention, the less solid our breath and body become. Every place we feel breath in our body can come alive with subtle vibrations, movement, tingles, flow. The steady power of our concentration shows each part of our life to be in change and flux, like a river, even as we feel it.

As we learn to let go into the present, the breath breathes itself, allowing the flow of sensations in the body to move and open. There can come an openness and ease. Like a skilled dancer, we allow the breath and body to float and move unhindered, yet all the while being present to enjoy the opening.

As we become more skillful we also discover that concentration has its own seasons. Sometimes we sit and settle easily. At other times the conditions of mind and body are turbulent or tense. We can learn to navigate all these waters. When conditions show the mind is tight, we learn to soften and relax, to open the attention. When the mind is sleepy or flabby, we learn to sit up and focus with more energy. The Buddha compared this with the tuning of a lute, sensing when we are out of tune and gently strengthening or loosening our energy to come into balance.

In learning concentration, we feel as if we are always starting over, always losing our focus. But where have we actually gone? It is only that a mood or a thought or doubt has swept through our mind. As soon as we recognize this, we can let go and settle back again in this next moment. We can always begin again. Gradually as our interest grows and our capacity to sense deepens, new layers of our meditation open. We will find ourselves alternating, discovering periods of deep peace like an undisturbed child and strength like a great ship on a true course, only to be distracted or lost sometime later. Concentration grows in a deepening spiral, as we return to our meditation subject again and again, each time learning more of the art of inner listening. When we are listening carefully, we can sense new aspects of our breath all the time. One

Burmese meditation teacher requires his students each day to tell him something new about the breath, even if they have been meditating for years.

Here, notice if you can, is there a pause between your breaths? How does it feel when your breath just starts? What is the end of the breath like? What is that space when the breathing has stopped? What does the impulse to breathe feel like before the breath even begins? How is the breath a reflection of your moods?

At first when we feel the breath, it seems like only one small movement, but as we develop the art of concentration, we can feel a hundred things in the breath: the subtlest sensations, the variations in its length, the temperature, the swirl, the expansion, the contraction, the tingles that come along with it, the echoes of the breath in different parts of our body, and so much more.

Sticking with a spiritual training requires an ocean of patience because our habit of wanting to be somewhere else is so strong. We've distracted ourselves from the present for so many moments, for so many years, even lifetimes. Here is an accomplishment in *The Guinness Book of World Records* that I like to note at meditation retreats when people are feeling frustrated. It indicates that the record for persistence in taking and failing a driving test is held by Mrs. Miriam Hargrave of Wakefield, England. Mrs. Hargrave failed her thirty-ninth driving test in April, 1970, when she crashed, driving through a set of red lights. In August of the following year she finally passed her fortieth test. Unfortunately, she could no longer afford to buy a car because she had spent so much on driving lessons. In the same spirit, Mrs. Fanny Turner of Little Rock, Arkansas, passed her written test for a driver's license on her 104th attempt in October 1978. If we can bring such persistence to passing a driving test or mastering the art of skateboarding or any one of a hundred other endeavors, surely we can also master the art of connecting with ourselves. As human beings we can dedicate ourselves to almost anything, and this heartfelt perseverance and dedication brings spiritual practice alive.

Always remember that in training a puppy we want to end up with the puppy as our friend. In the same way, we must practice seeing our mind and body as "friend." Even its wanderings can be included in our meditation with a friendly interest and curiosity. Right away we can notice how it moves. The mind produces waves. Our breath is a wave, the sensations of our body are a wave. We don't have to fight the waves. We can simply acknowledge, "Surf's up." "Here's the wave of memories from three years old." "Here's the planning wave." Then it's time to reconnect with the wave of the breath. It takes a gentleness and a kind-hearted understanding to deepen the art of concentration. We can't be present for a long period without actually softening, dropping into our bodies, coming to rest. Any other kind of concentration, achieved by force and tension, will only be short-lived. Our task is to train the puppy to become our lifelong friend.

The attitude or spirit with which we do our meditation helps us perhaps more than any other aspect. What is called for is a sense of perseverance and dedication combined with a basic friendliness. We need a willingness to directly relate again and again to what is actually here, with a lightness of heart and sense of humor. We do not want the training of our puppy to become too serious a matter.

The Christian Desert Fathers tell of a new student who was commanded by his master that for three years he must give money to everyone who insulted him. When this period of trial was over, the master said, "Now you can go to Alexandria and truly learn wisdom." When the student entered Alexandria, he met a certain wise man whose way of teaching was to sit at the city gate insulting everyone who came and went. He naturally insulted the student also, who immediately burst out laughing. "Why do you laugh when I insult you?" said the wise man. "Because," said the student, "for years I've been paying for this kind of thing, and now you give it to me for free!" "Enter the city," said the wise man. "It is all yours."

Meditation is a practice that can teach us to enter each moment with wisdom, lightness, and a sense of humor. It is an art of opening and letting go, rather than accumulation or struggle. Then, even within our frustrations and difficulties, a remarkable inner sense of support and perspective can grow. Breathing in, "Wow, this experience is interesting, isn't it? Let me take another breath. Ah, this one is difficult, even terrifying, isn't it?" Breathing out, "Ah." It is an amazing process we have entered when we can train our hearts and minds to be open and steady and awake through it all.

ESTABLISHING A DAILY
MEADITATION

First select a suitable space for your regular meditation. It can be wherever you can sit easily with minimal disturbance: a corner of your bedroom or any other quiet spot in your home. Place a meditation cushion or chair there for your use. Arrange what is around so that you are reminded of your meditative purpose, so that it feels like a sacred and peaceful space. You may wish to make a simple altar with a flower or sacred image, or place your favorite spiritual books there for a few moments of inspiring reading. Let yourself enjoy creating this space for yourself.

Then select a regular time for practice that suits your schedule and temperament. If you are a morning person, experiment with a sitting before breakfast. If evening fits your temperament or schedule better, try that first. Begin with sitting ten or twenty minutes at a time. Later you can sit longer or more frequently. Daily meditation can become like bathing or toothbrushing. It can bring a regular cleansing and calming to your heart and mind.

Find a posture on the chair or cushion in which you can easily sit erect without being rigid. Let your body be firmly planted on the earth, your hands resting easily, your heart soft, your eyes closed gently. At first feel your body and consciously soften any obvious tension. Let go of any habitual thoughts or plans. Bring your attention to feel the sensations of your breathing. Take a few deep breaths to sense where you can feel the breath most easily, as coolness or tingling in the nostrils or throat, as movement of the chest, or rise and fall of the belly. Then let your breath be natural. Feel the sensations of your natural breathing very carefully, relaxing into each breath as you feel it, noticing how the soft sensations of breathing come and go with the changing breath.

After a few breaths your mind will probably wander. When you notice this, no matter how long or short a time you have been away, simply come back to the next breath. Before you return, you can mindfully acknowledge where you have gone with a soft word in the back of your mind, such as "thinking," "wandering," "hearing," "itching." After softly and silently naming to yourself where your attention has been, gently and directly return to feel the next breath. Later on in your meditation you will be able to work with the places your mind wanders to, but for initial training, one word of acknowledgment and a simple return to the breath is best.

As you sit, let the breath change rhythms naturally, allowing it to be short, long, fast, slow, rough, or easy. Calm yourself by relaxing into the breath. When your breath becomes soft, let your attention become gentle and careful, as soft as the breath itself.

Like training a puppy, gently bring yourself back a thousand times. Over weeks and months of this practice you will gradually learn to calm and center yourself using the breath. There will be many cycles in this process, stormy days alternating with clear days. Just stay with it. As you do, listening deeply, you will find the breath helping to connect and quiet your whole body and mind.

Working with the breath is an excellent foundation for the other meditations presented in this book. After developing some calm and skills, and connecting with your breath, you can then extend your range of meditation to include healing and awareness of all the levels of your body and mind. You will discover how awareness of your breath can serve as a steady basis for all you do.

WALKING MEDITATION

Like breathing meditation, walking meditation is a simple and universal practice for developing calm, connectedness, and awareness. It can be practiced regularly, before or after sitting meditation or any time on its own, such as after a busy day at work or on a lazy Sunday morning. The art of walking meditation is to learn to be aware as you walk, to use the natural movement of walking to cultivate mindfulness and wakeful presence.

Select a quiet place where you can walk comfortably back and forth, indoors or out, about ten to thirty paces in length. Begin by standing at one end of this "walking path," with your feet firmly planted on the ground. Let your hands rest easily, wherever they are comfortable. Close your eyes for a moment, center yourself, and feel your body standing on the earth. Feel the pressure on the bottoms of your feet and the other natural sensations of standing. Then open your eyes and let yourself be present and alert.

Begin to walk slowly. Let yourself walk with a sense of ease and dignity. Pay attention to your body. With each step feel the sensations of lifting your foot and leg off of the earth. Be aware as you place each foot on the earth. Relax and let your walking be easy and natural. Feel each step mindfully as you walk. When you reach the end of your path, pause for a moment. Center yourself, carefully turn around, pause again so that you can be aware of the first step as you walk back. You can experiment with the speed, walking at whatever pace keeps you most present.

Continue to walk back and forth for ten or twenty minutes or longer. As with the breath in sitting, your mind will wander away many, many times. As soon as you notice this, acknowledge where it went softly: "wandering," "thinking," "hearing," "planning." Then return to feel the next step. Like training the puppy, you will need to come back a thousand times. Whether you have been away for one second or for ten minutes, simply acknowledge where you have been and then come back to being alive here and now with the next step you take.

After some practice with walking meditation, you will learn to use it to calm and collect yourself and to live more wakefully in your body. You can then extend your walking practice in an informal way when you go shopping, whenever you walk down the street or walk to or from your car. You can learn to enjoy walking for its own sake instead of the usual planning and thinking and, in this simple way, begin to be truly present, to bring your body, heart, and mind together as you move through your life.

PART II

PROMISES AND PERILS

TURNING STRAW
INTO GOLD

*To undertake a genuine spiritual path is not to
avoid difficulties but to learn the art of making
mistakes wakefully, to bring to them the transformative power of our heart.*

Every spiritual life entails a succession of difficulties because every
ordinary life also involves a succession of difficulties, what the Buddha
described as the inevitable sufferings of existence. In a spiritually
informed life, however, these inevitable difficulties can be the source of
our awakening, of deepening wisdom, patience, balance, and compassion. Without this perspective, we simply bear our sufferings like an ox
or a foot soldier under a heavy load.

Like the young maiden in the fairy tale "Rumpelstiltskin" who is
locked in a room full of straw, we often do not realize that the straw all
around us is gold in disguise. The basic principle of spiritual life is that
our problems become the very place to discover wisdom and love.

With even a little spiritual practice we have already discovered the need for healing, for stopping the war, for training ourselves to be present. Now as we become more conscious, we can see yet more clearly the inevitable contradictions of life, the pain and the struggles, the joys and the beauty, the inevitable suffering, the longing, the everchanging play of joys and sorrows that make up human experience.

As we follow a genuine path of practice, our sufferings may seem to increase because we no longer hide from them or from ourselves. When we do not follow the old habits of fantasy and escape, we are left facing the actual problems and contradictions of our life.

A genuine spiritual path does not avoid difficulties or mistakes but leads us to the art of making mistakes wakefully, bringing them to the transformative power of our heart. When we set out to love, to awaken, to become free, we are inevitably confronted with our own limitations. As we look into ourselves we see more clearly our unexamined conflicts and fears, our frailties and confusion. To witness this can be difficult. Lama Trungpa Rinpoche described spiritual progress from the ego's point of view as "one insult after another."

In this way, our life may appear as a series of mistakes. One could call them "problems" or "challenges," but in some ways "mistakes" is better. One famous Zen master actually described spiritual practice as "one mistake after another," which is to say, one opportunity after another to learn. It is from "difficulties, mistakes, and errors" that we actually learn. To live life is to make a succession of errors. Understanding this can bring us great ease and forgiveness for ourselves and others—we are at ease with the difficulties of life.

But what is our usual response? When difficulties arise in our life we meet them with blame, frustration, or a sense of failure, and then we try to get over these feelings, to get rid of them as soon as possible, to get back to something more pleasant.

As we quiet ourselves in meditation, our process of reacting to difficulties will become even more apparent. But instead of responding with automatic blame, we now have an opportunity to see our difficulties and how they arise. There are two kinds of difficulties. Some are clearly problems to solve, situations that call for compassionate action and direct response. Many more are problems we create for ourselves by struggling to make life different than it is or by becoming so caught up in our own point of view that we lose sight of a larger, wiser perspective.

Usually we think our difficulties are the fault of things outside us. Benjamin Franklin knew this when he stated:

Our limited perspective, our hopes and fears become our measure of life, and when circumstances don't fit our ideas, they become our difficulties.

A Buddhist writer I know began his practice with a well-known Tibetan teacher many years ago. The writer didn't know much about meditation, but after some preliminary instruction he decided that enlightenment was for him. He went off to a hut in the mountains of Vermont and brought his few books on meditation and enough food for six months. He figured six months would perhaps give him a taste of enlightenment. As he began his retreat he enjoyed the forest and the solitude, but in just a few days he began to feel crazy because as he sat all day in meditation his mind would not stop. Not only did it think, plan, and remember constantly, but worse, it kept singing songs.

This man had chosen a beautiful spot for his "enlightenment." The hut was right on the edge of a bubbling stream. The sound of the stream seemed nice on the first day, but after a while it changed. Every time he sat down and closed his eyes, he would hear the noise of the stream and immediately in tune with it, his mind would begin to play marching-band songs like "Stars and Stripes Forever" and "The Star-Spangled Banner." At one point the sounds in the stream got so bad he actually stopped meditating, walked down to the stream, and started moving the rocks around to see if he could get it to play a different tune.

What we do in our own lives is often not different. When difficulties arise, we project our frustration onto them as if it were the rain, the children, the world outside that was the source of our discomfort. We imagine that we can change the world and then be happy. But it is not by moving the rocks that we find happiness and awakening, but by transforming our relationship to them.

The Tibetan Buddhist tradition instructs all beginning students in a practice called Making Difficulties into the Path. This involves consciously taking our unwanted sufferings, the sorrows of our life, the struggles within us and the world outside, and using them as a ground for the nourishment of our patience and compassion, the place to develop greater freedom and our true Buddha nature. Difficulties are considered of such great value that a Tibetan prayer recited before each step of practice actually asks for them:

Grant that I may be given appropriate difficulties and sufferings on this journey so that my heart may be truly awakened and my practice of liberation and universal compassion may be truly fulfilled.

In this spirit, the Persian poet Rumi writes about a priest who prays for thieves and muggers on the streets. Why is this?

Because they have done me such generous favors.
Every time I turn back toward the things they want
I run into them. They beat me and leave me
in the road, and I understand again, that what they want
is not what I want.
Those that make you return, for whatever reason,
to the spirit, be grateful to them.
Worry about the others who give you
delicious comfort that keeps you from prayer.

Very often what nourishes our spirit most is what brings us face to face with our greatest limitations and difficulties. Milarepa was a famous Tibetan yogi who as a youth had harmed many people through the use of his psychic powers. Yet later, when he came to a genuine teacher, the master made him labor without his powers for years, building and tearing down three great stone houses by hand, one stone at a time. In this struggle he learned to be patient, humble, and grateful. These very difficulties prepared him to receive and understand the highest teachings.

My own teacher Achaan Chah called this "practicing against the grain," or "facing into one's difficulties." When he felt they were ready, he would send monks who were fearful to meditate in the cemetery all night, and those who were sleepy would inevitably be assigned to ring the 3:00 A.M. wake-up bell all over the monastery.

However, even without seeking them, or receiving special assignments, enough difficulties will arise for us! To practice with them entails great courage of spirit and heart. Don Juan calls this becoming a spiritual warrior and states that:

Only as a [spiritual] warrior can one withstand the path of knowledge. A warrior cannot complain or regret anything. His life is an endless challenge and challenges cannot possibly be good or bad. Challenges are simply challenges. The basic difference between an ordinary man and a warrior is that a warrior takes everything as a challenge, while an ordinary man takes everything as a blessing or a curse.

Every life has periods and situations of great difficulty that call on our spirit. Sometimes we are faced with the pain or illness of a child or a parent we love dearly. Sometimes it is a loss we face in career, family, or business. Sometimes it is just our own loneliness or confusion or addiction or fear. Sometimes we are forced to live with painful circumstances or difficult people.

One graduate student who had worked with meditation for five years was always struggling, with her practice, her relationships, and her work as well. In meditation she had some moments of balance, and certain insights arose, but she never found a deep stillness. She reacted strongly against any form of loving-kindness meditation, finding it frustrating and artificial. Then her younger brother was injured in a car accident. She went home to help and walked into the middle of a huge fight between her divorced parents, who until this accident had hardly spoken for eight years. Her brother hovered near death, and things did not get better between her parents. After visiting the hospital each day, the woman would try to meditate in her old room at home, sitting and weeping for her brother, for her parents, and for her own pain. One evening she came out of her room, her eyes all red, and her parents asked her what was going on. She burst into tears and babbled about how incredibly much pain there was in her family and how painful it must be for all of them. Her outburst didn't help much, but out of shame her parents did tone down their fights a bit. Gradually, her brother got better. Relieved, she returned to graduate school, to her work, to her relationship, and to her meditation at home. The first day she sat to meditate she burst into tears, this time for how isolated she was and how hardened she had made herself. She tried a loving-kindness and forgiveness practice, and her heart flooded with compassion for everyone in her life. After this opening, somehow her meditation, work, and relationship all changed for the better.

In difficulties, we can learn the true strength of our practice. At these times, the wisdom we have cultivated and the depth of our love and forgiveness is our chief resource. To meditate, to pray, to practice, at such times can be like pouring soothing balm onto the aches of our heart. The great forces of greed, hatred, fear, and ignorance that we encounter can be met by the equally great courage of our heart.

Such strength of heart comes from knowing that the pain that we each must bear is a part of the greater pain shared by all that lives. It is not just "our" pain but *the* pain, and realizing this awakens our universal compassion. In this way our suffering opens our hearts. Mother Teresa calls it "meeting Christ in his distressing disguise." In the worst of difficulties, she sees the play of the divine and, in serving the dying poor, she discovers the mercy of Jesus. An old Tibetan lama who was thrown into a Chinese prison for eighteen years said that he viewed his prison guards and torturers as his greatest teachers. There, he says, he learned the compassion of a Buddha. It is this spirit that allows the Dalai Lama to refer to the Communist Chinese who have occupied and destroyed his country as "my friends, the enemy."

What freedom this attitude shows. It is the power of the heart to encounter any difficult circumstance and turn it into golden opportunity. This is the fruit of true practice. Such freedom and love is the fulfillment of spiritual life, its true goal. The Buddha said:

> Just as the great oceans have but one taste, the taste of salt, so too there is but one taste fundamental to all true teachings of the Way, and this is the taste of freedom.

This freedom is born out of our capacity to work with any energy or difficulty that arises. It's the freedom to enter wisely into all the realms of this world, beautiful and painful realms, realms of war and realms of peace. We can find such freedom not in some other place or some other time but here and now in this very life. Nor do we have to wait for moments of extreme difficulty to experience the freedom. It is, in fact, better cultivated day by day as we live.

We can begin to find this freedom in the everyday circumstances of our life if we see them as a place of our practice. When we encounter these daily difficulties, we must ask ourselves: Do we see them as a curse, as the unfortunate working of fate? Do we damn them? Do we run away? Do fear or doubt overcome us? How can we start working with the reactions we find in ourselves?

Often we see only two choices for dealing with our problems. One is to suppress them and deny them, to try to fill our lives with only light, beauty, and ideal feelings. In the long run we find that this does not work, for what we suppress with one hand or one part of our body cries out from another. If we suppress thoughts in the mind, we get ulcers; and if we clench problems in our body, our mind later becomes agitated or rigid, filled with unfaced fear. Our second strategy is the opposite, to let all our reactions out, freely venting our feelings about each situation. This, too, becomes a problem, for if we act out every feeling that arises, all our dislikes, opinions, and agitations, our habitual reactions grow until they become tiresome, painful, confusing, contradictory, difficult, and finally overwhelming.

What is left? The third alternative is the power of our wakeful and attentive heart. We can face these forces, these difficulties, and include them in our meditation to further our spiritual life.

A professor of psychology came to meditation seeking peace and understanding. She was educated in psychological theory, had studied Eastern philosophy, and wanted to delve into the workings of the mind and understand the play of consciousness, but her body would not co-operate. She had had a lifelong struggle with a degenerative disease that caused periods of great pain and weakness in her body. In the back of her mind she had hoped the meditation would ease the pain, so that she could then go on to discover the deeper aspects of Buddhist psychology. Yet each time she meditated, aches and pains would fill her sitting and walking periods. She couldn't get over her pain, and after several retreats, as her frustration grew, her pain got worse. She wanted experiences, not the same old chronic pain.

She was regularly asked what her relationship was to the pain. "Oh, I'm just being aware of it," she would claim, still secretly hoping it would go away. One day after hours of frustrated sitting with the pain, she let go of her resistance and, with a truly open attention, she saw it all differently. She realized that she had spent her entire life trying to get outside her body completely. She hated her pain and she hated her body, and meditation was one more means she hoped to use to get out of herself. How deeply she wept when she finally saw this. How little love she had shown her body. This was the turning point in her spiritual practice. She decided that if the work given to her was to sit with a body in pain, she would bring to it all the tenderness and mercy she could. As she honored her body and sat with its pain, her body began to soften. But more than that, her whole life began to change. A great love and compassion grew in her eyes, and she herself became a teacher of the spiritual values she had once sought.

The poet Rumi put it this way:

The spirit and the body carry different loads and require different attentions. Too often we put saddlebags on Jesus and let the donkey run loose in the pasture.

Our difficulties require our most compassionate attention. Just as lead can be transformed into gold in alchemy, when we place our leaden difficulties, whether of body, heart, or mind, into the center of our practice, they can become lightened for us, illuminated. This task is usually not what we want, but what we have to do. No amount of meditation, yoga, diet, and reflection will make all of our problems go away, but we can transform our difficulties into our practice until little by little they guide us on our way.

The maturity we can develop in approaching our difficulties is illustrated by the traditional story of a poisoned tree. On first discovering a poisoned tree, some people see only its danger. Their immediate reaction is, "Let's cut this down before we are hurt. Let's cut it down before anyone else eats of the poisoned fruit." This resembles our initial response to the difficulties that arise in our lives, when we encounter aggression, compulsion, greed, or fear, when we are faced with stress, loss, conflict, depression, or sorrow in ourselves and others. Our initial response is to avoid them, saying, "These poisons afflict us. Let us uproot them; let us be rid of them. Let us cut them down."

Other people, who have journeyed further along the spiritual path, discover this poisoned tree and do not meet it with aversion. They have realized that to open to life requires a deep and heartfelt compassion for all that is around us. Knowing the poisoned tree is somehow a part of us, they say, "Let us not cut it down. Instead, let's have compassion for the tree as well." So out of kindness they build a fence around the tree so that others may not be poisoned and the tree may also have its life. This second approach shows a profound shift of relationship from judgment and fear to compassion.

A third type of person, who has traveled yet deeper in spiritual life, sees this same tree. This person, who has gained much vision, looks and says, "Oh, a poisoned tree. Perfect! Just what I was looking for." This individual picks the poisoned fruit, investigates its properties, mixes it with other ingredients, and uses the poison as a great medicine to heal the sick and transform the ills of the world. Through respect and understanding, this person sees in a way opposite to most people and finds value in the most difficult circumstances.

How have we met disappointment and obstacles in our life? What strategy have we brought to our difficulties and losses? What spirit of freedom, compassion, or understanding is yet to be found in the midst of these difficulties?

In each and every aspect of life, the chance to turn the straw we find into gold is there in our hearts. All that is asked is our respectful attention, our willingness to learn from difficulty. Instead of fighting, when we see with eyes of wisdom, difficulties can become our good fortune.

When our body is sick, instead of fighting the disease, we can listen to the information it has to tell us and use it to heal. When our children whine or complain, instead of shutting them out, we can listen to what is their deeper need. When we have difficulty with some aspect of our lover or partner, we might inquire how we treat that part in ourselves. Difficulties or weaknesses often lead us to the very thing we need to learn.

In meditation this spirit is essential. One student was plagued by frequent sleepiness in his meditation. He led a very active life, and by temperament he was always doing, creating, acting. When he started to meditate, he would sit up ramrod straight to fight the sleepiness, to ward it off. After many months of this battle he realized he was fighting himself. So he gave the sleepiness permission to arise. But then he found he was sleepy again and again at each meditation. Finally he began to inquire, to look with both wisdom and compassion at his situation. This began a whole long process. He discovered he was sleepy because his body was tired. He kept himself so busy, he never got enough rest. Then as he saw this he also realized that he was afraid to rest. Quiet scared him; he didn't know what to do if he wasn't active. Then he heard a voice (once his father's, now his own) telling him he was lazy, and he realized the voice was often there and that he believed it, so he could never let himself rest. He saw the weariness in his constant activity and felt a deep need to stop.

Simply investigating his sleepiness in meditation led him to a new vision of living. Over the course of a year he began to slow down. His whole life and schedule changed. He learned that inactivity was not laziness. He discovered peace and contentment in listening to music, taking walks, talking with friends. In his endless busyness he had been seeking fulfillment and well-being outside himself. Yet, the well-being he had sought was in him all the time, shining like gold, waiting only for his transformation, for a wise and accepting heart to bring it alive in his life.

Often from our seeming weaknesses we can learn a new way. The things we do well, where we have developed our greatest self-confidence, can become habitual, bringing a sense of false security. They are not where our spiritual life will best open. If it is our strength to think through things carefully, then thoughts will not be our best spiritual teacher. If it is already our way to follow our strong feelings, then feelings are not where we will learn best. The place where we can most directly open to the mystery of life is in what we don't do well, in the places of our struggles and vulnerability. These places always require surrender and letting go: When we let ourselves become vulnerable, new things can be born in us. In risking the unknown we gain a sense of life itself. And most remarkably, that which we have sought is often just here, buried under the problem and the weakness itself.

For example, meditation may bring us face to face with the longing that keeps many of our lives in motion. At first the longing will appear to be a poison to get rid of if we can. But if we investigate it, we will find built into our longing a yearning for its opposite, the wholeness and connectedness that we seek. Somehow we must already be able to sense this completeness within us. So our longing is a reflection of this possibility. When we open and accept our longings, then the longing and emptiness itself can become included in a greater loving whole.

Similarly, we can find gold in the judgment and anger we have, for within them is the valuing of justice and integrity. When we work with anger, it can be changed into a valuable medicine. Transformed, our anger and judgment give us clarity to see what is skillful, what needs to be done, what limits need to be set. They are the seeds of discriminating wisdom, and a knowing of order and harmony.

In the same way, denial and confusion are unsuccessful strategies we use to avoid conflict and seek peace. When we acknowledge them consciously they become transformed. They can lead to a spacious acceptance, a resolution that holds all the voices in conflict in harmony. Through working directly to transform their energy, we can find true peace.

The seeds of wisdom, peace, and wholeness are within each of our difficulties. Our awakening is possible in every activity. At first we may sense this truth only tentatively. With practice it becomes living reality. Our spiritual life can open a dimension of our being where each person we meet can teach us like the Buddha and whatever we touch becomes gold. To do this we must make our very difficulties the place of our practice. Then our life becomes not a struggle with success and failure but a dance of the heart. It is up to us.

Once a young and ambitious rabbi moved into the town of a famous master. Finding no interested students, he decided to challenge the old master in public and try to win some followers. He caught a bird and, with it hidden in his hand, strode up to the old master, who was surrounded by students. "If you are so great," he asked the master, "tell me if the bird is dead or alive." His plan was this: If the old master said the bird was dead, he would release it to fly away. If the master said it was alive, he would quickly crush it and then open his hand showing the dead bird. Either way the old master would be embarrassed and lose students.

So there he stood, confronting the old master, with all the students looking on. "Is the bird in my hand dead or alive," he asked again. The master sat quietly, then replied, "Really, my friend, it's up to you."

MEDITATION:
REFLECTING ON DIFFICULTY

Sit quietly, feeling the rhythm of your breathing, allowing yourself to become calm and receptive. Then think of a difficulty that you face in your spiritual practice or anywhere in your life. As you sense this difficulty, notice how it affects your body, heart, and mind. Feeling it carefully, begin to ask yourself a few questions, listening inwardly for their answers.

How have I treated this difficulty so far?
How have I suffered by my own response and reaction to it?
What does this problem ask me to let go of?
What suffering is unavoidable, is my measure to accept?
What great lesson might it be able to teach me?
What is the gold, the value, hidden in this situation?

In using this reflection to consider your difficulties, the understanding and openings may come slowly. Take your time. As with all meditations, it can be helpful to repeat this reflection a number of times, listening each time for deeper answers from your body, heart, and spirit.

MEDITATION: SEEING ALL BEINGS AS ENLIGHTENED

A traditional skillful (and at times humorous) reflection can be used to change our relationship to difficulties. The image of this meditation can be easily developed and brought to our daily life. Picture or imagine that this earth is filled with Buddhas, that every single being you encounter is enlightened, except one—yourself! Imagine that they are all here to teach you. Whoever you encounter is acting as they do solely for your benefit, to provide just the teachings and difficulties you need in order to awaken.

Sense what lessons they offer to you. Inwardly thank them for this. Throughout a day or a week continue to develop the image of enlightened teachers all around you. Notice how it changes your whole perspective on life.

7

NAMING THE DEMONS

The noonday demon of laziness and sleep will come after lunch each day, and the demon of pride will sneak up only when we have vanquished the other demons.

In ancient cultures shamans learned that to name that which you feared was a practical way to begin to have power over it.

We have words and rituals for many of our great outer events, birth and death, war and peace, marriage, adventure, illness, but often we are ignorant of the names of the inner forces that move so powerfully through our hearts and lives.

In the last chapter, we talked about the general principle of turning difficulties into practice. Recognizing these forces and giving them a name is a specific and precise way to work with them and develop our understanding. We can begin to name and acknowledge many beautiful states that grace our lives: joy, well-being, peace, love, enthusiasm, kindness. This is a way to honor and nurture them. In the same way, naming the difficulties we encounter brings clarity and understanding and can unlock and free the valuable energy bound up in them.

Every spiritual path has a language for the common difficulties we encounter. The Sufis call them Nafs. The Christian Desert Fathers, who practiced nearly two thousand years ago in the deserts of Egypt and Syria, called them demons. One of their masters, Evagrius, left a Latin text of instructions for those who meditate in the wilderness: "Stay watchful of gluttony and desire," he warned, "and the demons of irritation and fear as well. The noonday demon of laziness and sleep will come after lunch each day, and the demon of pride will sneak up only when you have vanquished the other demons."

For Buddhist meditators these forces are traditionally personified as Mara (the God of Darkness), and at retreats they are frequently named the Hindrances to Clarity. New students inevitably encounter the forces of greed, fear, doubt, judgment, and confusion. Experienced students continue to wrestle with these very same demons, although in clearer and more skillful ways.

Whether difficulties or pleasures, the naming of our experience is the first step in bringing them to a wakeful conscious attention. Mindfully naming and acknowledging our experience allows us to investigate our life, to inquire into whatever aspect or problem of life presents itself to us. Give each problem or experience a simple name, as Buddha did when difficulties would appear before him. Buddha would state, "I know you, Mara." In his instructions on mindfulness, he directed meditators to note, "This is a mind filled with joy," or "This is a mind filled with anger," acknowledging each state as it would arise and pass away. In the space of such awareness, understanding grows naturally. Then, as we clearly sense and name our experience, we can notice what brings it about and how we can respond to it more fully and skillfully.

HOW TO BEGIN NAMING

Begin by sitting comfortably, focusing awareness on your breathing. As you feel each breath, carefully acknowledge it with a simple name: "in-breath, out-breath," saying the words silently and softly in the back of your mind. This will help you keep track of the breathing, which gives your thinking mind a way to *support* awareness rather than wandering off in some other direction. Then as you get quiet and as your skill grows, you can notice and name more precisely, "long breath," "short breath," "tight breath," or "relaxed breath." Let every kind of breath show itself to you.

As you continue to develop your meditation, the process of naming can be extended to other experiences as they arise in your awareness. You can name the bodily energies and sensations that come up, such as "tingling," "itching," "hot," or "cold." You can name feelings, such as "fear" or "delight." You can then extend the naming to sounds and sights, and to thoughts such as "planning" or "remembering."

In developing the naming practice, stay focused on your breathing unless a stronger experience arises to interrupt your attention. Then include this stronger experience in the meditation, feeling it fully and naming it softly for as long as it persists—"hearing, hearing, hearing" or "sad, sad, sad." When it passes, return to naming the breath until another strong experience arises. Keep the meditation simple, focusing on one thing at a time. Continue to name whatever is most prominent in each moment, being aware of the everchanging stream of your life.

At first, sitting still and naming may seem awkward or loud, as if it interferes with your awareness. You must practice naming very softly, giving ninety-five percent of your energy to sensing each experience, and five percent to a soft name in the background. When you misuse naming, it will feel like a club, a way to judge and push away an undesirable experience, like shouting at "thinking" or "pain" to make it go away. Sometimes, in the beginning, you may also feel confused about what name to use, looking through your inner dictionary instead of being aware of what is actually present. Remember, the practice of naming is much simpler than that; it is just a simple acknowledgment of what is present.

Soon you will be ready to bring the practice of naming and inquiry directly to the difficulties and hindrances that arise in your life. The five most common difficulties that the Buddha described as the chief hindrances to awareness and clarity are grasping and anger, sleepiness and restlessness, and doubt. Of course, you will inevitably encounter many other hindrances and demons, and will even create new ones of your own. Sometimes they will besiege you in combinations, which one student called "a multiple hindrance attack." Whatever comes, you will need to begin to see these basic difficulties clearly as they arise.

GRASPING AND WANTING

Grasping and wanting are two names for the most painful aspects of desire. Because our language uses the word desire in so many ways, it is helpful to sort them out. There are beneficial desires such as the desire for the well being of others, the desire for awakening, the creative desires that express the positive aspects of passion and beauty. There are painful aspects of desire—the desires of addiction, greed, blind ambition, or unending inner hunger. Through meditative awareness we can bring an attention that can sort out and know the many forms of desire. As William Blake stated

> Those who enter the gates of heaven are not beings who have no passions or who have curbed the passions, but those who have cultivated an understanding of them.

In beginning to name the demons, we can especially look for the difficult sides of desire, the grasping and wanting mind. When the wanting mind first arises we may not recognize it as a demon because we are often lost in its allure. Wanting is characterized as a Hungry Ghost, a ghost with an enormous belly and tiny pinhole mouth, who can never eat enough to satisfy his endless need. When this demon or difficulty arises, simply name it as "wanting" or "grasping" and begin to study its power in your life. When we look at wanting, we experience the part of ourselves that is never content, that always says, "If only I had something more, *that* would make me happy"—some other relationship, some other job, some more comfortable cushion, less noise, cooler temperature, warmer temperature, more money, a little more sleep last night—"then I would be fulfilled." In meditation the voice of wanting calls to us and says, "If only I had something to eat now, I'd eat, then I'd be satisfied, and then I could get enlightened." The desire of wanting is the unconscious voice that can see an attractive meditator sitting nearby and imagine a whole romance fulfilled, a relationship, marriage, and divorce, and only half an hour later remember that we're meditating. For the voice of wanting, what is here now is never enough.

Naming the Wanting Mind

As we work to observe the wanting and grasping without condemning it, we can learn to be aware of this aspect of our nature without being caught up in it. When it arises we can feel it fully, naming our experience "hunger," "wanting," "longing," or whatever it is. Name it softly the whole time it is present, repeating the name every few seconds, five, ten, twenty times until it ends. As you note it, be conscious of what happens: How long does this kind of desire last? Does it intensify first or just fade away? How does it feel in the body? What parts of the body are affected by it—the gut, the breath, the eyes? What does it feel like in the heart, in the mind? When it is present, are you happy or agitated, open or closed? As you name it, see how it moves and changes. If wanting comes as the demon hunger, name that. Where do you notice hunger— in the belly, the tongue, the throat?

When we look, we see that wanting creates tension, that it is actually painful. We see how it arises out of our sense of longing and incompleteness, a feeling that we are separate and not whole. Observing more closely we notice that it is also fleeting, without essence. This aspect of desire is actually a form of imagination and accompanying feeling that comes and goes in our body and mind. Of course, at other times it seems very real. Oscar Wilde said, "I can resist anything but temptation." When we are caught by wanting it is like an intoxicant and we are unable to see clearly. In India they say, "A pickpocket sees only the saint's pockets." Our wanting and desire can become powerful blinders limiting what we see.

Do not confuse desire with pleasure. There's nothing wrong with enjoying pleasant experiences. Given the many difficulties we often face in life, enjoyment is wonderful to have. However, the wanting mind grasps at the pleasure. We are taught in this culture that if we can grasp enough pleasurable experiences quickly one after another, our life will be happy. By following a good game of tennis with a delicious dinner, a fine movie, then wonderful sex and sleep, a good morning jog, a fine hour of meditation, an excellent breakfast, and off to an exciting morning of work, happiness will last. Our society is masterful at perpetuating this ruse. But will this satisfy the heart?

What happens when we do fulfill wanting? It often brings on more wanting. The whole process can become very tiring and empty. "What am I going to do next? Well, I'll just get some more." George Bernard Shaw said, "There are two great disappointments in life. Not getting what you want and getting it." The process of such unskillful desire is endless, because peace comes not from fulfilling our wants but from the moment that dissatisfaction ends. When wanting is filled, there comes a moment of satisfaction, not from the pleasure, but from stopping of the grasping.

As you name the wanting mind and feel it carefully, notice what happens just after it ends, and notice what states then follow. The issue of wanting and desire is a profound one. You will see how often our desires are misplaced. An obvious example is when we use food to replace the love we long for. To explain this, one Buddhist teacher, Geneen Roth, who works with eating disorders, wrote a book called *Feeding the*

Hungry Heart. Through the practice of naming, we can sense how much of our surface desire arises from some deeper wanting in our being, from an underlying loneliness or fear or emptiness.

Often when people start their spiritual practice, the wanting mind will become more intense. As we take away some of the layers of distraction, we discover that underneath are powerful urges for food or sex, or for contact with others, or powerful ambition. When this happens, some people may feel that their spiritual life has gone awry, but this is the necessary process of unmasking the grasping mind. We get to face it and see it in all its guises, so that we can develop a skillful relationship to it. Unskillful desire causes wars, it drives much of our modern society, and as unknowing followers, we are at its mercy. But few people have ever stopped to examine desire, to feel it directly, to discover a wise relationship to it.

When we study Buddhist psychology, we discover that desire is divided into many categories. Most fundamentally these desires are then separated into painful desire and skillful desire, both aspects stemming from a neutral energy called the Will to Do. Painful desire involves greed, grasping, inadequacy, and longing. Skillful desire is born of this same Will to Do but directed by love, vitality, compassion, creativity, and wisdom. With the development of awareness, we begin to distinguish unhealthy desire from skillful motivation. We can sense which states are free from unskillful desire and enjoy a more spontaneous and natural way of being without struggle or ambition. When we are no longer as caught by unskillful desires, our understanding grows, and both healthy passion and compassion will more naturally direct our life.

Understanding, freedom, and joy are the treasures that naming the demon of desire brings us. We discover that underneath unskillful desire is a deep spiritual longing for beauty, for abundance and completeness. Naming desire can lead us to discover this truest desire. One old teacher of mine said, "The problem with desire is that you do not desire deeply enough! Why not desire it all? You don't like what you have and want what you don't have. Simply reverse this. Want what you have and don't want what you don't have. Here you will find true fulfillment." By studying desire, we begin to include all of its possibilities in our spiritual life.

ANGER

The second common demon we will encounter is more obviously painful than desire. While desire and the wanting mind are seductive, the opposite energy of anger and aversion is more clearly unpleasant. At certain times we might, for a short while, find some enjoyment in it, but even then it closes our heart. It has a burning, tight quality that we can't escape. As the opposite of wanting, it is a force that pushes away, condemns, judges, or hates some experience in our life. The demon of anger and aversion has many faces and guises, and can be found in forms such as fear, boredom, ill-will, judgment, and criticism.

Like desire, anger is an extremely powerful force. We can easily become caught up in it, or we can be so afraid of it that we act out its destruction in more unconscious ways. Unfortunately, too few of us have learned to work with it directly. Its force can grow from annoyance to deep fear, to hatred and rage. It can be experienced toward someone or something that is present with us now or that is far away in time or place. We sometimes experience great anger over past events that are long over and about which we can do nothing. We can even get furious about something that has not happened but that we only imagine might happen. When it is strong in the mind, anger colors our entire experience of life. When our mood is bad, no matter who walks in the room or where we go that day, something is wrong. Anger can be a source of tremendous suffering in our own minds, in our interactions with others, and in the world at large.

Naming Anger

All of this can be understood when we begin to name the faces of anger as it arises. We can feel for ourselves how fear, judgment, and boredom are all forms of aversion. When we examine them, we see that they are based on our dislike of some aspect of experience. Naming the forms of anger presents us with an opportunity to find freedom in their midst.

At first, name the state softly, saying "anger, anger" or "hate, hate" as long as it persists. As you name it, note how long it lasts, what it turns into, how it arises again. Name it and notice how anger feels. Where in the body do you sense it? Does your body become hard or soft with anger? Do you notice different kinds of anger? When anger arises, what is its temperature, its effect on the breath, its degree of pain? How does it affect the mind? Is the mind smaller, more rigid, tighter? Do you sense tension or contraction? Listen to the voices that come along with it. What do they say? "I'm afraid of this." "I hate that." "I don't want to experience that." Can we name the demon and make our hearts big enough to allow both the anger and the subject of the anger to show us their dance?

Printed on this page, it may look easy to name our experience and sense it with a balanced attention, but of course it is not always so easy. At one California retreat I taught years ago, there were some therapists who had been schooled in the primal scream tradition. Their way of practice was one of release and catharsis, to scream and let their feelings go. After meditating for a few days, they said, "This practice is not working." I asked, "Why not?" They replied, "It's building up [our inner energy and anger], and we need a place to release it. Could we use the meditation hall at a certain hour of the day to scream and release, because otherwise it gets toxic when we hold it in."

The suggestion that we made was that they go back, name it, and simply be aware of it, that it probably wouldn't kill them. Since they had come there to learn something new, we asked them to continue to meditate and see what might happen. They did. After a few days they came back and said, "Amazing." I said, "What is amazing?" They said, "After naming it for some time, it changed." Anger, fear, desire—the process of all of these forces can be studied. They arise according to certain conditions, and when they're here, they affect the body and mind in a certain way. If we are not caught up in them, we can observe them as if they were a storm and see that after they are here for a time, like a storm, they pass away.

As we listen, we can also sense the origins of anger. Almost always the roots of anger are in one of two difficult states, which arise just before the anger appears. We become angry either when we are hurt and in pain or when we are afraid. Pay attention to your own life and see if this is true. The next time anger and irritation spring up, see if just before they arose you felt fear or hurt. If you pay attention to the fear or pain first, does the anger even appear?

Anger shows us precisely where we are stuck, where our limits are, where we cling to beliefs and fears. Aversion is like a warning signal that lights up and says, "Attached, attached." The strength of our anger reveals the amount of our attachment. Yet we know our attachment is optional. We can relate more wisely. Our anger, conditioned by our viewpoint on that day, is impermanent; it's a feeling with associated sensations and thoughts that come and go. We do not have to be bound to it or driven by it. Usually our anger is based on our limited ideas of what should happen. We think we know how God should have made the world, how someone should have treated us, what is our just due. But what do we really know? Are we that in touch with the divine plan for the sorrows and difficulties, beauty and wonders that we are to be given? Instead of getting involved in how we want the story written, we can begin to face and understand the forces from which anger arises. As with desire, we can study anger and learn whether it can serve us skillfully. Is it ever valuable? Does it have value in protection, or as a source of strength? Is anger necessary to achieve strength, to set limits, or to grow up? Are there other sources besides anger for the strength we seek?

Many of us have been conditioned to hate our anger. As we try to observe it, we will find a tendency to judge and suppress it, to get rid of it, because it is "bad" and painful, or shameful and "unspiritual." We must be very careful to bring an open mind and heart to our practice, and to let ourselves feel fully, even if it means touching the deepest wells of grief, sorrow, and rage within us. These forces move our lives, and we must feel them in order to come to terms with them. Meditation is not a process of getting rid of something, but one of opening and understanding.

When we work with anger in meditation, it can become very strong. Initially, we may sense just a little anger, but for those who have learned to suppress it and hold it back, anger will then transform into rage. All the anger that has been held in the body will show itself as tension and heat in the arms, the back, or the neck. All the words that have been swallowed can arise, and powerful images, volcanic rage, tirades of abuse will pour into our consciousness. This opening process can last for days, weeks, even months. These feelings are fine, even necessary, but it is important to remember how to work with them. When the demons become unmasked, you may feel you are going mad or doing something wrong, but in fact you have finally begun to face the forces that keep you from living in a loving and fully conscious way. We face these forces over and over. We will probably work with anger a thousand times in practice before we come to a balanced, mindful way of living. This is natural.

FEAR

The spirit of naming and discovery can also be brought to understanding fear, another form of aversion. Americans spend fifty billion dollars a year on security systems and guards. We get caught and lost in fear so often in our life, but rarely have we examined and dealt with the demon of the fearful mind itself. Of course, as we work with the fearful mind, we will initially become afraid. We will encounter this demon over and over again. However, at some point, if we open our eyes and our heart to the fearful mind and gently name it, "fear, fear, fear," experiencing its energy as it moves through us, the whole sense of fear will shift, and later will simply come the recognition, "Oh, fear, here you are again. How interesting."

Naming Fear

When fear arises, name it softly and experience what it does to the breath, to the body, how it affects the heart. Notice how long it lasts. Be aware of the images. Notice the sensations and ideas that accompany it, the trembling, the coolness, the scary stories it tells. Fear is always an anticipation of the future, an imagination. Notice what happens to your sense of trust and well-being, your belief about the world.

When I was a young monk I traveled with my teacher Achaan Chah to a branch monastery on the Cambodian border eighty miles away from our main temple. We were offered a ride in a rickety old Toyota with doors that didn't close fully. Our village driver was really speeding that day, recklessly passing water buffalo, buses, bicycles, and cars alike around blind curves on a mountainous dirt road. As this continued I felt sure I would die that day, so for the whole time I gripped the seat-back and silently prepared myself. I followed my breath and recited my monks prayers. At one point I looked over and saw my teacher's hands were also white from gripping the seat. This reassured me somehow, even though I also believed him to be quite unafraid of dying. When we finally arrived safely, he laughed and said simply, "Scary, wasn't it?" In that moment he named the demon and helped me make friends with it.

BOREDOM

Another form of aversion that we can learn to be mindful of is boredom. Usually we are afraid of boredom and will do anything to avoid it. So we go to the refrigerator, pick up the phone, watch TV, read a novel, busy ourselves constantly in an attempt to escape our loneliness, our emptiness, our boredom. When we are without awareness, it has a great power over us and we can never be at rest. Yet we need not let boredom run our lives this way. What is boredom when it is experienced in itself? Have we ever really stopped to look at it? Boredom comes from lack of attention. With it we also find restlessness, discouragement, and judgment. We get bored because we don't like what is happening or because we feel empty or lost. In naming it, we can acknowledge boredom and let it be a state to explore.

Naming Boredom

When boredom arises, feel it in the body. Stay with it. Let yourself be really bored. Name it softly as long as it lasts. See what the demon is. Note it, feel its texture, its energy, the pains and tensions in it, the resistances to it. Look directly at the workings of this quality in the body and mind. See what story it tells and what opens up as you listen. When we finally stop running away or resisting it, then wherever we are can actually become interesting! When the awareness is clear and focused, even the repeated movement of the in- and out-breath can be a most wonderful experience.

JUDGMENT

The same spirit of naming can be brought to the aversion we call judgment. So many of us judge ourselves and others harshly, yet have little understanding of the whole judging process. With meditative attention, we can observe how judgment arises as a thought, a series of words in the mind. When we don't get caught up in the story line, we can learn from it a great deal about both suffering and freedom in our life. For many people judgment is a main theme in their life, and a painful one. Their response to most situations is to see what's wrong with it, and in their spiritual practice the demon of judgment continues to be strong.

Naming Judgment

How can we work with the pain of judging? If we try to get rid of it by saying, "Oh, I shouldn't be judging," what is that? It's just another judgment. Instead, acknowledge the judgment as it arises. Allow it to come and go. Sometimes it helps to give it a name. If your judgment reminds you of someone from the past, try saying, "Thank you, Dad." "I appreciate your opinion on that, Carol." "Thanks for your opinion, John." Judgments are simply a prerecorded tape that plays through the mind over and over again. Try to have a sense of humor about your judgments—this will keep them in perspective relative to the rest of your life.

To understand the judging mind, we need to touch it with a forgiving heart. If it's really difficult to get in touch with it, try the following exercise. Sit quietly for an hour and see how many judgments arise. Count each one. Someone walks in the door. "I don't like them. Judgment twenty-two. I don't like what they're wearing either. Judgment twenty-three. Gee, I'm getting good at finding all these judgments. Oh, twenty-four. Yeah, I'm going to tell some friends about this. This is really a good exercise. Oops, I'm thinking too much. Oh, judgment twenty-five." Then all of a sudden your knee starts to hurt. "I wish this knee pain would go away. Judgment twenty-six. No, I shouldn't be judging. Judgment twenty-seven," and so forth. We can spend a very fruitful hour meditating, just understanding the judging mind.

To become conscious, we must fully allow each difficult state we have rejected—the judging mind, the desiring mind, the fearful mind—to come and tell us its story until we know them all and can let them back into our heart. In this process of dealing with the demons, we need a container of wisdom, awareness, and compassion, a still point in the midst of the movement of mind. As we accept the impersonal and habitual nature of the demons, we can see the gold they conceal. We may notice directly how aversion and judgment arise from a deep longing for justice or strength, or from a clarity and discriminating wisdom that cuts through the illusions of the world. When we know the demons for what they are, they release their other powers and we find clarity without judgment and justice without hatred. Through a heartfelt attention, the pain of anger and hate can lead us to a deep awakening of compassion and forgiveness. When we feel anger toward someone, we can consider that he or she is a being just like us, someone who has also faced much suffering in life. If we had experienced the same circumstances and history of suffering as the other person, might we not act in the same way? So we allow ourselves to feel compassion, to feel his or her suffering. This is not just a papering over of anger: it is a deep movement of the heart, a willingness to go beyond the conditions of a particular point of view. In this way our anger and judgment can lead us to the true powers of clarity and love we seek.

SLEEPINESS

The next most common demon to learn to name is a subtle one, the quality of sleepiness and dullness called sloth or torpor. This arises as laziness, tiredness, lack of vitality, and fogginess. Our clarity and wakefulness fade when the mind is overcome with sleep, and our life or our meditation become unwieldy and cloudy. In our life we experience tiredness because of the breakneck speed of our culture, or because we have lost touch with our body. We experience laziness or reluctance in the face of difficult tasks.

Sleepiness usually comes upon us gradually. As we sit, we can feel the sleepiness begin, like tendrils of fog, curling around our body and then whispering in our ear, "Come on, let's just take a little snooze." The mind then becomes scattered and depleted, and we lose heart for what we have undertaken. This can happen many times in meditation. Much of our living is done while we are only half awake. Large portions of our life have been spent in sleep and sleepwalking. Meditation means waking up. So we can begin by bringing mindfulness to the sleepiness.

Naming Sleepiness

Be aware of how the body feels when it's tired: the heaviness, the softening posture, the sense of heaviness in the eyes. Of course, if we're sleepy and nodding off, it is difficult to see. Still, observe as much as you are able. Pay attention to the beginning, middle, and end of sleepiness, and to the various components of the experience. See the impersonal conditions that cause it. Is it tiredness or resistance? Sometimes just bringing an interested awareness to sleepiness itself will dispel it and bring clarity and understanding. Other times it will recur more strongly.

As we encounter it and name this demon, we will see that sleepiness has three causes. One is the tiredness that signals a genuine need for sleep. This often arises at home after a long day, when we sit after a period of great busyness or stress, or in the first days of a retreat. It is a signal that we must respect the needs of our body. Our life may be out of balance, and we may need to work less and spend more time in the country. This kind of sleepiness passes after we take some rest. The second kind of sleepiness comes as a resistance to some unpleasant or fearful state of body or mind. Sometimes when it is hard to feel something, when we don't want to remember or experience something, we get sleepy. A third kind of sleepiness is a result of becoming calm and quiet, but without enough wakeful energy for clear concentration.

The sleepiness that comes as a resistance should not be confused with laziness. We are rarely lazy—we are simply afraid. The demon of sloth and torpor follows the strategy of the ostrich, thinking, "What I don't look at won't hurt me." When sleepiness arises and our body is not actually tired, it is often a sign of resistance. We can ask ourself, "What is going on here, what am I avoiding by falling asleep?" Many times we will discover an important fear or difficulty just underneath it. States of loneliness, sorrow, emptiness, and loss of control of some aspect of our life are common ones that we fall asleep to avoid. When we recognize this, our whole practice can open up to a new level.

Some sleepiness can also be caused by the development of strong stillness and calmness in the mind. Our active and high-stimulus culture has not accustomed us to dealing with times of quiet and calm. Our mind may think it is bedtime! So when we begin to become concentrated but have not balanced the mind by arousing an equal amount of energy, we can be stuck in a calm but dull state. This requires the naming of dullness and a rousing of energy. When faced with this form of sleepiness, name it, sit up straight, and take a few deep breaths. When sleepy, meditate with your eyes open wide. Stand in place for a few minutes or do walking meditation. If it's really bad, walk briskly or walk backward, splash some water on your face. Sleepiness is something we can respond to creatively.

When I was going through a long period of dullness in practice, my teacher, Achaan Chah, had me sit in meditation while perched on the edge of a very deep well. The fear of falling in kept me quite awake! Sleepiness is workable. It helps to bring an accuracy to our watchfulness, focusing on "Just this breath," or "Just this step," in order to steady the attention. If we can note, "Just this breath," in every single moment, from moment to moment, the mind will become expansive and refreshed, and sluggishness will disappear. Underneath the sleepiness is the possibility of true peace and rest. However, in the meantime, if nothing else works, then it is time to take a nap.

RESTLESSNESS

Restlessness, the opposite of sleep, manifests as the fourth powerful demon, called the Pacing Tiger. With restlessness we feel agitation, nervousness, anxiety, and worry. The mind spins in circles or flops around like a fish out of water. The body can be filled with restless energy, vibrating, jumpy, on edge. When restless, we feel as though we simply have to get up and pace around, turn on the TV, eat, do anything but stay in our body. Like sleep, restlessness can come as a response to pain and sorrow that we don't want to feel. It can also come as the demon worry. We sit down to meditate and the mind gets caught in fears and regrets, and we spin out hours of stories. In all forms of restlessness, our meditation becomes scattered, and it is difficult to stay present.

Naming Restlessness

When this state arises, name it without judgment or condemnation. Note softly, "restless, restless," and let your body and heart be open to experience this aspect of human life with wisdom. Feel it fully in the body. What is this energy? How strongly does it vibrate? Is it hot or cold; does it expand or contract the body and the mind? What does it do as you open to it, as you name it? How long does it last? What story does it tell?

Let yourself experience restlessness without getting caught up in the content of its story. It can be terribly unpleasant; the body filled with nervous energy, the mind spinning with worry. It is not "my restlessness" but "restlessness," an impermanent state born out of conditions that are bound to change. If it gets very intense, say to yourself, "Okay, I'm ready. I'll be the first meditator to die of restlessness." Surrender to it and see what happens. Like everything else, restlessness is a composite process, a series of thoughts, feelings, and sensations, but because we believe it to be something solid, it has a great deal of power over us. When we stop resisting and with mindful attention simply allow it to move through us, we can see how transitory and insubstantial the state actually is.

When restlessness is very strong, in addition to naming you can try the practice of counting your breaths—one to ten, then start again at one—until the mind comes back to balance. If it helps, breathe more deeply than usual, as a way of collecting and softening the body and mind. Understand that restlessness is one of the normal cycles of practice. Accept it and you will develop insight and understanding and an inner sense of ease or comfort. When you make peace with restlessness, its deeper energy will become available to you. Restlessness is only the surface level of a beautiful wellspring of energy within us, an unrestricted flow of creativity. This creativity can move through us in wonderful ways when we become a clear channel, when we have learned to be spacious with all things.

DOUBT

The last of the five common demons to test our practice is doubt. Doubt can be the most difficult of all to work with, because when we fall prey to it, our practice just stops, we become paralyzed. All kinds of doubt can assail us; doubts about ourselves and our capacities; doubts about our teachers; doubts about the meditation itself—"Does it really work? I meditate and all that happens is that my knees hurt and I feel restless. Maybe the Buddha really didn't know what he was talking about." We might doubt that the path we have chosen is the right practice for us. "It's too hard, too serious. Maybe I should try Sufi dancing." Or we think it's the right practice but the wrong time. Or it's the right practice and the right time, but our body's not yet in good enough shape. It doesn't matter what the object is, when the skeptical, doubting mind catches us, we're stuck.

Naming Doubt

When doubt arises, name it and look at it carefully and objectively. Have you ever really observed the voice that says, "I can't do it. It's too hard. It's the wrong time. Where is this getting me anyway? Maybe I should quit." What do you see? Doubt is a string of words in the mind associated with a feeling of fear and resistance. We can become aware of doubt as a thought process and name it, "doubting, doubting." When we do not become involved in its story, a marvelous transformation occurs; doubt itself becomes a source of awareness. We can learn a great deal from doubt about the changing, unstoppable nature of mind. We can also learn what it means to be identified with and caught up in our moods and states of mind. When we are caught up in doubt, we experience a great deal of suffering, but the moment that we can feel it without grasping, our whole mind becomes freer and lighter.

What happens when we name doubt carefully? How long does it last? How long does it affect our body, our energy? Can we listen to its story with the same ease as if it were saying, "The sky is blue"? To work with doubt we must center ourselves and fully come back to the present moment with continuity, firmness, and steadiness of mind. Gradually, this dispels confusion.

Along with the naming, doubt can also be dissolved by developing faith. We can ask questions or read great books. We can reflect on the inspiration of the hundreds of thousands of people before us who have followed the path of inner awareness and practice. Spiritual practice has been valued by every great culture. To live with great wisdom and compassion is possible for anyone who genuinely undertakes a training of their heart and mind. What better thing to do with our life? While it is natural for the mind to doubt, our doubt can lead us to a deeper attention and a more complete seeking for the truth.

Initially, doubts may come as demons and resistance—"It's not working today," "I'm not ready," "It's too hard." These could be called *small doubts*. After some practice we can learn to work skillfully with them. Beyond them rises another level of doubt, one which is truly useful to us. It is called the *great doubt*, the deep desire to know our true nature or the meaning of love or freedom. The great doubt asks, "Who am I?" or "What is freedom?" or "What is the end of suffering?" This powerful questioning is a source of energy and inspiration. A spirit of true inquiry is essential to enliven and deepen our spiritual practice, to keep it from being imitative. Working with this spirit, we find that buried under doubt is hidden treasure. The demon of small doubts can lead to the discovery of our great doubt and to a clarity that awakens our whole life.

In the process of naming the demons, we may find that they show themselves to us more fully. There are phases in practice when all we will see is desire or anger. We may doubt ourselves, thinking, "Oh dear, I am simply filled with desire or anger," or "I've got so much doubt," or "I'm so restless," or "Fear is underneath whatever I do." For a year or two in my own meditation all I saw was my anger, judgment, and rage. When I really touched it, it exploded through me. I spent almost a week without sleeping at one point, four or five of those days throwing rocks around in the forest and warning friends to stay away from me. Gradually, though, it subsided, gradually it lost its power.

• • •

As we go deeper in our spiritual life we find the capacity to acknowledge and touch the hardest places in ourselves. All around us, we encounter the forces of greed, fear, prejudice, hatred, and ignorance. Those of us who seek liberation and wisdom are compelled to discover the nature of these forces in our own heart and mind; we will experience how we get caught in them, but eventually we will find freedom in relation to these basic and primary energies.

Sometimes when the demons are most difficult, we can use a variety of temporary practices that function to dispel them and act as antidotes. For desire, one traditional antidote is to reflect on the brevity of life, on the fleeting nature of outer satisfaction, and on death. For anger, an antidote is the cultivation of thoughts of loving-kindness and an initial degree of forgiveness. For sleepiness, an antidote is to arouse energy through steady posture, visualization, inspiration, breath. For restlessness, an antidote is to bring concentration through inner techniques of calming and relaxation. And for doubt, an antidote is faith and inspiration gained through reading or discussion with someone wise. However, the most important practice is our naming and acknowledging these demons, expanding our capacity to be free in their midst. Applying antidotes is like using Band-Aids, while awareness opens and heals the wound itself.

When we become skillful at naming our experience, we discover an amazing truth. We find that no state of mind, no feeling, no emotion actually lasts more than fifteen or thirty seconds before it's replaced by some other one. This is true of joyful states and painful ones. Usually we think of moods as lasting a long time, an angry day or a sad week. However, when we look really closely and name a state such as "anger, anger," then all of a sudden we discover or realize it's no longer anger, that after ten or twenty soft namings it has vanished. Perhaps it will turn into an associated state like resentment. As we name resentment, we notice it for a while, and then it turns into self-pity, followed by depression. Then we observe the depression for a little while and it turns into thinking, and then that turns back into anger or relief or even laughter. Naming the difficulties helps us name the joyful states as well. Clarity, well-being, ease, rapture, calm, all can be named as part of the passing show. The more we open, the more we can sense the ceaseless nature of this flow of feelings and discover a freedom beyond all changing conditions.

The purpose of spiritual life is not to create some special state of mind. A state of mind is always temporary. The purpose is to work directly with the most primary elements of our body and our mind, to see the ways we get trapped by our fears, desires, and anger, and to learn directly our capacity for freedom. As we work with them, the demons will enrich our lives. They have been called "manure for enlightenment" or "mind weeds," which we pull up or bury near the plant to give it nourishment.

To practice is to use all that arises within us for the growth of understanding, compassion, and freedom. Thomas Merton wrote, "True love and prayer are learned in the hour when love becomes impossible and the heart has turned to stone." When we remember this, the difficulties we encounter in practice can become part of the fullness of meditation, a place to learn and to open our heart.

MEDITATION ON MAKING THE DEMONS PART OF THE PATH

Choose one of the most frequent and difficult demons that arises in your practice, such as irritation, fear, boredom, lust, doubt, or restlessness. For one week in your daily meditation, be particularly aware each time this state arises. Carefully name it. Notice how it begins and what precedes it. Notice if there is a particular thought or image that triggers this state. Notice how long it lasts and when it ends. Notice what state usually follows it. Observe whether it ever arises very slightly or softly. Can you see it as just a whisper in the mind? See how loud and strong it gets. Notice what patterns of energy or tension reflect this state in the body. Soften and receive even the resistance. Finally, sit and be aware of your breath, watching and waiting for this demon, allowing it to come and go, greeting it like an old friend.

MEDITATION ON THE IMPULSES THAT MOVE OUR LIFE

The inner forces of your life, the forces of reaction and wisdom, move through you as a source of all your action. Before every voluntary action and movement of our body there is a thought, an impulse or direction that comes from our mind. Often this impulse is subconscious, below the level of awareness. You can learn about how you respond to these forces and impulses by observing their action within you. As you observe this process, the interrelationship of your body and mind will become clear. In this you will discover a whole new capacity to be free and at ease in the face of difficulties.

A simple way to learn about how impulses operate is to focus on the ones that pull you to get up from meditation. In your daily meditation practice, make a resolve that for one week you will not get up until a strong impulse to do so arises three times. Sit as you usually would, being mindful of your breath, body, and mind. But do not set a fixed time for the end of your meditation. Instead, sit until a strong impulse tells you to get up. Notice its quality. It may arise from restlessness, from hunger, from knee pain, from thinking about how much you have to do, or the need to go to the bathroom. Softly name the energy that has arisen and with it sense the impulse to move. Feel it carefully in your body, naming, "wanting to get up, wanting to get up," staying with it for as long as it lasts. (This is rarely more than a minute.) Then after this impulse has passed, notice what it feels like now and if your meditation has deepened from sitting through the whole impulse process. Continue to sit until a second impulse to arise pulls you strongly. Notice the whole process in the same way as before. Finally, after a third time of carefully being with the whole impulse process, allow yourself to get up. The depth of your attention and centeredness will gradually grow through this practice.

If you wish, you can extend your observation to other strong impulses, noting the whole process of wanting to scratch an itch, to move while sitting, to eat, or to do other things. Being aware in this way will gradually teach you to stay centered, to have a capacity to take a few breaths and feel the changing responses to situations in your life rather than reacting to them automatically. You will begin to discover a center of balance and understanding in the face of the forces of your life.

8

DIFFICULT PROBLEMS
AND INSISTENT VISITORS

*When any experience of body, heart, or mind
keeps repeating in consciousness, it is a signal
that this visitor is asking for a deeper and fuller
attention.*

In the course of our practice of naming the common demons and
hindrances, we may come to encounter the underlying forces that cause
them to return over and over again. Fear, confusion, anger, and ambition
often appear as insistent visitors in our meditation. Even after we feel
we should know better, they will come again anyway. Now we must look
more deeply into how to work with the repeated difficulties that arise
in our spiritual life.

Some years ago, at the end of a ten-day retreat, it was announced
that I would lead a closing meditation on loving-kindness. This involves
a long guided meditation evoking states of forgiveness and compassion
for oneself and others. Fifteen minutes before that meditation was to
begin I received a heated phone call from my girlfriend at the time. She
was very upset with me for demands she said I placed on her. I was

equally upset by things she had done. We argued until the bell rang announcing the meditation.

When I went in to sit in front of the large group of students, I could still feel the reverberations of our conversation, but nonetheless I dutifully began to guide the meditation, using my best gentle, loving-kindness voice. After teaching such phrases as "May my heart be filled with loving-kindness" or "May I be peaceful," I would pause so that the students would be able to sense these qualities inside. During the pauses, though, the conversation flooded back, and I found myself thinking, "When this is over, I'm going to call her and tell her a thing or two." Then I would say out loud, "Think of another person you love and extend your kindness to them." In the next pause would come, "That immature and neurotic woman. When I talk to her . . ." I began to recollect all the past injustices I would remind her of. Then I would say, "Extend your compassionate heart yet further . . ." And so it went on, like an absurd game of tennis in my mind. If the students in front of me only knew.

Though it was painful to feel the anger and hurt, yet it was also all I could do to keep from laughing out loud. Our mind hangs on to its hurts and fears even when another part knows better. The mind will do almost anything, and it has no pride. Fortunately, I had enough practice with anger to observe this whole process with space and kindness, as the two voices continued. At least by the end of the meditation I had come to a bit of peace and forgiveness for her, for myself, and for the contradictory nature of mind itself. With this in mind, I went to call her back.

The great mystic poet Kabir asks:

*Friend, please tell me what I can do about this world
I hold to, and keep spinning out!*

*I gave up sewn clothes, and wore a robe,
but I noticed one day the cloth was well woven.*

*So I bought some burlap, but I still
throw it elegantly over my left shoulder.*

*I pulled back my sexual longings,
and now I discover that I'm angry a lot.*

*I gave up rage, and now I notice
that I am greedy all day.*

I worked hard at dissolving the greed,
and now I am proud of myself.

When the mind wants to break its link with the world
it still holds on to one thing.

How can we understand what perpetuates the difficulties we encounter? Once we can name the demons as they come and go, our heart can hold them more lightly. Without judgment we become what Ram Dass calls a "connoisseur of our neuroses." Then we are ready for a deeper opening, for understanding what is at their root.

With more careful attention we will sense that each demon and hindrance is an emotional or spiritual contraction, and that each is generated out of fear. It is this contraction and grasping that the Buddha described as the source of all human suffering. In the first years of my own practice and teaching, like any normal student, I struggled with restlessness, lust, doubt, and anger. I somehow believed it was these forces that were at the root of my suffering. However, as I listened more carefully, I discovered in myself, and later in my students, that underlying all of these struggles was fear.

Our fear creates a contracted and false sense of self. This false or "small" self grasps our limited body, feelings, and thoughts, and tries to hold and protect them. From this limited sense of self arises deficiency and need, defensive anger, and the barriers we build for protection. We are afraid to open, to change, to live fully, to feel the whole of life; a contracted identification with this "body of fear" becomes our habit. Out of this fear all of our greed, hatred, and delusion arise. Yet underneath it we will find an openness and wholeness that can be called our *true nature,* or original state, our Buddha nature. But to come to our true nature we need to examine and untangle the workings of this "body of fear" in the most personal way.

One of the clearest places to observe the process of contraction in our life is in meditation. Frequently we will experience ourselves contracting around and reacting to a specific difficulty that comes like an insistent visitor over and over again in our meditation. This repeated pattern of thoughts, moods, and sensations can be sensed as somehow stuck or unfinished. I am not referring to the general problems of sleepiness, judgment, or irritation we spoke of in naming the demons, but very specific and often painful sensations, thoughts, feelings, and stories that arise repeatedly in our consciousness. These are called *sankaras* in

Sanskrit. When repeated difficulties do arise, our first spiritual approach has been to acknowledge what is present, naming, softly saying, "sadness, sadness," or "remembering, remembering," or whatever. Of course, certain patterns that repeat will call for a response, some wise action on our part. We must recognize these situations, and as one Zen master put it, "Not just sit there like an idiot." However, many insistent visitors, even when we have named them or responded to them, will continue to repeat themselves, arising again and again.

When any experience of body, heart, or mind keeps repeating in consciousness, it is a signal that this visitor is asking for a deeper and fuller attention. While the general rule in meditation is to stay open to the flow of whatever arises, when we encounter an insistent visitor, we must recognize that this is its way of asking us to give it more attention, to understand it more clearly. This process involves investigation, acceptance, understanding, and forgiveness.

EXPAND THE FIELD OF ATTENTION

There are a few basic principles for learning how to open our stuck places and release the contradictions of the body of fear. The first of these principles is called Expanding the Field of Attention. A repeated difficulty will be predominantly felt in one of the four basic areas of mindfulness. It will come either in the realm of the body, in the realm of feelings, in the realm of mind (thoughts and images), or in the realm of our basic attitudes (grasping, fear, aversion, etc.). Expanding the field of attention requires that we become aware of another dimension of the insistent visitor and not just notice its predominant face. This is because invariably we are stuck on a different level from the obvious one we have been noticing and naming. Release will only take place when we can shift from that which is obvious to one of the other levels of awareness.

On retreats, we call these insistent visitors or difficult repetitive thought patterns the Top Ten Tunes. Normally when thinking arises, we can simply name it "thinking, thinking," and in the light of awareness it will vanish like a cloud. However, the Top Ten Tunes, whether as words, images, or stories, will persist and return no matter how often they are noticed. They play like records, repeating a theme over and over. At first, to gain perspective, we can number them one through ten. "Oh, that is three on the hit parade this week." In that way, when we notice them, we don't have to play the record all the way through each time and we can more easily let them go. Or we can use a variation of this technique and give them a humorous name or title. I have given names to many now familiar aspects of myself, such as "The Hungry Survivor," "Mr. Achiever," "Attila the Hun," "Baby Jacky," "Fear of the Dark," "The Impatient Lover." In this way, the repeated patterns of fear, sorrow, impatience, or loneliness become more familiar, and I listen to their stories in a friendlier and openhearted way. "Hello, nice to see you again! What do you have to tell me today?"

However, this is not enough. Suppose we encounter a repeated story about the divorce of our parents. It talks over and over about which children got to keep which possessions, and who said what to whom. Such a story can play many times. As it does, we must expand our field of attention: How does this thought feel in our body? Oh, there is a tightness in the diaphragm and the chest. We can name this, "tightness, tightness," and stay meticulously attentive for some time. As we do, it may open to other sensations, and many new images and feelings will be released. In this way, we can first begin to release the physical contractions and bodily fear that we have held. Then we can expand the attention further to new feelings. What feelings arise along with this thought pattern and this tightness? At first they may be half hidden or unconscious, but if we sense carefully, the feelings will begin to show themselves. The tightness in the chest will become sadness, and the sadness may become grief. As we finally begin to grieve, the pattern will release.

In a similar way, when we encounter a repeated physical pain or difficult mood we can expand awareness to the level of thoughts, the story or belief that comes along with it. With careful attention, we may find a subtle belief about ourselves that perpetuates the pain or mood, perhaps a story about our unworthiness, such as "I'll always be this way." When we become aware of the story or belief, and see it as just that, often the pattern is released.

Repeated thoughts and stories are almost always fueled by an unacknowledged emotion or feeling underneath. These unsensed feelings are part of what brings the thought back time and again. Future planning is usually fueled by anxiety. Remembering of the past is often fueled by regret, or guilt, or grief. Many fantasies arise as a response to pain or emptiness. The task in meditation is to drop below the level of the repeated recorded message, to sense and feel the energy that brings it up. When we can do this, and truly come to terms with the feeling, the thought will no longer need to arise, and the pattern will naturally fade away.

A FULL AWARENESS OF THE FEELINGS

This is a second principle for releasing repeated patterns—Open to a Full Awareness of the Feelings. It is the feeling level that controls most of our inner life, yet often we are truly unconscious of our feelings. Our culture has taught us contraction and suppression—"showing emotions" is not seemly for a man, and only certain emotions are allowed for women. One cartoon depicting our ambivalence showed a woman consulting her fortune-teller about why her husband would not talk about his feelings. Looking into her crystal ball, the fortune-teller declared that "Next January, American men will begin to talk about their feelings. Women all over the country will be sorry within minutes." This is the conflict we face.

When we have not learned to talk about feelings or even to be aware of them, our life remains entangled. For many meditators, reclaiming an awareness of feelings is a long and difficult process. Yet in Buddhist psychology bringing consciousness to feelings is critical for awakening. In a teaching called the Cycle of the Arising of Conditions, the Buddha explains how humans become entangled. It is the place of feeling that binds us or frees us. When pleasant feelings arise and we automatically grasp them, or when unpleasant feelings arise and we try to avoid them, we set up a chain reaction of entanglement and suffering. This perpetuates the body of fear. However, if we learn to be aware of feelings without grasping or aversion, then they can move through us like changing weather, and we can be free to feel them and move on like the wind. It can be a very interesting meditation exercise to focus specifically on our feelings for several days. We can name each one and see which ones we are afraid of, which we are entangled by, which generate stories, and how we become free. "Free" is not free from feelings, but free to feel each one and let it move on, unafraid of the movement of life. We can apply this to the difficult patterns that arise for us. We can sense what feeling is at the center of each experience and open to it fully. This is a movement toward freedom.

DISCOVER WHAT IS ASKING FOR ACCEPTANCE

This may sound like a very complicated and busy way to meditate, but in practice it is very simple. The general rule is simply to sit and be aware of what arises. If there are repeated patterns, expand the field of awareness. Then sense what is asking for acceptance. This is the third principle. Repeated patterns remain because of some level of resistance:

an aversion, fear, or judgment locks them in. This contraction is built out of fear. To release it, we must acknowledge what is present and ask our heart, "How am I receiving this?" Do we wish it to change? Is there a difficult feeling, belief, or sensation we have contracted around that we want to be over or go away? Is there some attachment, some fear?

The Dalai Lama has pointed out that communism worldwide did not work because it was not based on compassion and love; it was based on class struggle and dictatorial control, which in the end just doesn't work. Struggle and dictating doesn't work in our inner life either. So we must inquire what aspect of this repeated pattern is asking for acceptance and compassion, and ask ourself, "Can I touch with love whatever I have closed my heart to?" This doesn't mean solving it or figuring it out—it is simply asking, "What wants acceptance?" In difficult patterns of thought, emotion, or sensation, we must open to feel their full energy in our body, heart, and mind, however strongly they show themselves. This includes opening to our reactions to this experience as well, noticing the fear, aversion, or contraction that arises and then accepting it all. Only then can it release.

In my earliest practice as a celibate monk I had long bouts of lust and images of sexual fantasy. My teacher said to name them, which I did. But they often repeated. "Accept this?" I thought. "But then they'll never stop." But still I tried it. Over days and weeks these thoughts became even stronger. Eventually, I decided to expand my awareness to see what other feelings were present. To my surprise I found a deep well of loneliness almost every time the fantasies arose. It wasn't all lust, it was loneliness, and the sexual images were ways of seeking comfort and closeness. But they kept arising. Then I noticed how hard it was to let myself feel the loneliness. I hated it; I resisted it. Only when I accepted this very resistance and gently held it all in compassion did it begin to subside. By expanding my attention, I learned that much of my sexuality had little to do with lust, and as I brought an acceptance to the feeling of loneliness, the compulsive quality of the fantasies gradually diminished.

OPEN THROUGH THE CENTER

Fundamentally the acceptance I have described should be enough. Healing, compassion, and freedom arise from a free and open awareness. However, sometimes an even more careful and directed attention is needed to open our repeated patterns and deepest knots. This is the fourth principle for working with insistent visitors, called Opening Through the Center. The patterns of holding in our body and mind are like knots of energy that have bodily contraction, emotions, memories, and images all intertwined. In this practice we carefully direct our awareness to each level of a knot, feeling into the very center of the pattern. In doing so, we can release our identification with it and discover a fundamental openness and well-being beyond the contraction.

How is this done in practice? The loneliness I encountered that was giving rise to sexual fantasies can be an example. It returned often and painfully even though I named it and felt it with care. Loneliness has been one of my deepest sources of pain for as long as I can remember. I am a twin, and sometimes I think I got my brother to come along in the womb so I could have some company. As with each of the practices I have described, it is best to start with awareness of the body. As the loneliness continued to arise, I brought more careful attention to where it was held. Mostly it felt centered in my stomach. I then tried to feel what are called the physical elements in it. The earth (hardness or softness), air (stillness or patterns of vibration), fire (temperature), and water (cohesiveness or fluidity), plus sometimes color and texture. It was a hard sphere, pulsing in the center, hot and fiery red. Next I shifted to sense deeply all the feelings interwoven in it. Fear, pain, sadness, longing, and hunger were all present, along with a general aversion to feeling these states. I named each one softly. Then, while feeling into the center of the fire, pain, and hunger, I allowed whatever images wished to arise. There came a whole series of memories and pictures of abandonment and rejection. Often such images will open to early childhood, or even to past lives (if one is willing to allow them). As I felt into this center, I asked myself what beliefs and attitudes I held about it. The story that came out sounded like a child who says, "There is something insufficient and wrong with me and I will always be rejected." It was this belief, along with the attendant feelings, that I had identified with and contracted around.

As each of these layers opened in awareness, the pain gradually eased, the feelings softened, and the fire subsided. As I continued to feel into the center of the loneliness, I seemed to sense a hole or space in my belly that the pain had closed around. I named this central hole softly and felt its deep hunger, longing, and emptiness. Then I let it open as much as it wanted, instead of closing around it as I had done for so many years. As I did, it got bigger and softer and all the vibrations around it became very fine. The hole changed to open space and its hungry quality shifted. Though it was empty, it became more like clear empty space.

Gradually this filled more of my body, and with it a sense of light and fulfillment arose. I was filled with a sense of ease and profound contentment and peace. Resting in this open space, the whole notion of rejection and insufficiency was totally unnecessary. I could see that all of it—the loneliness, pain, sadness, thoughts of rejection—was a contraction of my body and mind based on the frightened and very limited sense of myself that I had carried for a long time. I could even see with compassion the scenes and conditions that generated it. But here, resting in the spaciousness and wholeness, I knew it was not true. And while the pain of loneliness has certainly come again in my life, I now know for certain it is not who I am. I have learned that its beliefs and contractions are based on fear and that underlying it all is a genuine wholeness and well-being that is our true nature.

For a simpler example, one man who attended our annual three-month Insight Meditation retreat grew to have quiet and powerful meditations over the first six weeks. Then all of a sudden pain arose in his shoulder, and he became disoriented, sleepy, and unable to concentrate. He meditated with these states repeatedly over some weeks before coming to see me. After he described the repeated pain and sleepiness, I asked him to focus his attention on the center of the sensations in his body. He closed his eyes and with careful awareness began to describe the physical elements, the feelings, and the images in the very center of the pain. All of a sudden his face changed as he recalled a vivid memory of himself at age sixteen accidentally breaking another boy's arm in football. He said, "I was feeling like such a powerful football player when I rushed up to block him and I broke his arm. Immediately afterward I was filled with fear, sadness, and regret. I became afraid of my own power." "How does this connect to your meditation?" I asked. A shock of recognition came to him. "Just when I was beginning to feel like I was having the most powerful meditations, my shoulder started to hurt, it got foggy and dull, I contracted. I think I was unconsciously afraid of this new power, that I might also cause hurt with it."

As soon as he saw this clearly and felt the depth of fear, his shoulder pain eased, his mind cleared, and a sense of basic confidence arose in place of the fear, confusion, and sleepiness. His meditation opened again to include peaceful and powerfully concentrated states, but now he could stay with this process and be at ease. As we understand and release our difficult patterns, our consciousness clears and our meditation follows a more unimpeded and natural way. We become connected with our true nature.

When awareness truly investigates our contractions, we open. Underlying each area of contraction we will find ease and space. This space can be felt quite physically in the body, as a progressive opening of sensations until the sense of bodily solidity dissolves. It can be felt in the heart as an open compassionate acceptance, and in the mind as a clear space of awareness that contains all things. In this space we discover our true nature.

When we are not contracted, the space of our body and mind is naturally filled with qualities that reflect its wholeness. We experience well-being, joy, clarity, wisdom, and confidence—the jewel-like properties of clear consciousness. Each time we open beyond our contracted and fearful states, we will come to this. The qualities we will encounter are the complement, the completion for what was previously held in us. So the football player found confidence arising out of his fear, and my own loneliness released into the wholeness and contentment I had been seeking all along. Carl Jung knew this when he told the founders of Alcoholics Anonymous that what they were really seeking in the spirits in the bottle was the true healing of the spirit that is our home.

In opening we can see how many times we have mistaken small identities and fearful beliefs for our true nature, and how limiting this is. We can touch with great compassion the pain from the contracted identities that we and others have created in the world. From the universal and timeless perspective of opening, we can begin to see the whole human dance of birth and death with the compassionate eyes and understanding heart of a Buddha. We can see how the process of identification carries us through our life until we awaken.

What humankind longs for cannot be found in the realm of the contracted states, the wanting mind, and the struggles of our small self. Instead, spiritual practice offers us a profound shift of identity. With awareness we can learn to release ourselves from needy, fearful, or compulsive identities to discover a wholeness and well-being, a sense of freedom, and a natural flow of our being.

This level of spiritual practice is a revolutionary process of investigation and discovery. Our repeated difficulties can bring us to these new openings. The very conflict and pain we have carried can lead us to new levels of freedom. Each difficult circumstance has a lesson that can bring us to its own particular awakening. What is asked for is our willingness to go to the center of our being.

Keep in mind that facing our repeated patterns and exploring our identity is deep work. It often requires the facilitation of a teacher or guide. We will say more about this in a few chapters, when we look at how to find and benefit from a teacher.

FIVE MORE SKILLFUL MEANS

This life is a test—it is only a test.
If it had been an actual life, you would have received further
instructions on where to go and what to do.
Remember, this life is only a test.

In the same spirit of adventure and discovery, let us consider five further principles for working with difficult experiences that are traditionally taught in Buddhist practice. Each of these is a way to sense the patterns of our difficulties, repeating them more consciously, exploring them or releasing our entanglement with them. These five ways begin with the basic act of letting go and then become more energetic and challenging as they go along.

LETTING GO

Letting go is the first and most fundamental of these principles. When difficulties arise and we are able to do so, we can simply let them go. But beware! This is not as easy as it sounds. Often we find ourselves too attached and entangled with the story or feeling to do so. Other times we may try to "let it go," because we don't like something. But this is not letting go—it is aversion. In the early phase of spiritual practice, many of our attempts to let go of difficulties are misguided in this way. They are actually gestures of judgment and avoidance.

Only when there is balance in the mind and compassion in the heart can true letting go happen. As skill in meditation develops, it then becomes possible to simply let go of certain difficult states as soon as they arise. This letting go has no aversion in it—it is a directed choice to abandon one mind state and calmly focus our concentration in a more skillful way in the next moment. This ability arises through practice. It comes as our composure grows. It can be cultivated but never forced.

When letting go is not possible, it can be modified to a softer version of this practice called Let It Be. Whatever arises, whether it is pain, fear, or struggle, instead of letting go, be aware of it, let it come and go, "Let it be." Remember the Beatles' song, "There will be an answer. Let it be, let it be." "Letting be" does not mean getting rid of or avoiding, but simply releasing. Allow what is present to arise and pass like the waves of an ocean. If crying arises, let there be crying. If grief or anger arises, let there be grief or anger. This is the Buddha in all forms, Sun

Buddha, Moon Buddha, Happy Buddha, Sad Buddha. It is the universe offering all things to awaken and open our heart. The spirit of *letting it be* was expressed beautifully in a poster advertisement for meditation and yoga that I saw years ago. A famous Hindu guru with gray hair and a long flowing beard was standing exquisitely balanced on one foot in the yoga posture known as the tree pose. He wore only a small loincloth. Most amazingly, he stood in this pose balanced atop a surfboard coasting down a large wave. At the bottom of the poster it said in large letters, "You can't stop the waves, but you can learn to surf." In this way we can greet the contradictions of our life and let them go or let them be.

TRANSFORMING THE ENERGY

Sometimes, however, letting go or letting it be is too difficult. Perhaps you have tried to accept some difficulty; you've allowed it, you may have even tried to feel into it deeply, and still you're in a struggle with it. There are other alternatives for difficulties that arise over and over again. One is to transform the energy, to turn the energy of the difficulty into useful feelings and useful action. This can be done in an inner or an outer way. For example, when we work with the forces of rage and aggression that are deeply stored in many of our bodies and minds, they sometimes become very powerful. An outer way to transmute them would be to take this anger and chop firewood. We release it and skillfully redirect it, using its force to get some work done for the winter, and transforming the power of this energy through the movements of our body to a creative or beneficial purpose. In transforming it, we release it and see it clearly. We also benefit by learning to express it directly. Expression is particularly necessary for many of the people in our culture who have been so trained to suppress their emotions that they are scared to ever express them. If we have been afraid of anger all of our life, we need to explore it and experiment with it—not in ways that hurt or harm others, but in order to transform its energy. It is the same with other difficulties. We can begin to let them out and find a way to put them to good use.

Transformation can also be internal. As an example of internal transformation let us consider compulsive sexual desire, repetitive and powerful lust that arises so strongly that we're unable to be mindful of it. In the inner way of transforming, we sense this energy physically and move it from our genitals up to our heart. We can direct this energy through inner attention until we feel it connected to our heart instead of our sexual organs alone. Just as we can use anger to chop wood, we can take the power of this desire, which is really the desire to connect, and shift its energy from the place of attachment to the place of love. Then when our sexuality is expressed, it will be connected with this love instead of fear, compulsion, or need.

PUTTING ASIDE

A third traditional practice for working with difficulties is called Putting Aside. This means to suppress them temporarily. Conscious suppression does have its value. There are good times to work on our difficulties and there are bad times, proper occasions and improper occasions. For instance, a surgeon who was at home for the weekend and on call got into a big fight with her husband. All of a sudden her beeper went off, and she had to go to the hospital. She got in her car, drove to the hospital, and very shortly was all scrubbed up and gowned for the surgery. This was not a good time mentally to continue the argument with her husband. This was a good time to put it aside and be mindful of the operation.

While this is an extreme case, many times we find ourselves in circumstances with our families, our children, our loved ones, or our colleagues at work that are not the most suitable or safest for actually confronting our difficulties. Finding the proper time and place for inner work is important. Understanding that we can put difficulties aside is incredibly helpful. We don't need to face our problems all at once, and we don't need to do so in every circumstance. As with all aspects of nature, there is a proper place for our hearts and minds to grow.

Inevitably, times will occur in our spiritual journey when our inner process gets overwhelming and we cannot deal with our difficulties easily. We may be in the middle of a life crisis; we may be surrounded by unsympathetic people; we may lack a proper support system; or we may just be fatigued. This is the time to put difficulties on the back burner, to wait for a more suitable time to work with them. In this practice we consciously put our difficulties aside, recognizing that we must come back to them later with our full attention. It is important to honor our vulnerability and recognize that we each need a trusting situation in which to work with the deepest feelings that will arise within us. As human beings we have been wounded, and so we have created defenses around many of our difficulties. The key to opening is trust and love. We can melt our difficulties with love. We can't batter them down, but we can dissolve them open.

ACTING MINDFULLY AND IN IMAGINATION

Acting on impulses as soon as they come up is what we do in our life all the time. To make this into a spiritual practice, we must learn to act with mindful attention as a true skillful means. Without mindfulness, we will simply reinforce our conditioned habits and desires, keeping ourselves stuck in their patterns, giving unconscious power to the forces of grasping and anger. With mindfulness, our actions can lead us to freedom.

The fourth skillful way of working with difficulties is a practice called Acting in Imagination. Suppose we encounter strong fear, desire, doubt, or aggression. In this practice, we let ourselves act it out, exaggerating it in our imagination. For desire, we might imagine having it fulfilled to the maximum in every variation and flavor, over and over again, for a hundred or a thousand times. We sense it, imagine it, picture it, but we do so with mindfulness so that we don't simply reinforce it. If we encounter aggression, we might imagine biting that person, kicking them, or whatever. This practice lets us see the energy that is within us, as if we are saying, "Let me see how strong this desire is, how big this angry mind is." Imagine these difficult problems and sense them to their extreme. When allowed to go to this extreme, we discover that we are able to contain and relate to these forces. They lose their power over us. We can begin to see them as impersonal—"the pain," "the fear," "the longing," that we all share as humans.

The power of this inner attention is extraordinary. Through imagining and envisioning our inner difficulties, we are able to rework the wounds and struggles, the conflicts of the past. As we hold them in our consciousness and feel them in our body, we can finally allow ourselves to feel the full effect of their energies. In doing so, our consciousness opens. Instead of being quite so identified with just one part of the picture, we may see other perspectives. We may see it from the viewpoint of other people, from the viewpoint of other stages in our life. A deep and profound healing takes place through the active imagination of conflicts, difficulties, and desires within us. When we have imagined them and fully accepted them, we also see their limitations and we come to a deeper freedom of our consciousness.

One man who encountered a powerful and repeated sense of anger and frustration worked with this practice for many years. As we sat together I encouraged him to visualize how big was his anger. He said it felt like a bomb, then a nuclear explosion. I instructed him to let his anger open as much as it wanted, and he said it burned up the whole universe. The whole universe became dark and dead and full of ashes. A great fear arose in him. He felt that for a long time much of his life had been dead; now the deadness felt stronger, as if his life would be that way forever. I suggested he let the deadness and ashes fill the universe forever and see what would happen. He sat with it for some time and let himself imagine it lasting for ten, fifty, five hundred million years.

Then, to his amazement, there came a green light far off in the distance that frightened him, so he imagined the deadness lasting yet another hundred million years. Finally the green light became so strong that he couldn't ignore it. It was a new planet being born, with oceans, green plants, and young children. Seeing this he realized that even the greatness of his own pain had an end. The anger and frustration that had been there for so long began to lose its power over him and an inevitable renewal began to take place.

The Indian poet Ghalib wrote:

For the raindrop, joy is in entering the river. . . .
Travel far enough into sorrow, tears turn into sighing;
When after heavy rain, the storm clouds disperse,
Is it not that they've wept themselves clear to the end?

Just as we can explore our difficulties through visualization, we can also use visualization to evoke the great forces of universal wisdom and compassion that are within each of our hearts. Many of the advanced Buddhist practices of *samadhi* and *tantras* are based on this principle. In them we can inwardly embody the great symbols of awakening such as the Buddha or Jesus or visualize the extending of our heart's compassion to all living beings. In using skillful visualization with our heart and mind, we can begin to powerfully transform our world.

ENACTING MINDFULLY

The fifth skillful means for working with difficulties is called Enacting It Mindfully. Let's face it, we act out most of our desires anyway. In the fifth way, we take whatever difficulty has repeated itself, and fulfill it while being fully aware of what is happening throughout the whole process. There are two restrictions for taking this as a practice. First, it must not be genuinely harmful to yourself or any other being. Second, it must be done mindfully. Thus, if it is a desire, we act on it, paying meticulous attention the whole time. If it is something that needs to be expressed, we express it, observing our attention, the state of mind, the feeling in the body, the constriction or openness of heart as we do it. We observe the entire process and let the experience, the feelings in our body, and the consequences become our teacher. That is a powerful place where we can awaken. Remember, however, it is important not to harm yourself or another being in the process.

As a first step we may simply exaggerate our difficulty. In Thailand, Achaan Chah instructed one student who was often angry to begin this process by closing himself in a tiny tin hut on a hot tropical day. He directed him to wrap himself in his winter robes and stay angry, really letting himself feel it fully.

Enacting mindfully has another step. A teacher with whom I studied in India was hooked on sweets. He just loved *gulab jaman*. *Gulab jaman* is so sweet it makes baklava seem like dry toast. After trying inner discipline and meditation unsuccessfully, he decided to work with this by acting it out. One day he went to the market and ordered thirty rupees' worth of *gulab jaman*. This is a mountain of sweets floating in an ocean of sugary syrup. He sat down with this and mindfully made himself eat as much of it as he could, noticing all that happened to him in the process. He saw the peacefulness that came the moment the desire ended (at the first bite). He felt the pain of the desire. He felt the pleasure of the sweetness. He sensed the pleasure turn into oppression as he continued eating the same desired object, a mountain of *gulab jaman*. In the end he was never again plagued by the unquenchable desire for *gulab jaman*.

This is a somewhat advanced form of practice. It does not mean repeatedly binging or acting out our compulsion over and over. It means doing it once while being truly present and honestly awake for all that happens, learning from the first action to the last consequence.

As you can see, there are many ways to dance with our difficulties. Each one is a movement from unconsciousness to open attention. We can study them, or we can just let them go. We can transmute them and learn to make these energies a useful part of our practice. When we're unable to do this, we can put them aside and later find a safe and supportive circumstance in which to work with them. Beyond this, we can exaggerate them in our imagination to come to terms with them. We can mindfully enact them. All of these ways keep our practice growing, heartfelt, and alive.

When the Indian saint Ramakrishna was asked why there is evil in the world, he answered, "To thicken the plot." These very plot thickeners, often the most difficult and insistent ones, can lead us to open our bodies, hearts, and minds. In doing so, we discover that these were never our true identity. Under all the tears, the pain, the fear, and the anger we have contracted ourself around, we can find freedom, joy, and ease in the face of all life.

9

THE SPIRITUAL ROLLER COASTER: KUNDALINI AND OTHER SIDE EFFECTS

The dazzling effect of lights and visions, the powerful releases of rapture and energy are a wonderful sign of the breakdown of the old structures of our being, body, and mind. However, they do not in themselves produce wisdom.

How are we to understand the more spectacular and exotic spiritual experiences that fill the literature of the great mystical traditions? Do people in modern times still have them? What value do these experiences have? In the previous chapters, we have dealt with the physical energies, emotions, and thought patterns within our relatively ordinary state of consciousness. As these are released, new levels of calm and clarity take their place, and with continued practice, our whole state of consciousness itself sometimes changes. With further systematic spiritual practice, powerful experiences of altered states of body, heart, and mind can arise.

This chapter attempts to describe these fundamentally indescribable experiences and put them into perspective as part of our spiritual path.

ATTITUDES TOWARD ALTERED STATES

Before we can understand nonordinary states, we must realize that spiritual traditions hold two widely divergent perspectives on their value for transforming and liberating our consciousness. Certain spiritual paths insist that we need to attain profoundly altered states of consciousness in order to discover a "transcendent" vision of life, to open beyond our body and mind and realize the divine taste of liberation. These schools speak of the need to go to the mountaintop, to have a cosmic vision, to transcend the small self, to experience an enlightenment. Many traditions focus on such visionary and transcendent experiences. In Zen, the Rinzai School emphasizes powerful koan practices and rigorous retreats to break through ordinary consciousness and lead to experiences called *satori* and *kensho,* moments of profound awakening. Insight Meditation (vipassana) contains schools that use powerful concentration techniques and long intensive retreats to bring students to an awakening beyond their everyday consciousness. Raja and kundalini yogas, certain shamanic practices, the "dark night" of intensive Christian prayer are others that follow this spirit of practice. The techniques they use include repetition, intensity, pain, powerful breathing, narrowly focused concentration, koans, sleep deprivation, and visioning to help students transcend normal consciousness.

Many other schools, however, do not seek to climb the mountain of transcendence, but set out instead to bring the spirit of the mountaintop alive here and now in each moment of life. Their teachings say that liberation and transcendence must be discovered here and now, for if not here in the present, where else can it be found? Instead of seeking to transcend, the perspective of the "immanent" school teaches reality, enlightenment, or the divine must shine through every moment or it is not genuine.

The schools that focus on awakening "here and now" teach that the divine and enlightenment is ever present. Only our desire and grasping mind, including our desire for transcendence, keep us from experiencing this reality. The Soto School of Zen teaches this through a meditation called Just Sitting, a profound opening to what is true just now. In this practice one abandons the very notion of gaining enlightenment, satori, or of being anywhere else. In his teaching one of the greatest American

Soto Zen masters, Suzuki Roshi, never spoke of satori—his wife joked that it was because he never had it. All altered perceptions and visions in the Soto Zen tradition are called *makyo*, or illusion, and are ignored. Insight Meditation has many masters who hold a similar perspective. For them, altered states are just another experience, an impermanent phenomenon, or as Achaan Chah put it, "Just something else to let go of." The teachings of Advaita Vedanta, Krishnamurti, karma yoga, and the path of service to the divine, all follow this path.

Immanent and transcendent paths are both an expression of the Great Way. They are each expressions of practice that can lead to a profound letting go and true liberation. Most of you who pursue spiritual practice in a devoted way will at some time experience both perspectives. Each way has its value, and each has its dangers.

The value of transcendent states is the great inspiration and compelling vision that they can bring to our lives. They can provide a powerful vision of reality beyond our day-to-day consciousness and guide us to live from this highest truth. The experiences we have of them can, at times, be profoundly healing and transforming. But their dangers and misuses are equally great. We can feel ourselves special for having had them; we can easily get attached to having them; and the drama, the body sensations, rapture, and visions all can become addictive and actually increase the craving and suffering in our life. The most pervasive danger of all is the myth that these experiences will utterly transform us, that from a moment of "enlightenment" or transcendence, our life will be wholly changed for the better. This is rarely true, and attachment to these experiences can easily lead to complacency, hubris, and self-deception.

The value of the practice of immanence is its powerfully integrated approach. It brings the spirit alive here and now and infuses our whole life with a sense of the sacred. The dangers include delusion and complacency. We can easily believe we are "living in the present" and still be half asleep, following our old comfortable habits. Our initial sense of love and light can become an excuse to say that everything is already divine or perfect, and cause us to gloss over any conflict or difficulty. Some students practice this way for a long time without gaining much real wisdom. Stuck without knowing it, they may feel quite peaceful, but their lives have not been transformed and they may never fulfill the spiritual journey, never find true liberation in the midst of the world.

With both of these perspectives on altered states in mind, let us look at some of those that may arise and consider how best to work with them. It is important to remember, though, that because the mental, emotional, and spiritual territory covered by this chapter and the next is usually unknown to our ordinary consciousness, it is essential that we have a teacher or guide and proper support for staying balanced while navigating this territory. This is critical. One doesn't take a journey into the Himalayas without a guide who knows the ancient paths.

SOME COMMON ALTERED STATES

When we begin a spiritual practice, we struggle with the pains of our body and the armoring we have forged for it over the years, we face emotional storms, and we encounter a procession of the five common hindrances. But as we continue spiritual practice, and become more familiar and compassionate with our deepest difficulties, even the most ingrained patterns of holding and fear will gradually lose their power over us. We develop a spirit of calm and steadiness, whatever our means of practice.

This calm is not the end of practice but can be just a beginning. This collectedness and steadiness of heart and mind is a gateway to other realms of experience. Through our repeated meditation or prayer, through deep and consistent practice of yoga and concentration, through special breathing exercises—or sometimes in other extreme circumstances, such as physical accidents or the use of psychedelics—we find ourselves powerfully present, unimpeded by any inner distraction. With this newfound full attention, our consciousness actually shifts into different and radically new perceptions.

RAPTURES

Whenever powerful concentration and energy are evoked in spiritual practice, a great variety of new and exciting sensory experiences can begin to arise. They do not occur for everyone, nor are they necessary for spiritual development. These new states are more like side effects of meditation, and the better we understand them, the less likely we are to get stuck in them or confuse them with the goal of spiritual life.

First to arise for many people is a whole array of altered physical perceptions. Many of these are categorized in Buddhist texts as side effects called the five deepening levels of rapture. In this context, *rapture* is a broad term used to cover the many kinds of chills, movements, lights, floating, vibrations, delight, and more that open with deep concentration, as well as the enormous pleasure they can bring to meditation.

Rapture commonly arises during intensive periods of meditation or spiritual practice, but can also be stimulated by a powerful ceremony or powerful teacher. Sometimes rapture begins as subtle coolness or waves of fine and pleasurable vibrations throughout the body. Through concentration or other techniques of practice one often experiences a buildup of great energy in the body. When this energy moves, it produces feelings of pleasure, and when it encounters areas of tightness or holding, it builds up and then releases as vibration and movement. Thus, rapture may lead to trembling or the powerful spontaneous releases of physical energy which some yogic traditions refer to as *kriyas*. These are spontaneous movements that come in many different patterns. Sometimes they arise as a single involuntary movement felt together with the release of a knot or tension in the body. At other times they can take the form of prolonged and dramatic movements that can last for days.

Early in one year-long training retreat, I experienced a period of very powerful release where my head began shaking back and forth for hours. Some days later my arms started to involuntarily flap like a bird's wings. When I would try to stop them, I could barely do so. If I relaxed at all, they would flap continuously. They did so for several days. When I asked the teacher about it, he inquired whether I was being fully aware, and I said, "Certainly." Later he said, "You're not really being aware. Look more carefully and you will see that you don't like it. You subtly want it to go away." When I saw he was right, he said, "Simply go back and observe it," and over the next two days the movement subsided, and I sat there feeling my arms throb, bringing hours of deep bodily release.

These spontaneous bodily releases are neither enlightening nor harmful. They are simply what happens when the energy being generated in our practice encounters blocks and tightness where it cannot flow. It is part of the opening of the body that we first discussed in Chapter 4, Necessary Healing. When these spontaneous movements appear, we can begin to respect how deep our physical patterns of holding can be. For many students, physical releases and openings take place over months and years of their spiritual practice. It is best to meet these movements by softening, especially relaxing the back and the area at the base of the spine. If the release is only moderately strong, it is often best to try to relax and yet hold the body still in the face of it and allow the energy to push open new channels in the body, rather than be released in movement. For stronger release this is impossible, though there are ways to temper and soften the buildup and flow of energy. As we become concentrated, the energy of our body system will follow a natural process of opening and balancing itself. We will feel how the heat, pulsations, and vibrations spontaneously move through our spine to open blocked energy channels and then radiate out to every nerve and cell of our body. We can discover that some of the deepest healing and body work can take place as we sit still and meditate. Remember that this can be a long process, so be patient with your body.

Beyond *kriyas* and spontaneous movement, many other kinds of rapture can arise. These include pleasant kinds of thrills throughout the body, tingling, prickles, waves of pleasure, and delightful sparkles. At certain levels one may feel the skin vibrate or feel as if ants or small bugs were crawling all over it, or as if the skin were being stuck by acupuncture needles; at other levels one may feel hot, as if the spine were on fire. Some Tibetan yogis develop this into fire meditation so skillfully that their bodies will melt the snow in a circle around them as they sit. This heat can alternate with feelings of cold, beginning with slight chills, and turning to strong rapture with a profound deep cold. Sometimes these experiences of temperature change are so tangible and strong that we shiver on hot summer days.

Along with this kinetic rapture, one may see colored lights, initially blues, greens, and purples, and then, as concentration gets stronger, golden and white lights. Finally, many students will see very powerful white lights as if looking into the headlight of an oncoming train or as if the whole sky were illuminated by a brilliant sun. Different colored lights often arise in conjunction with specific states, such as green with compassion, red with love, blue with wisdom. Several systems of teachings discuss these inner colors, and while their explanations are not always consistent, they agree that seeing colors is usually the effect of a deep and pure opening of consciousness.

At still deeper states of concentration we may feel our entire body dissolve into light. We may feel tingles and vibrations so fine that we feel we are only patterns of light in space, or we may disappear into the colors of very strong light. These lights and sensations are powerful effects of the concentrated mind. They feel purifying and opening, and can show us that on one level the mind and body and the whole of consciousness is made of light itself.

A series of unusual sensory perceptions in addition to these forms of light and power may also arise. Many of these are associated with changes in the traditional physical elements of earth (hardness and softness), air (vibration), fire (temperature), and water (cohesiveness) in the realm of the physical senses. We may feel we have become very heavy, or hard and solid like a stone, or feel as if we are being squashed under a weight or a wheel. Our sense of weight may disappear and we may sense ourselves floating and have to open our eyes and peek to make sure we're still sitting in meditation. Similar experiences can also arise during walking meditation. When walking is concentrated, the whole room can appear to sway as if we were on a ship in a storm, or we might put our foot down and feel as if we were drunk. Sometimes everything starts to sparkle, and it seems as if we could walk through the floor or the wall itself. Our vision can swirl and create strange patterns and colors around us. The shape of the body may seem to shift. Temperature, solidity, and vibration may simultaneously change, with sensations of heat, melting, and movement all occurring at once.

The body may seem to stretch out gigantically tall or become very short. Sometimes it feels as if our head is located somewhere outside of our body or we may experience strange breathing rhythms or breathing in every cell of our body or feel that we are breathing through the soles of our feet. A hundred other variations of these altered physical perceptions may arise during practice.

Similarly, other senses may open to new experiences. Our hearing may become very acute, we may hear the softest sounds we have ever heard or powerful inner sounds such as bells, notes, or choruses of sound. Many people hear inner music. Sometimes voices will clearly speak. We may hear words or specific teachings. Our senses of taste and smell may open in ways never before experienced. One morning when I walked on my monk's alms-rounds to collect food, my nose became like that of the most sensitive dog. As I walked down the street of a small village, every two feet there was a different smell: something being washed, fertilizer in the garden, new paint on a building, the lighting of a charcoal fire in a Chinese store, the cooking in the next window. It was an extraordinary experience of moving through the world attuned to all the possibilities of smell. In similar fashion, our senses of sight, sound, taste, and touch can all reach profound new sensitivity.

Deep concentration can lead to all kinds of visions and visionary experiences. Floods of memories, images of past lives, scenes of foreign lands, pictures of heavens and hells, the energies of all the great archetypes, can open before our eyes. We can sense ourselves as other creatures, in other bodies, in other times and other realms. We can see and encounter animals, angels, demons, and gods. When such visions arise in the most compelling form, they become as real as our day-to-day reality. While such visions often arise spontaneously, they can also be developed through specific meditative exercises as a means to awaken the beneficial energy of a particular realm.

Along with the openings of vision, hearing, and physical senses, we can experience a release of the strongest kinds of emotions, from sorrow and despair to delight and ecstasy. Meditation may feel like an emotional roller coaster as we allow ourselves to be plunged into unconscious emotions. Vivid and profound dreams and many varieties of fear frequently appear. These are not just the emotions of our personal problems, but the opening of the whole emotional body. One encounters soaring delights and the darkness of isolation and loneliness, each feeling very real as it fills our consciousness. These releases require the guidance of a skilled teacher to help us through them with a sense of balance.

CHAKRAS

We may also encounter great changes through the opening of the energy centers in the body traditionally called chakras. This process does not happen for everyone, and it is in no way necessary for a full spiritual life. Indeed, openings of the energy body and chakras occur simply because a person has been blocked and held in these areas, and the experience arises as our inner energy tries to move and free itself in the body. There are yogic practices in Buddhist and Hindu traditions that can at times intentionally produce or direct these experiences, but often the opening is spontaneous. Here are some of the many ways we can experience the chakras:

The *first chakra*, at the base of the spine, is associated with the energy of security or groundedness. In meditation we can begin to experience it physically through powerful sensations in the bottom of the pelvis. As it opens, it brings a strong physical release and often triggers feelings and images associated with security and survival, our sense of safety. These images and fears may be connected to the valuing of our body and our life on earth, or they may bring up the opposite, fears of death and loss of control, loss of anything to which we are attached. When it opens, we can experience feeling at home in our body on earth and learn to rest in the true security of our being.

The *second chakra*, just above, is in the area of the genitals. Its energy usually opens us up to aspects of sexuality, reproduction, and generativity. When the energy of sexual release opens in this center, we may be flooded with sexual images and sensations for hours, days, or even weeks. For some, this may be pleasurable. For others, who may have issues of sexual abuse or painful sexual histories, it can require a confrontation with the fearful and destructive side of those energies.

The second chakra can produce visions of every kind of sexual encounter along with tremendous waves of lust and rapture. For one woman in a recent retreat, the opening of this chakra began with hours of powerful erotic and orgasmic vibrations. Then she saw visions of the copulation of humans and animals in every realm. It looked to her as if the trees were copulating with the sky, and when she sat in meditation she felt as if the entire world was being poured into and out of her vagina in an enormous sexual act. Initially this was overwhelming, but over some days she gradually relaxed and allowed the process to open to a sensitive and calm state filled with an exquisite sense of joining with all things. This chakra connects us with the boundless reproductive capacities of the world.

The *third chakra,* at the solar plexus, is often associated with will and power, and its opening may begin with experiences of tension and fear, pain and tightness, contraction, or difficulty in breathing. We may reexperience the ways we have held ourselves back from acting, or the ways we have held our breath in fear. As this chakra opens, outpourings of rage and frustration may arise. This may result in a tremendous freeing of energy: we may feel an enormous inherent strength in being; and our breath and actions may find a new clarity and spontaneity.

The *fourth chakra,* the heart, can open on both physical and emotional levels. Physically, we may first experience pain, bands of tension and holding around our heart that have been held for so many years. Many students report the heart opening feels as if they were having a heart attack and wonder if they need an ambulance. Profound grief, outpourings of compassion, and then laughter and joy may also arise as the emotional floodgates of the heart are opened. Issues of love, connection, loneliness, and the great patterns of our heart will surface here. Eventually sweetness and love fill our being. The opening of the heart can be slow or fast, occurring a petal at a time, or with great explosions of feeling. In the end, the heart can encompass the whole universe with love and compassion. It can become the center that moves all things.

The *fifth chakra,* the throat chakra, is often associated with creativity. As it opens, initially one may find arising the images and energy of all that has been held back, all that has not been said or honored in one's life. On a physical level, this opening can be accompanied by swallowing and coughing for hours or days or by spontaneous sounds that pour from us. As this center opens, we find our words and true voice, we can sense what it is like to have a clear channel for expressing our creative impulses.

The *sixth chakra,* between the eyes, is associated with vision and understanding. Again we may feel physical pain, burning, tension around the eyes, lights, even temporary blindness as this chakra opens. Visions may appear, or we may experience a powerful sense of clarity or an opening of our psychic sense. We may see colors, auras, chakras, and the subtle energies of life all around us. As this chakra clears, our thoughts may stop, we may become disoriented, losing a sense of who we are, or our direction and role in life. In this clear space of mind, we may then be able to see what is in another's mind, or have profound intuitions and understandings about ourselves and the world around us, as if a whole other sense had opened.

With the opening of the *seventh* or *crown chakra,* at the top center of the head, we may have the feeling of an open hole at the top of the head. At first we may feel pressure and tension, and as it opens we may be almost dizzy, but later we can learn to rest in the clarity of consciousness. Energy can pour into the head or out of it, and a profound sense of centeredness, well-being, and a connection with all of the world may arise. We may sense a powerful clear light pouring through this chakra, or feel as if the top of the head were a mandala or a many-petaled lotus in the center of the world. From this center, all things in life appear to dance in harmony.

Beyond the central chakras are other channels and lesser energy centers throughout the body that can open as our spiritual process continues. While there is a basic pattern to the opening of chakras and energy releases, it may happen in many different ways. The opening of chakras and the releases of energy in the body are described in all of the great spiritual traditions: in the Jewish mystical tradition of the Kabbalah; the tradition of the Sufi dervishes; the Christian mystical texts; and Buddhist practice manuals. One of the most complete descriptions of this energy release is found in the Hindu teachings of kundalini yoga. *Kundalini* is the name for the spiritual energy, or consciousness, that moves and illuminates all of life. It also specifically refers to the powerful energy releases in the spine and the chakras, and all of the subtle channels of the body that we have been discussing.

These energetic processes can take place in a period of hours or weeks or months, and for many students they are a process that goes on for years. They are all a part of an opening and purification that is the natural product of deep spiritual practice.

SKILLFUL MEANS OF WORKING WITH THE ENERGETIC AND EMOTIONAL OPENINGS

These energetic, visionary, and emotional openings can provoke powerful reactions of confusion and fear or ego-inflation and attachment. When they arise, we need the help of a specific spiritual path, with its accumulated wisdom, tradition, and practice, and most important, with a teacher who has personally encountered and understood these dimensions of the psyche. We must find someone whom we can trust and then rely on his or her skill and guidance.

ALL EXPERIENCES ARE SIDE EFFECTS

Even with a teacher, there are three principles to keep in mind in working with these unfamiliar realms of our spiritual life. The first principle is the understanding that All Spiritual Phenomena Are Side Effects. In the Buddhist tradition, the Buddha often reminded students that the purpose of his teaching was not the accumulation of special good deeds and good *karma* or rapture or insight or bliss, but only the sure heart's release— a true liberation of our being in every realm. This freedom and awakening, and this alone, is the purpose of any genuine spiritual path.

The dazzling effect of lights and visions, the powerful releases of rapture and energy, all are a wonderful sign of the breakdown of the old and small structures of our being, body, and mind. However, they do not in themselves produce wisdom. Some people have had many of these experiences, yet learned very little. Even great openings of the heart, kundalini processes, and visions can turn into spiritual pride or become old memories. As with a near-death experience or a car accident, some people will change a great deal and others will return to old constricted habits shortly thereafter. Spiritual experiences in themselves do not count for much. What matters is that we integrate and learn from the process.

"Unusual experiences" can create an obstacle course of repeated difficulties and pitfalls in our spiritual journey. Our reactions to them can even corrupt our meditation: we may grasp these experiences, or we may seek to repeat them and hold them and then think we are enlightened, which is called Settling for the Booby Prize, or we may find them disturbing and push them away. These are all traps.

One meditation student who practiced in India managed to come to a remarkable opening in his body after several long years of difficult and intensive practice. Each time he sat, his body would dissolve into tingles of rapture and light, and his mind would be open and profoundly peaceful. He was delighted. But then an emergency in his family called him back to England for several months. He couldn't wait to return to India. When he did get back, he found his body and mind were tight and blocked, filled with contraction, pain, and loss. So he undertook a series of intensive retreats to try to get back to the body of light and rapture, but it just wouldn't happen. Weeks and months went by, and his frustration grew along with his regret. If only he hadn't gone home from India! Now he tried even harder to clear himself. This struggle lasted for two years. Then one day it dawned on him that his two-year struggle with blocks, frustration, and difficulty was actually the result of his desire to repeat his past experience. His attachment to the old state and his resistance to what was present kept it all locked in. When he realized this and accepted his current state, his whole practice shifted. As he accepted his tension and pain a spacious equanimity arose all around it and his meditation began to flow into new territory again.

FINDING THE BRAKE

A second principle for working with these states could be called Finding the Brake. At times in intensive spiritual training, or in extreme or accidental circumstances, powerful altered states and energetic processes can open too rapidly for us to work with them skillfully. At these times, the degree of energy, the power of the experiences, or the level of release goes beyond our capacity to handle or hold it in a balanced or wise way. With a teacher and within ourselves, we must be able to acknowledge these limits and have the compassion to respond to them wisely. At this point, we must then find a way to slow down the process, to ground ourselves, to put on the brake. We can use spiritual technologies and practices to slow us down, just as we use other practices to open us up.

The processes that open up too rapidly in students can manifest as an extreme version of inner energetic opening, where the energy coursing through the body becomes so strong that it causes days or weeks of powerful agitation, loss of sleep, paranoia, disorientation, and even physical experiences such as painful sounds, fiery temperatures, or temporary blindness. (Those who do not believe that spiritual processes can affect the physical body should study the literature on phenomena such as stigmata.) A further manifestation of great difficulty can be experienced as a loss of boundaries, in which the sense of oneself and others dissolves to such an overwhelming extent that one feels the feelings of others, experiences the movement of traffic as though it were within one's own body, and finds it difficult to have any coherent sense of self in the welter of daily life. Here the experience is of intense vulnerability, loss of control, and body openings that threaten to tear us apart. Yet another realm of difficulty arises with the upsurging of powerful parts of oneself that are split off from our ordinary consciousness. These may manifest as hearing voices, unstoppable visions, hallucinations, and repetition of previous "psychotic" experiences in the case of those who have had them in the past.

A student who sat a three-month retreat that I taught was an over-zealous young karate student seeking the extremes of spiritual intensity. Rather than follow the instructions, he decided to get enlightened as quickly as possible in his own way. In the middle of the retreat he sat down and vowed to himself not to move for an entire day and night. After the first few hours he began to sit through sensations of fire and intense pain. He sat all afternoon, all night, and all the next morning. If one does this long enough, the pain and fire become so powerful that consciousness becomes disassociated and catapulted out of the body. There are many more gentle ways to have out-of-the-body experiences, but this happened to him very abruptly. As he continued to sit he began to experience all sorts of altered states. When he got up after twenty-four hours, he was filled with explosive energy. He strode into the middle of the dining hall filled with one hundred silent retreatants and began to yell and practice his karate maneuvers at triple speed. The whole room was bursting with his energy, and in the silence he could feel the fear that arose in many people around him, who were very sensitive after two months of silence. He made sounds with the movement, and his energy appeared to have flooded his third and sixth chakras. Then he said, "When I look at each of you, I see behind you a whole trail of bodies showing your past lives." He was living in a very different state of consciousness, which he had attained through pushing his body to such a limit. But he could not sit still or focus for a moment. Instead, he was very fearful and agitated, moving in a wild and manic state, as if he had temporarily gone crazy.

What did we do with him? Since he was an athlete, we started him jogging. We got him to run ten miles in the morning and afternoon. We changed his diet. While everyone else was eating vegetarian food, we put him on meat loaf and hamburgers. We made him take frequent hot baths and showers. We had him work and dig up a good part of the garden. And we kept at least one person with him all the time. After about three days he was able to sleep again. Then we started him off meditating slowly and carefully again. While his experiences may have been valid spiritual and psychic openings, they were not brought about in a natural or balanced way, and there was no way he could integrate them.

In putting on the brake to slow a powerful energetic process or re-create boundaries and bring balance back, first, stop meditating. Then focus on anything physical, whatever reconnects you with the body. Use whatever movements help release excess energy—digging in the earth, tai chi, running and walking, consciously bringing the attention down through the body, feeling the feet, visualizing the earth. Sexual orgasm can sometimes help. Receiving body work or massage can also be beneficial. Acupuncture and acupressure treatments can be very helpful for bringing balance. Change your diet; eat heavy foods, grains and meats, to ground your body. Try to restore your normal sleep by relaxing, using soothing herbs, baths, and massage after a day of tiring physical activity, such as hiking or gardening. All of this is best done in a supportive environment, with people nearby to provide additional grounding and connection.

There's a famous account of such a process undergone centuries ago by the great Zen master Hakuin recounted in a book called *The Tiger's Cave*. After years of committed practice, Hakuin experienced a profound enlightenment in which all things of the world became radiantly clear. But as he continued to practice, he lost his harmony. In both activity and stillness he was not free or settled. He threw himself further into practice with teeth clenched trying to free himself from floods of thoughts, disturbances, and sleeplessness, but it only got worse. His mouth was burning; his legs were freezing; in his ears were the sounds of a rushing stream; he sweated profusely and was unable to calm himself in any way. After seeking help unsuccessfully from the most reputable Zen teachers of his time, he heard of a wise old Taoist hermit in the mountains. He climbed the mountain and persevered in entreaties until the Taoist hermit saw his predicament and his sincerity. The hermit gave Hakuin two great teachings, for grounding and balancing his inner energy. One involves drawing energy from the top chakra down into the belly, using the belly and special breathing to ground the energy in the physical body. Secondly, the hermit gave him a series of energy-balancing exercises to circulate the energy through the body, all of which are spelled out in *The Tiger's Cave*.

Practitioners and yogis have encountered the difficulties inherent in spiritual experiences in all ages and all major methods of practice. In every case they found it essential to get help from someone who is skilled in this territory. Because these processes can take a long time, when they arise for us it is necessary to find a guide, someone who has touched their own madness, grief, and loss of boundaries, who can gradually and fearlessly direct us back to the ground of our own true nature.

AWARENESS OF THE DANCE

The third principle in working with altered states can be called Awareness of the Dance. When such experiences arise, the practitioner's primary responsibility is to open to the experience with a full awareness, observing and sensing it as a part of the dance of our human life.

We may become frightened by altered states, so that as they arise we resist and judge them: "My body is dissolving." "I have prickles all over." "I'm burning up." "I'm too cold." "The sounds are too loud." "My senses are too intense." "I cannot tolerate the many inner pains or waves of energy." Through fear, aversion, and misunderstanding, we can struggle with them for a long time, trying to avoid them, change them, get through them, or make them go away, and this very resistance will keep us caught in them.

Yet just as in beginning meditation we can learn to touch the pains and tension of the physical body with a healing and compassionate attention without resistance or grasping, so too the frightening and difficult altered states that arise can be met with the same compassionate and balanced attention. Just as in the beginning practice we learn to notice the seductive voices of the wanting mind without getting entangled, so too must we bring that balanced awareness to the sweet and powerful seduction of rapture, lights, and visionary experiences.

Our grasping or resistance to any experience stops our practice in that spot, stops our opening to the truth. One student had great fear of the sense of empty space that came to her in meditation, thinking she would lose herself, go crazy, or be unable to function. She spent two years resisting it, until in one guided meditation she finally let herself open to the fear and the space. It was marvelous. Her mind quieted, her heart softened, and her meditation opened to a new level of peace and ease.

As we encounter new experiences with a mindful and wise attention, we discover that one of three things will happen to our new experience: it will go away, it will stay the same, or it will get more intense. Whichever happens does not really matter. When we expand our practice to notice whatever states arise and our reactions to them, we can make them all a part of the dance. A great support for this perspective in practice is the tool we have worked with in naming the demons. Now we can consciously name the altered states as well, "rapture, rapture," or "vision, vision," as a way of acknowledging what is present, noticing it, and calling it by its true name. The moment we can say its name and create space for this experience to arise and pass, there comes a sense of trust in the process. We are reconnected with the understanding that seeks not to capture an experience, we open to what Alan Watts once called "the wisdom of insecurity," the wisdom of the ages.

A path with heart brings us to experience the phenomenal world in all of its infinite richness, to see, hear, smell, taste, touch, and think, and to find freedom and greatness of heart in the center of it all. Because each of us as a human flower will open in our own unique way in our own particular cycles, we need not direct the specific energies of our body and heart. Our path is neither to desire them nor fear them. The true path is one of letting go.

When we cultivate spaciousness, faith, and a broad perspective, we can move through all states and discover in them a timeless wisdom and a deep and loving heart.

MEDITATION: REFLECTING ON YOUR ATTITUDE TOWARD ALTERED STATES

What is your relationship to unusual and altered states in meditation? As you read about these experiences, notice which ones touch you, notice where you are attracted or what reminds you of past experiences. How do you meet such experiences when they arise? Are you attached and proud of them? Do you keep trying to repeat them as a mark of your progress or success? Have you gotten stuck trying to make them return over and over again? How much wisdom have you brought to them? Are they a source of entanglement or a source of freedom for you? Do you sense them as beneficial and healing, or are they frightening? Just as you can misuse these states through attachment, you can also misuse them by avoiding them and trying to stop them. If this is the case, how could your meditation deepen if you opened to them? Let yourself sense the gifts they can bring, gifts of inspiration, new perspectives, insight, healing, or extraordinary faith. Be aware of what perspective and teaching you follow, for guidance in these matters. If you feel a wise perspective is lacking, where could you find it? How could you best honor these realms and use them for your benefit?

IO

EXPANDING AND DISSOLVING THE SELF: DARK NIGHT AND REBIRTH

When we finally look at horror and joy, birth and death, gain and loss, things, with an equal heart and open mind, there arises a most beautiful and profound equanimity.

The territory of spiritual practice is as vast as the universe and the consciousness that created it. There are times in spiritual life when we move beyond the energetic and emotional phenomena described in the last chapter to experience openings of other extraordinary dimensions of consciousness. The psychologist William James wrote of such moments, "Our ordinary waking consciousness is but one form of consciousness. All around us lie infinite worlds, separated only by the thinnest veils."

In the Hindu yogic and devotional traditions, these realms are described as different levels of *samadhi*. In the Christian, Sufi, and Jewish mystical traditions, certain texts and maps—theoretical or practical descriptions or blueprints—describe the states of consciousness evoked through prayer, surrender, concentration, and silence. Among the guidebooks to these realms are *The Cloud of Unknowing, Dark Night of the Soul,* the mystical descriptions of the *Kabbalah,* and the Sufi journey of seven valleys in *Conference of the Birds.* The Buddhist tradition offers hundreds of techniques for the opening of consciousness, among them concentration on the breath and body, the use of visualization or sound, the repetition of mantras, and the use of *koans,* which are "unsolvable" questions that are repeated until the thinking mind stops and the realms of unknowing and silence appear.

New realms of consciousness can also open spontaneously through what is called grace, or they may occur under the press of a circumstance such as a near-death experience. They can be stimulated by sacred power spots, by the presence of powerful teachers, and by psychedelic substances, or they can be reached by the systematic and direct means of spiritual practice—by following strong spiritual discipline, through great continuity of meditation or prayer, or circumstances of profound silence. When our commitment to such forms of practice grows so deep that our whole being is consumed in the practice itself, the mind and body can open to previously unknown dimensions of life. The Sufi poet Rumi invites us there when he writes "Out beyond wrong doing and right doing there is a field of luminous consciousness. I'll meet you there."

In navigating these realms, we can be helped by teachers and maps that hold the knowledge of the many who have traveled there before us. One of the most comprehensive maps of Buddhist meditation is the Theravada (the Elders) map of higher consciousness. Theravada is the only one of the early schools of Buddhism to survive until this day. Their teachings are still the major form of Buddhism found in India and Southeast Asia. The map that follows is a distillation of the text and teachings of the Elders used to explain meditative states.

BUDDHIST MAPS OF ABSORPTION AND INSIGHT STAGES

The Elders' map divides the mystical realms into two broad areas: those attained by expanding the self and those attained by dissolving the self. For expanding the self, the Elders outline eight refined levels of consciousness, called the Realms of Absorption (also called the Higher Samadhis). Within these realms of absorption, they further describe how we can gain access to the *six realms of existence,* to experience all the forms that life can take. The eight realms of higher absorption and the six realms of existence are directly experienced by the expanded self through the power of meditative concentration. The realms bring us to states of celestial lights and expansion where we experience extraordinary feelings, visionary illuminations, and states of rarefied stillness.

Beyond these states, the map of the Elders describes another whole set of mystical realms called the Realms of the Dissolution of Self. This set of realms arises when we direct our consciousness deeper and deeper into the source of our being, gradually dissolving all identity and sense of individual self through a process of death and rebirth. In these realms, meditation is directed to unraveling the whole mysterious process by which consciousness creates separate identity, to come to selflessness and freedom in the midst of it all.

The map of the Elders is used in Insight Meditation. As you read about it in detail, keep in mind that such maps are both helpful and limiting. Depending on the form of practice used and the individual, meditation can progress in quite different ways. Mystical texts outside of Buddhism also describe the process of awakening, in hundreds of other languages and landscapes, although they all share common elements. So I offer this map with some caution, as an example of promises and perils we may encounter on our spiritual journey.

THE ENTRY TO EXPANDED CONSCIOUSNESS: ACCESS CONCENTRATION

The gateway to both the Realms of Absorption and the Realms of Dissolution is a stabilization of heart and mind called *access concentration*. Access concentration is the first strong level of presentness and steadiness that arises in prayer or meditation. When we attain access concentration, our spiritual practice for a time becomes unwavering and focused, undisturbed by inner hindrances or the mundane vicissitudes of our life. In access concentration we become merged and attentive in our meditation, so that a powerful shift of consciousness occurs, and clarity, ease, and concentration all begin to flow into our practice.

Attaining access concentration requires a natural ability to concentrate, combined with perseverance and discipline. For certain students in intensive training with a skillful teacher, the level of access concentration can arise in a matter of months or weeks of training. The meditative principles for attaining it are always the same: repetition, concentration, and surrender. One focuses on a prayer or a mantra, on a colored light or visualization, on the breath or the body, or on a feeling such as loving-kindness or compassion, refocusing on it or repeating it over and over and over again, through all the stages of resistance and difficulty, until the heart and mind begin to become still, unified, and virtually absorbed in the experience.

When we initially attain access concentration, we may feel shaky. We may feel strongly focused but, like a novice bicycle rider, still be occasionally unsteady and distracted by things in the background. Through continued repetition and patience we can gain balance in this state. Through repeated surrender to this experience, we can learn how to nurture and sustain a focused level of concentrated attention.

Access concentration was so named by the Elders because in it we develop enough steadiness of heart and mind to give us meditative entry to the higher realms. From access concentration we can then expand the self, level by level, refining consciousness to attain the eight levels of absorption, oneness with extraordinary states of luminous consciousness. Expanding the self into refined realms of absorption allows us to enter visionary states, including the six realms of existence, states of celestial lights and feelings, and rarefied states of consciousness even beyond these.

From access concentration we can also enter a whole other dimension of consciousness, the Realms of the Dissolution of Self. Here we do not expand and refine the self, but instead we look very deeply into the nature of self and consciousness, until even the most refined and highest sense of self and separateness is dissolved.

STATES OF ABSORPTION

To expand the self and enter the eight higher levels of absorption, we must consciously choose to give ourselves more fully to the subject of our meditation. From access concentration we must continue to concentrate until the quality of absorption in our meditation grows much stronger. As we do, many positive qualities, both calming and wakeful, will spontaneously begin to flood our heart and mind. These qualities are called by the Elders the Five Factors of Absorption, and they include directed and sustained attention, rapture, happiness, and concentration. These qualities will arise whenever the heart and mind are concentrated, pure, undistracted.

Through repetition of our meditation subject and a gentle focusing of the factors of absorption, we can let them fill and suffuse our consciousness. With careful attention we can learn to bring them into balance in our mind. Then by inner resolution, by consciously directing our mind toward the first level of full absorption, we can produce a discrete and strong shift of consciousness and find ourselves resting in a new and stable second state of absorption (called *samadhi* or *jhana* by the Elders). These are remarkable states. When well developed, they can be experienced as if we had been gradually removed from our senses and immersed into a new, completely whole and silent universe. The states of absorption are filled with rapture, happiness, light, and ease. Our body experiences a rapture that fills every cell. An enormous sense of peace and well-being arises, and an oceanic sense of wholeness and rest can envelop our consciousness. Absorptions are steady states, where our meditation proceeds effortlessly and our consciousness is strong, clear, stable, and balanced. Resting in the first level of absorption, our mind invariably feels refreshed and expansive, filled with delight and joy.

Through practice we can learn to rest in this first level of absorption for a short or long time. If we choose, we can continue to steady our attention and deepen our concentration, so that all of the factors grow yet stronger; our consciousness can become expanded and further suffused with light and well-being. Following the path of the Elders, this first level of absorption is then used as a gateway to enter higher and more refined states of absorption. To shift from the first level of absorption to the second, we must deliberately let go of directed attention and sustained attention, leaving only rapture, happiness, and concentration. Then to enter the next levels of refined absorption, we must let go of the rapture and then the happiness. Each time we direct our meditation to rest in higher and more refined levels of equanimity and luminous consciousness the next absorption arises. As we proceed, each level of absorption becomes more silent, expansive, and peaceful. This process may initially take days or weeks, but when mastered can be experienced in a single sitting.

These first four levels of absorption can be reached through concentration on dozens of meditation subjects: visualizations and images of Buddhas and gods, colors, feelings of love, meditations on the breath, body, chakras, even light itself. Each meditation subject will lend a unique quality to the basic states of absorption that develop from it, but the underlying experience of unified and expanded consciousness will be the same.

After developing skill in the first four levels of absorption that result from these fixed meditation subjects, it is possible to open to even more refined states. The Elders call the next four levels the Absorptions Beyond Forms, where consciousness releases any meditation subject altogether and expands to experience boundless dimensions of exquisite silent and pure awareness. The experience of these states is amazing. They are traditionally described as becoming one with the gods.

To enter these higher four levels, after attaining the first four levels of absorption, we must consciously release all previous happiness and equanimity, and direct our consciousness to become merged with boundless space. Boundless space is the first higher level of formless absorption. From there we can further refine our awareness, level by level, to melt into the limitless consciousness that pervades the entire universe, to become absorbed in a state of total emptiness or to attain a state beyond perception altogether. In opening to each higher level, the sense of self becomes merged into an ever more refined and expanded consciousness. These formless absorptions are powerful yogic attainments and require considerable skill to enter and master. Those who do master various levels of absorption may also direct them to develop a wide range of psychic powers. Such powers include telepathy, telekinesis, visioning of past lives, and many others. Though occasionally such powers will arise spontaneously, for the Elders the systematic development of such powers draws on the discipline and practice of concentrated absorption as its basis.

In Buddhist literature there are many detailed descriptions of the factors of absorption, the levels of absorption, and the development of psychic powers. One of the greatest is Buddhagosa's text, *The Path of Purification* (Shambhala, 1979). This thousand-page text gives a particularly fine description of forty concentration practices and how each leads to full absorption. It elaborately details the path to these eight higher levels of expanded consciousness, describing the many benefits and explaining the psychic powers that can come with their development. Buddhagosa also provides a precise description of the whole path of dissolution and insight.

While many benefits, including profound peace, healing, and well-being, can arise from the unified consciousness that is produced by these states of absorption, it is important to remember that there are dangers as well. When we begin to taste such states, a craving may arise for further higher and more extraordinary states. As we discussed, sometimes we grasp our insights and experiences in a way that increases our sense of pride, will, and self-delusion. We can become entranced with these states, finding them so powerful and compelling that we return to them again and again, thinking them to be the end of our path and the completion of our inner life, when, in fact, they are simply profound states of unity and rest, often unintegrated with the rest of our life. As we will see, we must direct them toward understanding and wisdom, or their value will remain limited.

THE REALMS OF EXISTENCE

As part of expanding the self, in addition to the eight levels of absorption, Buddhist maps of consciousness also include the experience of the six realms of existence. For the most part, refining consciousness into the realms of absorption is a rapturous and heavenly experience, but the power of concentration can also be directed to bring some students to the experience of the six great archetypal realms of life. When consciousness is expanded in this dimension, whether through concentration or spontaneously, visions will arise of great gods and goddesses, of past lives, of temples or ceremonies, of scenes of battle or warfare, of previous births and deaths. Not only Buddhist but also Hindu, Taoist, Christian, Jewish, and Islamic traditions describe such visionary experiences, and explain that the realms of beauty and horror, the heaven realms and hell realms, are to be understood as a real part of this universe.

Buddhist cartography and the map of the Elders describe six realms of life that can be experienced by consciousness. The most painful of the six realms is a variety of unending hell realms, domains characterized by an intensity of pain, fire, icy cold, and torture. The highest of the realms are the heaven realms, states filled with pleasure, angelic beings, rapture, celestial music, delight, and peace. Between these extremes are two visible realms, the animal and human realms. The animal realm is often characterized by fear (eat or be eaten) and dullness, while the human realm is said to have the right balance of enough pleasure and pain to be optimal for spiritual awakening. The final two realms are realms of spirits. One is a realm of power struggle called the realm of the jealous and warring gods, a domain of territoriality and titanic struggle. The other is a realm of intense desire called the realm of the Hungry Ghosts, characterized by beings with pinhole mouths and enormous bellies who can never be fulfilled in their seeking or longing. In a simple way, all these realms can be seen as mythological and poetic descriptions of human experience in this very life. Great anger and rage put us into the hell realm, strong addictions make us into hungry ghosts, and wonderful sense pleasures or beautiful thoughts transport us to heaven. We can see how humans even encounter these realms geographically. Perhaps the paradise of a South Sea island is the heaven realm and the starvation and warfare in sub-Sahara Africa is the hell realm. In this way, we encounter the realm of power and jealous gods in Washington, D.C., and that of the Hungry Ghosts in Las Vegas.

But these are not just metaphors. It is important to understand that these six realms can arise full-blown in spiritual life and become experiences as real and compelling as any that we experience in what we call our ordinary world. As our consciousness expands, we can find ourselves descending into a hell realm or delighting in the heavens; we can actually experience the consciousness of animals or the endless desire of the Hungry Ghosts. The power of certain spiritual practices to cast us into these realms requires us to learn to consciously traverse them as an essential part of our development.

One young friend, an American Buddhist monk living in Sri Lanka, discovered the limitations of states of concentration in a humorous and unexpected way. After some years of solitary training in concentration, he decided to travel to India to study further with other teachers. Traveling simply, with his robes and bowl, living on alms food, he visited various ashrams. Finally, he stopped at the huge temple of a renowned Hindu master. As a Westerner he was welcomed and granted an audience with the guru. After some pleasantries, the guru chastised him for being a monk who lived off the donations of others. In this guru's tradition everyone was expected to work for a living as part of a balanced spiritual life. The monk replied that begging was an ancient and honorable tradition of renunciates in India, dating back long before the Buddha. They argued about this for some time without any resolution.

Finally, the American asked if the master would still be willing to teach him the meditation practices of his lineage, and the master agreed. He instructed him in a practice of visualization and the sacred words of a mantra, and said that if the young monk would practice properly, these instructions would take him to a divine realm far above the sorrows of this human existence.

The American was given a small cottage, and being a diligent and skilled yogi, he set out to master this practice. Using his well-developed skill in concentration, after only four days he found his body and mind filled with the rapture and stillness of the first level of absorption. Practicing further, his consciousness opened and he found himself in a refined and heavenly realm filled with light, just as the master had predicted. Then he noticed the form of the master seated off at some distance. The monk approached him respectfully, and the master smiled back and acknowledged the young man, as if to say, *See, this is the realm I told you about.* "And by the way," the master spoke up, "I'm also right about the renunciate life. Being a monk is an outmoded and misdirected form of practice. You should throw those robes away." Hearing this, the American monk got upset and tartly answered back, and there and then, in the realm of light, for a period of time the two of them continued their argument.

This story illustrates how even these advanced levels are not *in themselves* a source of wisdom. In spite of such attainment, many divisions can still exist within us, and the highest states of consciousness can be used wisely or misused. Concentration practice, if it is misused, only suppresses our problems by bringing a temporary halt to fears and desires. When we emerge from these states, our underlying difficulties will arise again.

To enter the realms of absorption and the visionary realms requires understanding and guidance. Whether we find them powerfully enticing or frightening, we must bring to them an awareness and wisdom that can see them as the play of consciousness itself. In the Zen tradition, altered states and all visionary experiences are referred to as *makyo,* or illusion. The highest heavens and the lowest hells are transitory, like the seasons and the positions of the stars. No matter what yogic attainment might come to us in these states, it is temporary and does not bring us freedom in all the realms of life. Because of this, Buddhist tradition uses absorptions mainly as a preparation for further understanding. They are not considered necessary for most students, but for those who do attain them, they function to cleanse and harmonize the body and mind, and to quiet, purify, and unify consciousness. Subsequently, for true liberation, the direction of meditation must be shifted from the calming and expanding of self to investigating how consciousness creates the self and all its forms of experience. From the stillness of absorption, we must return to access concentration and direct our attention to the breath, the body, to sensory experiences, and the mind. In this way we begin the path of dissolving the self, the path of insight into the nature of self.

DISSOLVING THE SELF

Dissolving the self is the second major dimension of meditative consciousness described in the map of the Elders, and it is central to many forms of Insight Meditation. Instead of expanding the self to extremely refined states of absorption or traveling the six realms, this next dimension of spiritual practice directs consciousness to look into the very nature of self and separate identity. After a time, even attaining the realms of the gods, experiencing boundless light and peace, can be sensed as less than liberating, because each state, no matter how remarkable, has an end. In entering each state and returning, the question begins to arise, "To whom is this dance happening?" Then it is as if we turn away from a projection screen showing our changing experience (through which we have experienced all sorts of dramas, from heavens to hells) and begin to realize that these experiences are like a movie. We turn to discover the projector, the light and celluloid, the source of the whole drama before us.

There is a parable from the Buddha that illustrates the disenchantment with all forms that turns our minds toward the process of creation itself.

Some children were playing beside a river. They made castles of sand, and each child defended his castle, and said, "This one is mine." They kept their castles separate and would not allow any mistakes about which was whose. When the castles were all finished, one child kicked over someone else's castle and completely destroyed it. The owner of the castle flew into a rage, pulled the other child's hair, struck him with his hands, and bawled out, "He has spoiled my castle. Come along, all of you, and help me to punish him." The others came to his help. They hit the child as he lay on the ground. . . . Then they went on playing in their sand castles, each saying, "This is mine; no one else may have it! Keep away! Don't touch my castle!" But evening came; it was getting dark, and they all thought they ought to be going home. No one now cared what became of his castle. One child stamped on his, another pushed his over with both hands. Then they turned away and went back, each to his home.

In the same way, at some point we see that all forms of meditative experience have a limited nature. This recognition marks a fork in the road. Rather than expanding consciousness into any realm of experience, we must now turn and direct our attention to unravel the question of our very nature, and this begins the path of dissolving the self.

Spiritual traditions offer many ways to dissolve or transcend the self, the sense of our separate identity. One such practice is a repeated inquiry into the question, "Who am I?" Others involve transcendent surrender through prayer or devotional practices, or dissolving the self through profound rituals and vision quests. In Insight Meditation, a common path for dissolving the self begins, like expanding the self, from the level of access concentration. For most students this means developing the level of access concentration gradually, as we have previously described. Those who have developed the higher levels of absorption will need to return from these states and begin to direct the power of their concentration carefully and consciously on the life process itself.

From access concentration, the attention must now release all other meditation subjects and begin to examine the sensory experience of the present moment in an undistracted way. As we do so, the four elements of calm, concentration, rapture, and equanimity become naturally joined with the qualities of bright mindfulness, energy, and investigation. Together, these qualities are called the Seven Factors of Enlightenment, and their stillness and clarity grow in strength as the path of meditation proceeds. Their development is described in greater detail in my previous book, *Seeking the Heart of Wisdom*. For the path of dissolution, what is important is that the calm and concentration that produce a great steadiness of mind now be combined with an equal energy of inquiry and investigation.

When we use the power of concentration to begin to investigate the self, instead of expanding consciousness as if it were telescopic, our meditation and attention become more like a microscope. We turn our attention to examine our breath, body, sense experience, heart, and mind. It is as if we are silently inquiring: What is the nature of this whole process of life, how does it work? As we do so, wherever we turn our bright attention, the body and mind begin to show their changing nature. Because our attention is combined with strong concentration, whatever we sense in the body will no longer be felt solidly. It is as if we can suddenly sense the constant changes in our body on a cellular or molecular level. At the same time, the perception of our senses becomes undistracted. We directly feel the suchness of life, the moment-to-moment impressions of our senses, of sounds, tastes, feelings, without the elaboration of thought and the whole overlay of our usual identity.

This opening of the body and mind is the beginning of what the Elders described as the Insight Meditation path of dissolution. This map has more than a dozen levels that arise naturally with our steadily deepening attention. As they do, insight into our body and mind increases, and distinct states of consciousness arise, each with a unique perspective. Often these levels arise with a flash of insight, though sometimes we pass from one level to another in a gradual way.

After access concentration, the first key level of insight to arise is called *insight into the body and mind*. When the microscope of our attention becomes focused enough to dissect the distinct, individual processes of body and mind, we see and experience our whole life as a composite of simple physical elements and mental elements. There are only moments of sound and the knowing of it, moments of sensations and the thoughts or images that come together with them, moments of taste, moments of memory—only simple sense experiences and our momentary response to them, nothing more.

Although the description may sound commonplace, it is a remarkable state that experiences only this, for in it we can see that our ordinary continuous sense of life, with its plans, memories, and action itself, is constructed of layers of thought. Without thought, all that exists is moment-to-moment sense experiences and, with each sense experience, a momentary process of conscious perception. That is all.

As attention deepens further, the next level of insight shows how each of these mental and physical elements arises in a cause-and-effect sequence, how one moment of thought, image, or sound becomes the condition for the subsequent moment to arise. At this new stage, body and mind appear quite mechanical, and wherever we look, the universe shows the process of conditions, like seeds, being planted in one moment, sprouting in the next. Then even deeper attention, like a stronger lens in the microscope, brings us to a level of consciousness where life dissolves into more and finer tiny moments of experience, as in the paintings of the pointillist Seurat. What seemed our solid existence—feelings, objects, self, and others—changes more clearly now wherever we pay attention. Our body becomes only a river of sensations: our senses, feelings, and thoughts all begin to show their three most basic characteristics:

First, their transience, like shifting patterns of sand. Second, their unreliability and basic unsatisfactory nature; because our experience changes, no matter how pleasing or wonderful it may be for a moment, it cannot bring any security or lasting fulfillment. Third, their selflessness; all phenomena move and change on their own: there is no part that remains solid or separate that we can own or control, that we can point to as being "I" or "me," or "mine" or "yours."

Next, a still deeper and more stable level of awareness arises, called by the Elders the Realm of Arising and Passing. Here, our attention becomes quite balanced, and we experience life as a dance of momentary experiences, like raindrops. This realm has several qualities. First, in it we distinctly sense life as only arising and passing, being born anew and ending, moment after moment. Second, at this stage, attention and concentration become so strong that the heart and mind become clear and breathtakingly luminous. All the powers and factors of enlightenment arise spontaneously: rapture, energy, clear investigation, calm, concentration, insight, equanimity. In this state, awareness arises so automatically and easily that the mind feels as if it floats, free and unhindered by whatever appears. Tremendous joy arises; we can sense a wonderful freedom and balance. As we see more clearly into the nature of life, with this well-being comes incredible faith and clarity. The opening of mind and heart is so great that the need for sleep can diminish to one or two hours a night. Sometimes psychic abilities will open spontaneously at this stage. Dreaming will often become powerful, lucid, and conscious, and out-of-the-body experiences are common. From this level it is even possible to develop meditation consciously while dreaming.

With the arising of this stage, students often believe they are enlightened. This is called *tentative awakening* or *pseudo-nirvana*. It is pseudo-nirvana because when such wonderful meditative states arise, we feel we are free of our everyday identity, but then we unknowingly grasp these states and create a new spiritual sense of ourselves. Pseudo-nirvana feels like freedom, but it is also a sticking point in meditation where students may be caught for a long time. In pseudo-nirvana the genuine qualities of joy, clarity, faith, concentration, and mindfulness easily turn into *corruptions of insight*.

Corruptions of insight refers to our attachment to and misuse of the genuinely positive phenomena that arise in practice. Don Juan spoke of the dangers of the power and clarity that come to all men and women of knowledge. In pseudo-nirvana, students become stuck in positive states, trying to maintain them, grasping the clarity, power, or peace, using them to reinforce their subtle sense of being one who is awake, accomplished, free. The only release from this level of attachment is a radical letting go. Coming to this understanding is one of the greatest insights on the spiritual path. No matter what remarkable state arises, we must learn to allow it to come and go freely, recognizing that it is not the goal of meditation. Then, through our own understanding and the guidance of a teacher, we can begin to include even the states of joy, equanimity, and clarity as simply another part of our mindfulness, noticing how they too arise and pass. At this point, we are awakened to the profound realization that the true path to liberation is to *let go of everything*, even the states and fruits of practice themselves, and to open to that which is beyond all identity.

THE DARK NIGHT

According to the Elders' map of insight stages, when we release the corruptions of insight, our whole practice shifts. Our consciousness is now temporarily free from grasping at a spiritual identity, just as the earlier state of access concentration temporarily released us from our worldly thoughts and identity. This opening marks the beginning of a spontaneous and deep process of death and rebirth. Many forms of death and rebirth are encountered in the course of spiritual practice in every tradition. All the processes we have described throughout this book can be experienced in this way. Healing, expanding through the middle of knots, energetic awakenings, visions, and chakra openings can all involve a letting go of our old identities and a rebirth of a new sense of self. But at the level of Insight Meditation beyond pseudo-nirvana, the death-rebirth process becomes all-encompassing, involving our total being. After we abandon our spiritual identity, the meditation leads us through a total dissolution of our sense of self, through a *dark night*, like death itself. To enter this path consciously challenges all we know of our identity. Yet it is the path to freedom. The Zen teacher Karlfried von Durkheim spoke of the need for this process when he wrote:

> The person who, being really on the Way, falls upon hard times in the world, will not, as a consequence, turn to that friend who offers him refuge and comfort and encourages their old self to survive. Rather, he will seek out someone who will faithfully and inexorably help him to risk himself, so that he may endure the difficulty and pass courageously through it. Only to the extent that a person exposes himself over and over again to annihilation, can that which is indestructible be found within them. In this daring lies dignity and the spirit of true awakening.

The spiritual description of death and rebirth as a "dark night" comes from the writings of the great mystic St. John of the Cross. In an eloquent way, he describes the dark night as a long period of unknowing, loss, and despair that must be traversed by spiritual seekers in order to empty and humble themselves enough to receive divine inspiration. He put it this way: "The soul that is attached to anything, however much good there may be in it, will not arrive at the liberty of the divine."

Traditionally the dark night arises only after we have had some initial spiritual opening. In the first flush of practice, joy, clarity, love, and a sense of the sacred can arise, and with them we experience a great excitement at our spiritual progress. However, these states will inevitably pass away. It is as if they arise for us as initial gifts, but then we discover how much discipline and surrender are needed to sustain and live in these realms. Inwardly we often touch the light and then lose it, falling back into separateness, despair, or unconsciousness. This may happen many times in the repeated cycles of opening and letting go, of death and rebirth, that mark our spiritual path. Yet it is this very process of death and rebirth that leads us to freedom.

In Insight Meditation, once we have abandoned the luminous state of arising and passing, we open to a profound cycle of dissolution, death, and rebirth. As awareness releases its hold on the corruptions of insight, it becomes yet more precise and fine. Then it is as if the microscope of our concentration begins to see with exquisite clarity the dissolution of all life experience. We immediately feel the end of each moment, the end of each experience. Life begins to feel like quicksand. Everything we look at or feel is dissolving. In this stage, nothing around us seems solid or trustworthy. On all levels, our consciousness becomes attuned to endings and death. We notice the end of conversations, of music, of encounters, of days, of sensations in the body on a powerful cellular level. We sense the dissolution of life moment to moment.

Now the dark night deepens. As our outer and inner worlds dissolve, we lose our sense of reference. There arises a great sense of unease and fear, leading students into a realm of fear and terror. "Where is there any security?" "Wherever I look, things are dissolving." In these stages we can experience this dissolution and dying within our own body. We may look down and see pieces of our body seeming to melt away and decay, as if we were a corpse. We can see ourselves dying, or having died, in a thousand ways, through illness, battles, and misfortune. At this point other powerful visions can arise, visions of the death of others, visions of wars, dying armies, funeral pyres, or charnel grounds. Consciousness seems to have opened to the realm of death to show us how all creation moves in cycles, all ends in death. We experience how every aspect of the world comes into being and inexorably passes away.

From this realm of terror and death arises a very deep realization of the suffering inherent in life: the suffering of pain, the suffering of the loss of pleasant things and, hanging over it all, the enormous suffering of the death of whatever is created or loved by us. Out of this we can experience tremendous sympathy for the sorrows of the world. It seems that no matter where we look in the world—at our community, our family members and loved ones, our own self and body—all of it is fragile, all will be lost.

As the realm of terror deepens, periods of paranoia may arise. In this stage, wherever we look, we become fearful of danger. We feel that if we walk outdoors, something could run us over. If we take a drink of water, the microbes in it could kill us. Everything becomes a source of potential death or destruction in this phase of the dark night. People experience these feelings in many different ways: as pressure, claustrophobia, oppression, tightness, restlessness, or struggle, or as the unbearable endless repetition of experiences, one after another, dying all the time. We can feel as if we are stuck in meaningless cycles of life. Existence can seem flat, arid, and lifeless. It is as if there is no exit.

As you might expect, it is hard to meditate through these stages. But continuing to sense these new levels of consciousness with clarity and acceptance is the only way through them. We must name each one and allow it to arise and pass. Any other reaction will keep us stuck. As we learn to acknowledge each state, name each state, and meet it with mindfulness, we discover that we are dying over and over again. What we are being asked to do is to open to this death and become someone who has entered the realm of death and awakened in the face of it.

In traversing these painful stages, there next arises a deep and profound desire for freedom. In this state we long for release from the fear and oppression of continued birth and death. We sense that there must be a freedom that is not bound up in our seeing, hearing, smelling, tasting, and touching, something beyond our plans and memories, our body and mind, the whole identity we have taken to be ourselves. In fact, in each level of the dark night, the increasing power of awareness has been gradually unraveling our identity, releasing our grip on all that we have held in life.

Even though we wish for freedom, there often arises a sense of impossibility, that we cannot go any further, that we just cannot let go any more. We enter the stage of great doubt; we want to stop; we become restless. In one text this is called the rolling-up-the-mat stage. Here the world becomes too difficult; our spiritual practice asks too much of us; we wish we could quit and go home to our bed or our mother.

Because the powerful stages of fear and dissolution touch such painful chords in us, it is easy to get stuck in them or lose our way among them. In this process, it is important to have a teacher; otherwise, we will get lost or overwhelmed by these states and quit. And if we quit meditation in the middle of the stages of loss, death, dissolution, and fear, they will continue to haunt us. They can easily become entangled with our personal loss and fear in our everyday life. In this way, they can become undercurrents in our consciousness, and the unresolved feelings can last for months or years, until we do something to take ourselves back to this process and complete it.

The same thing can happen to people in shamanic journeys or at places in very deep therapy. If a process is incomplete, the effects stay underground and leak to the surface, and we can be depressed, fearful, or angry for a very long time, until we go back down to the deepest level and bring it to resolution. To bring things to resolution means we must go right into them. We must be able to look them straight in the eye and say, "Yes, I can open to this too," meeting them with an open heart that neither grasps nor resists them.

When we can finally look at the horrors and joys, our birth and our death, the gain and loss of all things, with an equal heart and open mind, there arises the state of the most beautiful and profound equanimity. We enter a realm where consciousness is fully open and awake, perfectly balanced. This is a level of wonderful peace. We can sit at ease for hours, and nothing that arises causes any disturbance in the space of consciousness. Consciousness becomes luminous even beyond the stage of pseudo-nirvana, because now everything is untangled, free, and we grasp at nothing. As it says in the Diamond Sutra, the world appears like a play of light and color, as a star at dawn, as a rainbow, as clouds, and as a mirage. Everything that appears is singing one song, which is the song of emptiness and fullness. We experience the world of phenomena and consciousness, of light and dark, playing themselves out in a dance without separation.

This state of profound balance the Elders called *high equanimity*. Our mind becomes like a crystal goblet or like the clear sky in which all things appear unhindered. We become completely transparent, as if every phenomenon just passes through our mind and body. We are simply space, and our whole identity opens to reveal the true nature of consciousness before we became identified with body and mind.

This state is described in many traditions. Certain Buddhist practices in the Zen and Tibetan traditions directly cultivate this spacelike perspective through practices of *shikan-taza, maha mudra,* and other higher tantras. In Hinduism, Advaita Vedanta calls it the nondual that contains everything and nothing, also referring to it as the Higher Self. The Christian mystical tradition refers to such a state as Divine Apathy. This consciousness is likened to the eye of God that sees the creation and destruction of the world, the light and dark, with a heart that embraces it all, that *is* all of that. From this perspective we see that we are nothing and that we are everything. From this place of balance, we get a taste of what it is like to be in the world but not caught by a single thing in it.

THE REALM OF AWAKENINGS

Whenever we come to rest in this perfect balance, whether through meditation or another deep spiritual process, we can encounter yet further extraordinary states of consciousness, spontaneous awakenings and profound realizations that come unbidden to the open heart and balanced mind, like grace from the divine or even like lightning. These realizations can come in many forms. Sometimes from high equanimity we enter the void, the silent emptiness out of which all things arise. The entire universe disappears and later reappears by itself. This release from all sense of self and form brings enormous peace and shows us a freedom beyond all form and all limited existence. Sometimes such realizations of the void are deeply restful and quiet; other times they shock like thunderbolts. Some students will go around dazed for weeks after a profound opening to the emptiness of the void, not yet sure how to put life back together. Sometimes experiences of cessation and the void will have the flavor of absolute emptiness; other times there will be a mystical sense of pregnant fullness. There are many dimensions possible in experiencing the void.

At this level of perfect equanimity, students understand the suffering and pain inherent in all forms of identity, in all existence. At earlier levels, we experience and see the suffering but we don't understand it. In equanimity, our understanding and acceptance brings a direct apprehension of freedom, of the deathlessness that lies beyond all existence, beyond all form and limitation. Whenever this arises, there comes an unquenchable joy and the knowledge that for eons we have wandered, entangled in life, and now our grasping has unraveled and we have tasted freedom at last.

Other equally illuminating realizations can appear, showing us the complete freedom and liberation found in the very midst of life itself. A luminous vision arises when our heart realizes the inherent completeness and perfection of all things. Like T. S. Eliot's "still point of the turning world," we can come to a wondrous sense of wholeness and completeness, transcendence and love, beyond self and other, beyond all endeavors. We wake up just here, as the mystics say, in the Body of Buddha, the Body of Christ, and even the limited things of the world are filled with an inexhaustible sweetness and purity.

At these deep levels of practice, profound satoris and mystical awakenings continue to unfold. The everchanging essence of life shows how consciousness itself can be experienced as the creator and container of all that is. We discover that we are the Reality we were seeking. Consciousness can be experienced as clear light or as jewels pouring out of the cornucopia of experience like galaxies of stars sending out their light. Our clarity of mind can illuminate the artificiality of time and space. We can see directly how all things exist right now, see that the whole sense of time and creation is but a trick of consciousness, where individual identity is done with mirrors and "Time is simply God's way of keeping everything from happening all at once." We can know the arising of the illusion of separateness in each moment and live in the great peace that underlies it all.

In all of this there comes a dying to the old way we have held ourselves and an amazing new vision of life. This process of death and rebirth can happen in any period of time. Weeks, months, or years of meditation and prayer may precede it or it may happen quickly, on the operating table, or through some powerful shamanic ritual or other exceptional circumstance. For some people it happens in the midst of daily life, the discovery of that perfect balance and greatness that is possible for the human heart. Whenever it is discovered, in whatever circumstances, it begins to transform us. Even though we do not always remain in such a state, as if we had climbed to the top of a mountain, we've had a taste of inner freedom that can inform and affect our whole life thereafter. We cannot ever again believe that we are separate. To the extent that we have died already, we are not afraid of dying in the old way. This is called *dying before death*. It brings to our life a wonderful kind of wholeness and equanimity.

In the end, the gift of this process is to realize the most fundamental teachings of the *dharma,* the law, the Tao. We see what the Buddha taught, that all suffering in life is caused by grasping, fear, and limited identification. In the midst of this we discover a freedom, a release from individual entanglement that empties us and yet leaves us connected with everything. We discover that liberation is possible for every human heart, that it has happened in ancient times and it happens to this day.

And finally we come to see that spiritual practice is really very simple. The whole process is a path of opening and letting go, of being aware and not attaching to a single thing. This teaching leads us past all the temptations and demons, through the whole process of death and rebirth. As my teacher Achaan Chah taught:

If you let go a little, you will have a little peace. If you let go a lot, you will have even more peace. So wherever you are attached, let go of that and come back to the center. Learn to see all movement of life with balance and openness.

As we end this chapter on expanding and dissolving the self, let me remind you that this map of the Elders describes only one path among many for spiritual opening. Even those who have a natural ability to enter these realms discover that these experiences have their benefits and their limits. No matter how tremendous the openings and how strong the enlightening journey, one inevitably comes down. Very often in coming back down, layer by layer, one again reencounters all of the difficulties of the journey.

Then, when we have returned to ordinary consciousness, we find that sometimes we are deeply transformed by such states and sometimes not! At best they leave us with a greater sense of balance and fearlessness, with an ease and tenderness of heart and mind. But finally there is nothing to do but to let go of them as well. This is what we will have learned if the lessons are true.

This is illustrated by a story of an old Chinese Zen monk who, after many years of peaceful meditation, realized he was not really enlightened. He went to the master and said, "Please, may I go find a hut at the top of the mountain and stay there until I finish this practice?" The master, knowing he was ripe, gave his permission. On the way up the mountain the monk met an old man walking down, carrying a big bundle. The old man asked, "Where are you going, monk?" The monk answered, "I'm going to the top of the mountain to sit and either get enlightened or die." Since the old man looked very wise, the monk was moved to ask him, "Say, old man, do you know anything of this enlightenment?" The old man, who was really the Bodhisattva Manjusri—said to appear to people when they are ready for enlightenment—let go of his bundle, and it dropped to the ground. As in all good Zen stories, in that moment the monk was enlightened. "You mean it is that simple; just to let go and not grasp anything!" Then the newly enlightened monk looked back at the old man and asked, "So now what?" In answer, the old man reached down and picked up the bundle again and walked off toward town.

This story shows both sides of spiritual practice. It teaches us to let go, to relinquish our grasping and identification with all things, and reminds us that we just rent this house for a while. Once we have realized that, it teaches us, we must reenter the world with a caring heart. We must pick up our bundle and carry it back into the realm of human life.

But now we can travel as a bodhisattva, as one who has traversed the terrain of life and death and is free in a new way. From this freedom we can bring a heart of understanding and compassion to a world that needs it so much.

MEDITATION ON DEATH
AND REBIRTH

When your vision clears and your heart opens, you will discover that you are living in a constant process of beginnings and endings. Your children leave home; your marriages may begin and end; your home is sold; a new career begins; your work ends in retirement. Every new year, every day, every moment is a letting go of the old and a rebirth of the new. Spiritual practice brings you into the most intimate contact with this mystery. Sitting still, you encounter the unstoppable arising and passing of your breath, your feelings, thoughts, and mental images. More deeply still, you discover that your consciousness itself can change, giving rise to a thousand different views and perspectives. Finally, all that you take yourself to be—your separate body, mind, and individuality—can unravel before you until you discover that your limited identity is not your true nature.

The great Buddhist text from *The Tibetan Book of the Dead* is a wonderful guide for moving through the process of death, rebirth, and awakening to our true nature. This text is intended to be read to one who has just died. But because there is fundamentally no division between birth and death, the teachings that apply to the movement from one physical life to another give us identical instructions for living in this life, from one day, one moment, one breath, to another. I have read them to friends who were dying, to friends in the midst of a divorce, to those on vision quests, and to students in retreat.

You can sit quietly and read them to yourself, you can record them on tape and play them back, or you can ask a friend to read them to you slowly. As you hear these words, let them sink into your consciousness, listening, being receptive and open with your whole being. They will lead you back to your own true nature.

Remember the clear light, the pure clear light, from which everything in the universe comes, to which everything in the universe returns. The original nature of your own mind, the natural state of the universe unmanifest. Let go into the clear light. Trust it, merge with it. It is your own true nature, it is home. The visions you experience exist within your consciousness. The forms they take are determined by your past attachments, your past desires, your past fears, your past karma. These visions have no reality outside of your consciousness. No matter how frightening some of them may seem, they cannot hurt you. Let them pass through your consciousness. They will all pass in time. No need to become involved with them, no need to be attracted to the beautiful visions, no need to be repulsed by the frightening ones, no need to be attached to them at all. Just let them pass. If you become involved with these visions, you may wander for a long time confused. So let them pass through your consciousness like clouds passing through an empty sky. Fundamentally they have no more reality than this. If you become frightened or confused, you can always call on any luminous being whom you trust for protection and guidance.

Remember these teachings, remember the clear light, the pure bright shining light of your own nature. It is deathless. When you can look into the visions you experience and recognize they are composed of the same pure clear light as everything else in the universe, you will be liberated. No matter where or how far you wander, the light is only a split second, a half a breath away. It is never too late to recognize the clear light.

II

SEARCHING
FOR THE BUDDHA:
A LAMP UNTO OURSELVES

When we are faced with a variety of spiritual teachings and practices, we must keep a genuine sense of inquiry. What is the effect of these teachings and practices on myself and others? In his last words, the Buddha said we must be a lamp unto ourselves.

These are extraordinary times for a spiritual seeker. Modern spiritual bookstores bulge with texts of Christian, Jewish, Sufi, and Hindu mystical practices. The past chapters on the spiritual roller coaster and expanding and dissolving the self become just one more account among hundreds of spiritual tales. Yet many of these accounts are contradictory. Already we have seen how strongly perspectives can differ within the Buddhist traditions, from schools that seek enlightenment through purification and altered states of consciousness to those that say it is this seeking itself that keeps us from realizing our true enlightenment here and now. The many contradictory perspectives we encounter pose one of the great dilemmas of spiritual life: What are we to believe?

Initially, in our enthusiasm for our practice, we tend to take everything we hear or read as the gospel truth. This attitude often becomes even stronger when we join a community, follow a teacher, undertake a discipline. Yet all of the teachings of books, maps, and beliefs have little to do with wisdom or compassion. At best they are a signpost, a finger pointing at the moon, or the leftover dialogue from a time when someone received some true spiritual nourishment. To make spiritual practice come alive, we must discover within ourselves our own way to become conscious, to live a life of the spirit.

Some years ago in Massachusetts a woman named Jean, who had been a meditation student, came to see me in a greatly confused state. She had been married to a doctor and they had two children. Her husband had been subject to bouts of depression, and in the midst of one of them during the preceding year had committed suicide. This was very sorrowful and painful for her and even more so for her children. The family had lived outside of Amherst and had been involved in many of the spiritual communities in their area. They had studied with the Tibetans and the Sufis, and after his suicide their whole spiritual network came to the family's aid. Each day for many weeks friends came to cook meals, to care for the children, to bring comfort and support. Many of them included spiritual ceremonies for the family and for the father who had died.

One day a close friend in the Tibetan community came over excitedly to Jean and said, "I've been doing the Tibetan prayers and visualizations of the dead over the past forty days, and last night I saw him. Your husband is fine. The vision was so clear. He was entering the bardo of light of the Western Realm with the Bodhisattva Amitabha. I could sense it so clearly. Everything is fine." Jean was greatly heartened by this. In town several days later, however, she encountered a friend from the local Christian mystical community where she had also practiced. This friend came over excitedly and said, "He's fine. I have seen him. I had this profound vision just last night in my prayer in meditation, and he is surrounded by white light in the heaven of the ascended masters." Jean was a little shaken and confused by this comment.

When she went home, she decided to call on an old and respected teacher of hers, a Sufi master. When she arrived there, before she could explain her dilemma, he announced to her, "Your husband is fine, you know. He has already entered a womb and will take birth in a female body through parents living in the Washington, D.C., area. I have been following his consciousness in my meditation." Confused and upset, trying to sort out what was true, she came to see me.

I asked her to consider carefully what she actually knew herself. If she put aside the Tibetan teachings, the Sufi teachings, the Christian mystical teachings and looked in her own being and heart, what did she already know that was so certain that even if Jesus and the Buddha were to sit in the same room and say, "No, it's not," she could look them straight in the eye and say, "Yes, it is." I was asking her to put away all her philosophies and beliefs, the maps of past and future lives and more, reminding her that what she knew might be very simple. Finally, out of the quiet she said, "I know that everything changes and not much more than that. Everything that is born dies, everything in life is in the process of change." I then asked her if perhaps that wasn't enough—could she live her life from that simple truth fully and honestly, not holding on to what inevitably must be let go. Perhaps this simple understanding would be enough to live a wise and spiritual life.

What I asked of Jean, to put aside all the teachings she had heard and to consider what she herself truly knew, is a task we must all do. Often the things we know are very simple yet in this simplicity that Korean Zen master Seung Sahn called Don't Know Mind, we can sense the living spirit. We can feel the mystery of being born into this body, of being here for the colors and sounds of this dance. In this simplicity something renews itself, something completes itself that is really already complete. What is beautiful can show itself in its silence. Elizabeth Kübler-Ross writes of finding this at the moment of death. Those who have the strength and the love to sit with a dying person in the silence that goes beyond words will know that this moment is neither frightening nor painful, but a peaceful cessation of the functioning of the body. Watching a peaceful death can remind us of the peace found in seeing a falling star.

Somehow, in the moment of recognizing that everything changes, Jean found her way again. Religion and philosophy have their value, but in the end all we can do is open to mystery and live a path with heart, not idealistically, not without difficulties, but as a Buddha did, in the very midst of our humanness in our life on this earth. It is worth asking ourselves: What is it that we can see and know directly for ourselves? Are these simple truths not enough? I have asked this question of many meditation groups and usually people answer with simple truths such as, "Whatever view or opinion I hold, I realize there is some other." "This world has night and day and light and dark and pleasure and pain. It is comprised of opposites." Or, "When I'm attached, I suffer." Or, "Love is what has really brought me happiness in this life."

Our liberation and happiness arise from our own deep knowing, and it doesn't matter what anyone says to the contrary. Our spiritual life becomes unshakable only when we are connected with our own realization of truth.

Modern times have some parallel to the spiritual climate of ancient India. At the time of the Buddha, historical accounts describe many other teachers, yogis, sages, and masters offering a variety of spiritual practices. And just as in our times, people at the time of the Buddha had become confused after meeting many of these masters. One of the most famous teachings of the Buddha's life was given in the village of the Kalamas. After they had hosted a succession of masters giving contradictory spiritual teachings they became confused. When the Buddha arrived and heard of this, he said:

> You may be puzzled, Kalamas, and in doubt, and your doubt has arisen about what should be doubted. Do not believe me either. If you wish to know spiritual truth, you must investigate it this way: Do not, O Kalamas, be satisfied with hearsay or tradition, with legends or what is written in great scriptures, with conjecture or logic, or with liking for a view or disliking it, or saying, "This comes from a great master or teacher." But look in yourselves. When you know in yourselves what teachings are unprofitable, blameworthy, condemned by the wise, when adopted and put into effect lead to harm and suffering, you should abandon them. If they lead to falsehood and greed, to thievery or obsession, to the increase of hatred or delusion, abandon them. Again, O Kalamas, do not be satisfied with hearsay or tradition, or any teachings, however they may come to you. Only when you know in yourself when things are wholesome, blameless, commended by the wise, and when adopted and practiced lead to welfare and happiness, should you practice them. When they lead to virtue, honesty, loving-kindness, clarity, and freedom, then you must follow these.
>
> Thus you can think: If there are other lives, the fruit of the goodness in this life will be goodness hereafter, and if there are no other lives, then the fruit of the goodness will be experienced here and now.

When we are faced with a variety of spiritual teachings and practice, we must keep a genuine sense of inquiry: What is the effect of this teaching and practice on myself and others? How is this working? What is my relationship to it? Am I getting caught, frightened, lost in confusion? Am I being led to greater kindness and greater understanding, to greater peace or freedom? Only we can discover whether our path must lead us through the highest states of *samadhi* or through healing the wounds of our heart. In his last words, the Buddha said we must be a lamp unto ourselves, we must find our own true way.

Spiritual practice can never be fulfilled by imitation of an outer form of perfection. This leads us only to "acting spiritual." While we may be genuinely inspired by the examples of wise teachers and traditions, their very inspiration can also create problems for us. We want to imitate them instead of being honest and true in ourselves. Consciously or unconsciously, we try to walk like them, talk like them, act like them. We create great struggle in our spiritual life when we compare the images we hold of ourselves with our images of enlightened teachers, of figures like Buddha, Jesus, Gandhi, or Mother Teresa. Our heart naturally longs for wholeness, beauty, and perfection, but as we try to act like these great masters, we impose their image of perfection on ourselves. This can be very discouraging, for we are not them.

In fact, initially, spiritual practice may feel like it is leading us in the opposite direction. As we awaken, we tend to see our faults and fears, our limitations and selfishness, more clearly than ever before. The first difficulties on the path include some rude awakenings. We may wonder if we are on a path with heart or even on the right road at all. Doubts may arise. Practice may feel more like manual labor than a labor of love, and the images of perfection we hold will leave us yet more discouraged with ourselves and our practice. When we begin to encounter our own limitations directly, we may then try to look for another form of practice, a faster way, or we may decide to change our life radically—move our home, get divorced, join a monastery.

In our initial discouragement, we may blame our practice or the community around us, or we may blame our teacher. This happened to me in my first year as a monk. I was practicing diligently, but I became quite frustrated after a time. The restlessness, doubt, reactivity, and judgmental mind I encountered were very difficult for me. While I knew part of this was my own fault, I sensed a lot of it was due to the environment in which I found myself. I was living in a forest monastery under the guidance of a renowned meditation master, and as part of our daily schedule, aside from five hours of meditation, we had to chant, draw water from the well, sew robes, attend community affairs, and walk together to collect alms food in the morning. All this was supposed to be part of our meditation. Yet I had learned about other styles of monasteries where one could lock oneself in a room and practice in undisturbed silence twenty hours a day. I began to feel that if I were only at a place like that, my meditation would deepen properly and I could get enlightened.

The more frustrated I became, the more the monastery looked sloppy and not conducive to enlightenment. Even my image of the master began to fit right in with this frame of mind. How could he run a monastery in this fashion? In fact, why wasn't he practicing meditation all the time to set a better example, instead of sitting around surrounded by monks all day and teaching all of the villagers who came? So I went to confront him. I bowed and paid my respects and told him I wanted to leave for a stricter monastery, that there wasn't enough time to meditate where I was. "Eh," he said, "there isn't enough time to be aware?" "No," I answered, somewhat taken aback by his question. But my frustration was strong, so I went on, "Besides that, the monks are too sloppy and even you aren't silent enough. You are inconsistent and contradictory. This doesn't seem like what the Buddha taught to me." Only a Westerner would say something like this, and it made him laugh. "It's a good thing I don't appear like the Buddha," he answered. Somewhat annoyed I replied, "Oh, yes, why is that?" "Because," he said, "you would still be caught in looking at the Buddha outside of yourself. He isn't out here!" With that he sent me back to continue my meditation.

"It is our very search for perfection outside ourselves that causes our suffering," said the Buddha. The world of changing phenomena, whose cycles he called endless samsara, is by its nature a frustration to any image of perfection we might place on it. Even the most perfect moment or thing will change just a moment later. It is not perfection we must seek, but freedom of the heart. Remember again the words of the Buddha: "Just as the waters of the great oceans all have one taste, the taste of salt, so too, all true teachings have but one taste, the taste of liberation."

The Third Patriarch of Zen Buddhism explained that liberation arises when we are "without anxiety about nonperfection." The world is not supposed to be perfect according to our ideas. We have tried so long to change the world, yet liberation is not to be found by changing it, by perfecting it or ourselves. Whether we seek enlightenment through altered states or in community or in our everyday life, it will never come to us when we seek perfection. If not, then where do we find the Buddha in the midst of this? The Buddha arises when we are able to see ourselves and the world with honesty and compassion. In many spiritual traditions there is only one important question to answer, and that question is: Who am I? When we begin to answer it, we are filled with images and ideals—the negative images of ourselves that we wish to change and perfect and the positive images of some great spiritual potential—yet the spiritual path is not so much about changing ourselves as it is about listening to the fundamentals of our being.

A modern story of Mullah Nasrudin, the Sufi teacher and holy fool, tells of him entering a bank and trying to cash a check. The teller asks him to please identify himself. Nasrudin reaches in his pocket and pulls out a small mirror. Looking into it, he says, "Yep, that's me all right."

Meditation and spiritual practice are like this—like looking in the mirror. Initially, we tend to see ourselves and the world in familiar ways, according to the images and models we have held for so long. "This is me." "I am clever" or "plodding." "I am lovable" or "unworthy." "I am wise and generous," or "I am fearful and timid." Then we may try to fix or redo our image, but so mechanical an approach doesn't work either. I have known people who have embraced austere meditation as the true way one year, only to turn around and sing songs of devotion as the true path the next year. Henry Miller realized how ludicrous fixed ideas can become, saying, "Everything I wrote about the man, I realized later I could have just as well written the opposite."

What images do we hold of ourselves, of our spiritual life, of others? Are all these images and ideas who we really are? Is this our true nature? Liberation comes not as a process of self-improvement, of perfecting the body or personality. Instead, in living a spiritual life, we are challenged to discover another way of seeing, rather than seeing with our usual images, ideals, and hopes. We learn to see with the heart, which loves, rather than with the mind, which compares and defines. This is a radical way of being that takes us beyond perfection. It is as if our spiritual practice, with its ups and downs, can be held in the heart of the Buddha. From this perspective, all can be included as our practice.

In the middle of our annual three-month retreat, a friend came to ask about a number of community members who were sitting. "How is Jill doing?" he asked. I said, "Good." "And how is Sam doing?" "He's doing all right." "How is Claudia doing?" "Well, she went through quite a rough time, but she's doing okay." I continued to answer about six people: each one was doing fine. Finally the questioner asked, "What do you mean when you say they're doing good?" I paused to consider for a moment and then I said, "What it means is that they haven't left yet." We both laughed, yet this was a serious answer, for what matters in the realm of awakening is not the particular experience we have but whether that too can be made into our practice, whether we can stay open to what is present, learn to love in this place as well.

From our first sitting and the necessary healing that we encounter in practice, we gradually open to a new and unfamiliar ground. There may come altered states, or there may not, but eventually what we have been seeking all along is found here, in the moment we come to rest, in our essential self, our Buddha nature or basic goodness. It is discovered when we are quite present, yet not seeking a thing, when we have come to rest in this moment. There then appears a sense of wholeness and integrity, of strength and beauty. That which we were running around the world seeking is here at our door. Over and over again we learn this simplicity.

If we had been seeking strength through control over ourselves and others, we discover that was only a false version of strength, that truth and inherent strength appear in moments of deep silence and wholeness when we rest unshakably with things as they are. If we had been seeking beauty or love through others or in states that perfect our mind, this too comes whole and unbidden when desires and longings themselves come to rest. This is awakening to our Buddha nature.

What we seek is who we are, and in the fulfillment of our practice, we discover that our understanding has been here all the time. Pope John XXIII tells what this is like, even for a pope:

> It often happens that I awake at night and begin to think about a serious problem and decide I must tell the pope about it. Then I wake up completely and remember that I am the pope.

This is meditation: To resume our true nature and discover an enormous sense of rest and peace, a spaciousness in our heart in the midst of life; to allow ourselves to become transparent to the light that is always shining. "It is not far away," says one Zen master. "It is nearer than near." This is not a matter of changing anything but of not grasping anything, and of opening our eyes and our heart.

Since this may sound too simple, let us go a step further. Let's take a situation of difficulty in our life and see how we might discover our Buddha nature even there. We will do a simple meditation that can evoke the universal archetypes, the energies of compassion and wisdom that are always there within us whenever we remember to open to their voice. After you have read through the next three paragraphs, close your eyes and picture yourself in the middle of an instance of one of the greatest difficulties of your life. It may be a difficulty at work or it may be in a personal relationship. You can remember it, picture it, imagine it, think about it, feel it—whatever way your own heart and mind best sense it. Let yourself reexperience the scene vividly, the people who are there, the difficulties and how you react to them. Let it reach its worst height. Notice how your body feels in the midst of this and how you act and what state your heart is in.

Then imagine that there is a knock on the door that you must answer. Excuse yourself and step outside, where you find waiting for you someone like the Buddha, Jesus, Mother Mary, or the great Goddess of Universal Compassion. One of these beings has come to visit you. They look at you kindly and ask, "Having a hard day? Here," they suggest, "let me trade places with you. Give me your body and let me show you how I might handle this situation. You can remain invisible while I show you what is possible." So you lend your body to the goddess or Buddha, Jesus or whomever, and invisibly follow them back into the thick of your difficulties. Let the conversation and problems continue as before, and simply notice what you are being shown. How does Jesus, Buddha, Mary, or whoever respond to the situation? With silence? With what energy? What words do they choose? What is the state of their heart in the circumstance? What is the state of their body? Let them show you the way. Stay with them while they teach you.

Then they will excuse themselves again for a moment and walk back to the place where you met them. They lovingly return your body to you, and before they leave they touch you gently in the most healing way and whisper a few words of advice in your ear. Listen to these heartfelt words of wisdom and kindness. Hear them, imagine them, sense them, know them in whatever way you can, and let them be just what you need to live wisely.

Not everyone can do guided meditations easily, but most people find that through practice they are able to remember their difficulties and to discover or imagine them in a whole new way. It may take a period of silent practice to gain access to this wisdom, or you may find it comes quite quickly and easily. No matter—it is there to be found within you.

After this exercise ask yourself the question: Where did the Buddha, Jesus, Mary, or the Goddess of Compassion come from? That extraordinary wisdom or compassion or whatever else you learned in this meditation was already there within you! It is here already. You don't have to create it or imitate it, but listen for it and discover it within you. The words of advice from our inner spiritual figure will often be simple ones. "Love everyone." "Remember kindness." "Stand up for yourself and the truth." But these words take on a new meaning when we hear them in our own heart. All problems take on a new meaning when we can sense another way to hold our bodies, when we can picture or feel what strength and wisdom, what compassion and clarity feel like in the midst of our very greatest difficulties.

Here are some of the simple solutions of this guided meditation that have come from groups I have led. Someone saw the Buddha coming to replace them to confront an angry boss about an overdue project. The Buddha stayed present and strong, yet kept his body soft. The only words he said were, "You must feel a great deal of responsibility for holding all this together." Immediately the boss softened, and the employee and he were able to talk. Another person was on a home visit with very critical parents. The Goddess of Compassion took over her body and instead of fighting them, simply sat down to watch TV with them and tried to love them anyway. As the goddess left, she whispered in the ear of the frustrated daughter, "Don't go home too often." Another image was of Mother Mary, who came to a mother who pictured herself harried in the morning with three demanding children, feeling there was no time for herself, struggling greatly with the situation. Mother Mary came in, got down on the floor and started to play with the kids. She set limits, mind you, and sent them off when it was time for them to go to school, but mostly she gave them what they wanted. When she left she whispered in the harried mother's ears, "Just love them a lot and don't worry about the housework."

Spiritual attainment is not the result of special esoteric knowledge, the study of great texts and sutras, and the systematic learning of great works of religion, nor is it found in the realm of control or power; it doesn't attach to things being a certain way; and it holds no blame. It involves neither the control over another person nor even control of ourselves. It stems rather from an abundant wisdom of heart.

Years ago, I met an old monk in a jungle monastery in Southeast Asia. We were in a clearing at night and saw a man-made satellite weave its way through the stars. He pointed to it, telling me that such stars were newcomers to the sky. I tried to explain to him about rockets and satellites, and to my great surprise he questioned the idea that the earth was round. It had always seemed flat to him. The second- or third-grade education he had received in the 1920s had apparently not convinced him differently, yet he was regarded by many as a sage. His heart was filled with compassion and wisdom that drew many people to him to pour out their troubles and ask his advice. His understanding of human nature and life was deep and wonderful, though he didn't even know that the world is round.

The wisdom of the heart can be found in any circumstance, on any planet, round or square. It arises not through knowledge or images of perfection or by comparison and judgment, but by seeing with the eyes of wisdom and the heart of loving attention, by touching with compassion all that exists in our world.

The wisdom of the heart is here, just now, at any moment. It has always been here, and it is never too late to find it. The wholeness and freedom we seek is our own *true nature*, who we really are. Whenever we start a spiritual practice, read a spiritual book, or contemplate what it means to live well, we have begun the inevitable process of opening to this truth, the truth of life itself.

Let me end this chapter with an encouraging story. A young man found his way up to the small apartment of Nisargadatta, my old Hindu guru in Bombay, asked him a spiritual question and then left after this one question. One of the regular students then asked, "What will happen to this man? Will he ever become enlightened or will he fall off the path and go back to sleep?" Nisargadatta said, "It's too late for him! He has already begun. Just the fact that he came up here and asked one question about what is his true nature means that that place in him that knows who he really is has started to wake up. Even if it takes a long, long time, there's no turning back."

MEDITATION: BECOMING SIMPLE AND TRANSPARENT

As you reflect on your spiritual life you can ask yourself: What do you know in your heart about the truth of life? Do you actually need more knowledge than this, or is this simple fundamental wisdom enough? What keeps you from living simple truths you know? What would you need to let go of to do so? What confusion and fear interfere with your compassion? What strength and trust would be needed to live wisely and well? How would you change your life so that your body, heart, and mind might become more unknowing, more transparent to this light within? Can you imagine knowing less and becoming wiser?

Let yourself sense a simple loving presence you can bring into each moment. Be aware of how your spiritual life can guide you toward this.

PART III

WIDENING OUR CIRCLE

12

ACCEPTING THE
CYCLES OF SPIRITUAL LIFE

*If we have ideas about how our practice should
unfold, these will often get in the way, preventing us from honoring the phase that is actually with us.*

Every ancient system of wisdom teaches that human life unfolds in
a succession of stages: childhood, a period of education and learning, a
period for family life and meaningful work, and a period for contemplative
practice. In the Native American traditions, these evolving cycles are
honored in rites of passage that enable each community member to enter
new stages of life with full consciousness and support. Modern psychologists, such as Erik Erikson, also speak of an inevitable succession of
stages that make up a wise and meaningful life.

Just as there is beauty to be found in the changing of the earth's
seasons and an inner grace in honoring the cycles of life, our spiritual
practice will be in balance when we can sense the time that is appropriate
for retreats and the time that is appropriate for travel, the time for settling
down and planting roots, and the time to have a family and children. By

honoring these cycles, we honor the natural law of the universe in the Tao or the dharma of our own lives. The poet Wendell Berry speaks of this in his poem called "The Law That Marries All Things."

The cloud is free only
to go with the wind.

The rain is free
only in falling.

The water is free only
in its gathering together,

in its downward courses,
in its rising into the air.

In law is rest
if you love the law,
if you enter singing into it
as water in its descent.

In the beginning we may erroneously imagine spiritual practice to be a linear journey, traveling over a certain landscape to a faraway destination of enlightenment. But it is better described as a widening circle or spiral that opens our hearts and gradually infuses our consciousness to include all of life as a spiritual whole. In earlier chapters we have spoken of the way that the same issue will recur for us over and over in our practice at each new level. Inevitably, the question of how to navigate transitions in both our life circumstances and our practice will also recur. Twenty-five years ago Ram Dass described the cycles of spiritual life in *Be Here Now*.

Practice is like a roller coaster. Each new high is usually followed by a new low. Understanding this, it makes it a bit easier to ride with both phases. . . . There is in addition to the up-and-down cycles an in-and-out cycle. That is, there are stages at which you feel pulled into inner work and all you seek is a quiet place to meditate and get on with it, and then there are times when you turn outward and seek to be involved in the marketplace. Both of these parts of the cycle are a part of one's practice, for what happens to you in the marketplace helps in your meditation, and what happens in your meditation helps you to participate in the marketplace without attachment. . . . At first you will think of practice as a limited part of your life. In time you will realize that everything you do is part of your practice.

Change comes to our lives not only from shifts in our inner needs, but also from shifts in our external circumstances. The nature of existence, the Buddha taught, is ceaseless transformation. How can we find a way to honor these natural cycles of life in spiritual practice? First, we must respect the changing cycles that life brings us and accept the inner tasks they bring. In this way, our spiritual growth can develop naturally along with them. While this may seem obvious, our society has lost touch with these rhythms, and in many ways we are taught to ignore them. Young children are force-fed discipline and early academic training instead of being free to play and learn in healthy ways. Many middle-aged men live out a prolonged adolescence, and many women struggle to stay young as if to avoid maturity altogether. Old age is seen as a defeat to be resisted and feared. We have few role models of wise men and women at any life stage, no helpful initiations, and few rites of passage.

When we respect the natural cycles of life, we find that each of life's stages has a spiritual dimension. Each stage contributes wisdom and experience that we will draw upon in our spiritual growth. For example, one of the major sources of our spiritual consciousness is found in our earliest life—the benevolent oneness of existence in our mother's womb. Our consciousness holds in its depths this memory and the possibility of oneness, and we draw on it in meditation. Then, as an infant, we experience the freshness of seeing, feeling, and touching the world for the first time, the immediate physical presence of our senses and our own needs. Reawakening this immediacy, recapturing a spontaneous unbroken trust in what we know and feel, is central to finding our spiritual ground in later practice.

Many people have their first spiritual experience in childhood, that of an innate and natural connection with what is sacred and holy. The playfulness, joy, and curiosity of our childhood can become a foundation for the delighted rediscovery of this spirit in our practice. If our relationship with our parents is respectful and loving, that too becomes a model and foundation for respect and trust in all other relationships. Of course, if our experiences in the womb, as an infant, or as a child are bad ones, we will have great healing to do to reclaim our natural well-being. But these painful experiences may stimulate our longing for true well-being, and inevitably certain moments of every childhood will contain the seeds of awakening.

The independence and rebelliousness of our adolescence offer us yet another quality essential to our practice: the insistence that we find out the truth for ourselves, accepting no one's word above our own experience. As we move into the responsibilities of a young adult, we develop a compassionate concern for others besides ourselves. This ripening can bring us a sense of interdependence, the need for mutual respect and social justice, that is a source of awakening to the path of universal compassion.

Adult life brings its own natural spiritual tasks and openings. We become more caring and responsible for our family, our community, our world. We discover the need for vision and feel a strong desire to fulfill our own unique expression of life. As we mature, a natural contemplative quality enters our life. We can sense a movement within to seek periods of reflection and to gain perspective, to stay in touch with our heart. As we age, having seen many cycles of birth and death, there is a detachment and wisdom that grows within us.

Each stage of our life holds the seeds for our spiritual growth. Our spiritual life matures when we consciously accept the life tasks appropriate for us. Unfortunately, in many spiritual communities there are some people who hope to avoid these tasks. These people may start at age twenty-five spending years trying to ignore their body or their creativity and then suddenly and painfully realize when they reach their forties that they did want a family or career. Or they may join a spiritual community and picture themselves living a lifetime like the Buddha, as a wanderer and hermit in splendid isolation. What they forget is that after a period of wandering, the Buddha settled down to spend twenty-five years in the same monastery, teaching and offering himself as a community leader. Even for those who commit their life to a monastery, there are necessary cycles, initial periods of training and solitude, followed by greater responsibilities for teaching, leadership, and administration.

Whether in a monastery, in our place of business, or in our family life, we need to listen to what each cycle requires for our heart's development and accept its spiritual tasks. The natural cycles of growth—developing right livelihood, moving to a new home, the birth of a child, entering a spiritual community—all bring spiritual tasks that require our heart to grow in commitment, fearlessness, patience, and attention. The cycles of endings—our children leaving home, the aging and death of our parents, loss in business, leaving a marriage or community—bring our heart the spiritual tasks of grieving, of letting go gracefully, of releasing control, of finding equanimity and openhearted compassion in the face of loss.

Occasionally we get to choose the cycles we work with, such as choosing to get married or beginning a career. At these times it is helpful to meditate, to reflect on which direction will bring us closer to our path with heart, which will offer the spiritual lesson that it is time for in our life.

More often we don't get to choose. The great cycles of our life wash over us, presenting us with challenges and difficult rites of passage much bigger than our ideas of where we were going. Midlife crisis, threats of divorce, personal illness, sickness of our children, money problems, or just running yet again into our own insecurity or unfulfilled ambition can seem like difficult yet mundane parts of life to get over with so we can become peaceful and do our spiritual practice. But when we bring to them attention and respect, each of those tasks has a spiritual lesson in them. It may be a lesson of staying centered through great confusion, or a lesson of forbearance, developing a forgiving heart with someone who has caused us pain. It may be a lesson of acceptance or a lesson of courage, finding the strength of heart to stand our ground and live from our deepest values.

Spiritual teachers and gurus also face these unexpected cycles, times when their unfulfilled longings arise in them or when their community encounters difficulty. One highly respected guru in India was forced to reevaluate all he had taught when he discovered how much jealousy and competition there was among his students. Another teacher had desperately longed for a sabbatical, several years of retreat in the mountains, only to be appointed abbot of a famous temple after his own guru died. Some teachers may have to face the dependency they have created in the community around them, or even face their own dependency on teaching, at certain cycles in their practice. Difficult cycles are everyone's practice.

Just as worldly life moves in cycles, each offering spiritual lessons, so too the techniques and forms of our inner spiritual discipline move through natural cycles. Usually we think that each different spiritual path follows a distinct practice, such as service to the poor, prayers and devotion, physical yoga, retreat from the world, or study and inquiry. But our spiritual journey will probably lead us to include many of these dimensions of practice in the course of our growth. At one period of our practice we may be greatly devoted to following a teacher, later we may find ourselves in a period of practice and investigation on our own. One phase of our spirituality may focus on detachment and solitude, while a later phase demands we extend our loving-kindness through service to others. We may experience periods of great attention to our body, periods of prayer and surrender, or periods of study and reflection.

As I noted in Chapter 6, my teacher Achaan Chah used to sense these cycles in his students and direct the conditions of their practice so they would consciously work with them. When he felt they were ready, he would assign students who were afraid of solitude and loneliness to a distant and isolated cave monastery far from the nearest village. Those who were attached to stillness and had difficulty with human interaction might be sent to a monastery along the Bangkok highway where hundreds of pilgrims stop daily to visit. Those who had difficulty with food might be sent to work in the kitchen, and those filled with pride might well end up cleaning bathrooms and toilets as their regular and mindful duty.

These cycles are formally incorporated into the training at certain Zen monasteries, where members of the community are assigned certain roles for a year or two as part of practice. These positions include being the master's attendant, who must learn the work of service, of responsibility and devotion, and who benefits by closeness with the teacher. Another position is the keeper of discipline. The keeper of discipline must carry the Zen stick and use it when students fall asleep at sitting. He shouts to keep order, forcibly pulls errant students in line, and allows no excuses for sloppy or lazy practice. The opposite role goes to the care-giver of the temple. The care-giver brings extra cushions for those who need them, tends to the sick, helps with the overall coordination of the retreats, and offers all kinds of nurturing support. A student is assigned each role and expected to fulfill it, regardless of his or her own temperament. An even more interesting aspect of this training is that it rotates. After a year as the strict and merciless disciplinarian, one may be assigned to become a care-giver and overnight have to learn how to be tender and kind. One is expected to learn all these roles as a spiritual practice, to chop wood or carry water when it is time, to sit like a mountain, cook like a grandmother, and laugh like a Buddha.

Our consciousness contains all these roles and more, the hero and lover, the hermit, the dictator, the wise woman, and the fool. Even without a teacher or community directing us into different dimensions of practice, we will naturally encounter them in meditation. Our body, heart, and mind seem to open in cycles, as if there were a natural intelligence that brings us to whatever most needs our acceptance and understanding. For some time our meditation may offer great stillness and a peaceful release from the drama of our life. Then a new awareness of our family trauma and early childhood pain may arise, followed by a long period of working with grief and forgiveness. Then we may enter a cycle of deep concentration and spacious insight. But then our body may open in a new way, presenting physical pains or energy releases as our practice. Then as personal healing continues, we may encounter visions of world suffering and feel compelled to respond and include it in our practice. In these cycles there is no fixed order, no higher or lower. As these inner cycles open, our spiritual task is to include each of them in our awareness, bringing to each the love, wisdom, and forgiveness that have been needed all along.

Some of the most valuable teachings in spiritual practice come when our plans are disrupted. Thus, one student, who was deeply touched by the experience of a ten-day meditation retreat, resolved to do a period of long intensive practice. For two years he saved all his money, garnered his time off, prepared himself for a three-month silent retreat followed by an extended trip to Thailand and Burma. The week after his retreat began, he received an emergency phone call. His father was in the hospital with a serious heart attack, and his mother and family needed him at home. He loved his father very much and was deeply motivated to return to be with him, but he was also tremendously disappointed. He had waited so long to do this year of spiritual practice at the retreat and go to Asia, and now it was being taken away from him, and who knew when he would get another chance. Yet I'm sure the readers can already guess the end of this story. The nine months that he spent at home caring for his father, tending to the needs of his family, and living in the face of the mystery of death as his father died, became as deep, meaningful, and liberating a period of spiritual practice as he might ever have in his life.

An opposite set of conditions faced a somewhat older man who came on retreat. He had created a successful business for himself, raised three children who were now teenagers, had done some intensive work in therapy on the grief from his own childhood and an alcoholic family background. He came to the retreat still very much in conflict with his teenage boys, who were in the midst of a stormy adolescence. His purpose for sitting was to focus on understanding himself and his boys better. But the experience proved to have a different focus than he intended. After only a few days, his consciousness turned toward a deep and profound meditative silence. He became filled with devotion, he saw his body become filled with light, the trees around him began to shimmer, and a deep mystical vision flooded his consciousness. He wanted to write poetry and songs. To his great surprise, he found himself longing to live in a spiritual community and decided to do so when he finished raising his children. He also discovered a whole new direction and set of values for his life. With this he was able to return home with a new centered calm to face his teenage children.

One young woman came to our Buddhist retreat center after living simply in the woods for many years. She did several years of intensive meditation with profound results. Through a natural ability to quiet herself, she touched deep states of freedom, joy, and a bountiful emptiness. Then she became involved in intimate relationships and reconnected with the world of work, using her meditation for delightful support. After a year or two of reentering the world, she returned again to sit a two-month retreat with a visiting teacher. This time the high and luminous states vanished, and she was besieged by terrifying visions from her own childhood. Abuse, abandonment, her parents' alcoholism, and enormous pain from the time of her conception onward nearly overwhelmed her. The five years she had previously spent in meditative bliss gave way to a new and painful five-year process. This required her to face, integrate, and live with the sorrow of her personal history as fully as she had entered the joyful states that had led up to this. This second five years focused on loving-kindness meditation, therapy, painting, and a deep inner healing. Completing this second cycle eventually led her into a new cycle of marriage and building a home. Each of these cycles came of themselves, and all she could do was accept and honor them.

If we have ideas about how our practice should unfold, these will often get in the way, preventing us from honoring the phase that is actually with us. Often we wish our emotional work was done so we could open to another level. Many times students have come to me at a retreat and said, "Why am I still grieving? I've grieved for months over this loss. It should be done now." But grief too arises in waves and cycles, and it's done in its own time. It is over when we have so deeply accepted it that it doesn't matter if it arises again or not. Similarly students will complain, "I've dealt with my sexuality. Why should these issues be arising again?" Or, "I thought I'd come to terms with suffering, and yet now I discover in my practice there are levels of suffering in life that I'm only beginning to face and understand."

Practice cannot follow our ideals; it can only follow the laws of life. In a naive way we might imagine our hearts can stay open like a giant sunflower filled with loving-kindness, compassion, and connection day after day in an unchanging way, but our hearts and feelings have their rhythms and cycles too. Our heart breathes like the rest of us, and sometimes it opens and sometimes it closes like the blossoms of a flower that closes its petals on cool evenings.

Our bodies reflect the spirals and movement of the stars. We wake and sleep, the earth turns, the sun rises and sets, women have menstrual cycles that parallel the moon, our hearts beat, our breath moves in and out, our cerebral spinal fluid washes our brain and spine, all in natural rhythms.

Like the heart, the cycles of our body present themselves, even if we hope to "transcend" them. When we honor them, our practice opens. One student who had tried to ignore her body over many years of meditative spiritual practice kept getting sick. In part, it was the compulsiveness of her spiritual striving that was making her sick. Finally, she became so sick she was compelled to incorporate a regimen of exercise, diet, and conscious yoga in her practice. As soon as she acknowledged and honored her body, it began to nourish her well-being in every other part of her life, and out of this her silent meditation itself became deeper, fuller, and more profound.

In an opposite way, another student who had been obsessed with his body, with exercise, weights, fitness, and looks, kept painfully encountering compulsive thoughts about this in meditation. This went on for years. Finally, he had to release this compulsion and let go of the body image he had striven to uphold. In releasing his body, he could now bring attention to his heart and to the fears that underlay his meditation for so long. Then, as though a fog were lifted, a whole new sense of compassion and well-being arose both in his life and in his meditation, integrated in a deep, new way.

LEAVING RETREAT: PRACTICE WITH TRANSITION

Whether we are encountering unexpected outer cycles or natural inner cycles, spiritual practice asks us to honor these changing circumstances in a wakeful way, to breathe in and out gracefully with the cycles of our practice. One of the clearest opportunities to learn how to do this is when we work with the transition time at the end of periods of retreats, spiritual seminars, or secluded practice. Modern spiritual practice often requires that we temporarily enter a spiritual community, only to return home after some days or weeks. This transition, from the openness and support of a retreat and a spiritual community to the complexity of our daily life, can be difficult, especially if we hold on to any notion that one phase is more spiritual than the other. Yet with attention, each part of the transition, inner and outer, can be made mindful and included in the practice of our heart.

When we leave a retreat, we face a natural loss as we change from one circumstance to another. If the retreat fostered a quieting of our mind, an opening of our heart, and a simplicity of living, we may fear losing this as we return to the complexities of everyday life. We may imagine that whatever spiritual sensibility has been awakened in the protected retreat environment will disappear. We may feel open or vulnerable, raw or delicate, in our senses and emotions, so that in returning to our home in the city or to the daily struggles of our families, work, and driving in traffic, we feel we will be overwhelmed. The more powerful the retreat, the stronger this fear may be. We may also be afraid that no one will understand us. We may want our life to remain the way it was at the end of the retreat. We may try to hold on to whatever beautiful states we had encountered. Even after a profound awakening, we can encounter the attachment and pride that Zen calls the *stink of enlightenment*. All of these forces of fear, grasping, and pride prevent us from opening to the next cycle of our practice. Yet this transition is a perfect circumstance to learn how to move through the cycles of our practice.

First it requires patience. We must recognize that transitions can be long processes. If our retreat was deep or we were away for some time, there can be weeks and months of difficulty and confusion before we again feel integrated back into our lives. The most important thing is to consciously acknowledge our loss. As we move from one part of our life in practice to another, we must allow ourselves to feel the loss and letting go. In this way we can allow our heart to feel its grief and inevitable attachment to what we have just completed. In honoring the feelings of loss and allowing ourselves to see the attachment, we bring awareness to our process of letting go.

In the same way we must also honor our vulnerability. Often spiritual retreats leave us very open, and the intensity of everyday life can feel grating and shocking. At times we can feel like newborn babies who need to be honored and protected when cast back into the world. Sometimes the baby needs a hot bath and soothing music as a bridge between the time spent in a Tibetan monastery last week and the nursing job in a hospital ward he or she must return to next week. To honor this sensitivity, we must take care in how we make the transition. This often means setting aside periods for silence, changing our schedule to allow for extra contemplative time, postponing the busiest or most difficult encounters, giving ourselves enough time to make a smooth transition from silence to great activity. It can help to regularly reconnect with others in our spiritual community. Together we can laugh and grieve and help each other through the cycles of change.

When we return from a quiet contemplative period, we will often see the pain of the world, our own and others', in a more clear and undeniable way. This is actually part of our spiritual path, to see clearly and open our hearts to it all. However, it may also seem overwhelming. We may find ourselves repeating old unconscious patterns or facing difficult and unfinished business and be in need of compassion for the many painful parts of ourselves. In looking with fresh eyes, the world around us can also seem very unconscious and driven. We may see more clearly on the faces of many we pass the haunted, lonely, irritated, or frightened looks that reveal the intensity and speed of modern life and the underlying folly and enormity of its pain. If we consciously allow this to touch our hearts, it too can be the source of enormous compassion.

Even when we leave a retreat without difficulty, we enter a new cycle. We may experience a transition of great light, one where we are floating and filled with delight and joy in the mystery of life. We may reemerge to wonder at life's evanescent beauty, or find our heart wide open with love for all beings. Then our task will be to extend this spirit into the action of our daily life.

Each state we encounter will succumb to the next. There is no way to avoid the transitions of our life. The chief means of entering them gracefully is to practice them mindfully over and over again. It is like learning to ride a horse: over and over again walking, trotting, cantering, over smooth and rough terrain, mounting and dismounting, starting and stopping, until it becomes possible for us to move through life in a graceful conscious way. In moving through the difficult stages of our lives, we can learn to trust our heart to these cycles and their unfolding as surely as we can trust roots to go down and leaves to push up through the earth in our garden. We can trust that each petal of a flower will open in the right order from outside to inside. We can trust that whatever calls our attention in practice—our body, our personal history, the community around us—in or out of retreat, it will bring us what we need to live fully and genuinely in the timeless here and now.

In one sense, we're not going anywhere. The wonderful and great story of the Buddha's enlightenment tells how he practiced the perfections of compassion and patience, of steadiness and equanimity, for one hundred thousand immense eons, or kalpas, leading up to his lifetime as a Buddha. To conceive of one kalpa, imagine a mountain even higher and wider than Mount Everest and then imagine that every hundred years a raven flies over it with a silk scarf in its beak, dragging the scarf across the top of the mountain. When such a mountain is worn down by the scarf, this is one kalpa.

We could say that the Buddha practiced for a long time, but the deeper meaning of this image is to point to the timelessness of practice. We are not trying to get somewhere better next year or in twenty years, or even the next lifetime. We are learning to open to the timeless unfolding of our lives, being in greater and greater harmony with what is, with a greater inclusiveness of our hearts to all the seasons of our life.

> *In the entire ten directions*
>   *of the Buddha's universe*
> *There is only one way.*
> *When we see clearly, there is no*
>   *difference in the teachings.*
> *What is there to lose? What is there to gain?*
> *If we gain something, it was there from*
>   *the beginning.*
> *If we lose anything, it is hidden nearby.*
>   *—Ryokan*

MEDITATION: REFLECTING ON THE CYCLES OF YOUR SPIRITUAL LIFE

Sit comfortably and naturally, letting yourself feel present and at ease. Let go of any plans and feel the natural rhythm of your breathing. Then, when you have become quiet, reflect back over your whole spiritual life. Remember how you first became awakened to the life of the heart and the spirit. Remember the sense you had at that time of the possibilities, of the mystery, of the divine. Bring to your mind the years that followed, the early spiritual teachers and the sacred places that inspired you. Look over the following years, remembering the systematic practices you have followed, the cycles you have gone through, the situations that have taught you the most, the unexpected lessons, the times of solitude, the times of community, your trials, your benefactors, your guides, your recent practice. Be aware of the problems you encountered as well, their difficulties, their teachings.

Enjoy this reflection, seeing it as a story, an adventure, appreciating its cycles and turns with a sense of wonder and gratitude. Then feel yourself resting in this moment today with an openness toward your life ahead. Let yourself sense what may lie ahead of you: the next natural stages of your life, the incomplete areas of your life, the dimensions of spiritual practice you may be called upon to include. As your own spiritual guide, become aware of what situation might be beneficial for you. If your present life allows, should you seek a period of solitude and aloneness or choose to become involved in a spiritual community? Does your spiritual practice call you to a period of service for others or is it the season to devote yourself to your career, creativity, home, and family? Do you need a teacher, or is it best now to rest on your own resources? If your present life doesn't allow you to make those choices, what cycle are you being presented with? How can you best honor both your choices and your life situation and include them in the opening of your heart and the cycles of your practice? Sense how you can be true to yourself and true to the dharma, the Tao that is unfolding in your life.

13

NO BOUNDARIES
TO THE SACRED

*The compartments we create to shield us from
what we fear, ignore, and exclude exact their
toll later in life. Periods of holiness and spiritual fervor can later alternate with opposite
extremes—binging on food, sex, and other
things—becoming a kind of spiritual bulimia.
Spiritual practice will not save us from suffering
and confusion, it only allows us to understand
that avoidance of pain does not help.*

To fulfill spiritual life we must cease dividing our life into compartments. Our life is divided into periods of work, vacation, and recreation.
We have separated business life, love life, and spiritual life from the time
set aside for the body with sports, exercise, and enjoyment. The society
around us reflects and exaggerates this same compartmentalization. We
have churches that house the sacred and commerce districts for the
secular and profane; we have split off education from family life; the
interests of business and profit-making are divorced from those of

the earth and its environment on which they depend. The habit of dividing up life is so strong that it fragments our vision everywhere we look.

Spiritual practice can easily continue the pattern of fragmentation in our lives if we set up divisions defining what is sacred and what is not, if we call certain postures, practices, techniques, places, prayers, and phrases "spiritual," while the rest of who we are is left out. We can compartmentalize even our innermost lives.

While traveling in Thailand I got to know a Buddhist teacher who demonstrated how powerful the compartments of spiritual life can become. He was a forty-four-year-old Burmese monk who had been involved in the pro-democracy upheavals and demonstrations in Rangoon and after years of difficulty had finally fled the repressive dictatorship in fear for his life. He landed in the border refugee camps of Burma and Thailand. In these camps he taught the dharma and worked actively to support justice, compassion, and a spiritual life in the face of tremendous hardships. Students and others around him were often near starvation or sick from tropical diseases without medicine or other support. Raids by the Burmese army came periodically as well. Yet in the face of all this, he remained a steady spiritual beacon. During this time he met and was attended to by a young Thai village woman in her early twenties. At first she came to give him food, offerings, and support, but gradually they fell in love, even though in his monk's mind he was simply being a good and available teacher for this young Thai woman. The next I heard of him, some months later, the monk had decided to immolate himself on the steps of the Burmese embassy in Bangkok to protest the great injustices and sufferings of those in the border camps and throughout his country.

I went to look for him, and we sat down for a long talk. As he spoke, I discovered an astonishing thing: although he planned to take his life to protest the great injustices he had fought against for many years, this was not the real reason for his decision. The true reason was that he had fallen in love with this young girl. He had been in monk's robes since age fourteen and for twenty-nine years he had given his life to the order. He had no other skills and couldn't imagine himself married, with a family, yet he loved her. He did not know what to do, so burning himself for political reasons seemed the best way out.

I couldn't believe my ears. Here was someone who had faced tremendous privation and worked courageously in the midst of great human suffering and danger, his own and others, but when it came to facing his own personal dilemma, in this case a close relationship with a woman and the powerful feelings it evoked, he was ready to burn himself. The compartmentalization of his spiritual practice had left him unprepared to deal with the strength of these feelings and the conflicts they brought up in him. Facing the struggle of a nation was easier than facing the struggle in his own heart.

We talked for some time about how he could remain a monk and still have these strong feelings of love and longing. He worked with this in his practice, and the young woman graciously withdrew to allow a cooling-off period. Although it was difficult for them both, he ended the relationship and she moved away. He recommitted himself to his teaching with a new awareness that began to include in his practice of the heart, his personal passion as well as his passion for the dharma. Over the years since, he has grown to become a remarkable teacher.

Perhaps this story gives you a sense of how strong are the forces we must deal with when we compartmentalize and how easy it is to use a "spiritual" rationale to reinforce them.

Wherever false separations exist, they inevitably lead to difficulty. Modern ecology has shown us the painful effects of a small and compartmentalized vision of life. The enormous amount of oil we use and the resulting hydrocarbon emissions have affected the air we breathe and the entire global climate. When we farm only to maximize yield, vast quantities of pesticides and chemical fertilizers pour into the water and soil which sustain our life. What happens in the rain forests or over the icy poles affects the elements from which our bodies are made. For too many years we have forgotten these and other interconnections, so that our hearts, our lives, and our spiritual practices are separated from one another.

Traveling in India several years ago, my wife and I visited a renowned yogi and teacher named Vimala Thakar at her ashram on Mount Abu. For many years she had been involved in the rural development of India, walking from province to province and working in the villages with Vinoba Bhave and other disciples of Mahatma Gandhi. Then, after meeting Krishnamurti, her spiritual life took a great turn. She followed him closely and was transformed by his teachings. With his blessings, she became a teacher of meditation in much the same spirit as Krishnamurti himself. Since then she has led retreats and seminars worldwide.

Yet when we visited her, we learned that she was back again working in the villages on rural development projects. I asked her whether she found that meditation practice was not enough, that now she needed to stop meditating and return to the practice of service to others as the real spiritual life. She was shocked by the question and answered in this fashion:

> I am a lover of life, sir, and as a lover of life I cannot keep out of any field of life. So when I walk through a poor village in India and people are hungry for food, or sick because they lack good clean drinking water, how can I not stop and respond to this suffering? We dig new wells, create clean water supplies, and learn to grow crops more abundantly.
>
> When I come to London or Chicago or San Diego, I also encounter suffering, not a lack of clean water, but the suffering of loneliness and isolation, the lack of spiritual nourishment or understanding. Just as one naturally responds to the lack of clean water in the villages, one responds to a lack of understanding and peace in the hearts of those in the West. As a lover of life, how can I separate any part from the whole?

Vimala's voice reflects the wholeness and interconnection with all life that is the mark of a mature spiritual being. Sometimes, however, the language and metaphors of spirituality lack this wholeness and reinforce our own compartments and misunderstanding of what is spiritual and what is not. We hear about transcending our ego, or seek to attain divine states and purity, beyond desire, beyond the body; we are taught that enlightenment is to be found through renunciation; we believe it is somewhere beyond or outside ourselves. The notion of attaining a pure and divine abode fits unfortunately well with whatever neurotic, fearful, or idealistic tendencies we may have. To the extent that we see ourselves to be impure, shameful, or unworthy, we may use spiritual practices and notions of purity to escape from ourselves. By rigidly following spiritual precepts and forms, we may hope to create a pure spiritual identity. In India this is called the Golden Chain. It's not a chain of iron, but it's still a chain.

The Tibetan teacher Chogyam Trungpa Rinpoche warned of this "spiritual materialism," describing how we can imitate the outer forms of spiritual practice, its costumes, beliefs, culture, and meditations to hide from the world or bolster our own egos.

For most of us who have experienced trauma and great pain in our lives, spiritual practice may seem to offer an escape, a way to leave our troubles with this body and mind altogether, to escape the pain of our history and the loneliness of our existence. The more glorified the spiritual vision, the more it fits those of us who don't want to be here anyway. In the depths of their silent listening, many meditation students have discovered that from an early age their life experience was so painful they did not want to be born and they did not want to be here in a human body. They look to spirituality to provide an escape. But where will the notions of purity, of going beyond or transcending our bodies, our worldly desires, our impurities lead us? Does it actually lead to freedom or is it only a strengthening of aversion, fear, and limitation?

Where is liberation to be found? The Buddha taught that both human suffering and human enlightenment are found in our own fathom-long body with its senses and mind. If not here and now, where else will we find it?

Kabir, the Indian mystic poet, says:

Friend, hope for the truth while you are alive.
Jump into experience while you are alive! . . .
What you call "salvation" belongs to the time before death.
If you don't break your ropes while you are alive,
do you think ghosts will do it after?
The idea that the soul will join with the ecstatic
just because the body is rotten—
that is all fantasy.
What is found now is found then.
If you find nothing now, you will simply end up with
an empty apartment in the City of Death.
If you make love with the divine now, in the next life
you will have the face of satisfied desire.

We have only now, only this single eternal moment opening and unfolding before us day and night. To see this truth is to realize that the sacred and secular cannot be divided. Even the most transcendent visions of spirituality must shine through the here and now and be brought to life in how we walk, eat, and love one another.

This is not easy. The power of our fear, the habits of judgment within us, repeatedly prevent our touching the sacred. Often we will unconsciously draw our spirituality back to the polarity of good and bad, sacred and profane. Unknowingly we re-create patterns of our early life that helped us survive the pain, trauma, and dysfunction many of us experienced as children. If out of fear our strategy was to hide, we may use our spiritual life to continue to hide and claim we have renounced life. If our childhood defense for pain was to get lost in fantasy, we may seek a spiritual life of visions to get lost in. If we tried to avoid blame by being good, we may repeat it by trying to be spiritually pure or holy. If we compensated for loneliness and feelings of inadequacy by being compulsive or driven, our spirituality may reflect that. We will have taken our spirituality and used it to continue to divide life.

One student, who had come from an abusive family in which his father was often and unexpectedly violent, dealt with this dangerous situation by creating a finely tuned antenna for any difficulty that might arise and along with it a strong sense of paranoia. In his spiritual practice he re-created this, dividing teachers and students into good guys and bad guys, those who were dangerous and those who were allies, those whom he disliked and those whom he put on a pedestal and tried to imitate. Anyone who acted as he had in his wild younger days was particularly judged, dismissed, or feared, much as he feared those parts of himself. In dividing the community around him in this way, he so antagonized a number of people that his paranoia and fears became justified—many were indeed angry with him—and in no time he had re-created the dangerous good-guy–bad-guy situation of his original family. What he read in spiritual texts he used to reinforce his division, judging which people, which acts, which practices were holy, and which were ignorant, based on desire, hatred, and delusion.

Without guidance, such a person could go on for years using his spiritual life to reenact his early trauma. What was necessary in his case was to direct very careful attention to how he created such a strong sense of good and bad, of paranoia and untrustworthiness on one side and ideals on the other, and what fears were at the root of this. Once directed to examine this, he shifted his practice from the troubles of the world outside him to the troubles and sorrows he created within himself. When he began to see that he was the one creating the fear, paranoia, division, and suffering in his life, his whole old sense of himself began to drop away and a new possibility awakened for him.

Another student, a young woman, came to practice with a tremendous sense of insecurity and fear. In the great pain of her own early childhood she had found peace by withdrawing into silence and daydreams. By being quiet, she had avoided trouble and conflict with the world around her. On entering spiritual practice she was greatly relieved. Here was a place that officially sanctioned her silence and introversion and supported her withdrawal from the world. To her teachers she initially seemed to be a very fine meditation student, having no difficulty with the rules and silence, quieting herself easily and speaking of deep insights into the transient nature of life and how to avoid the dangers of attachment. She came to retreat after retreat, but at some point it became clear that she was using her practice to avoid and run away from the world, that her meditation had simply re-created the fear of her early family life. Her life, like that of the student above, was limited to certain compartments. When this was brought to her attention, she complained bitterly. Didn't the Buddha speak of solitude, of sitting under trees in the forest, living a life of seclusion? Who were we as her teachers to recommend anything different?

Her denial was so difficult to break through that she wandered for many years meditating in different spiritual communities. Only after ten years, after her own frustration and dissatisfaction grew strong enough, was she motivated to begin to change her life, to break out of her compartments.

The walls of our compartments are made of fears and habits, of ideas we have about what should or shouldn't be, of what is spiritual and what is not. Because particular aspects of our lives have been overwhelming to us, we have walled them off. Most frequently we don't wall off the great and universal sufferings of the world around us, the injustice, war, and bigotry, but rather our own immediate and personal pain. We fear the personal because it has touched us and wounded us most deeply, and this is what we must examine to understand these compartments. Only when we have become aware of these walls in our own hearts can we develop a spiritual practice that opens us to all of life.

THE NEAR ENEMIES

There is a specific teaching in the Buddhist tradition that can help us understand how the compartmentalization and separation that operates in us is repeated in spiritual life. It is called The Near Enemies. The near enemies are qualities that arise in the mind and masquerade as genuine spiritual realization, when in fact they are only an imitation, serving to separate us from true feeling rather than connecting us to it.

An example of near enemies can be seen in relation to the four divine states the Buddha described of loving-kindness, compassion, sympathetic joy, and equanimity. Each of these states is a mark of wakefulness and the opening of the heart, yet each state has a near enemy that mimics the true state, but actually arises out of separation and fear rather than genuine heartfelt connection.

The near enemy of loving-kindness is attachment. We have all noticed how attachment can creep into our love relationships. True love is an expression of openness: "I love you as you are without any expectations or demands." Attachment has in it a sense of separation: "Because you are separate from me, I need you." At first, attachment may feel like love, but as it grows it becomes more clearly the opposite, characterized by clinging, controlling, and fear.

The near enemy of compassion is pity, and this also separates us. Pity feels sorry for "that poor person over there," as if he were somehow different from us, whereas true compassion, as we've explained, is the resonance of our heart with the suffering of another. "Yes, I, too, together with you, share in the sorrows of life."

The near enemy of sympathetic joy (the joy in the happiness of others) is comparison, which looks to see if we have more of, the same as, or less than another. Instead of rejoicing with them, a subtle voice asks, "Is mine as good as his?" "When will it be my turn?"—again creating separation.

The near enemy of equanimity is indifference. True equanimity is balance in the midst of experience, whereas indifference is a withdrawal and not caring, based on fear. It is a running away from life. Thus, with equanimity, the heart is open to touch all things, both the seasons of joy and sorrow. The voice of indifference withdraws, saying, "Who cares. I'm not going to let it affect me."

Each of these near enemies can masquerade as a spiritual quality, but when we call our indifference spiritual or respond to pain with pity, we only justify our separation and make "spirituality" a defense. This is reinforced by our culture, which often teaches us that we can become strong and independent by denying our feelings, using ideals and a strength of mind to create safety for ourselves. If we do not recognize and understand the near enemies, they will deaden our spiritual practice. The compartments they make cannot shield us for long from the pain and unpredictability of life, but they will surely stifle the joy and open connectedness of true relationships.

Like the near enemies, the force of compartmentalization separates our body from our mind, our spirit from our emotions, our spiritual life from our relationships. Without examining these separations, our spiritual life stagnates and our awareness cannot continue to grow.

This proved to be the case for a determined young man who went off to spend a number of years in Japanese Zen monasteries and a Buddhist monastery in Sri Lanka. He had come from a broken home, his father having died when he was young, and had an alcoholic stepfather and a sister who had become addicted to drugs. Through a very strong will and powerful motivation, he learned to quiet his mind and to con-

centrate deeply. In Japan he answered many koans and had strong realizations of the emptiness and interconnectedness of all things. In the
Sri Lankan monastery he did a practice where he learned to dissolve his
body into light. When his sister died, he was called back to this country
to face what was left of his family. He helped everyone through this
difficult period, but not long afterward he became ill and frightened.

Trying to understand his condition, he went to speak to a counselor.
The counselor asked him to tell his whole life story. As the young man
did this, the counselor would periodically stop him and ask how he felt.
Each time he would answer by precisely and meditatively describing his
body sensations. "My breath stops a little then and my hands get cold,"
or "There's a tightness in my stomach." At the next session, when asked
how he felt, he described "a pulsing in my throat" and "flushing with
heat throughout my body." Finally, after several sessions like this when
asked yet again, "But how did that *feel*," the young man burst into tears
and an enormous amount of unacknowledged grief and emotion began
to pour out of him. He had been aware of his body, he had been aware
of his mind, but he had used them in his meditation practice to build a
wall, to exclude from his awareness the painful emotions he had experienced for much of his life. From this point on, he realized the need to
change his way of spiritual practice to include his feelings. As a result,
many of the traumas of the past were healed, and his life took on a joy
he had never known before.

A collective example of compartmentalization in spiritual life was
described to me by a Catholic nun who had spent twenty-four years in
a cloistered order. For the first fourteen years she and her sisters kept
to the strict practice of silence, and in a superficial way the community
ran rather well. Then, with the opening of monastic orders in the years
following Vatican II, the nuns of her order took off their habits and began
speaking to one another. She said the first years of speaking were a
disaster for the entire community. Dissatisfactions, petty hatreds,
grudges, and all the unfinished business that had built up for decades
were now aired by people who had little skill in bringing awareness to
their speech. It was a long, painful period as they learned to include
speech in their practice, a process that almost destroyed the community.
Many of the nuns left in the middle of this process, feeling that they had
wasted a part of their lives by not dealing with their true relationships
to one another. Fortunately, those who stayed were able to re-create
the community with a new spirit of commitment to truth and sisterly
love. They brought in some wise mentors to help them and learned how

to bring their conflicts and speech into a life of prayer. Wholeness and grace returned to their community.

The compartments we create to shield us from what we fear exact their toll later in life. Periods of holiness and spiritual fervor can later alternate with opposite extremes—binging on food, sex, and other things—becoming a kind of spiritual bulimia. Even a society as a whole can act out in this way, having "spiritual" areas where people are mindful, conscious, and awake, and other places where the opposite is demonstrated through abusive drinking, promiscuity, and other unconscious conduct.

Compartmentalization creates an opposite shadow, an area that is dark or hidden from us because we focus so strongly somewhere else. The shadow of religious piety can hold passion and worldly longing. The shadow for a strong atheist may include a secret longing for God. We each have a shadow that in part is comprised of those forces and feelings that we outwardly ignore and reject. The more strongly we believe something and reject its opposite, the more energy goes into the shadow. As is commonly said, "The bigger the front, the bigger the back." A shadow grows when we try to use spirituality to protect us from the difficulties and conflicts of life.

Spiritual practice will not save us from suffering and confusion, it only allows us to understand that avoidance of pain does not help. Only by honoring our true situation can our practice show us a way through it. This was demonstrated in a painful segment of the life of a wonderful Tibetan teacher named Lama Yeshe, who was highly regarded as a meditation master and a compassionate and enlightened teacher. One day he had a heart attack and was hospitalized. Some time later he wrote a private letter to a lama he considered his brother. It said:

Never have I known the experiences and sufferings which attended my stay in Intensive Care. Due to powerful medicines, unending injections, and oxygen tubes just to breathe, my mind was overcome with pain and confusion. I realized that it is extremely difficult to maintain awareness without becoming confused during the stages of death. At its worst, forty-one days after I became ill, the condition of my body was such that I became the lord of a cemetery, my mind was like that of an anti-God and my speech like the barking of an old mad dog. As my ability to recite prayers and meditations degenerated, after many days I considered what to do. I did stabilizing meditation with strong mindfulness through great effort, and this was of much benefit. Gradually again I have developed immeasurable joy and happiness in my mind. The strength of my mind has increased and my problems lessened and ceased.

Even a great teacher cannot avoid the troubles of his body, cannot avoid sickness, old age, and death. In the same way, we cannot do away with feelings or the messiness of human relationships. Even the Buddha had some relationships that were easier than others; the most difficult ones brought him enemies who tried to kill him, troublesome students, and problems with his parents when he went home to visit. Keeping this in mind, how then might we practice?

We must see that spirituality is a continual movement away from compartmentalization and separation and toward embracing all of life. We must especially learn the art of directing mindfulness into the closed areas of our life. When we do, we will face the patterns from personal history, the conditioning that shields us from the pains of the past. To be free is not to rise above these patterns—that would only make new compartments—but to go into and through them, to bring them into our hearts. We must find in ourselves a willingness to go into the dark, to feel the holes and deficiencies, the weakness, rage, or insecurity that we have walled off in ourselves. We must bring a deep attention to the stories we tell about these shadows, to see what is the underlying truth. Then, as we willingly enter each place of fear, each place of deficiency and insecurity in ourselves, we will discover that its walls are made of untruths, of old images of ourselves, of ancient fears, of false ideas of what is pure and what is not. We will see that each is made from a lack of trust in ourselves, our hearts, and the world. As we see through them, our world expands. As the light of awareness illuminates these stories and ideas and the pain, fear, or emptiness that underlies them, a deeper truth can show itself. By accepting and feeling each of these areas, a genuine wholeness, sense of well-being, and strength can be discovered.

However strong the force of self-protection and fear that built the walls in our life, we discover another great and unstoppable force that can break them down. This is our deep longing for wholeness. Something in us knows what it is to feel whole and undivided, connected to all things. This force grows within us in our difficulties and our practice. It moves us to expand our spirituality beyond just silent prayers to respond to the homeless in our streets. It then draws us back to silence when an overactive life of service has made us lose our way. This force forgives our failures in the face of our pain.

True spirituality is not a defense against the uncertainties, pain, and danger in life, not "an inoculation," as Joseph Campbell called popular religion, to avoid the unknown. It is an opening to the entire mysterious process of life. Lama Yeshe's spiritual training and wisdom did not stop his body and mind from falling apart in the hospital, but his heart was able to include every part of his experience as practice.

We fragment our life and divide ourselves from it when we hold to ideals of perfection. In ancient China, the Third Zen Patriarch taught that "True enlightenment and wholeness arise when we are without anxiety about nonperfection." The body is not perfect, the mind is not perfect, our feelings and relationships will certainly not be perfect. Yet to be without anxiety about nonperfection, to understand that, as Elizabeth Kübler-Ross puts it, "I'm not okay, you're not okay, and that's okay," brings wholeness and true joy, an ability to enter all the compartments of our life, to feel every feeling, to live in our body, and to know a true freedom.

To end our compartmentalization we do not need to gain some special knowledge. We need less "knowing" about how life should be and more openness to its mystery.

The purity that we long for is not found in perfecting the world. True purity is found in the heart that can touch all things, enfold all things, and include all things in its compassion. The greatness of our love grows not by what we know, not by what we have become, not by what we have fixed in ourselves, but in our capacity to love and be free in the midst of all life.

In this spirit Zen master Suzuki Roshi called his students together as he lay dying of cancer and said:

If when I die, the moment I'm dying, if I suffer that is all right, you know; that is suffering Buddha. No confusion in it. Maybe everyone will struggle because of the physical agony or spiritual agony, too. But that is all right, that is not a problem. We should be grateful to have a limited body . . . like mine, like yours. If you had a limitless life it would be a real problem for you.

Even though our physical body is limited, our true nature opens us to the limitless, to that beyond our birth and death, to a wholeness and indivisibility with all things. Celebrating this timeless understanding Chuang Tzu wrote of the true men and women of old, "They slept without dreams and woke without worries. Easy come, easy go. They took life as it came gladly" because the Tao includes all things.

Let your heart be at peace
Watch the turmoil of beings,
but contemplate their return.

If you don't realize the source,
you stumble in confusion and sorrow.
When you realize where you come from,
you naturally become tolerant,
disinterested, amused,
kindhearted as a grandmother,
dignified as a king.
Immersed in the wonder of the Tao,
you can deal with whatever life brings you,
and when death comes, you are ready.

MEDITATION ON COMPARTMENTS
AND WHOLENESS

Sit in a way that is both comfortable and alert. Let your eyes close and feel the natural rhythm of your breathing, letting yourself become quiet and present. Feel how your breathing moves gently, how its movement can be sensed throughout your whole body. When you feel open and at rest, begin to reflect on the spiritual and the sacred in your life. How and where does a sense of the sacred most clearly show itself in your life? What activities (meditation, prayer, walks in nature, music) most bring it alive? What places do you most consider sacred? What people, what situations, most awaken this sense in you? Feel what it is like for you to live in this spirit.

Now direct your reflection toward the opposite experiences. What areas of your life do you least hold as sacred? Where do you sense compartments that your spirit and heart have not awakened? Dimensions of your life with little mindfulness and little compassion are the areas where you have forgotten the sacred. They may include any aspect of your body, your life as a man or woman, any aspect of your feelings and mind. They may be activities involved in work, business, money, politics, or community. They may be areas of

family life or may focus on particular people, family members, colleagues, or acquaintances. They may include particular activities
and places—your creative and artistic life, love life, shopping, driving, being in cities, hospitals, or schools—any place or any dimension you have excluded from the sacred.

Let each compartment that you have excluded from your spiritual life arise in your vision, one by one. As you sense each area,
hold it lightly in your heart and consider what it would mean to
bring this too into your practice. Envision how your sense of the
sacred could grow, to include this in your practice with full attention
and compassion, honoring these people, places, or activities. One
by one, picture them and feel the respect and wholeness that would
come about. Sense how each has a lesson to teach, how each area
will bring a deepening of your attention and an opening of your compassion until nothing is excluded. One by one, sense how your spirit
and loving respect can reinhabit every dimension of your being.
Then let yourself rest, feeling your breath and wholeness in this
moment. By living with this respectful attention and compassion
moment to moment, you sense the sacred in each part of your life.

14

NO SELF
OR TRUE SELF?

*There are two parallel tasks in spiritual life. One
is to discover selflessness, the other is to develop
a healthy sense of self. Both sides of that apparent paradox must be fulfilled for us to
awaken.*

Spiritual practice inevitably brings us face to face with the profound
mystery of our own identity. We have taken birth in a human body.
What is this force that gives us life, that brings us and the world into
form? The world's great spiritual teachings tell us over and over we are
not who we think we are.

Persian mystics say we are sparks of the divine, and Christian mystics
say we are filled with God. We are one with all things, say others. The
world is all illusion, say others. Some teachings explain how consciousness
creates life to express all possibilities, to be able to love, to know oneself.
Others point out how consciousness gets lost in its patterns, loses its
way, incarnates out of ignorance. Hindu yogas call the world a *lila*, or a
dance of the divine, much like Dante's phrase, "the divine comedy."

Buddhist texts describe how consciousness itself creates the world like a dream or a mirage. Modern accounts of near-death experiences are filled with reports of wonderful ease after leaving the body, of golden light and luminous beings. Perhaps these, too, confirm how we are unaware of our true identity most of the time.

When we look into the question of self and identity in spiritual practice, we find it requires us to understand two distinct dimensions of self: selflessness and true self. Let us consider selflessness first.

THE NATURE OF SELFLESSNESS

When the Buddha confronted the question of identity on the night of his enlightenment, he came to the radical discovery that we do not exist as separate beings. He saw into the human tendency to identify with a limited sense of existence and discovered that this belief in an individual small self is a root illusion that causes suffering and removes us from the freedom and mystery of life. He described this as *interdependent arising,* the cyclical process of consciousness creating identity by entering form, responding to contact of the senses, then attaching to certain forms, feelings, desires, images, and actions to create a sense of self.

In teaching, the Buddha never spoke of humans as persons existing in some fixed or static way. Instead, he described us as a collection of five changing processes: the processes of the physical body, of feelings, of perceptions, of responses, and of the flow of consciousness that experiences them all. Our sense of self arises whenever we grasp at or identify with these patterns. The process of identification, of selecting patterns to call "I," "me," "myself," is subtle and usually hidden from our awareness. We can identify with our body, feelings, or thoughts; we can identify with images, patterns, roles, and archetypes. Thus, in our culture, we might fix and identify with the role of being a woman or a man, a parent or a child. We might take our family history, our genetics, and our heredity to be who we are. Sometimes we identify with our desires: sexual, aesthetic, or spiritual. In the same way we can focus on our intellect or take our astrological sign as an identity. We can choose the archetype of hero, lover, mother, ne'er-do-well, adventurer, clown, or thief as our identity and live a year or a whole lifetime based on that. To the extent that we grasp these false identities, we continually have to protect and defend ourselves, strive to fulfill what is limited or deficient in them, to fear their loss.

Yet, these are not our true identity. One master with whom I studied used to laugh at how easily and commonly we would grasp at new identities. As for himself, he would say, "I am none of that. I am not this body, so I was never born and will never die. I am nothing and I am everything. Your identities make all your problems. Discover what is beyond them, the delight of the timeless, the deathless."

Because the question of identity and selflessness is subject to confusion and misunderstanding, let us go into it more carefully. When Christian texts speak of losing the self in God, when Taoists and Hindus speak of merging with a *True Self* beyond all identity, when Buddhists speak of emptiness and of *no self*, what do they mean? Emptiness does not mean that things don't exist, nor does "no self" mean that we don't exist. Emptiness refers to the underlying nonseparation of life and the fertile ground of energy that gives rise to all forms of life. Our world and sense of self is a play of patterns. Any identity we can grasp is transient, tentative. This is difficult to understand from words such as *selflessness* or *emptiness of self*. In fact, my own teacher Achaan Chah said, "If you try to understand it intellectually, your head will probably explode." However, the experience of selflessness in practice can bring us to great freedom.

In the chapter on dissolving the self, we saw how deep meditation can untangle the sense of identity. There are, in fact, many ways in which we can realize the emptiness of self. When we are silent and attentive, we can sense directly how nothing in the world can be truly possessed by us. Clearly we do not possess outer things; we are in some relationship with our cars, our home, our family, our jobs, but whatever that relationship is, it is "ours" only for a short time. In the end, things, people, or tasks die or change or we lose them. Nothing is exempt.

When we bring attention to any moment of experience, we discover that we do not possess it either. As we look, we find that we neither invite our thoughts nor own them. We might even wish them to stop, but our thoughts seem to think themselves, arising and passing according to their nature.

The same is true of our feelings. How many of us believe we control our feelings? As we pay attention, we see that they are more like the weather—moods and feelings change according to certain conditions, and are neither possessed nor directed by our consciousness or desires. Do we order happiness, sadness, irritation, excitement, or restlessness to come? Feelings arise by themselves, as the breath breathes itself, as sounds sound themselves.

Our body, too, follows its own laws. The body which we carry is a bag of bones and fluid that cannot be possessed. It ages, gets sick, or changes in ways we might not wish it to, all according to its own nature. The more we look, in fact, the more deeply we see that we possess nothing within or without.

We encounter another aspect of the emptiness of self when we notice how everything arises out of nothing, comes out of the void, returns to the void, goes back to nothing. All our words of the past day have disappeared. Similarly, where has the past week or the past month or our childhood gone? They arose, did a little dance, and now they've vanished, along with the 1980s, the nineteenth and eighteenth centuries, the ancient Romans and Greeks, the Pharaohs, and so forth. All experience arises in the present, does its dance, and disappears. Experience comes into being only tentatively, for a little time in a certain form; then that form ends and a new form replaces it moment by moment.

Shakespeare in *The Tempest* describes it to us like this:

Be cheerful, sir:
Our revels now are ended:
These our actors,
As I foretold you were all spirits and
Are melted into air, into thin air:
And, like the baseless fabric of this vision
The cloud-capped towers, the gorgeous palaces,
The solemn temples, the great globe itself,
Yea, all which it inherit, shall dissolve,
And, like this insubstantial pageant faded,
Leave not a rack behind:
We are such stuff
As dreams are made on, and our little life
Is rounded with a sleep.

In meditation we have described how precise and deep attention shows us emptiness everywhere. Whatever sensation, thought, whatever aspect of body or mind we focus on carefully, the more space and the less solidity we experience there. Experience becomes like the particle waves described in modern physics, a pattern not quite solid, everchanging. Even the sense of the one who is observing changes in the same way, our perspectives shifting from moment to moment as much as our sense of ourselves shifts from childhood to adolescence to old age. Wherever we focus carefully, we find a veneer of solidity that dissolves under our attention.

Sri Nisargadatta says:

The real world is beyond our thoughts and ideas; we see it through the net of our desires, divided into pleasure and pain, right and wrong, inner and outer. To see the universe as it is, you must step beyond the net. It is not hard to do so, for the net is full of holes.

As we open and empty ourselves, we come to experience an interconnectedness, the realization that all things are joined and conditioned in an interdependent arising. Each experience and event contains all others. The teacher depends on the student, the airplane depends on the sky.

When a bell rings, is it the bell we hear, the air, the sound at our ears, or is it our brain that rings? It is all of these things. As the Taoists say, "The between is ringing." The sound of the bell is here to be heard everywhere—in the eyes of every person we meet, in every tree and insect, in every breath we take.

Holding up a piece of paper, Zen master Thich Nhat Hanh expresses it this way:

If you are a poet, you will see clearly that there is a cloud floating in this sheet of paper. Without a cloud there will be no water; without water the trees cannot grow; and without trees, you cannot make paper. So the cloud is in here. The existence of this page is dependent on the existence of a cloud. Paper and cloud are so close. Let us think of other things, like sunshine. Sunshine is very important because the forest cannot grow without sunshine, and we as humans cannot grow without sunshine. So the logger needs sunshine in order to cut the tree, and the tree needs sunshine in order to be a tree. Therefore, you can see sunshine in this sheet of paper. And if you look more deeply, with the eyes of a *bodhisattva*, with the eyes of those who are awake, you see not only the cloud and the sunshine in it, but that everything is here, the wheat that became the bread for the logger to eat, the logger's father— everything is in this sheet of paper. . . .

This paper is empty of an independent self. Empty, in this sense, means that the paper is full of everything, the entire cosmos. The presence of this tiny sheet of paper proves the presence of the whole cosmos.

When we truly sense this interconnectedness and the emptiness out of which all beings arise, we find liberation and a spacious joy. Discovering emptiness brings a lightness of heart, a flexibility, and an ease that rests in all things. The more solidly we grasp our identity, the more solid our problems become. Once I asked a delightful old Sri Lankan meditation master to teach me the essence of Buddhism. He just laughed and said three times, "No self, no problem."

MISCONCEPTIONS ABOUT SELFLESSNESS

Misconceptions about selflessness and emptiness abound, and such confusions undermine genuine spiritual development. Some people believe that they can come to selflessness by struggling to get rid of their ego-centered self. Others confuse the notion of emptiness with inner feelings of apathy, unworthiness, or meaninglessness that they have carried from a painful past into spiritual practice. We have described how some students use emptiness as an excuse for a withdrawal from life, saying it is all illusion, trying to make a "spiritual bypass" around life's problems. But each of these diseases of emptiness misses the true meaning of emptiness and its liberating freedom.

To try to get rid of the self, to purify, root out, or transcend all desire, anger, and centeredness, to vanquish a self that is "bad," is an old religious idea. This notion underlies the ascetic practices, such as wearing hair shirts, extreme fasting, and self-mortification, that are found in many traditions. Sometimes such practices are used skillfully, to induce altered states, but more often they only reinforce aversion. Worse, what comes with them is the notion that our body, our mind, our "ego," is somehow sinful, dirty, and deluded. "I (the good part of me) must use these techniques to get rid of the self (the lower, bad part of me)." But this can never work. It can never work because there is no self to get rid of! We are a changing process, not a fixed being. There never was a self— only our identification makes us think so. So while purification, kindness, and attention can certainly improve our habits, no amount of self-denial or self-torture can rid us of a self, for it was never there.

When emptiness is confused with the deficiency and emotional poverty that many students bring to spiritual practice, it can perpetuate difficulties in other ways. As we have discussed, spiritual practice attracts a great many wounded people who are drawn to such practice for their own healing. Their numbers appear to be increasing. The spiritual impoverishment of modern culture and the number of children raised without a nurturing and supportive family is growing. Divorce, alcoholism, traumatic or unfortunate circumstances, painful child-rearing practices, latchkey children, and child-rearing by day care and television all can produce people who lack an inner sense of security and well-being. These children grow up to have adult bodies but still feel like impoverished children. Many such "adult children" live in our society. Their pain is reinforced by the isolation and denial of feelings that is common in our culture.

Many students come to spiritual practice with this problem, what some psychologists call a "weak sense of self" or a "needy ego," with holes in their psyche and heart. This deficient sense of self is carried for years by our habits and bodily contractions, by the stories and mental images we have learned to tell ourselves. If we have a deficient sense of self, if we perennially negate ourselves, then we may easily confuse our inner poverty with selflessness and believe it to be sanctioned as the road to enlightenment.

Confusion of selflessness with inner poverty can be especially difficult for women. In our male-dominated culture, a woman can grow up feeling that she doesn't really count, that she will not amount to much in this man's world, that a woman's fate and work is not of value. This powerful conditioning can lead to an identity riddled with depression, fear, and a pervasive feeling of inadequacy.

One woman who came to meditation practice feeling this way believed she had a deep understanding of emptiness. For five years, she had studied with a young teacher who himself was confused about emptiness. When she came to see me, she talked about how deeply she had under-stood the teachings of selflessness and the impermanent, insubstantial nature of life. She stated that whenever she practiced walking meditation or sitting meditation, she experienced selflessness very clearly. But to me she simply looked unkempt and depressed, so I inquired further. I asked her to describe exactly how she experienced emptiness. Then I asked her to do her walking meditation in front of me and tell me precisely what she noticed. As she walked, I pointed out a heaviness in her walk and a contracted quality of her body. Soon she could see it too. As she explored her experience, it turned out not to be emptiness at all, but numbness and deadness. As we talked, it became clear that her body and feelings had been shut down for years. Her self-esteem was low, and she felt herself incapable of doing worthwhile things in the world. She confused this inner feeling with the profound teachings of insub-stantiality. Sorting out this confusion began to bring her back to life.

Similar confusion happens when "emptiness" is misunderstood as "meaninglessness." This misperception can reinforce our underlying depression and fear of the world, justifying our inability to find beauty or our lack of motivation to participate in life.

The difference between true emptiness and the emptiness of depression can be illustrated by two salutations: An awakened person might say, "Good morning, God," whereas a depressed or confused person would be more likely to say, "Good God, morning." Confusing the two can lead to a kind of passivity: "It's all the illusion, it's all a spiritual dream unfolding. I don't have to do anything. We don't do anything ourselves anyway." This kind of passivity is related to indifference, the near enemy of equanimity, which was discussed earlier. An understanding of the mystical emptiness of things is not at all passive; the mark of true emptiness is joy; it enlivens the appreciation of the mystery of life as it appears to us each moment out of the void.

A final confusion around emptiness can appear when we imagine that in feeling emptiness we are impervious to the world or above it all. A samurai who believed this came to a Zen master and boasted, "The whole world is empty; it is all emptiness." The Zen master answered, "Hah, what do you know of this? You're a dirty old samurai," and threw something at him. The samurai in an instant drew his sword—he was truly insulted—and an insult to a samurai is made at the cost of your life. The Zen master just looked up and said, "Emptiness is quick to show its temper, isn't it?" The samurai understood, and the sword returned to its scabbard.

FROM NO SELF TO TRUE SELF

Dissolving the sense of self or experiencing the selfless nature of life is only one side of the coin in our spiritual life. As I said in the beginning of this chapter, there are two parallel tasks in spiritual life. One is to discover selflessness, the other is to develop a healthy sense of self, to discover what is meant by *true self*. Both sides of this apparent paradox must be fulfilled for us to awaken.

Achaan Chah spoke of this paradox one evening in his monastery in a way that was quite astonishing for a Buddhist master. He said, "You know, all this teaching about 'no self' is not true." He went on, "Of course, all the teachings about 'self' are not true either," and he laughed. Then he explained that each of these sets of words, *self* and *no self*, are only concepts or ideas that we use in a very crude approximation, pointing to the mystery of a process that is neither *self* nor *no self*.

In trying to show how to approach this paradox, Jack Engler, the Buddhist teacher and psychologist at Harvard, put it this way: "You must be somebody before you can be nobody." By this he means that a strong and healthy sense of self is needed to withstand the meditative process of dissolution and come to a deep realization of emptiness. This is true, but do not take it in a linear way—the development of self and the realization of the emptiness of self can actually happen in any order. Like all aspects of spiritual life, self and emptiness evolve together as a spiral in our practice, with new and deeper ways of understanding, each succeeding one another.

A Zen master who understood both sides of this process found on one of his annual visits to America that a senior student was stuck in the selfless "empty" half of practice. The student had learned to meditate for hours in a clear, empty silence, and could solve most Zen koans easily, but in the world he was passive and calm, and neglected his family life. His household was too quiet and serious, his children were shushed or ignored, and his marriage was falling apart. His wife complained to the Zen master and the student said, "Isn't this where spiritual practice leads?" The Zen master knew better.

He asked both the student and his wife to attend the next retreat together. And while the other students were meditating on traditional Zen questions such as "What is the sound of one hand clapping?" he gave this couple a different koan. "How do you realize Buddha while making love?" He told them to do it two, three, four times a day while the other students were sitting and walking, and to report their answer to him in interviews each morning and evening.

As the retreat went on, there was a growing concentration and silence. As in such retreats, most of the students became quiet, clear, and empty, except for one couple at the end of the hall. Although they missed some sittings, when they came in each successive day, this couple would glow with a fuller rosier energy. And each day the master would speak to them about wholeness, encouraging them to find true fulfillment as the Buddha in action.

The retreat saved their marriage, helped restore their family life, and taught the students about fullness of self as well as emptiness of self.

How can our practice help us develop a healthy and full sense of self? How can we come to true self? There are several aspects of this process to understand. Our initial sense of self or positive ego strength, as it is described in Western psychology, comes from our early development. Our birth temperament or karmic tendencies are shaped by early feedback and mirroring from our childhood environment to create a sense of who we hold ourselves to be. If we have good bonding with and respect from our parents, a healthy sense of self develops. Without it, a deficient and negative sense of self is established. Then this initial sense of self is reinforced by teachers, school, our social condition, and continuing family life. A habitual sense of self grows through this repeated conditioning, layered on our earliest childhood patterns and re-created as we continue to grow in healthy and unhealthy ways. If our sense of self is unhealthy, our spiritual work of self is initially a work of reclamation and healing. This means understanding and releasing a deficient or wounded sense of self and reawakening the lost energy and authentic connection to ourselves. When we have reclaimed some measure of ourselves, the next task becomes the further development of character, of our wisdom, strength, skill, and compassion. This development is described in the teachings of the Buddha as the cultivation of skillful qualities such as generosity, patience, mindfulness, and kindness.

The development of self then leads to a more fundamental level, the discovery of true self. This is the discovery that the positive qualities of character that spiritual life works so hard to cultivate are already present as our true nature. From this sense of true nature, we can also discover and honor our individual or personal destiny, our self for this life, the unique patterns through which our awakening will express itself. Only when we combine the development and discovery of self with a realization of the emptiness of self, do we complete our understanding of true self.

There is a remarkable moment in the practice of the Buddha that can shed some light on this paradox. In seeking liberation, the Buddha at first followed the practices of two great yogis of his time but found them limited. Then he entered a five-year period of self-denial and ascetic practice in which he tried to use his strength of character to uproot and overcome all that was unskillful in him. If you remember, this was described when we talked of his lion's roar. During those five years of austerities, he tried to subdue and force his body, mind, desires, and fears into submission and so discover freedom. When he came to the end of this road without success, the Buddha sat down to reflect. At this point a wonderful realization arose that showed the path to his enlightenment. He remembered himself as a child seated under a rose apple tree in his father's garden. He remembered how in that childlike state a natural sense of wholeness and sufficiency was present. Seated as a child he had already experienced the calm, clarity, and natural unity of body and mind he was seeking. After remembering this profound sense of wholeness, the Buddha changed his entire way of practice. He began to nourish and honor his body and spirit. He remembered that he could rest in the universe rather than fight it. He realized that awakening is never the product of force but arises through a resting of the heart and an opening of the mind.

In this central moment, the Buddha could draw upon a healthy childhood to bring him back to a natural wisdom. It is said he also drew upon the spirit of lifetimes spent developing patience, courage, and compassion. Unlike the Buddha, many of us who enter practice do not have a healthy childhood or a strong sense of self to draw upon. With a weak or shaky sense of self, even when we are able to rise temporarily above our deficiency and touch states of openness and selflessness, we are unable to integrate them and fulfill these realizations in our life.

Thus, the first level of self-development for many students is reclamation. We have talked about meditation as a process of healing. In reclamation, we bring attention to understanding the painful conditions that created our weak, deficient, or barricaded sense of self. We begin to see how our own defenses and the wishes of others have eclipsed a true grounding in our own deepest experience. Gradually, we can cease to identify with these old patterns and allow for the creation of a healthier sense of self. As the fearful and deficient self is let go, we must start over like a child, recognizing and reclaiming our own body and heart wherever we were abused or cut off from ourselves. We reclaim our feelings, our own unique perspective, our voice that can speak what is true for us. In this process we usually need the help of a skilled person as a guide so that we can use that relationship as a model to learn the love, honesty, and acceptance that create a healthy self.

Undertaking this reclamation of our lost self is a major part of any Westerner's spiritual journey, and much has been written about it in psychological and feminist literature. This portion of the poem "Now I Become Myself" by May Sarton expresses it:

> Now I become myself. It's taken
> Time, many years and places,
> I have been dissolved and shaken,
> Worn other people's faces,
> Run madly, as if Time were there,
> Terribly old, crying a warning,
> "Hurry, you will be dead before—"
> (What? Before you reach the morning?
> or the end of the poem is clear?
> Or love safe in the walled city?)
> Now to stand still, to be here,
> Feel my own weight and density! . . .
> Now there is time and Time is young.
> O, in this single hour I live
> All of myself and do not move

I, the pursued, who madly ran,
Stand still, stand still, and stop the Sun!

It may take years of deep work to stop running, to reclaim our unspoken voice, the truth within us. Yet this is necessary to come to wholeness and true self.

The next aspect of the development of self is the development of character. The Buddha very frequently described spiritual practice as the cultivation of good qualities of heart and character. These include such qualities as restraint (restraining from acting on impulses that cause harm), kindness, perseverance, wakefulness, and compassion. He exhorted his followers to cultivate the Factors of Enlightenment and, by repeated effort, to strengthen the spiritual faculties of energy, steadiness, wisdom, faith, and mindfulness. The Buddha's model of an enlightened being was a noble warrior or skilled craftsman who had developed a character of integrity and wisdom through patient training. We too can choose to develop ourselves, working patiently with the patterns of our mind and heart, gradually shaping the direction of our consciousness.

Repeated cultivation is a basic principle of most spiritual and meditative paths. We have seen how we can practice concentration and gradually train the puppy. In the same way we can frequently recite prayers and through them strengthen our faith. In repeated meditations we can learn how to skillfully let go of fearful or contracted identities, how to calm our hearts, how to listen instead of react. We can systematically direct our attention to reflect on compassion, to purify our motivations with each act, and gradually we will change. "Like the arrowsmith who turns his arrows straight and true," said the Buddha, "a wise person makes his character straight and true." Whatever we practice we will become. In this way we must rely on ourselves. "Self is the true refuge of self," said the Buddha. Understanding this, we can choose to strengthen our courage, loving-kindness, and compassion, evoking them in ourselves through reflection, meditation, attention, and repeated training. We can also choose to abandon pride, resentment, fear, and contraction when they arise, leaving flexibility and openness as the ground for healthy development.

As our development of self grows and our heart becomes less entangled, we begin to discover a deeper truth about the self: We do not have to improve ourselves; we just have to let go of what blocks our heart. When our heart is free from the contractions of fear, anger, grasping, and confusion, the spiritual qualities we have tried to cultivate manifest in us naturally. They are our true nature, and they spontaneously shine in our consciousness whenever we let go of the rigid structures of our identity.

Once spiritual faculties such as faith and awareness are awakened, they take on a life of their own. They become spiritual powers that fill us and move through us unasked. The pure, clear space of consciousness is naturally filled with peace, clarity, and connectedness; the great spiritual qualities shine through when our fearful sense of self is released. These qualities show our fundamental goodness and our true home.

One man, a gruff old engineer who had held his breath tight for many years, came to Insight Meditation with a rigid body. In meditation he allowed his experience of holding and fear to grow stronger until he began to see the ancient images and painful sense of abandonment that he continually carried with him. He could feel how he had contracted his body in order to be strong in the face of the pains of life and how underneath that defense was a terrible sense of weakness and vulnerability that the rigidity had covered. Eventually, through days of allowing himself to feel the weakness and inadequacy, his whole being opened into a vast and silent space.

At first he felt somewhat fearful of this unaccustomed sensation, but then as he breathed and experienced it deeply and more easily, he found in it a great peace and rest. Resting in this space, he discovered in it an inherent completeness and wholeness that was its own great strength. He knew unmistakably that this well-being and strength was his true nature. It was what he had sought for so long. Once he had touched it, it began to grow in him through a process of awareness and letting go. From this, the spirit of his life changed from struggle, one of trying to make up for his weakness and insufficiency, to one that enjoyed and rested upon a sense of belonging and wholeness.

The Persian poet Rumi reminds us of this possibility with great love and humor. He says:

In times of sudden danger most people call out, "O my God!"
Why would they keep doing this if it didn't help?
Only a fool keeps going back where nothing happens.

The whole world lives within a safeguarding, fish
inside waves, birds held in the sky, the elephant,
the wolf, the lion as he hunts, the dragon, the ant,
the waiting snake, even the ground, the air,
the water, every spark floating up from the fire,

all subsist, exist, are held in the divine. Nothing
is ever alone for a single moment.

All giving comes from There, No matter who
you think you put your open hand out
toward, it's That which gives.

Beneath our struggles and beyond any desire to develop self, we can discover our Buddha nature, an inherent fearlessness and connectedness, integrity, and belonging. Like groundwater these essential qualities are our true nature, manifesting whenever we are able to let go of our limited sense of ourselves, our unworthiness, our deficiency, and our longing. The experience of our true self is luminous, sacred, and transforming. The peace and perfection of our true nature is one of the great mystical reflections of consciousness described beautifully in a hundred traditions, by Zen and Taoism, by Native Americans and Western mystics, and by many others.

THE UNIQUE EXPRESSION OF TRUE SELF

In awakening our Buddha nature, we find that there is one further aspect of self to understand, the need to honor our personal destiny. This discovery is an essential task, especially for those of us in the West. In traditional Buddhist stories, it is taught that an individual might make a great vow to fulfill over the ages, to become the chief attendant to a Buddha or to become a yogi of unsurpassed psychic powers or a bodhisattva of limitless compassion. The intention of many lifetimes creates a specific character and destiny for each of us according to our karma. This needs to be recognized.

As Martha Graham put it:

There is a vitality, a life force that is translated through you into action. And because there is only one of you in all time, this expression is unique, and if you block it, it will never exist through any other medium and be lost.

The universal qualities of our Buddha nature must shine through each of us, evolving out of the individual set of patterns in each person. This unique set of patterns we could call our character, our destiny, our individual path to fulfill. To discover our destiny is to sense wisely the potential of our individual life and the tasks necessary to fulfill it. To do so is to open to the mystery of our individual incarnation.

While we cannot know our karmic past, we can recognize the deep patterns and archetypes that make up our individuality. Then these unique patterns and character types we discover can be honored and transformed in practice from rigid identifications to transparent jewels. This allows the qualities of enlightenment to shine through our own particular expression. Our critical intellect can turn into discriminating wisdom; our desire for beauty can turn into the force that brings harmony to our environment; our intuitive capacity can lead to sensitive parenting and great gifts of healing. To sense the patterns and gifts given to us and to fulfill them is a wondrous part of the development of self. It is an honoring of our potential and our unique destiny. In this we can bring together our practice, our particular tasks in our family and community, fulfilling our capacities, our gifts, and our heart as a unique individual. As we do so, our individual nature reflects the universal.

Then when these qualities of Buddha nature and personal self are combined with a deep realization of the emptiness of self, we can be said to have fully discovered the nature of self. This true self is both unique and universal, both empty and full.

The emperor of China asked a renowned Buddhist master if it would be possible to illustrate the nature of self in a visible way. In response, the master had a sixteen-sided room appointed with floor-to-ceiling mirrors that faced one another exactly. In the center he hung a candle aflame. When the emperor entered he could see the individual candle flame in thousands of forms, each of the mirrors extending it far into the distance. Then the master replaced the candle with a small crystal. The emperor could see the small crystal reflected again in every direction. When the master pointed closely at the crystal, the emperor could see the whole room of thousands of crystals reflected in each tiny facet of the crystal in the center. The master showed how the smallest particle contains the whole universe.

True emptiness is not empty, but contains all things. The mysterious and pregnant void creates and reflects all possibilities. From it arises our individuality, which can be discovered and developed, although never possessed or fixed. The self is held in no-self, as the candle flame is held in great emptiness. The great capacities of love, unique destiny, life, and emptiness intertwine, shining, reflecting the one true nature of life.

The *I Ching* speaks of having a well that is finely constructed and closely lined with stones, so that clean, deep, and pure water will always fill it. This purity, our true nature, is found beneath all images of self and emptiness, in the great silence of our being. The qualities we develop are not to be named or possessed. As soon as we try to fix them, they become distorted. Instead, the development of our spirit and the release of our spirit come together, a mystery of form and formlessness. Then, like the water in the well, everything becomes clear and drinkable, and clear water is seen everywhere, in the earth and the sky above.

MEDITATION: WHO AM I?

In many spiritual traditions, repeatedly asking yourself the question "Who am I?" or a variation such as "Who is carrying this body?" is the central practice offered for awakening. Teachers like Ramana Maharshi and great Zen masters from China and Japan have used the repetition of this simple and profound question to guide students to discover their *true nature*. In the end, it is a question we must all ask ourselves. Without being aware of it, you take many things as your identity: your body, your race, your beliefs, your thoughts. Yet very quickly with sincere questioning, you will find yourself sensing a deeper level of truth.

While the question "Who am I?" can be asked alone in your own meditation practice, it can also be done with a partner. One of the most effective ways to inquire into this question is to sit together with another person and ask this question over and over, letting the answers deepen as you go on.

To do this, let yourself sit comfortably facing a partner, prepared to meditate together for thirty minutes. Decide who will ask the question for the first fifteen minutes. Look at your partner in a relaxed way and then allow the questioner to begin asking the question "Who are you?" Let the answers from the person responding arise naturally, saying whatever comes to mind. Once an answer has been given, after a brief pause, the questioner can ask again, "Who are you?" Continue asking this question over and over for a full fifteen minutes. Then you can switch roles, giving your partner equal time.

As this question is repeated, all sorts of answers may arise. You may first find yourself saying, "I am a man" or "I am a woman" or "I am a father," "I am a nurse," "I am a teacher," "I am a meditator." Then your answers may become more interesting: "I am a mirror,"

"I am love," "I am a fool," "I am alive," or whatever. The answers themselves do not matter, they are part of a deepening process. Just keep gently listening for an answer each time you are asked. If no answer arises, stay with that empty space until one comes. If confusion, fear, laughter, or tears arise, stay with them too. Keep answering anyway. Keep letting go into the process. Let yourself enjoy this meditation.

Even in this short time your whole perspective can change and you can discover more about who you truly are.

15

GENEROSITY, CODEPENDENCE, AND FEARLESS COMPASSION

When our sense of self-worth is still low, we cannot set limits, make boundaries, or respect our own needs. Our seemingly compassionate assistance becomes mixed with dependence, fear, and insecurity. Mature love and healthy compassion are not dependent but interdependent, born out of a deep respect for ourselves as well as for others.

Near the great Temple of the Buddha's Enlightenment in Bodh Gaya, India, is a long line of beggars who seek money from the stream of pilgrims who visit each day. Years ago on the first day of a month-long visit to Bodh Gaya, I naively gave money to the beggars. As a consequence, each day after that, as I walked from the market to the temple, I would be surrounded by beggars yelling at me, pulling at my clothes, and even crying for money because they knew I was one who gave to them. It made it a difficult month, and I felt quite sad, as I had really wanted to give them support, but not in this way.

On my next visit I made a new plan. I decided to wait until just before leaving and then give to the beggars all the money I could spare. The morning of my departure I changed forty dollars to one- and two-rupee notes and planned to give four rupees to every beggar in a respectful way. I began to walk down the line of the hundred and fifty beggars in front of the temple, offering money into each hand, feeling pleased with how sensible this was. But then, as I neared the middle of the line, pandemonium broke loose. The beggars at the far end of the line were afraid I would run out of money before I reached them, so they all charged toward me at once, hands outstretched, angrily grabbing my body, my clothes, the money, whatever they could touch. I quickly turned to run and be free of their grasping, and I threw the remaining money over their heads into the air.

Looking back from a safe distance, I saw a painful scene quite different from what I had intended. All the beggars were on their hands and knees in the dirt, fighting one another for the rupees that had fallen there. I realized that I had much to learn about skillful generosity and the art of giving.

When we look at the world's religious traditions, we find them filled with noble gestures and sacrifices of great generosity. Jesus told the disciples to give all their riches away and "follow me." Mother Teresa tells her nuns, who serve the poorest of the poor, "Let them eat you up." In a story of one of his past lives, the Buddha-to-be saw a sick and hungry tigress unable to feed her two young cubs. He felt a profound compassion arise in him and he threw himself off a cliff to become food for the tigress and her cubs.

His Holiness Karmapa, one of the leaders of Tibetan Buddhism, visited America to give blessings and instructions. He was said to be able to embody the Buddha of Compassion. At one ceremony he taught a thousand participants the traditional practice for cultivating compassion, where a student breathes in the pain of the world and breathes out compassion. At the end, an older psychologist stood up to ask, "Should we take it all in? What if the person in front of you has cancer?" Karmapa gave him a look of profound kindness and said simply, "You take it all in. You let the pain of the world touch your heart and you turn it into compassion." What no one in the room knew was that Karmapa himself had just been diagnosed with cancer, but his teaching was uncompromising—you take it all in and you turn it into compassion. He died a year later.

How can we understand such remarkable teachings of extreme generosity and compassion? Compassionate generosity is the foundation of true spiritual life because it is the practice of letting go. An act of generosity opens our body, heart, and spirit and brings us closer to freedom. Each act of generosity is a recognition of our interdependence, an expression of our Buddha nature. But for most of us, generosity is a quality that must be developed. We have to respect that it will grow gradually; otherwise our spirituality can become idealistic and imitative, acting out the image of generosity before it has become genuine. While it can be good to give beyond our means, if this is done unconsciously and repeatedly, it will become unhealthy. Whether it is generosity with our time, our possessions, our money, or our love, the principles are the same. True generosity grows in us as our heart opens, grows along with the integrity and health of our inner life.

Traditionally it is taught that generosity can open on three levels. The first is called *tentative giving*. This initial generosity comes with hesitation. We fear that what we are giving away may be needed by us later. We think about saving it in our attic but then realize that it is time to give it away. After we pass our initial reluctance, we realize happiness and freedom—the first joys of giving.

The second level of giving is called *brotherly or sisterly giving*. It is an open equal sharing that offers both energy and material assistance as if to a loved one. "I have this, so let us all share in it." We do not hesitate. An easy spirit motivates this generosity, and with it the spirit of joy, friendship, and openness grows in us.

The most developed level of giving is called *royal giving*. In this we take such delight in the welfare and happiness of others that our generosity is spontaneous and immediate. This goes beyond equal sharing. We enjoy the well-being of others so deeply that we give of the best we have so that others may enjoy. Our own joy becomes greater with such generosity. It is as if we become a natural channel for the happiness of all around us. We discover in our own heart the abundance of a king or queen.

We can feel how opening to each of these levels brings increasing joy and light into our life. Yet our capacity for manifesting true generosity will often be limited by an incomplete development of the healthy self discussed in the last chapter. Great generosity springs naturally out of a sense of health and wholeness of our being. In the best of traditional cultures, where people are embraced and nourished on both the physical and spiritual levels, they grow up with a sense of ample inner and outer resources. Generosity, sharing, and interdependence become a natural way of life. In many tribal cultures, one never turns away a stranger from the door—they are always invited in to share a meal. One Native American ceremony showers young children with food, drink, and clothing. Then members of the tribe cry out, "I'm hungry, I'm thirsty, I'm cold." From their abundance, the children are then led to distribute their bounty to others in need.

As we have seen, though, many students do not have a sense of abundance or a strong inner sense of self. When the conditions of deficiency and wounding are still not healed, we have a very hard time knowing what it feels like to give in a genuine way. Because our inner experience is still one of need, giving is usually done with a subtle expectation of getting in return. Before we reclaim ourselves, our attempts at noble generosity often become a veneer over an unhealthy dependence.

When misunderstood, ideals of compassion and generosity reinforce dependency and attachment based on a contracted, fearful sense of self. In these situations, compassion and generosity are misused, and we give ourselves away or lose ourselves in the unskillful support of another. Alcoholics Anonymous and other Twelve Step groups use the term *co-dependence* to describe such misuse of generosity, in which our unskillful assistance helps others avoid facing the true difficulty in their life. The most classic example is the spouse of an alcoholic who tells lies and covers up for the partner's drinking in order to "protect them." "Helping" in this way only allows the partner to continue to drink and to escape learning from the painful consequences of his or her actions. Such "codependent helping" is always done out of our own fear and dependency. We are afraid to face the pain of our partner's drinking or afraid that bringing the truth out in the open might cause the loss of our relationship.

As we will see later, much as with alcoholism, codependence can cause students of a spiritual community to cover up the unhealthy behavior of their own teachers in order to maintain a myth of security and belonging, in order to avoid the conflict that would arise if such things were brought out in the open.

In many relationships our fears and dependence may leave us afraid to tell the truth. We may be unable to set limits, afraid to say no. Or generosity that is initially healthy may degenerate into compulsion. For instance, the woman who gives long hours over many years to support volunteer, spiritual, or nonprofit organizations (where the work seems endless) and over these same years neglects her own body, health, development, and self-esteem. There are also men who have trouble saying no, no matter what is asked of them. After many years of this they find themselves filled to the brim with resentment without understanding how they got that way.

The question that we must face in our practice is how can we know when our actions are compassionate and when they are codependent. One answer may lie in the story the Buddha tells of a family of acrobats. A grandfather and granddaughter traveled and made their living by performing balancing acts. They came to the Buddha to discuss what was the best way to safeguard and care for each other. The grandfather put forth the idea that each should care for the other, that he should care for his granddaughter in the balancing, and she should take care of him. Thus they would protect one another. The granddaughter asked the Buddha if that was not backward. "Would it not be better for each of us to care for ourselves, and in that way we safeguard the other, and our acrobatics will prosper?" After listening to the little girl, the Buddha replied, "Though she is young, she is wise. If you as a grandfather guard yourself with care and pay attention to what you do, you will also guard the safety of your grandchild; and if you as a child guard yourself with awareness, with care, with respect, then you guard both yourself and those around you."

Codependence and unhealthy compassion arise when we have forgotten our *own* role in the balancing act of human relationships or when we disregard the true consequences of the actions of others around us. The roots of codependence were described in the last chapter when we spoke of inner wounds, low self-esteem, and unworthiness. Codependence also arises when we discount our own intuitions and emotions (because of low self-esteem) or out of fear of the disapproval of others.

Many of us are so out of touch with ourselves that we can easily lose a sense of what is a skillful action in a situation. We can be so intent on caring for others or on pleasing them or pacifying them or avoiding conflict with them that we don't clearly face our own needs, our own situation. A current joke about this phenomenon is the conversation between two research scientists trained in "objective observation," which necessitates leaving themselves out. They make love, and afterward one research scientist turns to the other and says, "It was okay for you, how about me?"

Losing touch with ourselves and lack of self-respect are also the source of addictive dependencies in practice. Stories of unhealthy dependence in spiritual life are common. Sometimes students combine spiritual practice with chemical addiction, such as the alcoholic priest or the meditation student who alternates his meditation with drugs to stay high, using spiritual language to justify his own unhealthy life-style. Sometimes spirituality itself functions as an addiction.

We have already seen how certain meditators practice to get high and avoid dealing with life. One woman who worked as a nurse married a man whose whole life was focused on his spiritual practice. He wanted to "get enlightened" and then teach others. She took care of her patients all day and then came home to take care of him. He went to frequent retreats and between them would read spiritual books, smoke dope, and have spiritual discussions with friends, while she continued to work to support him. She wanted someday to have her own home and children but felt guilty about wanting things that might take him away from his practice.

For a long time she supported and defended him, thinking this was spiritually correct, meanwhile feeling unconsciously resentful yet afraid to speak up. She didn't know how to say no. Finally, she came to see me. When I suggested that she speak honestly, her painful feelings poured out. She finally ended up throwing him out of the house. After a few retreats where he felt miserable about himself, he went home, got a job, and began to include his wife, home, and the possibility of children as part of his spiritual life.

As the Buddha's dialogue with the acrobats pointed out, when we leave ourselves out of the sphere of compassion, a false security or unwise compassion is the result. All unhealthy or overly idealistic generosity arises from this error, when a deep respect for ourselves is left out of the equation. When our sense of self-worth is still low, we cannot set limits, make boundaries, or respect our own needs. Our seemingly compassionate assistance becomes mixed with dependence, fear, and insecurity. Mature love and healthy compassion are not dependent but interdependent, born out of a deep respect for ourselves and others. They can say yes and they can say no. Like a parent who raises a child wisely, they know when to set limits, when to say no. They love and serve the child but also respect what the child needs to learn for itself. Sometimes a firm "no" or "I can't" or "I won't allow that; it is beyond my limit" is the most spiritual thing we can say.

Setting boundaries and limits, shifting from a dependent and entangling love to one based on mutual respect, learning to give while honoring one's own needs, all of these can entail a profound growth in self-esteem and self-awareness that parallels the healthy development of self. Some students have to pull back from giving for a time while they practice the art of setting boundaries. Others who have felt too impoverished to give at all can start with small acts of generosity at whatever level is natural for them. A tentative gift from one unaccustomed to giving can be regal in its own way. We can learn to cultivate a wise generosity that is sensitive to our own needs and those of others.

In his instructions on mindfulness the Buddha recommended that we give careful attention to the states of the heart that prompt our actions. It is too idealistic to expect that we will always just want to do good; we must listen to know when the heart is attached, to know when the heart is afraid, to know when the heart is dependent. By listening deeply, we can begin to sort out dependence from love. Similarly, we can distinguish when the heart is open, when we are free of attachment, when mutual respect and caring is present. Based on this, our acts can be wise and compassionate.

Learning to distinguish wisdom from dependence can be aided by understanding our own early history. We can reflect on how needs were met in our family, how limits were set, how insecurity was treated. Until we become aware of them, we will repeat these family patterns in our spiritual life. Twelve Step meetings offer participants a chance to hear the personal stories of other members. This honest telling of our family story can be a powerful process in our sorting out health from dependence, respect from fear, and finding a wise and true compassion.

Recognizing our family patterns can also be a part of meditation. In a group interview at one meditation retreat, a student could not stop obsessing about his relationship. Jim ran a food co-op in the day and worked at an AIDS project at night. He lived in the Santa Cruz mountains with another man, his lover. He was always thinking about his customers and clients, and worrying about how his lover was doing without him. He wondered whether meditating for ten days wasn't selfish. I asked him about his family. His father left his mom and three kids after Jim was born, and they never saw him again. His mom drank a bit and worked all the time to hold the family together. At age five Jim started trying to help keep the family together and keep his mom in a good mood. He led a life of caretaking, all run by duty and guilt. He was becoming very tired of holding it all together.

As he told his own story, he wept for himself, for how he had measured his life by others. Others in the group wept too. I asked him how old he felt. "Five," he said, and I asked him if he could hold this child inside him and listen to his needs: could he find compassion for himself as well as for others. He did so, and over time, by gradually developing a caring attitude toward his own life, his meditation, his relationship, and his work, all improved.

Compassion for oneself is often neglected in spiritual practice. In my first few years of leading retreats, I would find myself periodically overwhelmed. After three or four retreats in a row, with hundreds of individual interviews, I would gradually become drained, irritable with students and colleagues. At its worst there were days I felt burnt out and did not want to hear another student's problem. During this period, I had a chance to see His Holiness Dujom Rinpoche for advice and instruction on my practice. I told him about this difficulty. Because he was a renowned tantric master, I hoped he would offer me a special visualization and mantra whereby I could surround myself with light, recite sacred phrases, and be untouched by the intensity and path of seeing too many students and dealing with their problems. He asked for many details about how I practiced and taught, and then said, "Yes, I can help you." I waited for his higher tantric teaching, but then he said, "I recommend you teach shorter retreats and take longer vacations." This, I guess, is the higher teaching.

The ground for compassion is established first by practicing sensitivity toward ourselves. True compassion arises from a healthy sense of self, from an awareness of who we are that honors our own capacities and fears, our own feelings and integrity, along with those of others. It is never based on fear or pity but is a deep supportive response of the heart based on the dignity, integrity, and well-being of every single creature. It is a spontaneous response to the suffering and pain we encounter. It is our feeling of mutual resonance and natural connectedness in the face of the universal experience of loss and pain. As our own heart is opened and healed, it naturally seeks the healing of all it touches. Compassion for ourselves gives rise to the power to transform resentment into forgiveness, hatred into friendliness, and fear into respect for all beings. It allows us to extend warmth, sensitivity, and openness to the sorrows around us in a truthful and genuine way.

Compassion may at times give rise to action, and at times it may not. It doesn't arise in order to solve problems. Yet out of compassion flows action whenever it need be taken. True compassion arises from a sense that the heart has the fearless capacity to embrace all things, to touch all things, to relate to all things. Chogyam Trungpa called this the spiritual warrior's tender heart of sadness. He said:

> When you awaken your heart, you find to your surprise that your heart is empty. You find that you are looking into outer space. What are you, who are you, where is your heart? If you really look, you won't find anything tangible or solid. . . . If you search for the

awakened heart, if you put your hand through your rib cage and feel for it, there is nothing there but tenderness. You feel sore and soft, and if you open your eyes to the rest of the world, you feel tremendous sadness. This sadness doesn't come from being mistreated. You don't feel sad because someone has insulted you or because you feel impoverished. Rather, this experience of sadness is unconditioned. It occurs because your heart is completely open, exposed. It is the pure raw heart. Even if a mosquito lands on it, you feel so touched. . . . It is this tender heart of a warrior that has the power to heal the world.

The power of the compassionate heart, of genuine compassion, to transform the pain we encounter is extraordinary.

I recently read of a couple who were unable to conceive a child. They decided to adopt one and sought a child from a poor country, thinking this would be of greater service. They adopted a beautiful two-month-old baby boy from India. During the first year, it became evident that the child had grave health problems. First, it was discovered that he was profoundly deaf and would never hear. Second, he had cerebral palsy that, though it would not affect his intelligence, could cripple the development of his body. They taught him sign language so they could speak to him, and then they got him a small wheelchair when he was old enough to walk so that he might move about. After this, they created a support network of parents who adopted disabled children. Because they were afraid their son would be isolated, they did a most astonishing thing. They wrote to India to ask if they might adopt another child who was also deaf. Along with this press story was a picture of the two children together, radiant with wide smiles, hugging one another. Imagine this for yourself. Imagine adopting a child and learning that he or she was deaf and crippled, and then imagine a response that answers back without self-pity or fear and says, "I have one child like this, now please send me another."

The fearlessness of compassion leads us directly into the conflict and suffering of life. Fearless compassion recognizes the inevitable suffering in life and our need to face the suffering in order to learn. Sometimes only the fire of suffering itself and the consequences of our actions can bring us to deeper understanding, to feel kindness for all beings, and to liberation.

When I formally asked to join Achaan Chah's monastery, he replied that I was welcome if I was not afraid to suffer! The role of a great teacher is to help students learn in the face of suffering. The power of this fearless compassion can be as tough as it is kind. When we watch the nature shows on public television, we can see this enacted very well. There are times when the mother lion and the mother wolf will make any kind of sacrifice for their babies and do anything to protect them. Then there is another season when she will have nothing to do with them; she runs away, leaves them on their own, or kicks them out of the cave. At a certain point the mother bird tosses her babies out of the nest. Even when the baby cries, "But I can't fly," the mother knows better. "That's all right, you're going to learn, and today's the day."

Sometimes compassion for ourselves and others requires us to set great limits and boundaries, to learn to say no and yet not put another person out of our heart. A woman friend who was studying in India was traveling through the dark streets of Calcutta one night on the way to the train station. For many months she had been practicing both Insight Meditation and the complementary practices of loving-kindness and compassion. That night she was on her way to a meditation retreat with a friend. Suddenly a man jumped on her rickshaw and tried to pull her off. She and her friend managed to push him away, and still frightened, they continued on to the railway station. When she told her story to her teacher, he expressed his concern and said, "Oh, dear, with all the loving-kindness and compassion in your heart, you should have taken your umbrella and hit that man over the head."

In the paradox of life sometimes our compassion requires us to say yes and sometimes it requires us to say no. These may seem like opposites but they are not. Each can express a respect for all beings, including ourselves. So when my codirector at an international Buddhist gathering gave away her new and beautiful birthday gift to try to show great generosity, her mood became sad and irritable. Finally, one Tibetan lama took her aside and asked her what was going on. He discovered she had given away this beautiful gift to please her friend but was sorry she had done it for she had never had time to enjoy it herself. The lama looked at her and said, "Go and get that back right now, and don't give it away until you are ready." Then they both laughed and the laughter brought relief. She went and got it back, and her day changed very much for the better.

There is no formula for the practice of compassion. Like all of the great spiritual arts, it requires that we listen and attend, understand our motivation, and then ask ourselves what action can really be helpful. Compassion exhibits the flexibility of a bamboo bending with the changing circumstances, setting limits when necessary and being flexible at the same time.

Compassion allows life to pass through our hearts with its great paradoxes of life, love, joy, and pain. When compassion opens in us, we give what we can to stop the war, to heal the environment, to care for the poor, to care for people with AIDS, to save the rain forests. Yet true compassion also loves ourselves, respects our own needs, honors our limits, and our true capacity.

Even the Buddha had to face such limits. One of his titles was The Teacher of Those Who Can Be Taught. Usually he brought great benefit to those around him, but this was not always the case. Once, after the monastic order had been established and many rules of conduct for monks and nuns agreed upon, fighting and powerful disagreement broke out in one of his forest monasteries. Certain of the monks accused others of having broken a rule, others denied it and claimed their accusers were breaking the rules by making false accusations.

When the Buddha came to speak with them, he recommended that they all apologize to one another, but his own monks ignored his advice. He tried in a number of ways to get them to listen to him and finally realized there was nothing he could do but leave them to their own consequences. So he left the unruly monks and spent a peaceful rainy season retreat far in the forest, living with the animals around him. He did what he could and no more.

When genuine compassion and wisdom come together, we honor, love, praise, and include both ourselves and others. Instead of holding the ideal that we should be able to give endlessly with compassion for all beings "except me," we find compassion for all beings including ourselves. The separation of self and others melts away. Then, like the sun rising, the strength of generosity and compassion will grow in our practice and we will discover it to be our true nature. Like the pictures we see of parents who pick up cars that have rolled onto their children, we will find that in certain moments the power of our love grows even greater than the physical realities that confront us. When such compassion arises, it moves through us as a grace, bringing together a tenderness and fearlessness that could never come by any other means.

A single mother I admire told me how she struggled to raise her four children alone, with little money and no free time. It seemed she was doing all she could do. Then quite unself-consciously the energy of the great mother of compassion entered her when her youngest daughter, at fourteen, was paralyzed as the result of an accident. Her daughter couldn't speak or move. The doctors at the hospital said they didn't think there was much chance for her to ever move again. Yet her mother knew that her daughter was still conscious inside. As mothers do, she felt deep in her being that her daughter could be rehabilitated. The mother moved into the hospital room and began working with her daughter. She spent a year in the hospital and two years after that at home almost every day with the daughter, just picking up the girl's hand, putting it down, picking it up and putting it down, moving something in front of her eyes, back and forth, day after day, until her daughter's hands and eyes began to move again. After three years the girl was well enough to return to school. Now full grown, she has finished law school and is about to be married. Such loyal generosity cannot be forced; it moves through us when we are deeply connected and deeply empty. Our hearts then move of themselves, as if to music of the divine.

MEDITATION: TRANSFORMING SORROW INTO COMPASSION

The human heart has the extraordinary capacity to hold and transform the sorrows of life into a great stream of compassion. It is the gift of figures like Buddha, Jesus, Mother Mary, and Kwan Yin, the Goddess of Mercy, to proclaim the power of this tender and merciful heart in the face of all the suffering of the world. Whenever your own heart is open and uncovered, the awakening of this stream of compassion begins within. Compassion arises when you allow your heart to be touched by the pain and need of another.

To cultivate this quality, you may wish to practice the traditional meditation for the practice of compassion and for the transformation of sorrows in the fire of the heart.

Let yourself sit still in a centered and quiet way. Breathe softly and feel your body, your heartbeat, the life-force within you. Feel how you treasure your own life, how you guard yourself in the face of your sorrows. After some time, bring to mind someone close to you whom you dearly love. Picture them and your caring for them. Notice how you can hold them in your heart. Then let yourself be aware of their sorrows, their measure of suffering in this life. Feel how your heart opens naturally, moving toward them to wish them well, to extend comfort, to share in their pain, and meet it with compassion.

This is the natural response of the heart. Along with this response, begin to actively wish them well, reciting the traditional phrases, *May you be free from pain and sorrow, may you be at peace,* while holding them in your heart of compassion. Continue reciting these phrases in this way for some time.

As you learn to feel your deep caring for this person close to you, you can then extend this compassion to others you know, one at a time. Gradually you can open your compassion further, to your neighbors, to all those who live far away, and finally to the brotherhood and sisterhood of all beings. Let yourself feel how the beauty of every being brings you joy and how the suffering of any being makes you weep. Feel your tenderhearted connection with all life and its creatures, how it moves with their sorrows and holds them in compassion.

Now let your heart become a transformer for the sorrows of the world. Feel your breath in the area of your heart, as if you could breathe gently in and out of your heart. Feel the kindness of your heart and envision that with each breath you can breathe in pain and breathe out compassion. Start to breathe in the sorrows of all living beings. With each in-breath, let their sorrows touch your heart and turn into compassion. With each out-breath wish all living beings well, extend your caring and merciful heart to them.

As you breathe, begin to envision your heart as a purifying fire that can receive the pains of the world and transform them into the light and warmth of compassion. *This is a powerful meditation that will require some practice. Be gentle with yourself.* Let the fire of your heart burn gently in your chest. Breathe in the sorrows of those who are hungry. Breathe in the sorrows of those who are caught in war. Breathe in the sorrows of ignorance. With each out-breath, picture living beings everywhere and breathe out the healing balm of compassion. With every gentle in-breath, over and over, let the sorrows of every form of life touch your heart. With every out-breath, over and over, extend the mercy and healing of compassion. Like the mother of the world, bring the world into your heart, inviting all beings to touch you with each breath in, embracing all beings in compassion with each breath out.

After some time, sit quietly and let your breath and heart rest naturally, as a center of compassion in the midst of the world.

16

YOU CAN'T DO IT ALONE: FINDING AND WORKING WITH A TEACHER

Some teachers are rascals and coyotes who trick and surprise their students; some are harsh task-masters trying to whittle down ego and pride; others teach more through honoring and en-couragement, nurturing the best in a student; some teachers lecture like a professor; others can melt us open with their love and compas-sion. The greatest and simplest power of a teacher is the environment of their own freedom and joy.

As we have seen, there are times when it is important in the growth of spiritual life to develop a relationship with a teacher or spiritual guide. Whether you have been working with a teacher or are considering doing so, it is worth reflecting carefully on this key relationship. While Americans are most conscious of their need to be self-sufficient, the spirit of the pioneer and the cowboy is not necessarily a skillful way to approach spiritual life. We have already described the profound process of healing that takes place in meditation: the inevitable hindrances, the skills needed to work with obsessive states, the powerful physical openings of chakras and energy systems, the realms of the dark night and the death-rebirth experience, the many cycles of spiritual life. How are we to find our way in these realms on our own? Even when we have a spontaneous awakening in our lives, in times of great change or near-death experiences, we find these painful or ecstatic experiences and visions will very often fade without the support of a teacher and a systematic practice.

Having a map and directions from spiritual books and texts is not enough. We do not know where our spiritual life will lead us, but it always requires us to go into that which is difficult and unknown. Those who attempt to practice alone are almost inevitably more confused or lacking in spiritual depth than those who have practiced under a skillful teacher.

It is a basic principle of spiritual life that we learn the deepest things in unknown territory. Often it is when we feel most confused inwardly and are in the midst of our greatest difficulties that something new will open. We awaken most easily to the mystery of life through our weakest side. The areas of our greatest strength, where we are the most competent and clearest, tend to keep us away from the mystery. To go into this territory beyond our own self, to enter these realms without a guide, can be like trying to lift ourselves by our own bootstraps.

Rumi warns us about this with a story.

A certain man caught a bird in a trap.
The bird says, "Sir, you have eaten many cows and sheep
in your life and you're still hungry. The little bit
of meat on my bones won't satisfy you either.
If you let me go, I'll give you three pieces of wisdom.
One I'll say standing on your hand. One on your roof.
And one I'll speak from the
limb of that tree."

The man was interested. He freed the bird and let it stand
on his hand.

"Number one: Do not believe in absurdity, no
matter who says it."

The bird flew and lit on the man's roof. "Number two:
Do not grieve over what is past; it's over.
Never regret what has happened.

By the way," the bird continued, "in my body there is a huge
pearl weighing as much as ten copper coins. It was meant
to be an inheritance for you and your children,
but now you've lost it. You could have owned
the largest pearl in existence, but evidently,
it was not meant to be."

The man started wailing like a woman in childbirth.
The bird said, "Didn't I just say 'Don't grieve
for what's in the
past' and also 'Don't believe
in absurdity'? My entire body doesn't weigh
as much as ten copper coins. How could I have
a pearl that heavy inside me?"

The man came to his senses. "All right.
Tell me number three."

"Yes, you've made such good use of the first two!

"Don't give advice to someone who is
groggy and falling asleep. Don't throw seeds on the
sand."

Rumi wants us to see how easy it is to get caught.

Even when we do receive good advice, it is easy to ignore it or misinterpret it. The places where we are stuck, those difficult layers of fear and attachment, the points of self-delusion and unworthiness we will encounter, are many. They come in everyone's practice, and the more educated and competent we believe ourselves to be, the slower the climb and the more foolhardy our falls.

As Ray Bradbury quipped, "The first thing you learn in life is you're a fool. The last thing you learn is you're the same fool. Sometimes I think I understand everything. Then I regain consciousness."

Our worldly education doesn't help much in meditation.

Once in Boston, the director of a new hospice, a fairly spiritually sophisticated doctor, asked me to lead a retreat for his entire staff. On the fourth day of sitting and walking intensively, this doctor came to see me in an interview. He was quite alarmed, for he was experiencing strong pains in his heart that radiated up through his shoulders. While the pain was acute, he found it even more difficult to deal with his fear. All his symptoms had him believing he was having a heart attack. His only question for me was whether to call an ambulance or whether to have someone drive him to the hospital. I asked him a number of pointed questions about the sensations in his body, his energetic experiences, and his state of mind. After listening carefully, I told him that in fact the signs were of the opening of his heart chakra, which is often a physical and muscular release of armor around the heart as well as an emotional and spiritual opening. I had experienced it myself and seen it many times before. Then I said, "Besides, you've started a new, spiritually oriented hospice, haven't you? Perhaps it's time at this retreat to really face your own death, even if it really is a heart attack." (I was quite sure it wasn't.) "Didn't you come here to learn about death and dying? What better place to die than at a meditation retreat?" Then I sent him back to sit. Without a teacher he would have remained confused about his experience and probably would have gone to the hospital. (Of course, if you do experience severe pains of this kind and are not practicing with a teacher, *do* get yourself to a hospital.)

Because the spiritual process is not a random one, guides and teachers drawing on ancient traditions can understand and assist our journey when we ourselves are lost. However, even when we recognize the need for a teacher, we can be confused about what to look for. Our culture gives us few or no models for how to find or work with spiritual teachers, gurus, or guides. The old, wonderful spirit of apprenticeship has been lost in our time, and most of our education comes in large impersonal settings or, increasingly, through videos and computers. Still, we have all heard guru stories and Zen master tales, and when we first imagine a relationship to such a person, we will often exaggerate or distort the reality of learning from a teacher. Some students have an overly inflated idea of a spiritual master, so they imagine finding a teacher who is an all-knowing, omniscient, and omnipotent god, and many spiritual communities promote this exaggerated concept. Their students speak as if the master does everything, saying, "My teacher helped me get this job," or "My teacher made this accident happen to teach me a lesson," or "My teacher through his magic powers has created the situation I'm now experiencing." "The master is doing it." "The master guides all and is responsible for all." "The master will enlighten me in due time."

The opposite exaggerated view of a teacher will come from those students who are very cautious and have difficulty respecting or elevating another person in any way, who cannot accept that someone might actually know more than they do. They find it hard to let themselves be taught by anyone. After hearing stories about false gurus or teachers gone bad, such a person feels there is no need for a teacher and no real way to trust. Often this attitude stems from unfinished problems with authority figures and shows itself as the inability to be at ease in different roles, at times the inability to learn as a student and at other times to be comfortable as a teacher. Even without such problems, we might simply be awkward and afraid because we don't know what to do with a teacher or how we should respond. Over the long run, whatever difficulties we have in our other relationships will probably arise as well with our teacher, from issues of trust—trusting too easily or being unable to trust—to issues of boundaries, fear, doubt, and need.

Underlying most of the difficulties students have with teachers is the deep longing we all have to be loved and accepted in a whole and total way. Few of us have ever been loved in this way. Yet we are afraid of it as well. The pains of our past losses and abandonment are still with us, leaving us confused and afraid. This fear causes us either to underestimate the value of teachers to protect our self from the strength of our longing, or to inflate and idealize and seek only the most perfect master, one who would never hurt us or disappoint us. Yet what we really need is to learn how to love and be loved. It is this love that is central to the relationship between teachers and students, and only within this container are other teachings passed along.

The best teachers know this and can teach us how to love and trust ourselves; they can teach us how to love the truth, to love life. They can be a model and bring to us a genuine and fearless relationship. A relationship with a skillful spiritual teacher, whether a brief encounter or a lifelong association, can often become an intensely intimate and valuable communion of spirit. The genuineness of a teacher and teachings becomes a sacred vessel that holds the truth that leads us to awaken our heart.

The respected Zen master Suzuki Roshi was described by his student Trudy Dixon in this way: "Because he is just himself, he is a mirror for his students. When we are with him, we feel our own strengths and shortcomings without any sense of praise or criticism from him. In his presence we see our original face, and the extraordinariness we see is only our own true nature."

When I am asked how someone can find a teacher, the most honest thing I can say is that this is a mysterious process. Very often we simply run into them, hear about them, or are drawn to them in some unplanned or unexpected way. Many times we will have seen a picture, read a book, or heard from a friend about a teacher who inspires us, presents a possibility of greatness, who touches our heart or awakens some longing or vision in us; such inspiration can pull us powerfully, mysteriously, and even reluctantly into the orbit of a teacher or spiritual community. We can visit various spiritual centers, try their teachings, go to lectures or ceremonies, and from all of this find ourselves drawn to a certain teacher. Nowadays there are even guidebooks for the many Buddhist, Hindu, Christian, and Jewish practice centers in the West. These too can help give us a sense of what is available.

There are many wonderful and strange stories about the way fellow seekers and friends have come to their teachers. One man I knew who had intended to take LSD underneath the Buddha's bodhi tree at the main temple in India "accidentally ran into" a wonderful teacher on the way, threw away the LSD, and practiced with him for ten years. Another man simply looked under Z in the phone book, found *Zen*, called, and asked if he could speak with the master at the local Zen center. An older woman I know had her master walk up to her at a conference and say, "I want you to study with me." Another young American man, who knew nothing of spiritual life, had a dream of a Tibetan lama while sick in the hospital. Two years later, while traveling in Nepal, he met the very lama who appeared in his dream. This lama smiled and said, "I have been expecting you."

The range of styles of spiritual teachers is great. In the Buddhist tradition, this is exemplified by the two poles of *guru* and *spiritual friend*. *Spiritual friend* comes from a Sanskrit term that denotes the friendly guidance and support we take from another in our spiritual path. Some teachers prefer this role, unencumbered by a need for devotion, surrender, or the traditional student-teacher hierarchy. One great forest master in Thailand, Buddhadasa Bikkhu, does not want students to bow to him, even though this is the custom when meeting any monk or master. Instead, he has them come and sit next to him and treats them as "a spiritual friend," engaging in warmhearted conversation and inquiry, encouraging students to respect themselves and their own vision.

The opposite style of teacher is the traditional guru. There are Buddhist teachers, lamas, Zen masters, Hindu teachers, and masters of Hasidic and Sufi traditions who express their teachings through this role. The guru is a great, wise master who embodies spiritual practice, guides us through specific teachings, and to whom we surrender for our own freedom. With a guru we tend to listen and obey, more than talk over and question. Sometimes we are asked to worship a guru as a divinity in human form or as an all-enlightened master, fully awake, whose every act is skillful. In working with a guru we undergo a process of surrender, a stripping away of our own self-centered ways, as a vehicle to develop an openness and selflessness infused with the guru's spirit.

Between the poles of spiritual friend and guru is a wide range of styles. Teachers will teach through a combination of their own personalities and the methods that brought their own awakening. In one famous dialogue, the Buddha shows a visitor the clusters of teachers and students in his forest monastery. "Students who have an interest in inquiry are gathered there with my wisest disciple, Sariputtra, and those who are inspired by the practice of monastic discipline are there with Upali, foremost master of the monk's life. Those drawn by psychic development are there with the great psychic Mogallana, and still others who are naturally drawn to concentration and samadhi are over there with Mahakassapa."

In the Spiritual Roller Coaster chapter we spoke about the traditions and teachers who stress the need for mystical visions, ecstasy, or powerful altered states and about others who seek to bring the sacred alive in the midst of our everyday activity. Some teachings focus their practices on the body, such as hatha and kundalini yoga or Sufi breath practices; others focus on action, bringing compassion and the sense of sacredness alive through service; others may focus on directly opening or transforming the heart and mind through meditation, prayer, or visions and concentration. Some teachings stress powerful altered states, a deep questioning of who we are and what is the nature of consciousness and life itself. For others there is the path of surrender, the path of devotion, a moment-to-moment letting go of our small self-centered way, saying to God or the universe, "Not my will, but thine."

To the surprise of many, this variety of teaching styles cannot be neatly divided by tradition. Within each great tradition we will find teachers who emphasize these contrasting ways. There are Zen masters who are caring and devotional, and there are Zen masters who require fierce discipline and mind-shattering inquiry. There are strict hatha yoga physical purists, and others who teach hatha yoga simply as a vehicle for a sacred awareness to dance through the body.

In each tradition some teachers are rascals and coyotes who trick and surprise their students; some are harsh taskmasters who point out a student's every fault, trying to whittle down ego and pride; others teach more through honoring and encouragement, nurturing the best in a student; some teachers lecture like a professor; others can melt us open with their love and compassion or show us the space and humor in all things.

A teacher should be an exemplar and a master of the tradition of practice they present. It is also helpful if they know enough of a range of teachings to fit the variety of students who come to them. Otherwise, one may encounter the difficulty of a student who practiced sincerely under a great kundalini yogi in India, but whose practice kept making him more tense, agitated, and scattered. In desperation, he asked a famous Tibetan lama what was wrong, and after some careful discussion the lama replied, "It's simple. Your teacher has given you the wrong practice." Quite surprised, the student then said, "But my teacher only teaches this one practice!"

If we already have a teacher, it can be interesting to reflect back to what drew us to them and to their particular way of practice. What expectations did we bring and how has it turned out? What have we learned, and what are our disappointments? Is it still serving us to remain?

If we are seeking a new teacher, we should inquire directly about how they teach. How do they view the path of practice, and what is the goal? What form does their practice take? How do they guide students? Will we be able to spend time with this teacher? Will we actually get their direct assistance? What kind of support does the teacher give to students through the arduous parts of the spiritual journey? What is the sense of the community around the teacher? Then we need to look at what is asked of us. Does what is asked feel healthy and appropriate? What commitments are necessary? What kind of relationship is expected? How much time is required? What does it cost?

In seeking a teacher, we must listen to our heart, and we must look at ourselves with honesty. What are we really seeking? Is this what is offered by this teacher and by this way of practice? What draws us to this teacher? Does this teacher and way of practice fit my temperament and serve me, or conversely, does it reinforce my fears and neuroses? Would it serve me to go into a large and extroverted group community when I'm a very shy person who has hidden for years, or might I get overwhelmed and stuck further in my shyness? Do I need the discipline of a strict Zen master, and the stick that is used to keep students sitting straight, or was I abused and beaten as a child, and would this only re-create and reinforce a painful and negative sense of myself? What cycle of my spiritual life is it time for—silence or service, meditation or study?

We cannot always answer these questions, but just by posing them we can help ourselves avoid the grossest and most unskillful mistakes. Very often we can begin to practice and give ourselves a period for trial and error. A trial period may be for one month, one or two retreats, even a year, however long it takes to get a sense of the teacher, their relationship to other students and to ourselves, and to get a feeling for the practice.

Whether choosing or reviewing our choice, we must sense a trust and respect for the integrity and wisdom that our teacher embodies. Look for teachers who offer a sense of maturity in their spiritual and personal life, an integration of the physical, worldly, emotional, and mystical dimensions. Look for humor. Even strict disciplinarians should also embody a spirit of joy, ease, and love in their own being. Like choosing a partner in marriage, choosing a teacher also asks for a deep respect of our own inner knowing, and a willingness to commit when the circumstances seem right.

Over the years our relationship with a teacher will change. In time our teacher may fulfill many roles. They can be mentor and priest, confessor and guide, spiritual midwife and critic, mirror and exemplar of a radiant presence. From a skillful teacher, we can borrow courage, assurance, strength, and clarity. We can use their guidance, energy, and love to resonate with and inspire our own. Two older women masters with whom I had the privilege of studying brought to their teaching so much joy and love of the spirit, it would wash over me and fill my cells when I was with them. A great hug from one would bring rapture for days. They had both led long lives with a full measure of sorrows and triumphs, grandchildren and students. In their teaching, they were demanding and uncompromising; in their manner, wise and understanding.

Another teacher I worked with was full of the unexpected, always bringing surprising and sometimes shocking new ways of looking at things. He embodied courage and a willingness to turn one's life upside down if that was what it took to live in the truth. His whole being was so devoted to awakening the mind and heart in the spirit of the Buddha, that he truly empowered all those around him to question, change, and awaken as well.

Remember that as we select a teacher, we join a tradition and lineage as well. Lineages are the carriers of ancient wisdom. In every great tradition, the shamans, the healers, the yogis, the wise women of the mystery schools, the great rabbis or desert fathers, live within their lineage. Lineage and tradition are the sacred containers for preserving practices and wisdom that have been discovered and accumulated over generations. Lineages are the form through which the light of awakening is passed from one generation to the next. Lineages contain formal scriptures, ancient chants, rituals, meditation techniques, and teaching stories, all as vehicles to awaken our hearts and spirits. Skillful teachers use the practices and rituals of a lineage to create a sacred space that awakens devotion and wisdom and that allows consciousness to transcend its normal limitations.

When we choose a teacher, we are drawn into the powerful current of a lineage and partake of its worldview, its visions, its possibilities, and its limitations. Every lineage and tradition has both possibilities and limitations. In the wisest traditions, the higher teachings will guide its members to recognize and transcend the very limitations of the tradition's own form, to discover the sacred that is within themselves beyond all form. Thus in devotion to a guru, students must ultimately see the guru in themselves, or in the tradition of Zen koans, students must go beyond all questions and all answers.

The choosing of a lineage or set of practices, like choosing a teacher, is a mysterious process in which we are drawn or attracted to a spiritual stream. Again, trust yourself, and look for integrity, joy, and maturity in the community. I usually recommend to students that they choose "name brands," those traditions that have been around for hundreds or thousands of years, where the teachings, disciplines, and visions have been refined for many generations by the wise hearts of teachers and students.

As we consider joining a teacher, we might look at their place in their lineage or tradition. How are they regarded by other spiritual leaders? Are they empowered and respected within their own tradition? If all this feels like shopping in the American supermarket of the spirit—unfortunately, in a way it is. But this is not shopping for a color that pleases us or for a car that fits our image. This is deeply seeking an honest and genuine way to follow our intuition and spiritual longings. When we honor those we encounter and ourselves with attention, honesty, and care, good things will inevitably result.

Once we have chosen to follow one, how then are we to work best with a teacher? The beginning may not be easy. We will encounter unfamiliar customs and practices, new languages, new prayers, chants, and perspectives. We will also have to work with the awkwardness of entering a new community. As if this were not enough, along with these difficulties, we are often given initial rites of passage. Some Zen monasteries will not accept students until they have sat, unmoving, outside the gates (in the snow in some parts of Japan) all day long, for one, two, or more days. This is to demonstrate the genuine spirit with which they ask for teachings. Most traditions have initial retreats, ceremonies, or practices given to provide entrance for the newcomer. In return for receiving spiritual teachings, we are often required to show that we will value them.

There are two qualities that are most important to bring to our work with a spiritual teacher. They are our common sense and our sincere commitment. With common sense, we will not overidealize the teacher or practice; we will not betray ourselves or our own good judgment. Common sense is a respect for ourselves and a willingness to see things clearly.

Sincere commitment is the second key to working with a teacher, no matter what their style of practice. This is the gold that a teacher looks for in the best of students. With commitment we bring our full energy to follow a path and its discipline, such as prayer, through its inevitable difficulties and confusions. When we combine an earnest and sincere commitment to practice with the skillful guidance of a teacher, the joys and difficulties we encounter continue to illuminate our path.

In working with a teacher to learn a spiritual practice, we are simultaneously developing a relationship with the teacher. The relationship, too, asks for our commitment. In it we learn to trust the teacher, the practice, and ourselves in deeper and deeper ways. We are asked, over and over, to persist in its development, to stay with it, to give ourselves to it, to bring our full heart and energy to the practice and the teacher. We can ask whatever questions we feel necessary and then give it our best shot and see for ourselves what happens in a few years of sincere practice.

The Dalai Lama says we can best tell if our practice is working by looking at its results after five, ten, or twenty years. Perhaps that is easy for him to say after fourteen lifetimes as the Dalai Lama. In this vein, Mullah Nasrudin told a woman who proudly announced that her son had completed his studies, "No doubt, madam, God will send him some more!" It is in our perseverance and commitment that real spiritual growth takes place.

How can we most benefit from our relationship with a teacher? In Asia and in traditional Western spiritual cultures, people know how to behave outwardly: how to bow, the forms of respect, what is to be offered, and what might be received. They also know what questions are most skillful to ask a teacher or a guru and what to actually expect from their guidance of us. Unlike cultures where there is a common knowledge of the rules of one spiritual tradition, here in America students do not know what to expect. It helps to inquire directly of the teacher and elder students what the best way is to enter the community; what the forms of regular contact between teachers and students are; how available the teacher will be; what we should do in times of difficulty. To benefit from a teacher, we want to find out how best to be known by this person, when and where to speak to them, so that they can guide our own personal path. We must make ourselves available to receive their guidance, to get feedback and help in the places where we are stuck or frightened, to bring a sense of balance when we are out of balance.

The ability to bring students back to balance is one of the gifts of a skillful teacher. My own forest master, Achaan Chah, said that was most of what he did as a teacher. I asked him one day why he seemed to give such contradictory instructions from one student to another, from one season to another. It didn't seem consistent or straightforward, it didn't seem really enlightened to me. Achaan laughed and replied, "The path is not like that. The way I teach is more like this: I look down a path which I know well, but it may be dark or foggy, and the student in front of me is about to fall off in a ditch on the right-hand side or get lost in a side track to the right. So I call out to them, 'Go to the left, go to the left.' Then some time later, the same student or another following the foggy path may be ready to fall in a ditch on the left-hand side or get lost on a side track in that direction. Again I call out, 'Go to the right, go to the right.' I remind them whenever they get off the path. In a way, that is all I do."

Skillful guidance in our practice keeps us present, helps us to open. A wise teacher calls forth the strength and wisdom of the student. Such a teacher can compassionately point out the greatest difficulties in our own character, ask hard things of us, and care enough to awaken our greatness.

Achaan Chah would often ask hard things of his students: traditional ascetic discipline, great renunciations, or the hard practice of doing that which was called for day in and day out, whether or not it was what we wished to be doing. Then he would wander around the monastery, and if it looked like someone was having a hard time, he would sidle up to them and inquire, "Are you suffering today?" If they said no, then he would say, "Well, then, have a fine day." But if we said yes, he would say, "I wonder whose fault that is," and smile and walk away. Or he might say, "Gee, I wonder if anyone around here is attached," and walk away. He kept directing us back to an understanding of our own inner experience, to discover how we were entangled and how we, too, could learn to be free.

A fine teacher brings the spirit of awakening alive through their very being. One of the warmest and most heart-touching memories of my years with Achaan Chah, who guided monks in the jungles and forests of Thailand at sixty monasteries for over thirty years, was how present he was with us in our own difficulties. When we sat up all night without sleep, he sat there with us. When we were cleaning the walkways of the forest, he taught us how to make bamboo brooms and how to make sweeping a beautiful meditation. When we swept and cleaned the whole monastery before a holiday celebration, he was there with us. Even in a remote cave monastery, where a wealthy patron had offered to build an enormous meditation hall atop a mountain, he came with us as the monks cleared the way for a road to create the new center. During the cold season in one of the coldest parts of Thailand, I remember walking barefoot more than five miles through the forest with him and several other monks to receive meager food offerings in our bowls from a poor village nearby. It was so cold (just above the freezing point), my teeth were chattering, my bald head felt icy, and I had wrapped my one towel under the cotton cloth of the monk's robe for just a little extra protection against the winter wind. When we got to the village, Achaan Chah turned to me and smiled. "Cold?" he asked. "Yes, I am freezing," I said. "I don't know if I can stand any worse." He smiled at me and said, "Well, this is as cold as it gets; this is as cold as it gets." I was so grateful he was there with me.

The same spirit came through an old Rinzai Zen master with whom I studied. I attended a number of rigorous week-long retreats, where we sat motionless from early morning until late at night, working with a koan, with only short breaks for walking and eating. At first, I was disappointed that the master did not sit with us, but then I found out why. He sat in a room off the meditation hall giving four or five interviews every day to each of the fifty students. Though he gave over two hundred interviews a day, each time I saw him he was more fully present and clearer than I was at any time during the retreat. He really was there with us.

When we are supported and given teachings in this way, we realize how much of spiritual life is our growing ability to give. It is wise to look at whatever spiritual practice and teacher we wish to join from the perspective of what we can offer. In spiritual life, what finally makes us happy is not what we get, but what we can give, what we can give to a community and what we can give of ourselves. We give of ourselves when we give up our old views, our fears, our limitations, the barriers that we have held for a long time, and discover a fundamental and radically new way of being as we allow ourselves to be reborn as children of the spirit. We give to a community when we bring our energy, our creativity, our heart to the whole.

There is an immense joy that arises in a community when together we give of ourselves. We have it in our American tradition too. It is the spirit of village barn-raising, the beauty of singing the *Messiah* with one hundred other voices, the coming together to serve a greater purpose. To give of our own spirit, to serve, is a wonderful and fulfilling part of joining a spiritual community. This giving and receiving heart, this honoring of the sacred, creates the spirit of sangha or *satsang* that characterizes those who are gathered together in the name of that which is holy. The community is created, not when people come together in the name of religion, but when they come together bringing honesty, respect, and kindness to support an awakening of the sacred. True community arises when we can speak in accord with truth and compassion. This sense of spiritual community is a wondrous part of what heals and transforms us on our path.

As we contemplate joining a community, sensing what we can give and the ways the community awakens its members, we should look to the senior students. How do students mature in this community? Are they respected, given higher practices, opportunities to serve or teach? Is there a way to fulfill the teachings as the master has done? Are the older students happy and wise?

You will notice that in discussing teachers and communities I speak of joy, wisdom, skill, and compassion, but not of powers and miracles. It is true that around some powerful teachers we may see visions, feel rapture and energy awaken in our bodies, even have our consciousness transformed for a time. This power, when it is genuine, can be helpful, or it can be intoxicating or confusing, depending on how it is used. However, such power is never necessary. Beyond the problems that arise when such power is misused, which we will speak of later, it is more important to realize one basic fact: No one can enlighten us; no one can mature for us; no one can let go for us; no one can ever do it for us. They can point, inspire, touch, even give us a sense of the true way, but most of all, our teachers can create the sacred space where our awakening can happen.

An eighty-year-old Swiss woman, a spiritual master with whom I had the privilege to study, spoke about the need for a true teacher to create a free and protected environment in which the heart and the spirit could open and blossom as they have longed to since the beginning of time. A teacher's capacity to create such a sacred space, to transmit a sense of trust and act as a compassionate container strong enough to allow old parts of us to die and new ones to be born, is an extraordinary gift. Through it we are offered not only the ancient wisdom of a lineage but also our own true selves. The greatest and simplest power of a teacher is the environment of their own freedom and joy.

For some years I visited an old Hindu guru in India. He was wise and filled with a joyful energy of the spirit. He asked many things of us, to inquire deeply, to meditate, and to surrender and trust deeply. But the best thing about him was the sense he gave us of being loved totally by someone who did not want anything back, who had not the slightest single shred of desire for anything from us. In him there was no sense of attachment, no wanting of students, not even wanting our awakening— just a clear and joyful space that invited truth and opening from us in whatever we encountered. Being loved in that way was an extraordinary experience: my whole body, mind, heart, and spirit came to a space of openness, and peace.

After he felt that a student had truly understood the reality and heart of his teaching, he would send them home. For some this was after a few weeks; for some it was after a few months. "Go home and bring this spirit to life, there is no need to stay with the outer guru all the time."

Just as it is important to stay with a teacher and practice, it is also important to know that we can leave when the time is right. Sometimes it will be because we will have completed the lessons that are there for us; sometimes circumstances will have made it become the wrong place or wrong cycle; often, we may need additional or different teachings beyond those we can receive from our teacher.

Our obligation and patient commitment to a teacher does not mean we must follow their way for the rest of our life. Over the long run, we must take a teacher or a practice, join a community, and then see how it serves us. Even though teachers and communities may expect us to swear fealty, to take vows, to join for life, we do not need to take a permanent spiritual vow. Even permanent vows must be renewed. Yes, we must be patient and committed, but the true vow of the spirit is to honor our own integrity, awakening, and compassion, no matter what changes of circumstances they call for.

After completing an initial period of training, most of the best Western teachers I know have studied extensively with a number of other great masters. Moving from one teacher to another can be difficult if we have made extended commitments. Many students who have come to see me have felt in a bind about the question of vows. They had taken teachings from great Tibetan lamas that required a lifetime commitment of practice, or they had taken vows to be ordained for life in a particular tradition or to follow a certain way as if forever. But sometimes they reached a point where these vows seemed to be hindering the development of their spiritual practice. In our discussion we would look carefully to make sure they were not simply running away from their commitment in an unconscious fashion. If our inquiry together showed that the skillful support from those vows had truly ended for them or that their life circumstances had changed so that their previous commitments no longer served their spiritual growth, I would send them back to their lamas and teachers to ask for a ceremony to release them from these vows. Then they could move on as they needed in their spiritual life.

Even in traditions where one makes a lifelong commitment, this must be reviewed and renewed periodically in terms of the individual's well-being. Some Buddhist traditions ask students to commit for an initial period of five years with one teacher. Then after gaining some understanding in this tradition, one is encouraged to visit other masters and to broaden one's understanding and skillful means.

In the end, the true purpose of a teacher is to guide us to discover our inherent freedom of heart. All spiritual teaching has this end, and the gift of all wise teachers is encouragement to find within ourselves our Buddha nature—free, independent, and joyful in the midst of all life.

Whether we stay with a teacher for months, years, or decades, it is a blessing to encounter a true spiritual benefactor, a mentor and guide to our own freedom. We are blessed by their presence, which is a reminder of what is possible. We are blessed by their direct guidance. We are blessed by the discipline and practices that they offer us. We are blessed by their skill in teaching us how to use spiritual discipline and in fostering the patience that we need so that we, too, can master it. We are blessed by the depth of their love that gives us inspiration in facing our wounds and holds our best and highest interest in their hearts.

When we find a skillful teacher and a lineage we can trust and respect, this becomes a beacon to illuminate our hearts and our path. It gives us an opportunity to discover that which is genuine and timeless for ourselves and to carry that light into all the world.

17

PSYCHOTHERAPY
AND MEDITATION

*The best of modern therapy is much like a pro-
cess of shared meditation, where therapist and
client sit together, learning to pay close attention
to those aspects and dimensions of the self that
the client may be unable to touch on his or her
own.*

Each time Buddhist teachings have traveled to new countries, such
as China, Japan, and Tibet, they have been profoundly influenced by
the encounter with other native cultures and religions. Out of these
encounters, whole new forms of practice, such as Zen and tantra, have
developed. This process is now happening in the West. Of the Western
"inner practices," the one that is having the most significant impact on
Buddhism and on all contemporary spiritual life is the understanding
and practice of Western psychology. Many serious students and teachers
of the spiritual path in the West have found it necessary or useful to turn
to psychotherapy for help in their spiritual life. Many others who have
not done so would probably benefit by it.

What does Western psychotherapy do that traditional spiritual practice and meditation doesn't? We have seen how frequently students in the West encounter the deep wounds that result from the breakdown of the Western family system, the traumas of childhood, and the confusion of modern society. Psychotherapy addresses in directed and powerful ways the need for healing, the reclamation and creation of a healthy sense of self, the dissolution of fears and compartments, and the search for a creative, loving, and full way to live in the world.

We have acknowledged that these issues cannot be separated from spiritual life. It is not as if we get our psychological house in order and then strike out to attain nirvana. As our body, heart, mind, and spirit open, each new layer we encounter reveals both greater freedom and compassion and deeper and more subtle layers of underlying delusion. Our deep personal work and our meditative work must necessarily proceed together. What American practice has to come to acknowledge is that many of the deep issues we uncover in spiritual life cannot be healed by meditation alone. Problems such as early abuse, addiction, and difficulties of love and sexuality require the close, conscious, and ongoing support of a skillful healer to resolve. In large spiritual communities, the guru, lama, or teacher rarely has the time to guide us closely through such a process. Many spiritual teachers also are not skilled in working with these areas. Some have not even dealt with them in themselves.

By contrast, the best of modern therapy is much like a process of shared meditation, where therapist and client sit together, learning to pay close attention to those aspects and dimensions of the self that the client may be unable to touch on his or her own. More than the profound concentration of many meditation practices, therapy has the quality of investigation and discovery. In this joint meditation, the therapist joins in the listening, sensing, and feeling and may direct the client toward ways to pay a deeper attention to the roots of his or her suffering, entanglements, and difficulty. I have benefited in this way by working with several excellent therapists who have allowed me to understand and heal levels of my heart and mind that were never touched in years of meditation.

Even the great Mahasi Sayadaw, Burma's most renowned meditation master, recognized that Western students must face these new problems. When first teaching in America, he exclaimed on how many students seemed to be suffering from a range of problems unfamiliar to him in Asia. He called it "psycho-logical suffering." The Dalai Lama, too, in dialogue with Western psychologists, expressed shock at the amount of low self-esteem, wounding, and family conflict that arise in the practice of Westerners. These problems have to be addressed.

All too often the mistaken belief that enough sincere practice of prayer or meditation is all that is needed to transform their lives has prevented teachers and students from making use of the helpful teachings of Western psychology. In an unfortunate way, many students of Eastern and Western spirituality have been led to believe that if they experience difficulties, it is simply because they haven't practiced long enough or somehow have not been practicing according to the teachings.

A second erroneous belief is that good students should be capable of facing the whole spiritual path by themselves and that to turn to an outsider for assistance is an indication of weakness or failure. This can be threatening to some communities who feel that to turn to outside methods such as Western psychology would be admitting that their system and teacher did not have all the answers. Confusion about the place of therapy in practice arises from a false idea that the "spiritual" and the "worldly" are separate realms, that the spiritual is "higher" and the worldly somehow "lower." We may have been taught that experiences we have at the "spiritual" level in meditation, as if by magic, will have the power to transform all the other levels of our being. Thus, if we have a great "awakening" in Buddhist practice or the experience of grace or oneness with the divine in Christian or Hindu devotional practice, we think this will be enough to change our vision, heal our hearts, and bring us into harmony with the deepest truths of our lives.

The reason for this belief is that during such an experience we feel in great harmony, and some echo of that feeling will remain with us for quite a long time. Yet such experiences in our spiritual journey mark only an initial success; inevitably the experience spirals back, requiring that we learn to integrate each new insight fully into the course of our lives. In this process there are no higher or lower levels, no areas that are more sacred than any other. There is simply the encountering of whatever patterns of contraction, fear, and identification cause our suffering and discovering an awakening and freedom from them.

In truth, the need to deal with our personal emotional problems is more the rule in spiritual practice than the exception. At least half of the students at our annual three-month retreat find themselves unable to do traditional Insight Meditation because they encounter so much unresolved grief, fear, and wounding and unfinished developmental business from the past that this becomes their meditation. In every tradition, even the most successful Western seekers will, after periods of powerful meditation and deep insights, reencounter painful patterns, fear, and unconsciousness in whole other parts of their lives. We may experience understanding and peace in meditation, but when we return to the problems of daily life or visit our families or even fall in love, suddenly old patterns of suffering, neurosis, attachment, and delusion can be as strong as ever. We have to find ways to include them on our path.

Recently, the successful Western teacher of a large Hindu community turned over teaching responsibility to two senior students. In short order, much turmoil and conflict arose. One senior student began to abuse his role; the other was remote and insensitive. In the heated meetings that followed, it became evident that not only the senior students had such problems. Many loyal students stated reluctantly that the teacher himself, though not abusive, was painfully insensitive, distant, and un-available. With great integrity, after thirty years of teaching, at age sev-enty-four, this teacher decided to begin psychotherapy to address these issues in his life.

After decades of experience with Eastern practices in the West, we have now begun to see quite clearly the results of failing to include the area of personal problems in our practice. Much of the discussion in the next chapter, The Emperor's New Clothes, examines the way such fail-ures, with quite disastrous results in some cases, can occur in the rela-tionship of teachers and communities. Because the issues of personal life are often the source of our greatest suffering and neurosis, of our deepest attachments and greatest delusion, we fear them and may unconsciously use spiritual practice to avoid dealing with them. How disappointed certain students become when they leave their ashrams and monasteries (Buddhist or Christian) and find that after ten or fifteen years they still have not really faced their life, not faced the root fears and the areas of suffering that limit and entangle them.

A skilled psychotherapist can offer specific practices and tools for addressing the most painful areas of our life. He or she can bring to a problem or difficulty a knowledge of the common patterns, the specific developmental processes and unhealthy defenses that create much of the suffering in our Western culture. The therapist's familiarity with the family systems, beliefs, stories, and identifications that underlie these problems makes releasing them possible within the safety of regular meetings committed to focusing on whatever areas of life are difficult. There are many kinds of examples of how psychotherapy has assisted those involved with spiritual practice. Let me recount several.

One student who stayed in a spiritual community for years had no confidence that he could be successful at obtaining a livelihood outside of the community; he was also fearful and confused about money, seeing it as unspiritual and dangerous. Finally, as many of his friends became established in careers and families, he realized he wanted help. At first he sought counseling to consider simply whether he should stay in the community or leave and get some job training. But the counseling led him to face deeper fears, insecurities, and regrets for the way he had lived. The therapy showed him how much of his life had been dominated by his reaction to his cold businessman father. He discovered a lifetime pattern of avoiding money and success and saw how this had become confused with his spiritual life. This had gone on for many years. Finally, facing these fears and reactions, he was able to see that he had many unused gifts and many choices. He moved out of the community, went to art school, and became a very successful designer. He still meditates and is serving on the board of directors of his old community, where he can now bring to it and his practice a new strength instead of his old insecurity.

Another student, who had spent ten years of his life traveling and meditating in India and Japan, decided to try therapy after a string of painful relationships. His therapy was a long process of untangling childhood abuse, sexual fear and compulsion, and deep shame and anger. In his years of meditation, he had successfully avoided these issues, but every time he tried to establish an intimate relationship, he became flooded with these problems. He realized how much of his life, even the meditation career, had been a reaction to his early abuse. In therapy he began to focus on his deep longing for love, his shame, and his confused sexuality. For him it was a slow process of learning to trust the close relationship of the therapy. He stopped traveling, and while he is still learning about intimate relationships, he is now happier and more complete than at any time in his adult life.

A third student, who turned to psychotherapy in the middle of her spiritual training, had begun meditating when very young. She was an avid practitioner who delighted in the calm of meditation and the nurturance of the community, but she was also somewhat passive, insecure, and self-conscious. When she declared that she wanted to become a teacher of meditation, her teacher told her that she had much personal maturing to do before that would be possible. He suggested that she establish a nourishing livelihood outside the meditation community and at the same time explore her timidity and inner insecurity with a respected woman therapist in her community. Soon after starting therapy, it became clear that the fact that she was adopted, which she had ignored in her spiritual life, was a key to much of her passive identity. Unworthiness, grief, and confusion poured out when she looked at the knot of her childhood. She began to question the foster parents who had adopted her at age two, and through a long search process was able to find her birth mother. A tearful though difficult reunion began the start of a new life for her. She realized that she had been a dutiful daughter and meditation student to make sure that she would not lose her home again. But now, through continuing both therapy and meditation, she began to find her own way and her own voice for the first time. As her old identity was released, a great space of new freedom opened in her life, and she began a process of truly maturing and flowering that may someday lead her to become a fine meditation teacher.

When we have not completed the basic developmental tasks of our emotional lives or are still quite unconscious in relation to our parents and families, we will find that we are unable to deepen in our spiritual practice. Without dealing with these issues, we will not be able to concentrate during meditation, or we will find ourselves unable to bring what we have learned in meditation into our interaction with others.

Whether our patterns of contraction and unhealthy sense of identity have their roots in our childhood or even in the more ancient patterns of karma, they will continue to repeat themselves in our lives and the lives of our children if we do not face them. It is simply not true that time alone will heal them. In fact, over time they may well become more entrenched if we continue to ignore them.

Because awareness does not automatically transfer itself from one dimension of our life to another, compartments remain in the areas where our fears, our wounds, and our defenses are deepest. Thus, we encounter graceful masters of tea ceremonies who remain confused and retarded in intimate relations, or yogis who can dissolve their bodies into light, but whose wisdom vanishes when they enter the marketplace.

In comparing the practices of psychotherapy and meditation, it is important to recognize that all techniques are simply tools for learning and never ends in themselves. Just as meditation and prayer foster the practices of careful attention and balance, of inquiry, of surrender and letting go, all of these may be directed by a skilled partner in a conscious way and applied specifically to difficult areas of our lives. We could call this psychotherapy. We must learn to recognize when our spiritual life might benefit from this. Just as deep meditation requires a skilled teacher, at times our spiritual path also requires a skilled therapist. Only a deep attention to the whole of our life can bring us the capacity to love well and live freely.

Sigmund Freud wrote that the whole purpose of his work was to enable people to learn how to love and how to give meaningful work to the earth. The German poet Rilke puts it this way: "For one human being to love another: that is perhaps the most difficult task of all . . . the work for which all other work is but preparation." If our spiritual practice does not enable us to function wisely, to love and work and connect with the whole of our life, then we must include forms of practice that heal our problems in other ways.

One last example may show how the depths of spiritual life and psychotherapy can come together. A meditation student who was a divorced single mother of a seven-year-old son spoke to me because she felt stuck in her job and depressed in her life. Her meditation practice had provided her with some tranquility and insight about loss and letting go, but I recommended she undertake psychotherapy along with it.

In the therapy she immediately had to face how much her marriage and divorce had repeated her early childhood. Her husband left her when her son was four, just as her dad had left when she was three. In her therapy she used deep breathing to open her body and feelings. As she breathed and paid attention, deep fear, grief, and feelings of abandonment arose in their turn—strong feelings she could never let herself face in meditation. With the support of the therapist, after months of learning trust and opening to her feelings, she had a session where she faced the center of the pain of her father's abandonment. She saw herself at age three standing at the top of the stairs while he turned away and walked out of her life, never to return. The pain of this abandonment had been overwhelming for her.

She felt how she carried this abandonment in her body, and saw how she replayed it over and over on the playground, in college, in her marriage. Her conclusion from that moment at age three was that she was unlovable. The therapist had her breathe and feel all her feelings. Then when she was ready, he invited her to look closely at her father— the man she believed had left her because he did not love her. As she did, she saw a man frightened and in pain. In this deep state the therapist asked her to imagine being in her father's body—what did it feel like? She felt the tension and overwhelming sorrow of an unhappy man trapped in a disastrous marriage—fleeing for his life.

Then why did he not turn to say good-bye? Did he not love her? "No," she answered with a startled sob—"No, he loved me too much, and he just could not bear to look." The therapist then had her feel all parts of the scene and imagine it in still other ways.

Finally, he had her return to her three-year-old self and ask deeply: Was her lifelong belief that she was abandoned because she was unlovable true? She saw that it was a story made up by a grieving three-year-old.

"What did it mean to be a daughter of your particular mother and father?" the therapist asked. She saw the whole identity this had created. "Is this who you are, is this your true identity?" he then asked. At this, an extraordinary space opened up. She saw how her own mind contained her parents and all other possibilities, how the consciousness of mind carried them all. Breathing and letting go, she opened further to a mind and heart of peace and pure awareness, timeless, beyond her limited identity. A profound sense of rest and healing filled her heart.

For a number of months her therapy sessions focused on the identity she had constructed and on other possibilities. Through this process her depression gradually lifted, and she brought a fresh new energy to parenting and work. Her meditation deepened greatly as well. Since then, several years later she met another meditation student and began the first healthy relationship of her life.

On hearing such a story, we might well ask the question: Are meditation and psychotherapy the same thing? Can psychotherapy lead to the same insights and freedom promised in spiritual work? To answer, we must acknowledge that there are many kinds of therapy, just as there are many kinds of meditation. Some students may be put off by old-fashioned and erroneous ideas about what therapy is. They may envision lying on a couch, free-associating and rehashing childhood stories week after week, for years on end, or being encouraged by an analyst to deepen past resentments and anger, giving vent to rage and blame. They fear it will lead only to a "rearranging of the deck chairs on the *Titanic*," adjusting the problems of their life, yet never coming to a freedom beyond their small, limited identity.

While there will always be limited kinds of therapy and mediocre practitioners, the wisest forms of therapy offer understandings much beyond this. Both Eastern and Western psychologies recognize the power of the unconscious and of past conditioning in the maintaining of fear, greed, aggression, and delusion. Good therapy addresses our underlying fear and attachment, shame and compulsion, and rigidity, providing ways to release them. Each of them is part of a false identity. The skillful means for addressing the roots of these problems may include visualization, role-playing, storytelling, the use of the arts, dream work, body work, and more. A skilled therapist will be aware of a number of maps of early childhood development and what is necessary for the structures of a healthy self to come into place, as well as the processes of awakening moral development, self-acceptance, and individuation.

Like the traditional spiritual disciplines, Jungian therapy, Reichian therapy, psychosynthesis, the transpersonal psychologies, breath and body work of many kinds, have each developed ways to open consciousness to a deep understanding of the self below the realm of thought and words. When these processes are combined with a close and conscious relationship with a therapist, they allow old patterns and fears to arise and be healed within a realm of safety, love, and trust, free of attachment. In this relationship, a sense of openness and a more transparent understanding of the self can be awakened, and the truths of spiritual life can be brought into personal practice.

Naturally, it is important to select a skillful and wise therapist. If the Buddha were your therapist, there would be no problem. Selecting a therapist requires the same conscientious attention that we have described for selecting a teacher.

The therapist should not only be skilled but also demonstrate an obvious sense of integrity and kindness. It is not so important that he or she share the particular spiritual path of the client, but that he or she respect spiritual life and the principles of attention, compassion, and forgiveness that underlie both therapy and good meditation. In the end, it is not the particular techniques of therapy but a deep relationship, conducted within awareness and compassion, that in itself is the source of healing. The touching of our hearts and minds in this way can be a profound channel to the understanding of the sacred and the healing of our limitations.

When we have for so long been judged by everyone we meet, just to look into the eyes of another who does not judge us can be extraordinarily healing. The well-known spiritual teacher Ram Dass does this in the occasional therapy he conducts, sitting, holding his hand on the heart of a client for three to five hours. As he does, he looks into their eyes and listens with his heart to whatever needs to open, and then listens to the exquisite silence beyond that. To touch and be touched by another person in this way can create a whole new sense of what is possible in our relationships. In it we can tell our story and sense our usual fears and limitations and the contracted identity of our body and mind. Then we can ask, in the presence of another, if this is who we really are. In the best of therapy, we can find the deep realization of selflessness and nonattachment that comes in any spiritual path.

Does this mean that we can turn to therapy as the solution to all our suffering and our delusions? Not at all. Like meditation, psychotherapy is sometimes successful and sometimes not. It depends on what we bring to it, our readiness and commitment. It depends on the skill of the therapist. It depends on whether it is the right approach at the right time in our life. And even when it is "successful," like the deep openings that can happen in meditation, the healing is usually only partial and simply the beginning of the process of opening that is lifelong. In this process, neither meditation nor therapy is the solution—consciousness is. Just as the insights of meditation practice are not wholly sufficient for finding our way on a spiritual journey, neither are those of therapy.

Many students come to meditation after a long course of therapy, seeking a silence, depth of understanding, and freedom that they did not find there. Yet many meditation students discover the need for a healing in therapy and turn to it after years of meditation.

It is our commitment to wholeness that matters, the willingness to unfold in every deep aspect of our being. Perhaps, with this understanding we can draw on the strength and tools of Eastern and Western psychology together in a skillful way to live a spiritual life in twentieth-century society and find our heart's release in every realm.

18

THE EMPEROR'S
NEW CLOTHES:
PROBLEMS WITH TEACHERS

*In general these problems arise when spirituality
ignores or denies our own humanity.*

*As far as Buddha Nature is concerned, there is
no difference between sinner and sage. . . . One
enlightened thought and one is a Buddha, one
foolish thought and one is an ordinary person.*
—Zen Patriarch Hui Neng

No discussion of the perils and promises of spiritual life can ignore
the problems with teachers and cults. The misuse of religious roles and
institutions by TV evangelists, ministers, healers, and spiritual teachers,
both foreign-born and Western, is a common story. As a leader of a
spiritual community, I have encountered many students who were painfully affected by the misdeeds of their teachers. I have heard such stories

about Zen masters, swamis, lamas, meditation teachers, Christian priests, nuns, and everybody in between.

William James called religion a monumental chapter in the history of human egotism. Mark Twain saw religion as what people try to believe and wish were true. The idealistic belief of students combined with the personal problems of teachers can create the phenomenon depicted in the old tale of the emperor's invisible new clothes. Because no one wants to speak about what is really going on, the misdeeds of teachers are perpetuated. Just as spiritual practice requires us to work with areas of unconsciousness in our personal lives, we must also become aware of the unconsciousness in spiritual communities as a whole and in the teachers who lead them. Otherwise we will be following ideals instead of a path with heart, and we may well end up with spiritual pain, personal wreckage, and a broken heart.

When Soto Zen founder Dogen said, "A Zen master's life is one continuous mistake," he was pointing out how mistakes and openhearted learning from them are central to spiritual life. An unintended meaning of Dogen's statement is that many large and painful mistakes have been made when teachers have at times misled their communities. Great sadness and pain have come from these mistakes, because the role of spiritual teachers is to protect the welfare and hearts of their students and guide their awakening with compassion.

The problems of teachers cannot be easily separated from the communities around them. A spiritual community will reflect the values and behavior of its teachers and will participate in the problems as well. Because spiritual community is so important, only when our community life is made a conscious part of our practice can our own heart and spiritual life become integrated and whole.

Unaddressed community problems are often such a painful area that we will need all our spiritual skills, great sensitivity, compassion, and deep commitment to the truth in order to face them and deal with them. We will need to apply the same principles as we have in our personal practice: naming the demons, healing attention, ending compartmentalization, examining insistent repetitions, and finding the seeds of transformation in our own heart of understanding.

Not all communities suffer from abuse. Wise, integrated dharma teaching can become the way of our practice if teachers and students are truly committed to conscious living. In order to discover how to do this, let us truthfully look at the problems that do arise. We can begin by naming them clearly.

NAMING THE DIFFICULTIES

There are four major areas where teachers and communities most often get into difficulties. The first centers around the misuse of power. This happens most often in communities where all the power is centered around one teacher and their wishes are followed no matter what the consequence to students. Ultimately power replaces love in the teachings. Sometimes teachers manipulate the lives of students for their own ends, decreeing marriages, divorces, life-styles, and even abusing students who will not follow their wishes. The abuse of power can be coupled with a teacher's self-aggrandizement and self-inflation and with the establishment of whole hierarchies in which there are students who are in and out of favor, those who will be "saved" and those who will not, secret cliques, intimidation, fear, and the creation of dependence and spiritual dictatorship.

When sectarianism is mixed with this misuse of power, false pride, a cult mentality, and paranoia can grow into an "us against them" isolationism. At its worst, this can end up with weapons, spies, and survivalist scenarios. In one community where such power abuses developed, I visited friends who had brought their children there to live. The teacher was famous for his spiritual powers, and thousands of students admired him, loved him, and were in awe of him. As an older, celibate yogi who had lived a life of renunciation, his virtue went unquestioned. So did his authority. Around him grew several large ashrams and an unquestioning hierarchy. Closer to the teacher were in-groups, lots of money, and spiritual glamour. After some years stories started to surface of young girls procured for the teacher and select members of his entourage, of secret bank accounts, drugs, and guns. My friends, like most of the students, were true believers who dismissed these tales out of hand. With such a teacher how could they be true? Only later, when their teenage daughter gave them firsthand accounts of many of the rumors did they see how painfully entrapped they had been. They immediately left the community for good. To this day, however, even after lots of publicity, many members of the community remain with the teacher, and as if nothing had ever happened, they never bring up these issues. While this story combines elements of many areas of abuse, the misuse of power was at the center of the problem.

Like misuse of power, money is a second difficult area. Encountering spiritual teachings can have such a powerful impact on people's lives that they want to give generously. This can bring a great deal of money into spiritual communities. If the teachers have led simple lives and are unused to great abundance, or if their desires become inflated, this can lead to either naive or conscious misuse of money. I have met teachers from Asia who became overwhelmed by American wealth and began soliciting money and expecting only the best cars and the finest of accommodations. Certain teachers of Eastern spiritual communities have overvalued their own importance and misused their community's funds and its trust, although rarely to the extent that some TV ministers have. In extreme cases, both Eastern and Western spiritual teachings have been used to make large profits, accompanied by secret bank accounts, high living, and fraudulent use of student money.

A third major area of difficulty is harm through sexuality. Sexual abuse is prevalent throughout our culture, and spiritual communities are not exempt. The teacher's role can be misused in hypocritical or clandestine sex that contradicts the vows or tenets of the teachings, in forms of exploitation, adultery, and abuse, or other behavior that endangers the physical and emotional well-being of students. I have encountered this in many ways, from Zen masters who solicit sexual favors as part of their meditation instruction sessions ("Come sit on my lap"), to swamis who have created a secret harem. One Indian teacher I knew who came from the very strictest sect, where celibacy was unquestioned, ended up having secret affairs with many of his married students. Many other lamas, Zen masters, swamis, and gurus have done the same, eventually wreaking havoc on the lives of students and their community.

Sometimes a secret sexual encounter is carried out in the name of "tantra," or in the name of special teachings. At its worst, there have been cases involving underage boys or girls or the transmission of AIDS to students. All too easily, unconscious sexuality can be mixed up with sincere teachings. One Insight Meditation teacher who recently died used to give naked meditation interviews throughout some retreats and combined his very real gift for teaching with a very confused sexuality.

A fourth area of problems with teachers and communities involves addiction to alcohol or drugs. Sometimes this is clandestine, sometimes public. (The Zen tradition has a history of famous drunken poets and masters.) Public encouragement for drinking in several communities where the teacher was alcoholic has led many students to follow suit, and certain Buddhist and Hindu communities have needed to start AA groups to begin to deal with their addiction problems. Drug addiction, though less frequent, is also an occasional problem among teachers or in communities. At its worst, clandestine addiction to alcohol and drugs is combined with misuse of sexuality and power.

Students who enter spiritual communities do not imagine they will encounter these kinds of difficulties. Idealism, fantasies, and hopes fail to include these shadow areas as part of their work. However, recent newspaper stories, articles in Eastern journals, and the tenor of our times have made students more aware of these problems, and they are beginning to address them. Power, money, sex, alcohol, and inflated egos are difficulties for humanity at large. Should spiritual teachers be exempt from them? Of course, many spiritual teachers do not abuse their role and are exemplars of virtue and compassion. But because the problems are widespread, it is important to consider how and why these problems arise in order to create more conscious communities in the future.

WHY PROBLEMS OCCUR

In general these problems arise when spirituality ignores or denies our own humanity. The training of most teachers and gurus in monasteries and ashrams in Asia or the United States is a mystical and inner training that almost never touches upon the difficult issues of power and its potential abuse. Teachers are thrown into the role of administrator, minister, guide, and confidant, in which they have tremendous responsibility and power. Yet, many of their spiritual systems and practices explicitly exclude the human areas of sexuality, money, and power from what is considered spiritual. This compartmentalization can produce teachers who are awakened and skillful in certain areas (meditation skills, koan practice, prayers, studies, blessings, and even powerful loving-kindness) but are underdeveloped in great areas of their personal lives.

Students also have to remember what we have discussed before, that there are many degrees of awakening and the mystical visions and revelations that come with it. Awakening is a process marked by both profound experiences and periods of integration. However powerful an initial opening is, it inevitably leaves many aspects of our personal life unaffected. A mystical vision or a taste of "enlightenment," an experience of satori, or awakening, is just the beginning of deep spiritual practice, but these initial experiences can be so powerful that many people begin teaching based on them alone. These unintegrated experiences can easily lead to grandiosity and inflation.

Most teachers (whether they acknowledge it or not) are only partially enlightened, only partially awake. Buddhist teachings name distinct stages of awakening, in which understanding changes first and character much later. So, after our first experiences, we can give inspiring and genuine lectures on awakening, but only much later on the path will we have transformed the roots of our deepest desires, aggressions, fears, and self-centeredness.

Nowhere is this more obvious than in the area of sexuality. The power of sexuality is enormous—it produces all of humanity; it is that creative force that dances through all of life. Yet its exclusion from much of spiritual life has been disastrous.

Hoping to bring greater openness and awareness to this area of community life, some years ago I wrote an article for *Yoga Journal* called "The Sex Lives of Gurus." I interviewed fifty-three Zen masters, lamas, swamis, and/or their senior students about their sex lives and the sexual relations of the teachers. What I discovered was quite simple. The birds do it, the bees do it, and most gurus do it too. Like any group of people in our culture, their sexual practices varied. There were heterosexuals, bisexuals, homosexuals, fetishists, exhibitionists, monogamists, and polygamists. There were teachers who were celibate and happy, and those who were celibate and miserable; there were those who were married and monogamous, and those who had many clandestine affairs; there were teachers who were promiscuous and hid it; and there were those who were promiscuous and open about it; there were teachers who made conscious and committed sexual relationships an aspect of their spiritual lives; and there were many more teachers who were no more enlightened or conscious about their sexuality than everyone else around them. For the most part the "enlightenment" of many of these teachers did not touch their sexuality.

Traditionally, in Asia, vows and moral precepts have protected teachers and students from sexual and other forms of misconduct. In Japan, Tibet, India, and Thailand, the precepts against harm by stealing, lying, sexual misconduct, or abuse of intoxicants are understood and followed by all members of the religious community. Even where certain precepts have been relaxed or modified (such as allowable drinking in China or Japan), everyone understands certain strict cultural norms for the behavior of teachers. Whole communities support this, for example, by dressing modestly to protect the teacher and student from sexual interest, by jointly knowing the appropriate limits concerning the use of intoxicants or power.

In modern America these rules are often dispensed with, and neither TV preachers nor Eastern spiritual teachers have clear rules of behavior regarding money, power, and sex. Our society brings money to teachers or offers them enormous power without any clear guidelines. Alcohol and drugs are freely used in the West without any great moral compunction; lacking a clear commitment to traditional monastic guidelines, who is to say how much a teacher should drink? Spiritual practice without any common commitment to traditional precepts and vows can lead both teachers and students astray. Communities need to clarify their vows for the long-term benefit of teachers and students alike.

The temptations of sexuality, power, money, and intoxicants are great. One forty-five-year-old Burmese master whom we brought to a large Buddhist retreat in the Southern California desert was shocked by the way Americans dressed. It was his first retreat in the West, and a heat wave led most students to wear T-shirts and shorts. For this teacher, who had only seen women dressed in long skirts and long-sleeved blouses since his ordination at age fourteen, it was like attending a burlesque show. For several days he wouldn't even look up in the meditation hall or during interviews. Though shaky, he finally adjusted somewhat, but it was still a challenge to his equanimity.

TRANSFERENCE AND PROJECTION

To further understand the difficulties of teachers and communities, we must acknowledge the intense forces of idealism and projection that operate in spiritual relationships. "Transference," as it is called in Western psychology, is the unconscious and very powerful process in which we transfer or project on to some authority figure, a man or a woman, the attributes of someone significant in our past, often our parents. Like young children, we tend to see them as all good or all bad, as we did before we could understand how complex human beings can be. We hope they will take care of all of our problems, or fear they will judge us the way our parents did, or look to them for what we wanted to get from our parents.

People project a great deal on to their teachers. A good image for understanding this is that of falling in love. We "fall in love" with spiritual teachers. We seek a place for love, perfect goodness, and perfect justice, and in longing for it so deeply, we project it on to another person. In spiritual romanticism, we imagine that our teachers are what we want them to be, instead of seeing their humanness. For students whose families and schooling taught them never to question but to hand over their power to authorities, this tendency is particularly strong.

Transference is rarely addressed in spiritual communities, whereas in psychological, therapeutic relationships it is purposely discussed so that clients can eventually come to relate realistically to the therapist and the world around them.

Transference and idealization have a powerful effect on teachers as well as students. They create a climate of unreality, and often feed the teacher's isolation. When the teacher is insecure or lonely, student projections increase these feelings. When students see a teacher as perfect, the teacher may become similarly deluded.

A teacher may be surrounded by adoring devotees and yet have no peers, no one with whom he or she can have an open and honest conversation. They may have little private life and always be on duty for the spiritual needs of the community. They will often be mother, father, confessor, healer, administrator, master, and camp counselor all rolled into one. Few people realize the extent to which teachers can be isolated in their role, especially in communities where they are the sole acknowledged leader. The process of transference increases this isolation and is one of the key reasons for teacher misconduct. After some time, the unmet needs and unfinished business in a teacher will arise and be drawn into the fire of the community.

One mild-mannered, middle-aged married man I knew was suddenly catapulted into the role of teacher after his guru in India told students to follow him. At first he taught them with admirable strength and humility, but as many more students came to see him, he got swept away in the role, and his insecurities led him to try to demonstrate psychic powers he didn't have and to seek comfort through sexual contact with his women devotees. He justified both of these behaviors as part of his "higher teaching." He had become caught in the transference.

The problem of transference is sometimes made even greater by the nature of the students who come to spiritual communities. We have already noted how often spiritual centers draw lonely and wounded people. People come to spiritual practice looking for family, looking for love, for the good mother or father they never had. They look for healing, for friendship and support, in the difficult task of living in our society. They hope their spiritual community will provide the wonderful family they never had. But if the practice of the community doesn't address the unfinished family issues and pain of its members, then these deficiencies will continue to intensify. When a number of unconscious and needy community members live and practice together, they can easily re-create their old painful family system in the spiritual center. In an unconscious way, they may live out their fear, anger, or depression in a new "spiritual" version. Margaret Mead put it this way: "No matter how many communes anybody invents, the family always creeps back."

Even when students become aware of community problems, they may be afraid to confront them or leave because they don't want to lose their "family" again, just as abused children choose to go back to their abusive parent because the feeling of belonging is so important.

But if members of a community are unable to deal with their dependence, insecurity, and other threatening issues, further dependence, hypocrisy, and isolation will result. Genuine spiritual communities must acknowledge and make conscious these difficulties. Almost every community will inevitably have some difficulties and problems. Some will be ordinary, some will involve teacher misconduct. Although the great majority of teachers are not unscrupulous, whenever idealism, inflation, compartmentalization, and confusion of teacher role and needs exist, abuse and exploitation can still result.

HOW TO WORK WITH
TEACHER-COMMUNITY PROBLEMS

HONEST QUESTIONING

Both teachers and communities contribute to areas of misconduct, and both must be part of the solution. The key to understanding these difficulties is awareness. As a first step, this involves an honest questioning. Here are some questions you can use to cut through the delusions of grandeur and spiritual romanticism when they cover serious problems.

In the spiritual community, are you asked to violate your own sense of ethical conduct or integrity? Is there a dual standard for the community versus the guru and a few people around him? Are there secrets, rumors of difficulty? Do key members misuse sexuality, money, or power? Are they mostly asking for your money? Are they asking for your body? Are you not allowed to hang out with your old friends? Do you feel dependent? Addicted? Is the practice humorless? (This is an important sign.) Does the community have a heaviness and an antilife feeling about it? Are you asked to believe blindly without being able to see for yourself? Is there something powerful going on that may not really be loving? Is there more focus on the institution and membership than on practices that lead to liberation? Is there a sense of intolerance? When you look at the oldest and most senior students, are they happy and mature? Do they have a place to graduate to, to teach, to express their own dharma, or are people always kept in the role of students and children?

Look to see if the community is based on sectarianism or separation or has a fundamentalist quality to it. This may be difficult to do if we have fallen in love with a community or a teacher. We may feel intoxicated that we are the chosen, the elected ones, the ones who really see better than all the rest of those on earth. Yet this belief inevitably brings isolation, addiction, and a loss of genuine wisdom and compassion.

The vehemence with which students proclaim the "one true way" is usually a sign of unacknowledged insecurity; there is often great unconscious or hidden fear or doubt that underlies it. There is a story told of the Persian St. Rabia. One day Rabia was sick, and her friends came to visit. They began denigrating all the things of the world, to show how holy they truly were. She laughed at them. "You must be pretty interested in this world," she said. "Otherwise, you wouldn't talk about it so much. Whoever breaks the merchandise has to have bought it first." The claim that only some small chosen set of people will awaken or will be liberated on this earth is never true. Awakening is the birthright of every human being, every creature. There is no one right way.

Each of us must learn to become our own authority. This and this alone will liberate us. Remember the Buddha's advice to the confused villagers of Kalamas. We must look for ourselves at our own lives, regardless of the views of others, and only when that practice is clearly beneficial should we follow it. With a loving heart we must ask: Am I becoming more isolated, obnoxious, lost, or addicted? Am I increasing my suffering? Are clarity and freedom growing in me? Is there a greater capacity to know what is true for myself, to be compassionate and tolerant?

In answering these questions, we must do something even more difficult than posing them. We must tell the truth to ourselves, and we must speak the truth in our communities. To tell the truth in a community is to make the community itself conscious. In these situations, it becomes a great practice to name the demons and to learn to speak out loud with both compassion and clarity. We must speak with the teacher to see if they understand and will be part of righting the difficulty. We must insist that exploitive behavior be stopped. In this spirit, many years ago I had to fly to Asia on behalf of our board of directors, to directly question one of our senior teachers when he was unwilling to respond to the accusations of his sexual misconduct in America. We insisted that he speak truthfully to our community and teachers, explaining, apologizing, and reaffirming his ethical standards in order to be included again in our community. In some communities to question the guru or lama, the master or priest, is considered unspiritual or ungrateful, and to question the direction of the community is considered a sign of delusion and immaturity. Yet we must be willing to ask our community, "How are we lost, attached, and addicted, and how are we benefiting, awakening, and opening?" Each troubling area of belief, any illusions about the practice and teacher, exploitive behavior, or unclear moral code must be addressed. Speaking openly and honestly with the well-being of the community in our heart is extraordinarily beneficial. It is healing and transforming. Naming the demons with honesty and kindness has the power to dispel illusion.

Addressing these problems can be so painful and explosive that often they are poorly handled. Angry or secret meetings filled with blame, fear, and paranoia benefit no one. The spirit of mercy and concern for all is critical. It may take a while for a community to learn this. Getting the support of wise elders from outside the community to create a safe container for meeting is often necessary if understanding and restitution are to follow. Still, if the teacher is somewhat open-minded, the teacher and community will gradually mature together.

To do this, teachers have to be able to deal with the underlying roots of problems in themselves, whether old wounds, cultural and family history, isolation, addiction, or their own grandiosity. In some communities masters have ended up attending AA meetings or seeking counseling. In others, decision-making councils were formed to end the isolation of the teacher.

As we have said, practicing with the difficulties of teachers and communities calls on the same fundamental principles that we have learned in our meditation. We must repeatedly name the difficulties, discover the roots of insistent problems, and acknowledge the fears operating in everyone. We must bring awareness and honesty, coupled with a deep compassion for ourselves and all concerned, in order that we may learn from these situations as our practice.

TAKE WHAT'S GOOD

When dealing with the humanness and the complexity of teachers, it is helpful to keep a few other principles in mind. One is called *take what's good*.

After studying with my first teacher, Achaan Chah, who was impeccable in conduct, in many ways a model guru, gracious, insightful, and loving, I went to study with a famous old Burmese master for a year-long retreat. He was a grouchy old slob who threw rocks at the dogs, smoked Burmese cigars, and spent the morning reading the paper and talking with the loveliest of the young nuns.

In private interviews he was a very fine teacher. After training thousands of students, he truly was a skillful guide to inner meditation. But when I saw him in other situations, I became filled with doubts, thinking,

"He couldn't be enlightened." It took weeks of inner struggle before it dawned on me that he was a great meditation teacher but otherwise a poor role model. I realized that I could take what was beneficial and not buy the whole package. I didn't have to imitate this man. Then I became rather fond of him. I think of him now with affection and gratitude. I wouldn't want to be like him, but I'm grateful for the many wonderful things he taught me.

RECOGNIZE THE HALO EFFECT

In order to take what's good, we need to recognize a second principle of wise relationship and disentangle ourselves from the *halo effect*. The halo effect is the unexamined assumption that if a meditation master or spiritual teacher is good in one area, they must be good in all areas, that if they know about inner vision, they will equally know about child-rearing and car mechanics. It is easy to see this fantasy enacted repeatedly in spiritual communities.

One starry-eyed couple asked their teacher, a famous Tibetan lama, about childbirth. This lama was a celibate, raised in a monastery, who really knew nothing about it. But he gave them some advice he had heard from Tibetan mountain folklore. Based on this, they tried a home delivery up in the mountains with disastrous results—both mother and child nearly died.

Another student followed a charismatic Indian guru whose powerful love and teachings brought great joy and peace into his life. The student was a gay man, who had lived in a caring and committed partnership for more than ten years, and when the guru later stated that all homosexuality was a terrible sin that leads to hell, the student's life was nearly destroyed. His relationship was torn apart, and the secret guilt and self-loathing that had plagued this man throughout his childhood returned. Finally, with outside help, the student came to see that while his guru might bring him visions and wonderful meditation teachings, he was really quite ignorant about homosexuality. Only when he realized this, was he able to hold both the teachings he so valued and his own life with equal loving-kindness.

We can see over and over again how one dimension of life does not automatically bring wisdom in other dimensions. Every teacher and every practice has its strong points and its weaknesses.

KNOW THAT POWER IS NOT WISDOM

To further sort out the gold from the dross in spiritual life we must distinguish between wisdom and power. Powers can include psychic ability, special spiritual energy, creating visions for students, or just plain charisma. There are many powerful people who are not wise at all. There are many wise people who have no special powers other than their love and openness. Don't be fooled. Sometimes these two qualities come together in a wise, powerful teacher, but often they are confused. A powerful teacher may be wise and loving or not—the powers prove nothing. When the teacher serves the dharma, the divine, the truth, then things go well for everyone, but when the powers are used to serve the teacher, this is a formula for problems.

ESTABLISH CLEAR ETHICAL GUIDELINES

The most obvious principle in the maintenance of a wise spiritual community is the establishment of clear ethical guidelines that are followed by all. Each great spiritual tradition has some version of these. The question is: Are these precepts acknowledged, valued, and followed? One Zen master told me that the moral precepts were very important for students to follow, but, of course, Zen masters didn't need to bother with them since they were "free." You can imagine what troubles later visited that community.

If in your own community the guidelines for teachers and students are not yet clear, ask about them, figure them out. If you need to, get outside help from respected elders of your tradition or wise friends of the community. In the Insight Meditation community, we have formal guidelines, for students and teachers alike, that follow the five Buddhist precepts. They explicitly address the common areas of teacher misconduct and include commitment to refrain from harm to others through misuse of money, sexuality, or intoxicants. They also establish an ethics council and method for addressing difficulties that involve students or teachers. For a sample of such guidelines see the Appendix.

In the traditional rules for Buddhist monasteries, the resolution of ethics violations is seen as a healing process, one of seeking restitution and reconciliation. Sometimes confessions and apologies to the community are needed, sometimes vows must be taken again, sometimes a period of penance and reflection is called for. In creating guidelines, include a clear process for how to address misconduct, a place for honest words, for compassionate and ongoing support for ethical standards. Create regular community meetings, ethics ombudsmen, and the channels and skills of useful communication.

If in trying to bring form to the emperor's new clothes I've made these issues sound straightforward or easily dealt with, I assure you they're not! These can be the most painful and stormy areas of a community's life, and they ask for enormous perseverance and wisdom of everyone involved. Only with this spirit will healing prevail.

THE PLACE OF FORGIVENESS

Inevitably in working with the mixed difficulties of communities, teachers, and ourselves, we will be asked for a certain measure of forgiveness. Forgiveness does not condone the behavior of students, community members, or teachers who have caused suffering, nor does it mean that we will not openly tell the truth and take strong action to prevent future abuse. In the end, forgiveness simply says that we will not put someone out of our hearts. From the perspective of forgiveness, we recognize that we have all been wronged and we have all caused suffering to others. No one is exempt. When we look into our hearts and we see what we cannot forgive, we also see how we believe the person who was wrong is different from us. But is their confusion, fear, pain really different from our own?

Years ago, as our Buddhist community was going through a painful period dealing with a teacher who had gotten sexually involved with a student during a celibate retreat, we had a series of confused and angry meetings. We were trying to understand how this had happened, and what we needed to do about it. But these important questions were often asked with a tone of outrage and indignation. Then in the middle of one of the most difficult community meetings, one man stood up and asked a question of the group in a tone of great kindness. "Who among us in this room," he asked, "has not made an idiot of himself or herself in relation to sexuality?" The room broke into smiles as everyone realized we were all in it together. It was at that point that we began to let go of some of the blame and look for a wise and compassionate response to everyone concerned in this painful circumstance.

LEAVING A COMMUNITY

Even while attempting to bring understanding and forgiveness to these problems, sometimes the situations we encounter are so bad, our best response is to leave. Some teachers and some communities become so grandiose, so unconsciously duplicitous and fearful, that they are unwilling or unable to face their difficulties. Some unhealthy systems are exploitive and abusive beyond repair. Sometimes we sense the danger signals just after we join. Sometimes only later, in the face of real problems and persistent denial by the teachers and community, do we know we must move on.

As Thomas Merton warns us:

> The most dangerous man in the world is the contemplative who is guided by nobody. He trusts his own visions. He obeys the attractions of an inner voice, but will not listen to other men. He identifies the will of God with his own heart. . . . And if the sheer force of his own self-confidence communicates itself to other people and gives them the impression that he really is a saint, such a man can wreck a whole city or a religious order or even a nation. The world is covered with scars that have been left in its flesh by visionaries like these.

When we leave a spiritual community in the midst of difficulties, or when the teacher and community are unwilling to deal with their problems, we will experience extraordinary pain. In the course of our spiritual practice, our hearts are likely to be broken in a number of ways, but this betrayal is one of the most challenging. When a teacher we have trusted or a community we love proves to be hypocritical and harmful, it touches the deepest sense of loss and rage in many students. We feel as if we are young children again, reexperiencing divorce or the death of a parent, or our first experience of injustice or betrayal. For those of us who have felt the intensity of such failure by a teacher or a community, we might ask ourselves, "How old do I feel inside when I react to this loss?" Often we feel very young, and we will see that our intense feelings are not just about the current situation but point to what is unresolved in our own past. Perhaps this feeling is even part of a pattern of abuse or abandonment we have repeated many times in our life. Perhaps we have given ourselves away before or at other times hoped to be saved. If so, we must ask ourselves some hard questions. What attracted me to this system? Didn't I suspect what was going on? How did I participate in the unconsciousness?

Disillusionment is an important part of the spiritual path. It is a powerful and fiery gate, one of the purest teachers of awakening, independence, and letting go that we will ever encounter. To be disillusioned is to be stripped of our hopes, imaginings, and expectations. But while it opens our eyes, the resulting pain all too often closes our hearts. The great challenge of disillusionment is to keep our eyes open and still remain connected with the great heart of compassion. Whether our heart is torn open in the dark night of our inner practice or the dark night of community difficulties, we can use this experience to learn a deeper consciousness and a wiser love.

The process of healing from spiritual betrayal and loss can take a very long time. After the rage and grief, there comes a tremendous emptiness in the heart, as if something has been wrenched out of us. However, this emptiness is not just the result of betrayal by the teacher or the group. It has been there all along in the ways we may have betrayed ourselves. Finally, we have to come back to face ourselves and feel the holes we have tried to fill up from the outside. We have to find our own Buddha nature and discover in these difficulties the lesson that we really needed to learn.

For some people, disillusionment and difficulty, though very hard, are what they most needed before they could come back to themselves. I do not mean that we should seek to be abused, but sometimes it takes a misguided or a false teacher to create a wise student. Even if students feel they have lost their faith, the truth is we can never lose our faith— we just give it away for a while. "I lost my heart," we say. We gave our heart away for a while, but our heart, like our faith and the eternal truth, is always here with us.

The truth doesn't belong to the Buddha or to any master. As Achaan Chah used to say, "The dharma, the True Path, is like underground water. Any time we dig we will find it there."

The crucible of our relationship with spiritual communities and teachers can transform our initial idealism into wisdom and compassion. We will shift from seeking perfection to expressing our wisdom and love. Then we may come to understand the remarkable statement of Suzuki Roshi when he said, "Strictly speaking, there is no such thing as an enlightened person. There is only enlightened activity." Because liberation can never be possessed, for anyone to think, "I am enlightened," is a contradiction in terms. Wisdom, compassion, and awakening are never an attainment, a thing of the past. If they are not alive here in ourselves and our communities, then our task is obvious. Take whatever is in front of us, here and now, and in our hearts transform that too into wisdom and compassion.

MEDITATION: REFLECTING ON THE SHADOW OF YOUR FORM OF PRACTICE

Just as every community has a shadow, every set of teachings will also have and areas of shadow, aspects of life that they do not illuminate wisely. Every style of teaching will also produce its near enemy, the way that particular teaching can be most easily misused or misunderstood. It can be useful to take some time to reflect on the strengths and limitations of the practice you have chosen to follow. You can then consider to what extent these are issues in your own spiritual life. The following examples hint at the possible shadows you may encounter.

Insight Meditation and similar Buddhist practices can lead to quietude, to withdrawal from and fear of the world. The emptiness taught in Zen and nondualist Vedanta can lead to a related problem, to being disconnected and ungrounded. Any form of idealistic, otherworldly teaching that sees life on earth as a dream or focuses on higher realms can lead one to live with complacency, amorality, and indifference. Physical practices such as hatha yoga can lead to bodily perfection instead of awakening of the heart. Kundalini yoga can lead students to become experience junkies in search of exciting sensations of body and mind rather than liberation. Those such as Krishnamurti and others who teach against any discipline or method of practice can lead people to remain intellectual about spiritual life without providing any deep inner experience. Practices that involve a great deal of study can do the same. Moralistic practices with strong rules about what is pure and what is not can reinforce low self-esteem or lead to rigidity and self-righteousness. Practices of tantra can become an excuse to act out desires as a pseudo form of spiritual practice. Devotional practices can leave clarity and discriminating wisdom undeveloped. Powerful gurus can make us think we can't do it ourselves. Practices of joy and celebration such as Sufi dancing may leave students lacking an understanding of the inevitable loss and sorrows of life. Practices that emphasize suffering can miss the joy of life.

As you reflect on these shadows, consider your own spiritual path and tradition. Let yourself sense its strengths and weaknesses, its gifts and the ways it can be misused. Notice where you may be caught and what more you might need. Remember that there is nothing wrong with any of these practices per se. They are simply tools for opening and awakening. Each can be used skillfully or unknowingly misused. As you mature in your own spiritual life, you can take responsibility for your own practice and reflect wisely on where you are entangled and what can awaken you to freedom in every realm.

19

KARMA: THE HEART IS OUR GARDEN

The heart is our garden, and along with each action there is an intention that is planted like a seed. We can use a sharp knife to cut someone, and if our intention is to do harm, we will be a murderer. We can perform an almost identical action, but if we are a surgeon, the intention is to heal and save a life. The action is the same, yet depending on its purpose or intention, it can be either a terrible act or a compassionate act.

We are called upon to act night and day, alone or in community, in wonderful circumstances or confronting difficulties. How can we put our inner understanding into practice, and how can we know when our actions are wise? The key to wise action is an understanding of karma.

Karma has become a common word in our language. There are many examples of this. We say, "It's his karma," or "He'll get his karma." I even heard an ad on the radio for an automobile dealership that was selling cars in Berkeley at a low price last season because, they said, it was their karma to do so, and: "It's your karma to come in and get one of these good deals." One local paper even advertised a $15.95 service to ensure better karma and more money in the next life, "The Reincarnation Next Lifetime Guarantee" (Guaranteed Wealth or Your Money Back). This is the level to which the idea and use of the word karma has deteriorated in our culture.

The Avatamsaka Sutra is the Buddhist text that describes the laws that govern the thousands of possible realms of the universe—realms of pleasure and realms of pain, realms created by fire, by water, by metal, by clouds, or even by flowers. Each universe, the sutra tells us, follows the same basic law: In each of these realms if you plant a mango seed, you get a mango tree, and if you plant an apple seed, you will get an apple tree. It is so in every realm that exists in the world of creative phenomena.

The law of karma describes the way that cause and effect govern the patterns that repeat themselves throughout all life. Karma means that nothing arises by itself. Every experience is conditioned by that which precedes it. Thus our life is a series of interrelated patterns. The Buddhists say that understanding this is enough to live wisely in the world.

Karma exists at many different levels. Its patterns govern the large forms of the universe, such as the gravitational forces of galaxies, and the smallest, subtlest ways that our human choices affect our moment-to-moment state of mind. At the level of physical life, for example, if one looks at an oak tree, one can see "oak tree" manifesting in several different stages of life's patterns. In one stage of the oak tree pattern, an oak tree exists as an acorn; at a subsequent stage it exists as a sapling; in another stage as a large tree; and in yet another, as the green acorn growing on that large tree. Strictly speaking, there is no such thing as a definitive "oak tree." There is only the oak tree pattern through which certain elements follow the cyclical law of karma: a particular arrangement of water, minerals, and the energy of sunlight that changes it from acorn to sapling to large tree over and over again.

The tendencies and habits of our mind are similarly karmic patterns that we repeat over and over, like the acorn and the oak tree. When the Buddha spoke of this, he asked, "Which do you think is larger, the highest mountain on earth or the pile of bones that represents the lives that you have lived over and over in every realm governed by the patterns of your own karma? Greater, my friends, is the pile of bones than the highest mountain on earth."

We live in a sea of conditioning patterns that we repeat over and over, yet we rarely notice this process. We can understand the workings of karma in our lives most clearly by looking at this process of cause and effect in our ordinary activities and by observing how the repetitive patterns of our own mind affect our behavior. For instance, being born in a certain culture at a certain time, we learn certain habit patterns. If we are born into a taciturn fishing culture, we learn to be silent. If we grow up in a more expressive Mediterranean culture, we may express our feelings with gestures and loud talk. Our social karma—parental, school, and linguistic conditioning—creates whole patterns of consciousness that determine the way we experience reality and the way we express ourselves.

These patterns and tendencies are often much stronger than our conscious intentions. Whatever our circumstances, it is old habits that will create the way we live. I remember visiting my grandmother in an apartment building for seniors. Life there was quiet and sedentary for most residents. The only place where anything happened was in the lobby, and interested residents would go there to watch who came in and went out. In the lobby, there were two groups of people. One group regularly sat there enjoying themselves. They played cards, they said hello to everyone who came by. They had a pleasant and friendly relationship with one another and with the circumstances around them. In another part of the lobby were people who liked to complain. For them there was something wrong with everyone who came through the door. In between visitors they complained, "Did you taste the terrible food they served us today?" "Did you see what they did to the bulletin board?" "Have you heard what they're doing with our rent?" "Do you know what my son said the last time he was here?" This was a whole group of people whose main relation to life was to complain about it. Each group brought to the building a pattern they had lived with for many years.

Long-repeated circumstances and mental attitudes become the condition for what we call "personality." When Lama Trungpa Rinpoche was asked what was reborn in our next lives, he joked, "Your bad habits." Our personalities become conditioned according to past causes. Sometimes this is apparent, but very often habits that stem from the distant and unremembered past go unnoticed.

In Buddhist psychology, the karmic conditioning of our personality is categorized according to three basic unconscious forces and automatic tendencies of our mind. There are *desire types*, whose most frequent states of mind are associated with grasping, with wanting, not having enough. There are *aversion types*, whose most common state of mind is to push away the world through judgment, dislike, aversion, and hatred. Then there are the *confused types*, whose most fundamental states are lethargy, delusion, and disconnection, not knowing what to do about things.

You can test which type predominates in you by observing how you typically enter a room. If your conditioning is most strongly that of desire and wanting, you will tend to look around a room and see what you like about it, what you can get; you will see what you are attracted to; you will notice what is beautiful; you will appreciate a beautiful flower arrangement; you will like the way certain people are dressed; you will find someone sexually interesting or imagine that others would be stimulating people to know. If you are an aversion type, you tend to enter a room and, instead of first seeing what you want, you see what is wrong: "It's too loud. I don't like the wallpaper. People aren't dressed right. I don't like the way the whole thing is organized." If you are a confused personality, you may walk into a room, look around, and not know how to relate, wondering, "What is going on here? How do I fit in? What am I supposed to do?"

This primary conditioning is actually a very powerful process. It grows into the forces that bring whole societies into war, create racism, and drive the lives of many around us. When we first encounter in ourselves the forces of desire and aversion, of greed and hatred, we might think that they are harmless, a bit of wanting, of dislike, a bit of confusion. However, as we observe our conditioning, we see that fear, grasping, and avoidance are in fact so compelling that they govern many aspects of our personality. Through observing these forces we can see how the patterns of karma operate.

When we begin to look closely at our personalities in meditation, our first impulse is often to try to get rid of our old habits and defenses. Initially most people find their own personality difficult, unpleasant, even unsavory. The same thing can happen when we look at the human body. It is beautiful at the right distance, at the right age, and in the right light, but the closer we look, the more flawed it becomes. When we see this, we try dieting, jogging, skin care, exercise, and a vacation to improve our body. But even though these may be beneficial, we are still basically stuck with the body we were born with. Personalities are even more difficult to alter than our bodies, but the purpose of spiritual life is not to get rid of our personality. Some of it was there when we were born, some has been conditioned by our life and culture, and no matter what, we can't do without it. On this earth we all have a body and a personality.

Our task is to learn about this very body and mind and awaken in the midst of it. Understanding the play of karma is one aspect of awakening. If we are not aware, our life will simply follow the pattern of our past habits over and over. But if we can awaken, we can make conscious choices in how we respond to the circumstances of our life. Our conscious response will then create our future karma. We may or may not be able to change our outer circumstances, but with awareness we can always change our inner attitude, and this is enough to transform our life. Even in the worst external circumstances, we can choose whether we meet life from fear and hatred or with compassion and understanding.

Transforming the patterns of our life is always done in our heart. To understand how to work with the karmic patterns in our life, we must see that karma has two distinct aspects—that which is the result of our past and that karma which our present responses are creating for our future. We receive the results of past action; this we cannot change. But as we respond in the present, we also create new karma. We sow the karmic seeds for new results. The word *karma* in Sanskrit is usually paired with another word, *vipaka—karma vipaka. Karma* means "action," and *vipaka* means "result."

In dealing with each moment of our experience, we use either skillful (awakened) or unskillful (unconscious) means. Unskillful responses such as grasping, aversion, and confusion all inevitably create more suffering and painful karma; skillful responses, based on awareness, love, and openness, will inevitably lead to well-being and happiness. Through skillful means, we can create new patterns that transform our life. Even the powerful patterns based on grasping, aversion, and delusion have within them the seeds of skillful responses. Desire for pleasure can be changed into a natural and compassionate action that brings beauty into the society and world around us. The judgmental-aversion temperament can, through awareness, become transformed into what is called *discriminating wisdom:* a clarity associated with compassion, a wisdom that sees clearly through all the delusions of the world, and uses the clarity of truth to help and heal. Even confusion and the tendency to be disconnected from life can be transformed into a wise and spacious equanimity, a wise and compassionate balance that embraces all things with peace and understanding.

Traditionally, karma has often been discussed in Buddhist teachings in terms of death and rebirth. The Buddha told of a vision on the night of his enlightenment in which he saw thousands of his own past lives, as well as those of many other beings, all dying and being reborn according to the lawful karmic results of their past actions. But we do not need to see with Buddha's vision to understand karma. The same karmic laws he described act in our lives from moment to moment. We can see how death and birth take place each day. Each day we are born into new circumstances and experiences as if it were a new life. In fact, this happens in each moment. We die every moment and we are reborn the next.

It is taught that there are four kinds of karma at the moment of death, or in any moment of transition: *weighty karma, proximate karma, habitual karma,* and *random karma.* Each represents a stronger karmic tendency than the one that follows it. The traditional image used to explain this is one of cows in a field when the gate is opened. Weighty karma is like a bull. It is the force from the most powerful good or bad deeds we have done. If a bull is there and you open the gate, the bull always goes through first. Proximate karma is the cow that is nearest the gate. This refers to the state of mind that is present at the moment of transition. If the gate is open and there is no bull present, the cow that is closest goes through. If no cow is particularly near the gate, habitual karma arises. This is the force of our ordinary habit. Without some strong state of mind present, the cow that usually goes first will go through the gate first. Finally, random karma arises if there is no strong habit operating. If no stronger force arises, our karma will be the random result of any number of past conditions.

As each action (or birth) arises, there are forces that sustain it and forces that finally bring it to an end. These karmic forces are described by the image of a garden. The seed that is planted is the *causative karma.* Fertilizing and watering the seed, taking care of the plants, is called *sustaining karma.* When difficulties arise, this is *counteractive karma* portrayed by a drought: even if we plant a viable seed and fertilize it, if there is no water, it will wither away. Then finally, *destructive karma* is like fire or gophers in the garden, which burn it or eat it all up.

This is the nature of life in every realm, in every creative circumstance. One condition follows another, yet all of this is subject to change. The karma of our outer circumstances can change with the flick of a horse's tail. In any day, great good fortune or death can come to any one of us.

What brings the karmic result from the patterns of our actions is not our action alone. As we *intend* and then act, we create karma: so another key to understanding the creation of karma is becoming aware of *intention.* The heart is our garden, and along with each action there is an intention that is planted like a seed. The result of the patterns of our karma is the fruit of these seeds.

For example, we can use a sharp knife to cut someone, and if our intention is to do harm, we will be a murderer. This leads to certain karmic results. We can perform an almost identical action, using a sharp knife to cut someone, but if we are a surgeon, the intention is to heal and save a life. The action is the same, yet depending on its purpose or intention, it can be either a terrible act or a compassionate act.

We can study the power of intention to create karma in our day-to-day life. We can start by paying attention to our many actions that arise throughout the day in response to problems. In an automatic way, we may ignore difficult circumstances or respond critically or harshly. We may try to protect or defend our own way. In all of these cases, the intention in our heart will be bound up with grasping, aversion, or delusion, creating a karma of suffering in the future that will bring back an equivalent response.

When these difficult circumstances arise in our life, if we instead bring to them the desire to understand, to learn, to let go, or to bring harmony and create peace, we will speak and act with a different intention. Our actions might be very similar, our words might be similar, but if our intention is to create peace or bring harmony, it will create a very different kind of karmic result. This is easy to see in close business or personal relationships. We can say the same sentence to our partner or friend, and if the unspoken spirit in saying it is, "I love you and I want us to understand what is going on," we will get one kind of response. If we say the same thing with an underlying attitude of blame, defense, and criticism, with the slightest tone of, "What's wrong with you?" it will create a whole different direction in the conversation and could easily escalate into a fight.

Two short dialogues from *Do I Have to Give Up Me to Be Loved by You* by psychologists Jordan and Margaret Paul illustrate this.

DIALOGUE NO. 1:

JIM: (distant, voice slightly hard) "What's wrong? . . ."
MARY: "Nothing."
Jim then plunks himself down in front of the TV and nothing more is
   said. The distance between them continues, even widens.

DIALOGUE NO. 2:

JIM: (genuinely soft and curious) "You seem upset. What's wrong?"
MARY: (still closed and hard) "Nothing."
JIM: "Look, hon, I hate this distance. It makes me feel awful. Have I
   done anything that hurts you?"
MARY: (angry and accusing) "Yes. How come you told Sam and Annie

we'd go out with them Saturday and you never even asked me or told me about it? . . ."

JIM: "Mary, I'd like to talk about this but it's hard to understand what the problem is when you're yelling at me. Do you think we could just talk about it for a while?"

MARY: "Yes, I guess we do need to talk about it."

The intention or attitude that we bring to each situation of life determines the kind of karma that we create. Day to day, moment to moment, we can begin to see the creation of the patterns of karma based on the intentions in our heart. When we pay attention, it becomes possible to become more aware of our intentions and the state of our heart as they arise in conjunction with the actions and speech that are our responses. Usually we are unconscious of them.

For example, we may decide to stop smoking cigarettes, then partway through the day the desire to have a cigarette may arise and we find ourselves reaching in our pocket, pulling out a pack, taking out a cigarette, lighting it up to inhale. All of a sudden we wake up and remember, "Oh, I was going to stop smoking." While on automatic pilot and without awareness, we went through all of the habitual motions of reaching for a cigarette and lighting it. It is not possible to change the patterns of our behavior or create new karmic conditions until we become present and awake at the *beginning* of the action. Otherwise it has already happened. As the old saying goes, "This is like closing the door after the horse has left the barn."

The development of awareness in meditation allows us to become mindful enough or conscious enough to recognize our heart and intentions as we go through the day. We can be aware of the different states of fear, wanting, confusion, jealousy, and anger. We can know when forgiveness or love or generosity is connected with our actions. When we know what state is in our heart, we can begin to have a choice about the patterns or conditions we will follow, the kind of karma that we create.

Try working with this kind of awareness in your life. Practice it with your speech. Pay very careful attention and notice the state of your heart, the intention, as you speak about even the smallest matter. Is your intention to be protected, to grasp, to defend yourself? Is your intention to open out of concern, compassion, or love? Once you've noticed the intention, then become aware of the response elicited. Even if it is a difficult response, stay with the skillful intention repeatedly for a while and observe the kinds of responses it brings.

If your intention was unskillful or unkind, try changing it and see what happens after a while. At first you may only experience the results of your previously defensive attitude. But persist in your good intention and observe the kinds of responses it eventually elicits. To understand how karma works you need only look at your most personal relationships or your simplest interactions. You can pick a specific relationship or a specific place and experiment there. Try responding only when your heart is open and kind. When you don't feel this way, wait and let the difficult feelings pass. As the Buddha instructed, let your speech and actions arise gently, with kindly intent, in due season, and to their benefit. As you cultivate kind and skillful intention, you can then practice it at the gas station or the supermarket, in the workplace, or in traffic. The intention that we bring creates the pattern that results.

As we become more aware of our own intention and action, karma shows itself to us more clearly. Karmic fruit even seems to come more quickly, maybe simply because we notice it. As we pay attention, the fruit of whatever we do, both skillfully and unskillfully, seems to manifest more quickly. As we study this law of cause and effect we will see that whenever we or someone else acts in a way that is based on grasping, hatred, prejudice, judgment, or delusion, the results will inevitably bring some suffering. We begin to see how those who harm us also create inevitable suffering for themselves. It makes us want to pay closer attention, and as we observe the law of cause and effect we can see directly the skillful and unskillful states in our own heart.

Attention to karma shows us how lives are shaped by the intention in the heart. When asked to explain the law of karma in the simplest way, Ruth Denison, a well-known vipassana teacher, put it this way: "Karma means you don't get away with nothin'." Every day we are sowing the seeds of karma. There's only one place where we can exercise any influence on karma, and that is in the intention of our actions. In fact, there is only one person's karma that we can change in the whole world—our own. But what we do with our heart affects the whole world. If we can untie the karmic knots in our own heart, because we are all interconnected, we inevitably bring healing for the karma of another. As one ex–prisoner of war said when visiting a fellow survivor, "Have you forgiven those who imprisoned you yet?" The survivor said, "No, I haven't. Never." The first veteran said, "Then somehow they still have you in prison."

When my wife and I were traveling in India some years ago, she had a very painful vision of one of her brothers dying. At first I thought it was part of a death-rebirth process in her meditation. The following day she had a second vision of her brother as a spirit guide, coming along with two Native Americans to offer her support and guidance. About one week later a telegram arrived at the ashram where we were staying on Mount Abu in Rajisthan. Sadly, it told my wife that her brother had in fact died in the fashion that she had seen in her vision. The telegram was dated the day she had her vision. How could she see her brother's death halfway around the world? She could because we are all connected. And because this is so, changing one heart affects all of our hearts, and the karma of all the world.

At one retreat I taught some years ago, a woman was wrestling with the painful results of early abuse in her life. She'd been angry, depressed, and grieving for many years. She had worked in therapy and meditation through a long process to heal these wounds. Finally in this retreat she came to a place of forgiveness for the person who had abused her. She wept with deep forgiveness, not for the act, which can never be condoned, but because she no longer wished to carry the bitterness and hatred in her heart.

She left the retreat and returned home and found a letter waiting in her mailbox. It had been written by the man who had abused her, with whom she had no contact for fifteen years. While in many other cases, abusers will deny their actions to the last, in spite of forgiveness, something had changed this man's mind. He wrote, "For some reason I felt compelled to write to you. I've been thinking about you so much this week. I know I caused you great harm and suffering and brought great suffering on myself as well. But I simply want to ask your forgiveness. I don't know what else I can say." Then she looked at the date at the top of the letter. It was written the same day she completed her inner work of forgiveness.

There's a famous Hindu story of two kingdoms that were each being governed in the name of Krishna. Looking down from heaven, Lord Krishna decided to visit them and see what was being done in his name. So he went and appeared before the court of one king. This king was known to be wicked, cruel, miserly, and jealous. Lord Krishna appeared in his court in a blaze of celestial light. The king bowed to him and said, "Lord Krishna, you've come to visit." Krishna said, "Yes. I wish to give you a task. I would like you to travel throughout the provinces of your kingdom and see if you can find one person who is truly good." This king went out through all his provinces. He talked to high castes and low castes, to priests and farmers, to artisans and healers. Finally he came back to his throne room and waited for Lord Krishna to reappear. When Lord Krishna arrived, he bowed down and said, "My Lord, I've done your bidding. I've gone from low to high throughout my kingdom, but I have not found one truly good person. Though some of them performed many good deeds, when I got to know each person, even their best actions ended up being selfish, self-interested, conniving, or deluded. Not a single good person could I find."

Then Lord Krishna went to the other court ruled by a famous queen named Dhammaraja. This queen was known to be kind, gracious, loving, and generous. Here again Lord Krishna set her to a task. "I would like you to go throughout your kingdom and find one truly evil person for me." So Queen Dhammaraja went through her provinces speaking to low castes and high castes, farmers, carpenters, nurses, and priests. After a long search she returned to her court, whereupon Lord Krishna reappeared. She bowed and said, "My Lord, I have done as you asked, but I have failed my task. I have gone throughout the land, and I've seen many people who act unskillfully, who are misguided, and act in ways that create suffering. Yet when I really listened, not one truly evil person could I find, only those who are misguided. Their actions always came from fear, delusion, and misunderstanding."

In both kingdoms the circumstances of life were governed by the spirit of the rulers, and what they encountered was a reflection of their heart. As we pay attention and understand our own heart and grow in the skillful responses of wisdom and compassion, we do our part to make the whole of the earth peaceful. Through our work and creativity, we can bring about beneficial circumstances outwardly in our life. However, most of the great things that happen to us, where we are born, when we die, the great changes that sweep our lives and the world around us, are the result of ancient and powerful karmic patterns. These we cannot change. They come to us like the wind and the weather. The only weather forecast that we can guarantee is that conditions will continue to change.

In understanding karma, we must answer a simple question: How do we relate to these changing conditions? What type of universe we create, what we choose to plant, what we bring forth in the garden of our heart, will create our future. The Buddha begins his teachings in the great Dhammapada by saying:

We are what we think.
All that we are arises with our thoughts.
With our thoughts we make the world.
Speak or act with an impure mind
And trouble will follow you
As the wheel follows the ox that draws the cart.

We are what we think.
All that we are arises with our thoughts.
With our thoughts we make the world.
Speak or act with a pure mind
And happiness will follow you
As your shadow, unshakable.

In the long run we possess nothing on this earth, not even our own body. But through our intentions we can shape or direct the patterns of our heart and mind. We can plant seeds in our heart that will create the kind of kingdom the world will be, whether it be wicked and evil or good and compassionate. Through simple awareness of our intention from moment to moment, we can plant a splendid garden, we can create patterns of well-being and happiness that last far beyond our personalities and our limited life.

Vipassana teacher Sylvia Boorstein illustrates this power with a story of a good friend, a famous doctor who for many years had served as president of the American Psychiatric Association. He was known as a gentleman, a man of integrity and kindness, who brought great joy to everything in his life. He always offered a deep respect to his patients and colleagues. After he retired and grew older, he started to become senile. He lost his memory and his ability to recognize people. He still lived at home, and his wife helped take care of him. Being longtime friends, Sylvia and her husband Seymour, who is also a psychiatrist, were invited to his home for dinner one evening. It had been some time since they had last seen him, and they wondered if his senility had increased. They arrived at the door with a bottle of wine and rang the doorbell. He opened the door and looked at them with a kind of blank stare that showed no recognition of who they were even though they had been friends for many years. Then he smiled and said, "I don't know who you are, but whoever you are, please come in and enjoy my home," and he offered them the same graciousness with which he had lived for his whole life.

The karmic patterns that we create through our hearts transcend the limitations of time and space. To awaken the heart of compassion and wisdom in a response to all circumstances is to become a Buddha. When we awaken the Buddha within ourselves, we awaken to a universal force of spirit that can bring compassion and understanding to the whole of the world. Gandhi called this power Soul Force. It brings strength when powerful action is needed. It brings tremendous love and forgiveness, yet stands and speaks truth as well. It is this power of our heart that brings wisdom and freedom in any circumstance, that brings the kingdom of the spirit alive here on earth.

For Gandhi this spirit was always connected to his heart, always open to listen and ready to respond to the world by sharing the blessings of compassion with all beings.

Beyond my non-cooperation there is always the keenest desire to cooperate, on the slightest pretext, even with the worst of opponents. To me, a very imperfect mortal is ever in need of God's grace, ever in need of the Dharma. No one is beyond redemption.

MEDITATION ON FORGIVENESS

If we could read the secret history of our enemies, we should find in each person's life sorrow and suffering enough to disarm all hostility.

—Longfellow

Forgiveness is one of the greatest gifts of spiritual life. It enables us to be released from the sorrows of the past. Although it can arise spontaneously, it can also be developed. Like the loving-kindness meditation and compassion practice offered in earlier chapters, there is a way to cultivate forgiveness through an ancient and systematic practice. Forgiveness is used as a preparation for other heart-centered meditations, as a way to soften the heart and release the barriers to our loving-kindness and compassion. Through repeated practice, over and over, we can bring the spirit of forgiveness into the whole of our life.

Before you can do forgiveness practice, you must be clear about what forgiveness means. Forgiveness does not in any way justify or condone harmful actions. While you forgive, you may also say, "Never again will I knowingly allow this to happen." You can resolve to sacrifice your own life to prevent further harm. Forgiveness does not mean you have to seek out or speak to those who caused you harm. You may choose never to see them again.

Forgiveness is simply an act of the heart, a movement to let go of the pain, the resentment, the outrage that you have carried as a burden for so long. It is an easing of your own heart and an acknowledgment that, no matter how strongly you may condemn and have suffered from the evil deeds of another, you will not put another human being out of your heart. We have all been harmed, just as we have all at times harmed ourselves and others.

For most people forgiveness is a process. When you have been deeply wounded, the work of forgiveness can take years. It will go through many stages—grief, rage, sorrow, fear, and confusion—and in the end, if you let yourself feel the pain you carry, it will come as a relief, as a release for your heart. You will see that forgiveness is fundamentally for your own sake, a way to carry the pain of the past no longer. The fate of the person who harmed you, whether they be alive or dead, does not matter nearly as much as what you carry in your heart. And if the forgiveness is for yourself, for your own guilt, for the harm you've done to yourself or to another, the process is the same. You will come to realize that you can carry it no longer.

To practice the formal forgiveness meditation, let yourself sit comfortably, allowing your eyes to close and your body and breath to be natural and easy. Let your body and mind relax. Breathing gently into the area of your heart, let yourself feel all the barriers and holding that you have carried because you have not forgiven, not forgiven yourself, not forgiven others. Let yourself feel the pain of keeping your heart closed. Then after breathing softly into the heart for some time, begin asking and extending forgiveness, reciting the following words and allowing them to open your forgiving heart. Let the words, images, and feelings grow deeper as you repeat them.

Forgiveness from others: *There are many ways that I have hurt and harmed others, betrayed or abandoned them, caused them suffering, knowingly or unknowingly, out of my pain, fear, anger, and confusion.* Let yourself remember and visualize these many ways you have hurt others. See and feel the pain you have caused out of your own fear and confusion. Feel your own sorrow and regret, and sense that finally you can release this burden and ask for forgiveness. Picture each memory that still burdens your heart. And then one by one, repeat, *I ask for your forgiveness, I ask for your forgiveness.*

Forgiveness for yourself: Feel your own precious body and life. *There are many ways that I have betrayed, harmed, or abandoned myself through thought, word, or deed, knowingly or unknowingly.* Let yourself see the ways you have hurt or harmed yourself. Picture them, remember them, visualize them. Feel the sorrow you have carried from all these actions, and sense that you can release these burdens, extending forgiveness for them one by one. Then say to yourself, *For each of the ways I have hurt myself through action or inaction, out of my fear, pain, and confusion, I now extend a full and heartfelt forgiveness. I forgive myself, I forgive myself.*

Forgiveness for those who have hurt or harmed you: *There are many ways I have been wounded and hurt, abused and abandoned, by others in thought, word, or deed, knowingly or unknowingly.* Let yourself picture them, remember them, visualize these many ways. Feel the sorrow you have carried from this past and sense that you can release yourself from this burden by extending forgiveness if your heart is ready. Now say to yourself, *In the many ways others have hurt or harmed me, out of fear, pain, confusion, and anger, I see these now. To the extent that I am ready, I offer them forgiveness. I have carried this pain in my heart too long. For this reason, to those who have caused me harm, I offer you my forgiveness. I forgive you.*

Let yourself gently repeat these three directions for forgiveness until you can feel a release in your heart. Perhaps for some great pains you may not feel a release, but only the burden and the anguish or anger you have held. Touch this softly. Be forgiving of yourself in this as well. Forgiveness cannot be forced; it cannot be artificial. Simply continue the practice, and let the words and images work gradually in their own way. In time, you can make the forgiveness meditation a regular part of your practice, letting go of the past and opening your heart to each new moment with a wise loving-kindness.

20

EXPANDING OUR CIRCLE:
AN UNDIVIDED HEART

*Suppose you considered your neighborhood to
be your temple—how would you treat your temple, and what would be your spiritual task
there?*

All of spiritual practice is a matter of relationship: to ourselves, to
others, to life's situations. We can relate with a spirit of wisdom, compassion, and flexibility, or we can meet life with fear, aggression, and
delusion. Whether we like it or not, we are always in relationship, always
interconnected.

Much of the past nineteen chapters has focused on relating wisely to
our inner self, through healing, training, and understanding the cycles
and possibilities of a spiritual life. Because expressing spiritual practice
in all aspects of our life is so important, there could well be a companion
volume to this one that spells out traditional practices such as right
livelihood and conscious sexuality, as well as practices for marriage and
family life, for politics, economics, community life, and art. Yet in this

book we have already touched on the major principles we need to understand and live with awareness in each of these areas.

The laws that govern wise relationships in politics, marriage, or business are the same as in inner life. Each of these areas requires a capacity for commitment and constancy, for taking the one seat. In each of these relationships we will encounter the familiar demons and temptations, and again we will be called upon to name them and dance with our difficulties. Each area will have its cycles, and in each we must learn to be true to ourselves.

To extend our practice we must learn to consciously bring the spirit of wakefulness and loving-kindness to every act. Albert Einstein, one of our modern wise men, described spiritual life in this way:

> A human being is a part of the whole called by us "the universe," a part limited in time and space. He experiences himself, his thoughts and feelings, as something separate from the rest—a kind of optical delusion of his consciousness. This delusion is a kind of prison for us, restricting us to our personal desires and affection for a few persons nearest to us. Our task must be to free ourselves from this prison by widening our circle of understanding and compassion to embrace all living creatures and the whole of nature in its beauty.

Expanding our spiritual practice is actually a process of expanding our heart, of widening our circle of insight and compassion to gradually include the whole of our life. Being on earth here in human bodies, this year, this day, is our spiritual practice.

It used to be that most of Eastern spiritual practice was preserved by monks and nuns in monasteries and temples. For centuries much of Western contemplative practice in Europe took place in cloisters as well. In our modern times, the monastery and temple have expanded to include the world itself. Most of us are not going to live as monks and nuns, and yet as lay people we seek a genuine and profound spiritual life. This is possible when we recognize that where we are is our temple, that just here in the life we are leading we can bring our practice alive.

My old guru in Bombay would teach us in this way. He would let students stay just long enough to come to some genuine understanding of life and love and how to be free in the midst of it all. Then he would send them home, saying, "Marry the boy or girl next door, get a job in your own community, live your life as your practice." On the opposite coast of India, Mother Teresa sends home the hundreds of volunteers who come to help in Calcutta, saying, "Now that you have learned to see Christ in the poor of India, go home and serve him in your family, on your street, in your neighborhood."

From a traditional Buddhist view, it is taught that we have all been reborn since the beginning of time over countless lifetimes in every form. We are instructed to reflect on this perspective and see that lifetime after lifetime we have been born as mothers, fathers, brothers, and sisters for one another in every form. Thus, we are instructed to treat each person we meet as if they were our beloved children or our parents or our grandparents. In Buddhist countries it is common to refer to everyone with the honorific title of some relative: Uncle President, Auntie Mayor, Uncle General, Grandfather Teacher, and so forth. We are all one family.

This can be felt most directly in the silence of an undivided heart. When the mind is still and the heart open, the world is undivided for us. As Chief Seattle reminded our ancestors when he surrendered his land:

> This earth is our mother. Whatever befalls the earth befalls the sons and daughters of the earth. This we know. All things are connected like the blood which unites one family. All things are connected.
>
> Whatever befalls the earth befalls the sons and daughters of the earth. We did not weave the web of life, we are merely a strand in it. Whatever we do to the web we do to ourselves.

When the heart is undivided, whatever we encounter is our practice. There is no difference between sitting in meditation in dedicated silence or acting in every realm. They are like breathing in and breathing out, two inseparable aspects of our life. The Zen tradition says this explicitly when it states:

> In spiritual practice there are only two things: you sit and you sweep the garden. And it doesn't matter how big the garden is.

We take time to be quiet, to open and awaken, and then we manifest that awakening in the garden of the world.

Sometimes we must heal our own wounds first, to come to some inner well-being, but eventually we experience a natural movement to serve, a longing to give back to the world. This spirit of service needn't be based on ideals, on trying to fix all that is wrong in the world. When we have touched our inner garden, we bring a grace to all we touch. This poem by Lynn Park expresses it so well.

Take the time to pray—
it is the sweet oil that eases the hinge into the garden
so the doorway can swing open easily.
You can always go there.

Consider yourself blessed.
These stones that break your bones
will build the altar of your love.

Your home is the garden.
Carry its odor, hidden in you, into the city.
Suddenly your enemies will buy seed packets
and fall to their knees to plant flowers
in the dirt by the road.
They'll call you Friend
and honor your passing among them.
When asked, "Who was that?" they will say,
"Oh, that one has been beloved by us
since before time began."
This from people who would have trampled over you
to maintain their advantage.

Give everything away except your garden,
Your worry, your fear, your small-mindedness.
Your garden can never be taken from you.

When we expand our garden, our actions become the natural expression of our heart filled with gratitude, love, and compassion. These feelings arise when we recognize the blood of our own family in everything that lives. We receive physical and spiritual sustenance from the world around us; this is like breathing in. Then because each of us is born with certain gifts, part of our happiness is to use these to give back to the earth, to our community, family, and friends; this is like breathing out. As we grow in interconnectedness, the integrity and responsibility of a world citizen naturally grows in us.

DAILY LIFE AS MEDITATION

In expanding our circle of practice, we may feel that we haven't enough time. Modern life is already very fast-paced and getting more so all the time. Saving time is even beginning to replace sex as a means of selling products on television. Do we have enough time to expand our practice? Remember how someone complained to Achaan Chah that there wasn't enough time to practice in his monastery because there were so many chores—sweeping, cleaning, greeting visitors, building, chanting, and so forth—and Achaan Chah asked back, "Is there enough time to be aware?" Everything we do in life is a chance to awaken.

We can learn to see here and now those places where we are afraid or attached or lost or deluded. We can see in the very same moment the possibility of awakening, of freedom, of fullness of being. We can carry on this practice anywhere—at work, in our community, at home. Sometimes people complain about how difficult it is to practice in family life. When they were single, they could take long periods of silent retreats or spend time in the mountains or travel to exotic temples, and then these places and postures became confused in their mind with the spirit of the sacred itself. But the sacred is always here before us. Family life and children are a wonderful temple. Children can become fantastic teachers for us. They teach us surrender and selflessness. They bring us into the present moment again and again. When we're in an ashram or monastery, if our guru tells us to get up early in the morning to meditate, we may not always feel like it. Some mornings we may roll over and go back to sleep thinking we'll do it another day. But when our children awaken in the middle of the night because they are sick and need us, there's no choice and no question about it—we respond instantly with our entire loving attention.

Over and over we are asked to bring our whole heart and care to family life. These are the same instructions a meditation master or guru gives us when we face the inevitable tiredness, restlessness, or boredom in our meditation cell or temple. Facing these at home is no different from facing them in the meditation retreat. Spiritual life becomes more genuine when things become more difficult. Our children have inevitable accidents and illnesses. Tragedies occur. These situations call for a constancy of our love and wisdom. Through them we touch the marrow of practice and find our true spiritual strength.

In many other cultures the nurturing of wise and healthy children is seen as a spiritual act, and parenting is considered sacred. Children are held constantly, both physically and in the heart of the community, and each healthy child is seen as a potential Leonardo, Nureyev, Clara Barton, a unique contributor to humanity. Our children are our meditation. When children are raised by day care and television, in a society that values money-making more than its children, we create generations of discontented, wounded, needy individuals. A key to extending practice into the demanding areas of child rearing and intimate relationships is the same development of patience or constancy as in following our breath, bringing our heart back a thousand times. Nothing of value grows overnight, not our children, nor the capacity of our hearts to love one another. I saw the power that grows from loving respect on a family sabbatical to Thailand and Bali. My daughter Caroline studied Balinese dance for two months with a wonderful teacher, and when she finished he proposed to stage a farewell recital for her at his school, which is also his home. When we arrived they set out a stage, got the music ready, and then started to dress Caroline. They took a very long time dressing a six-year-old whose average attention span is about five minutes. First they draped her in a silk sarong, with a beautiful chain around her waist. Then they wrapped embroidered silk fifteen times around her chest. They put on gold armbands and bracelets. They arranged her hair and put a golden flower in it. They put on more makeup than a six-year-old girl could dream of.

Meanwhile I sat there getting impatient, the proud father eager to take pictures. "When are they going to finish dressing her and get on with the recital?" Thirty minutes, forty-five minutes. Finally the teacher's wife came out and took off her own golden necklace and put it around my daughter's neck. Caroline was thrilled.

When I let go of my impatience, I realized what a wonderful thing was happening. In Bali children are held in great respect as members of society. Whether a dancer is six or twenty-six, she is equally honored and respected as an artist, one who performs not for the audience but for the gods. The level of respect that Caroline was given as an artist inspired her to dance beautifully. Imagine how you would feel if you were given such respect as a child. Just as the Buddha cultivated patience, respect, and compassion to mature his heart over one hundred thousand lifetimes, we can bring a bit of this to our families and love relationships.

Spiritual practice should not become an excuse to withdraw from life when difficulties arise. Meditation practice of any sort would not get very far if we stopped meditating every time we encountered a difficulty. The capacity for commitment is what carries our practice. In a love relationship such as marriage, commitment is the necessary down payment for success. Commitment does not mean a security pact where love is a business exchange—"I'll be here for you if you don't change too much, if you don't leave me." The commitment in a conscious relationship is to remain together, committed to helping one another grow in love, honoring and fostering the opening of our partner's spirit.

In both child rearing and love relationships, we will inevitably encounter the same hindrances as we do sitting in meditation. We will desire to be somewhere else or with someone else. We will feel aversion, judgment, and fear. We will have periods of laziness and dullness. We will get restless with one another, and we will have doubts. We can name these familiar demons and meet them in the spirit of practice. We can acknowledge the body of fear that underlies them and, together with our partner, speak of these very difficulties as a way to deepen our love.

MOVING INTO THE WORLD

As our life circumstances change and we learn to find balance in a succession of difficulties, we discover the true meaning of wakefulness and freedom. What better temple can we ask for? We can extend these same principles from family life to the work of our community, to politics, to economics, to global peace work, or to service to the poor. All of these spheres ask us to bring to them the qualities of a Buddha. Can we bring the Buddha into the voting booth where we live; can we act as the Buddha, writing letters to our congressmen and congresswomen; can we share in feeding the hungry; can we walk like the Buddha to demonstrate for peace or justice or care for our environment? The greatest gift we can bring to the challenges of these areas is our wisdom and greatness of heart. Without it, we perpetuate the problems; with it, we can begin to transform the world.

I remember the first anti–Vietnam War demonstration I attended, how the protestors brought the same aggression and hate to the generals and politicians as the generals brought to their battles. We were simply re-creating the war. Yet I believe we can be on the barricades, make strong political statements, place our hearts and bodies in the service of justice, without basing actions on hatred, without creating "us" and "them." Martin Luther King, Jr., reminded us never to succumb to the temptations of making people our enemy. "As you press on for justice," he said, "be sure to move with dignity and discipline, using only the weapons of love."

A well-known writer friend was gravely disturbed by the mass destruction of the Persian Gulf War. She wished to respond in as personal and direct a way as possible. So she took her meditation practice out into the square in the center of her town. Every day at noon, in rain, snow, or sun, she would sit peacefully and meditate next to a sign that asked for peace in the Persian Gulf. Some days people shouted at her, some days they joined her, some days she was alone. But no matter, she continued to demonstrate the peace she wanted in her square, day by day.

One Zen master is currently training thousands of ecological and political demonstrators in the principles of sitting and nonviolence. They learn about working with the inevitable conflict and demons that arise, and how to bring the peace and integrity they desire to the process of change. Another spiritual peace worker, in an important meeting with the general who heads the European nuclear forces, began his conversation by saying, "It must be very difficult to bear responsibility for the defense of all the people in Europe." Starting from this initial sense of mutual respect, the dialogue went very well.

We can enter the realm of politics with the integrity of world citizens and the wisdom of a bodhisattva, a being committed to the awakening of all. We can bring our spiritual practice into the streets, into our communities, when we see each realm as a temple, as a place to discover that which is sacred. Suppose you considered your neighborhood to be your temple—how would you treat your temple, and what would be your spiritual task there? Perhaps you would simply pick up litter when you saw it or move rocks out of the road before anyone could strike them. Perhaps you would drive in a mindful sacred way or drive less and use less gas. Perhaps you would greet neighbors with the hospitality that you greet your brothers and sisters within the temple. Perhaps you would organize care for the sick or hungry.

No one says this will be easy. Sitting in meditation is difficult and acting in meditation is equally difficult. It may take years of practice to learn how to enter the family arena or the political arena and stay connected with our deepest compassion. Staying connected takes a particular and conscious effort. Yet, what is sacred and what is true is found here as much as anywhere.

We may be confused initially because our world is complex. When we sit alone, we face only our own suffering. When we act in our families and in the world community, we must also face the suffering that connects us with all of life. Hundreds of millions of our brothers and sisters live in situations of great injustice or great poverty. At times the injustice and the sorrow of it all seems overwhelming, beyond our capacity to face. Yet something in us knows that this, too, is part of our spiritual life and that we can respond to this suffering as a part of our own, which in fact it is! None of us can avoid tyranny, loss, sorrow, or death. We are all interconnected in the destruction or saving of our planetary environment.

We must remember that the world's current problems are fundamentally a spiritual crisis, created by the limited vision of human beings—a loss of a sense of connection to one another, a loss of community, and most deeply a loss of connection to our spiritual values.

Political and economic change have never been sufficient in themselves to alleviate suffering when the underlying causes are not also addressed. The worst problems on this earth—warfare, poverty, ecological destruction, and so forth—are created from greed, hatred, prejudice, delusion, and fear in the human mind. To expand the circle of our practice and to face the sorrow in the world around us, we must face these forces in ourselves. Einstein called us nuclear giants and ethical infants. Only when we have found a compassion, a goodness and understanding, that transcends our own greed, hatred, and delusion, can we bring freedom alive in the world around us.

A wide and open heart gives us the strength to face the world directly, to understand the roots of our sorrows and our part in them. President Dwight Eisenhower reminded us of this responsibility when he stated:

> Every gun that is made, every warship launched, every rocket fired signifies, in the final sense, a theft from those who are cold and not clothed. This world in arms is not spending money alone. It is spending the sweat of its laborers, the genius of its scientists, the hopes of its children. This is not a way of life at all in its true sense . . . it is humanity hanging from a cross of iron.

It is *our* society that does this. Each of us in a modern society must acknowledge our part in the world dilemma. There are many important levels from which we can address global suffering. We must do what we can in every arena, bringing compassion and skill to economics, to education, to government, to service, and to world conflict. Underlying all this work we must find a strength of heart to face injustice with truth and compassion.

There are two sources of strength in our world. One is the force of hatred, of those who are unafraid to kill. The other and greater strength comes from those who are unafraid to die. This was the strength behind Gandhi's marches against the entire British Empire, the strength of Dorothy Day's tireless work for the poor on the streets of New York.

This strength of heart and being is that which has reclaimed and redeemed human life in every circumstance.

Awakening compassion and freedom on this earth will not be easy. We need to be honest in dishonest times, when it is easier to fight for our principles than to live up to them. We must awaken in a time when the Tao, the dharma, the universal laws are often forgotten, when materialism, possessiveness, indulgence, and military security are widely advertised as the correct basis for human action. These ways are not the dharma, they do not follow timeless laws of human harmony and human happiness. This we can see for ourselves. We must find or discover in ourselves the ancient and eternal law of life based on truth and compassion to guide our actions.

CONSCIOUS CONDUCT: THE FIVE PRECEPTS

To widen our understanding and compassion, our action must be in harmony with these ancient laws of conscious conduct. These laws alone are the basis of conscious spiritual life, and to follow and refine them in every circumstance is itself a practice leading to liberation of all beings. I saw one of the clearest examples of these laws demonstrated in the Cambodian refugee camps. I was with a friend and teacher Mahaghosananda, an extraordinary Cambodian monk, one of the few to survive, when he opened a Buddhist temple in a barren refugee camp of the Khmer Rouge communists. There were fifty thousand villagers who had become communists at gunpoint and had now fled the destruction to camps on the Thai border. In this camp the underground Khmer Rouge camp leaders threatened to kill any who would go to the temple. Yet on its opening day more than twenty thousand people crowded into the dusty square for the ceremony. These were the sad remnants of families, an uncle with two nieces, a mother with only one of three children. The schools had been burned, the villages destroyed, and in nearly every family, members had been killed or ripped away. I wondered what he would say to people who had suffered so greatly.

Mahaghosananda began the service with the traditional chants that had permeated village life for a thousand years. Though these words had been silenced for eight years and the temples destroyed, they still remained in the hearts of these people whose lives had known as much sorrow and injustice as any on earth. Then Mahaghosananda began chanting one of the central verses of the Buddha, first in Pali and then in Cambodian, reciting the words over and over:

Hatred never ceases by hatred
but by love alone is healed.
This is an ancient and eternal law.

As he chanted these verses over and over thousands chanted with him. They chanted and wept. It was an amazing moment, for it was clear that the truth he chanted was even greater than their sorrows.

Every great spiritual tradition recognizes and teaches the basic laws of wise and conscious human conduct. Whether called virtues, ethics, moral conduct, or precepts, they are guidelines for living without bringing harm to others; they bring sanity and light into the world. In every human being, there is the capacity to take joy in virtue, in integrity, and in uprightness of heart. When we care for one another and live without harming other beings, we create freedom and happiness.

Buddhist practice requires the undertaking of five basic precepts as the minimum commitment to not harming others through our speech and actions. These precepts are recited regularly to remind students of their commitment. The precepts are:

I undertake to refrain from killing and harming living beings.
I undertake to refrain from stealing and taking that which is not mine.
I undertake to refrain from causing harm through sexual misconduct.
I undertake to refrain from false speech, harmful speech, gossip, and slander.
I undertake to refrain from the misuse of intoxicants or substances such as alcohol or drugs that cause carelessness or loss of awareness.

The positive power of virtue is enormous. When we don't live by these precepts, it is said we live like wild beasts; without them, all other spiritual practice is a sham. Imagine trying to sit down to meditate after a day of lying and stealing. Then imagine what a different world this would be if everyone kept even one precept—not to kill, or not to lie, or not to steal. We would truly create a new world order.

These simple teachings are a perfect way to enact our practice, to expand our circle of understanding and compassion into the world around us. To follow precepts is to train our attention and respect. It takes attention and care to avoid harm to others. The precepts clearly signal us when we are about to lose our way, when our fears and delusion entangle us so that we might harm another being. Buddhist monks follow not just five but several hundred training precepts, and out of this practice arises exquisite mindfulness and respect, in speech, in decorum, in all action.

The basic precepts are not passive. They can actively express a compassionate heart in our life. Not killing can grow into a reverence for life, a protective caring for all sentient beings who share life with us. Not stealing can become the basis for a wise ecology, honoring the limited resources of the earth and actively seeking ways to live and work that share our blessings worldwide. From this spirit can come a life of natural and healing simplicity. Out of not lying we can develop our voice to speak for compassion, understanding, and justice. Out of nonharming sexuality, our most intimate relations can also become expressions of love, joy, and tenderness. Out of not abusing intoxicants or becoming heedless, we can develop a spirit that seeks to live in the most awake and conscious manner in all circumstances.

At first, precepts are a practice. Then they become a necessity, and finally they become a joy. When our heart is awakened, they spontaneously illuminate our way in the world. This is called Shining Virtue. The light around someone who speaks truth, who consistently acts with compassion for all, even in great difficulty, is visible to all around them. Better than perfume, its fragrance rises to the gods. Viktor Frankl, the well-known psychologist, has written of this power:

> Those of us who lived through the concentration camps can remember very clearly the men and women who walked through the huts comforting those in need and giving away their last piece of bread. They may have been few in number but they are a testimony to the possibilities of the human spirit.

Each of us has this spirit in us—sometimes hidden, sometimes more available. This light and this generosity and this peace are our greatest gift to the earth. In expanding our practice, we become the center of a circle, like a stone thrown into a pond that sinks softly to the bottom while ripples move to touch each shore. As the center of the circle, we become peaceful in ourselves and bring alive this same peace to others no matter what changes of life are before us. Suzuki Roshi says, "To find perfect composure in the midst of change is to find ourselves in nirvana."

REVERENCE FOR LIFE

In widening our circle of practice, we learn the art of honoring life in each encounter, moment by moment and person by person. This is not an idealistic practice but an immediate one.

William Blake put it this way:

If one is to do good, it must be done in the minute particulars. General good is the plea of the hypocrite, the scoundrel, and the flatterer.

Living a spiritual life does not demand high ideals or noble thoughts. It requires our caring and kind attention to our breath, to our children, to the trees around us, and to the earth with which we are so interconnected.

The monks following the Buddha were prohibited from cutting plants or trees. Their nonharming and reverence was extended to embrace all of the life around them. In these modern times the forests of Asia are being destroyed as rapidly as the rain forests in the Amazon. Recognizing that soon there will be no forests left for forest monks and forest monasteries, some meditation masters have led villagers out into the forests to tie monks' robes from their temples around the oldest and greatest of the trees. An ordination ceremony is then performed as if the tree itself were formally becoming a follower of the Buddha. The Thai and Burmese people have such reverence for this ordination ceremony that they spare these trees and the whole area of the forest is saved.

This kind of repeated caring and attention becomes our spiritual practice. When we remember that every being we meet has been our uncle and our aunt, our son and our daughter, our heart becomes responsive and flexible.

More than any idea we may have about how things should be, the key to flexibility and respect is a listening heart. As Gandhi says, "We must care for the truth in front of us more than consistency." A modern peace project that follows this principle is called The Compassionate Listening Project. This group of Americans and Europeans have trained themselves in listening with care, attention, and deep compassion to every side of difficult situations. They have recently sent out teams to listen to some of the most cut-off people in the world. One team went to Libya and sat and listened in a compassionate way to the views and stories of Libyan army officers and the followers of Muammar Qaddafi. This listening was to try to understand the situation from their point of view. Another team was sent to Nicaragua to listen to both the peasants and to the armed commandos of the Contras, to hear from each their point of view, their suffering, their difficulties, and their perspectives. Another team was sent to the Middle East to listen to the factions in Lebanon.

When we listen as if we were in a temple and give attention to one another as if each person were our teacher, honoring his or her words as valuable and sacred, all kinds of great possibilities awaken. Even miracles can happen. To act in the world most effectively, our actions cannot come from our small sense of self, our limited identity, our hopes, and our fears. Rather, we must listen to a greater possibility and cultivate actions connected with our highest intentions from the patient and compassionate Buddha within us. We must learn to be in touch with something greater than ourselves, whether we call it the Tao, God, the dharma, or the law of nature. There is a deep current of truth that we can hear. When we listen and act in accordance with this truth, no matter what happens, our actions will be right.

One of the best examples of this listening heart came after Gandhi's death, when the whole Gandhian movement of his followers was in disarray. Within a year or two of the establishment of India, a number of his followers decided to have a nationwide meeting to see how best to continue his work. They hoped to convince one elder, Vinoba Bhave, Gandhi's closest disciple and heir apparent, to lead this conference, but he declined. "We cannot revive the past," he stated. After much pleading, they finally convinced Vinoba to lead their gathering, but only on the condition, as he requested, that it be postponed for six months, giving him enough time to walk on foot from where he lived to the meeting site, halfway across India.

He began to walk from village to village. As he stayed in each village, he would call a meeting as Gandhi had done. He would listen to their problems and at times advise the villagers. Naturally, he walked through a series of very poor villages, there being many of them in India. In one, many people spoke of the hardship, of their hunger and how little food they had to eat. He asked them, "Why don't you grow your own food," but most of them were untouchables, and they said, "We would grow our own food, sir, but we have no land." Upon reflection, Vinoba promised them that when he returned to Delhi he would speak to Prime Minister Nehru and see if a law could be passed giving land to the poorest villagers in India.

The village went to sleep, but Vinoba, struggling with the problem, did not rest that night. In the morning he called the villagers together and apologized. "I know government too well." He said, "Even if after several years I'm able to convince them to pass a law granting land, you may never see it. It will go through the states and provinces, the district head man and the village head man, and by the time the land grant reaches you, with everyone in the government taking their piece, there probably will be nothing left for you." This was his honest but sad predicament.

Then one rich villager stood up and said, "I have land. How much do these people need?" There were sixteen families, each needing five acres apiece, so Vinoba said, "Eighty acres," and the man, deeply inspired by the spirit of Gandhi and Vinoba, offered eighty acres. Vinoba replied, "No, we cannot accept it. You must first go home and speak with your wife and children who will inherit your land." The man went home, got permission, and returned saying, "Yes, we will give eighty acres of our land." That morning eighty acres of land was given to the poorest families.

The next day Vinoba walked to another poor village and heard the plight of hunger and landlessness from its lowest caste members. In the meeting he recited the tale of the previous village, and from his story another rich landowner was inspired. He offered one hundred and ten acres for the desperate twenty-two poorest families and again was directed to get permission from his family. Within the day the land was granted to the poor.

Village by village, Vinoba held meetings and continued this process until he reached the council several months later. In the course of his walk, he had collected over 2,200 acres of land for the poorest families along the way. He told this story to the council, and out of it, many joined him to start the great Indian Land Reform Movement. For fourteen years that followed, Vinoba Bhave and thousands of those inspired by him walked through every state, province, and district of India, and without any government complications or red tape, collected over ten million acres of land for the hungriest and most impoverished villagers.

All this began from the spirit of listening, a caring for truth, and a compassionate beginner's mind brought to an old and difficult situation. To live in this way takes a courage and simplicity, a courage to listen honestly and face the world as it presents itself, and a simplicity to see what life asks of us with unclouded eyes and heart.

This courage recognizes that no one has ever lived our life before. There is no exact plan or model we can follow, even from the greatest inspiration. We all follow an unknown path and an uncharted stream, and it takes great courage to move ahead with our eyes and our hearts open. When we look with deep compassion, we may find it necessary to change our life again and again, to let go of unwise parts of ourselves or to extend our compassion in new ways to the world around us.

To live a path with heart in this way is called Living the Life of a Bodhisattva. *Bodhisattva* is a Sanskrit word of two parts. *Bodhi* means "awakened" and *sattva* means "a being." Together they mean a person who is committed to awakening, a being committed to the freedom and well-being of every creature, who like a Buddha uses every circumstance to express the human capacity for understanding and compassion. It is said that even if the sun were to arise in the west and the world turned upside down, the bodhisattva has only one way. Even in the face of the greatest difficulties, the way of the bodhisattva is to bring a spirit of understanding and compassion alive there too.

In widening our circle of practice, we discover the capacity of our heart to bear witness to the suffering of the world and experience our heart expanding, connecting in compassion to all life.

The bodhisattva within us knows that true love is irresistible and unconquerable and that it transforms whatever it touches. Amazingly, to live a life as a bodhisattva is not grand or idealistic. It is simply bringing to every circumstance a spirit of love, openness, and freedom. Then our very being transforms the world around us.

When Mahatma Gandhi was asked by a reporter for a message to the Indian people, just as his train was pulling out, he scrawled on a piece of paper, "My life is my message."

To expand our circle of practice is to let our life be our message.

MEDITATION ON SERVICE

Pick a quiet time. Let yourself sit comfortably, being at ease and yet awake. Feel your body sitting and feel the gentle movement of your breath. Let your mind be clear and your heart be soft. Reflect on the bounteous gifts and blessings that support all human life: the rain, the plants of the earth, the warm sunshine. Bring to mind the many human benefactors: the farmers, parents, laborers, healers, postal workers, teachers, the whole society around you. As you feel the world around you, be aware of its problems as well: the needs of its people, its animals, its environment. Let yourself feel the movement in your heart that wishes to contribute, the joy that could come with the offering of your own unique gift to the world.

Then, when you are ready, pose the following questions inwardly to yourself. Pause after each one and give your heart time to answer, allowing a response from the deepest level of your compassion and wisdom.

Imagine yourself five years from now as you would most like to be, having done all the things you want to have done, having contributed all the things you want to contribute in the most heartfelt way. What is your greatest source of happiness? What is the thing you've done by which you feel the world is most blessed? What is the contribution you could make to the world that would give you the most satisfaction? To make this contribution to the world, what unworthiness would you have to relinquish? To make this contribution to the world, what strengths and capacities would you have to recognize in yourself and others? What would you have to do in your life today to begin this service, this contribution? Why not begin?

UNDERTAKING THE FIVE PRECEPTS: NONHARMING AS A GIFT TO THE WORLD

Every great spiritual system offers guidelines for ethical conduct as a statement that spiritual life cannot be separated from our words and actions. A conscious commitment to virtue and nonharming is the foundation for living a harmonious and compassionate life. At first, following a moral code can be seen as a protection for yourself and others. With further practice and reflection, you can see how each basic area of truthfulness and integrity can be developed into a meditation itself, bringing you awakening and sowing seeds of inner freedom. As you develop each area of your virtue, it can become a spontaneous gift, an offering of caring from your heart to all other beings.

In Buddhist practice, one way to establish virtue and integrity is to formally repeat and undertake The Five Precepts. This can be done regularly, as a reminder and a recommitment of your intentions.

To undertake the five precepts, sit in a quiet and alert fashion in your regular place of meditation. If you have an altar, you may wish to light a candle or offer incense or flowers. Then rest with your body still and your heart open. When you are ready, recite the following precepts:

> I undertake the training precept of refraining from killing and harming living beings.
>
> I undertake the training precept of refraining from stealing and taking that which is not mine.
>
> I undertake the training precept of refraining from causing harm through sexual misconduct.
>
> I undertake the training precept of refraining from false speech, harmful speech, gossip, and slander.
>
> I undertake the training precept of refraining from the misuse of intoxicants such as alcohol or drugs that cause careless-ness or loss of awareness.

As you recite each precept, feel the intention in your heart. Sense the strength and well-being it can offer you and the compassion it holds for all beings in the world.

Then at some time in your practice, if you wish to explore further ways to work with these precepts, you can do the following exercise:

> Pick and refine one of the five precepts as a way to cultivate and strengthen virtue and mindfulness. Work with that precept meticulously for one week. Then examine the results and choose another precept for a subsequent week. Here are some possible ways to work with each precept.
>
> 1. *Refraining from killing: reverence for life.* Undertake for one week to purposely bring no harm in thought, word, or deed to any living creature. Particularly become aware of any living beings in your world whom you ignore (people, animals, even plants), and cultivate a sense of care and reverence for them too.
>
> 2. *Refraining from stealing: care with material things.* Un-dertake for one week to minimize consumption—driving less, spending less, letting each physical act be one of caring steward-ship and respect. Then undertake for one week to act on every

single thought of generosity that arises spontaneously in your heart.

3. *Refraining from false speech: speech from the heart*. Undertake for one week not to gossip (positively or negatively) or speak about anyone you know who is not present with you (any third party).

4. *Refraining from sexual misconduct: conscious sexuality*. Undertake for one week to observe meticulously how often sexual feelings and thoughts arise in your consciousness. Each time, note what particular mind states you find associated with them, such as love, tension, compulsion, caring, loneliness, desire for communication, greed, pleasure, aggression, and so forth.

5. *Refraining from intoxicants*. Undertake for one week or one month to refrain from all intoxicants and addictive substances (such as wine, liquor, marijuana, cigarettes, and caffeine). Observe the impulses to use these, and become aware of what is going on in the heart and mind at the time of those impulses.

PART IV

SPIRITUAL MATURITY

21

SPIRITUAL MATURITY

As one matures in spiritual life, one becomes more comfortable with paradox, more appreciative of life's ambiguities, its many levels and inherent conflicts. One develops a sense of life's irony, metaphor, and humor and a capacity to embrace the whole, with its beauty and outrageousness, in the graciousness of the heart.

Fruit falls from a tree naturally when ripe. After due time in spiritual life, the heart, like fruit, begins to mature and sweeten. Our practice shifts from the green hard growth of seeking, developing, and improving ourselves to a resting in mystery. It shifts from reliance on form to a resting in the heart. One young woman who had struggled greatly in the early years of her practice in the face of family difficulties and the fundamentalist church to which her parents belonged wrote, "My parents hate me when I'm a Buddhist, but they love me when I'm a Buddha."

To mature spiritually is to let go of rigid and idealistic ways of being and discover a flexibility and joy in our life. As spiritual maturity develops, it brings kindness to the heart. Ease and compassion become our natural movement. The Taoist Lao Tzu celebrated this spirit when he wrote:

> She who is centered in the Tao can go where she wishes without danger. She perceives the universal harmony, even amid great pain, because she has found peace in her heart.

When Eastern spirituality in America began to be popular in the 1960s and 1970s, its practice was initially idealistic and romantic. People tried to use spirituality to "get high" and to experience extraordinary states of consciousness. There was a belief in perfect gurus and complete and wonderful teachings that if followed would lead to our full enlightenment and change the world. These were the imitative and self-absorbed qualities that Chogyam Trungpa called "spiritual materialism." By undertaking the rituals, the costumes, and the philosophy of spiritual traditions, people tried to escape their ordinary lives and become more spiritual beings.

After a few years it became clear to most people that being high would not last forever and that spirituality was not about leaving our life to find existence on an exalted, light-filled plane. We discovered that transformation of consciousness required a great deal more practice and discipline than we initially imagined. We began to see that the spiritual path *asked* more of us than it appeared to offer. From romantic visions of practice, people began to wake up and realize that spirituality required an honest, courageous look into our real-life situations, our family of origin, our place in the society around us. Individually and in communities, through growing wisdom and disillusioning experience, we began to give up the idealistic notion of spiritual life and community as a way to escape from the world or save ourselves.

For many of us this shift has become the foundation of a more deeply integrated and wiser spiritual work, a work that includes right relationships, right livelihood, right speech, and the ethical dimensions of the spiritual life. This work has required the end of compartmentalization, an understanding that whatever we seek to push into the shadow or avoid must eventually be included in our spiritual life, that nothing can be left behind. Spirituality has become more about who we are than what ideal we pursue. Spirituality has shifted from going to India or Tibet or Machu Picchu to coming home.

This kind of spirituality is filled with joy and integrity; it is both ordinary and awakened. This spirituality allows us to rest in the wonder of life. This mature spirituality allows the light of the divine to shine through us.

Let us look at the qualities of spiritual maturity:

1. *Nonidealism.* The mature heart is not perfectionistic: it rests in the compassion of our being instead of in ideals of the mind. Nonidealistic spirituality does not seek a perfect world; it does not seek to perfect ourselves, our bodies, our personalities. It is not romantic about teachers or enlightenment based on images of the immense purity of some special being out there. Thus, it does not seek to gain or attain in spiritual life, but only to love and be free.

The frustration of seeking perfection is illustrated by a story of Mullah Nasrudin. One day in the marketplace he encountered an old friend who was about to get married. This friend asked the Mullah whether he had ever considered marriage. Nasrudin replied that years ago he had wanted to marry and had set out to find the perfect woman. First he traveled to Damascus, where he found a perfectly gracious and beautiful woman but discovered she was lacking a spiritual side. Then his travels took him farther to Isfahan, where he met a woman who was deeply spiritual yet comfortable in the world and beautiful as well, but unfortunately they did not communicate well together. "Finally in Cairo I found her," he said, "she was the ideal woman, spiritual, gracious, and beautiful, at ease in the world, perfect in every way." "Well," asked the friend, "did you then marry her?" "No," answered the Mullah, "unfortunately, she was looking for the perfect man."

Mature spirituality is not based on seeking perfection, on achieving some imaginary sense of purity. It is based simply on the capacity to let go and to love, to open the heart to all that is. Without ideals, the heart can turn the suffering and imperfections we encounter into the path of compassion. In this nonidealistic practice, the divine can shine through even in acts of ignorance and fear, inviting us to wonder at the mystery of all that is. In this there is no judgment and no blame, for we seek not to perfect the world but to perfect our love for what is on this earth. Thomas Merton saw it this way.

Then it was as if I suddenly saw the secret beauty of their hearts, the depths where neither sin nor desire can reach, the person that each one is in God's eyes. If only they could see themselves as they really are. If only we could see each other that way there would be no reason for war, for hatred, for cruelty . . . I suppose the big problem would be that we would fall down and worship each other.

2. A second quality of mature spirituality is *kindness*. It is based on a fundamental notion of self-acceptance, rather than guilt, blame, or shame, for the ignorant acts we've committed or the fears that still remain within us. It understands that opening requires the warm sun of loving-kindness. It is all too easy to turn spirituality and religion into what Alan Watts called "a grim duty." Poet Mary Oliver wrote:

You do not have to be good.
You do not have to walk on your knees
for a hundred miles through the desert, repenting.
You only have to let the soft animal of your body
love what it loves . . .

In deep self-acceptance grows a compassionate understanding. As one Zen master said when asked if he ever gets angry, "Of course I get angry, but then a few minutes later I say to myself, 'What's the use of this,' and I let it go." This self-acceptance is at least half of our spiritual practice. We are asked to touch with mercy the many parts of ourself that we have denied, cut off, or isolated. Mature spirituality is a reflection of our deep gratitude and capacity for forgiveness. As the Zen poet Edward Espe Brown writes in *The Tassajara Recipe Book:*

Any moment, preparing this meal,
we could be gas thirty thousand
feet in the air soon
to fall out poisonous on leaf,
frond and fur. Everything
in sight would cease.

And still we cook,
putting a thousand cherished
dreams on the table, to nourish
and reassure those close and dear.

In this act of cooking, I bid farewell.
Always I insisted you alone were to blame.
This last instant my eyes open
and I regard you with all
the tenderness and forgiveness
I withheld for so long.

With no future
we have nothing
to fight about.

3. The third quality of spiritual maturity is *patience*. Patience allows us to live in harmony with the dharma, the Tao. As Chuang Tzu stated:

The true men of old
Had no mind to fight Tao
They did not try by their own contriving
To help Tao along.

Zorba the Greek tells of his own lesson in patience:

I remember one morning when I discovered a cocoon in the bark of a tree just as the butterfly was making a hole in its case and preparing to come out. I waited awhile but it was too long appearing and I was impatient. I bent over it and breathed on it to warm it. I warmed it as quickly as I could and the miracle began to happen before my eyes, faster than life. The case opened, the butterfly started slowly crawling out, and I shall never forget my horror when I saw how its wings were folded back and crumpled; the wretched butterfly tried with its whole trembling body to unfold them. Bending over it, I tried to help it with my breath. In vain. It needed to be hatched out patiently and the unfolding of the wings needed to be a gradual process in the sun. Now it was too late. My breath had forced the butterfly to appear, all crumpled, before its time. It struggled desperately and, a few seconds later, died in the palm of my hand.

Spiritual maturity understands that the process of awakening goes through many seasons and cycles. It asks for our deepest commitment, that we take the one seat in our heart and open to every part of life.

True patience is not gaining or grasping, it does not seek any accomplishment. Patience allows us to open to that which is beyond time. When Einstein was illustrating the nature of time, he explained, "When you sit with a pretty girl for two hours, it seems like a minute, and when you sit on a hot stove for a minute, it seems like two hours. That's relativity." When the Buddha spoke of practicing for one hundred thousand *mahakalpas* of lifetimes, he did not mean that it takes forever to awaken, but that awakening is timeless. Awakening is not a matter of weeks or years or lifetimes, but a loving and patient unfolding into the mystery just now.

"The problem with the word *patience*," said Zen master Suzuki Roshi, "is that it implies we are waiting for something to get better, we are waiting for something good that will come. A more accurate word for this quality is 'constancy,' a capacity to be with what is true moment after moment, to discover enlightenment one moment after another." In the deepest way it understands that what we seek is what we are, and it is always here. The great Indian teacher Ramana Maharshi said to students who were weeping as his body died, "But where do you think I could go?" Maturity of spiritual life allows us to rest just here in the truth that has always been and always will be.

4. A fourth quality of spiritual maturity is *immediacy*. Spiritual awakening is found in our own life here and now. In the Zen tradition they say, "After the ecstasy, the laundry." Spiritual maturity manifests itself in the immanent as well as the transcendent. It seeks to allow the divine to shine through our every action. Altered states, extraordinary experiences of the mind, great openings of consciousness are valued, not for their own sake, but only to the extent that they return us to our human incarnation to inform our wisdom and deepen our capacity for compassion. As Achaan Chah said, "Even the extraordinary experiences are of no use, only something to let go of, unless they are connected with this moment here and now." Spiritual states are honored when they clear the vision and open the body and mind, but only as a passage to return to the timeless present. As Kabir says of whatever we seek, "what is found then is found now."

In the immediate present, mature spirituality allows us to "walk our talk," to act and speak and touch one another as a reflection of our deepest understanding. We become more alive and more present. We discover that our very breath and body and human limitations are a part of the divine. This maturity listens to our body and loves it all, the body of joy and of grief; it listens to the heart and loves the heart's capacity to feel. This immediacy is the true source of compassion and understanding. "Only within our own body, with its heart and mind," said the Buddha, "can bondage and suffering be found, and only here can we find true liberation."

5. A fifth quality of spiritual maturity is a sense of the sacred that is *integrated and personal*. "Integrated" in that it does not create separate compartments of our life, dividing that which is sacred from that which is not; "personal" in honoring spirituality through our own words and actions. Otherwise, our spirituality is not of any true value. Integrated

and personal spiritual practice includes our work, our love, our families, and our creativity. It understands that the personal and the universal are inextricably connected, that the universal truths of spiritual life can come alive only in each particular and personal circumstance. How we live is our spiritual life. As one wise student remarked, "If you really want to know about a Zen master, talk to their spouse."

An integrated sense of spirituality understands that if we are to bring light and compassion into the world, we must begin with our own lives. Our personal life becomes more genuinely our spiritual practice than any set of experiences we have had or philosophy we espouse. This personal approach to practice honors both the individual and universal in our life, respecting life as an impermanent dance between birth and death, yet also honoring our particular body, our particular family and community, and the personal history and joys and sorrows that have been given to us. In this way, our personal awakening is a matter that affects all other creatures.

In the Amazon jungle there are nine hundred different species of wasps, each of which pollinates a different shape and species of fig tree. These fig trees are the main source of nutrition for all the smaller mammals of the rain forest, and these smaller mammals in turn provide the basis of life for jaguars, monkeys, peccaries, and others. Each species of wasp keeps a chain of other animals alive. In the same way, every individual in the world has a unique contribution. Fulfilling spiritual life can never come through imitation, it must shine through our particular gifts and capacities as a man or woman on this earth. This is the pearl of great price. In honoring our own unique destiny, we allow our most personal life to become an expression of the Buddha in a new form.

6. A sixth quality of spiritual maturity is *questioning*. Rather than adopting a philosophy or following blindly a great teacher or compelling path, we come to recognize that we must see for ourselves. This quality of questioning is called by the Buddha *Dhamma-vicaya*, our own investigation into the truth. It is a willingness to discover what is so, without imitation or without following the wisdom of others. Someone once told Picasso that he ought to make pictures of things the way they are— objective pictures. When Picasso said he did not understand, the man produced a picture of his wife from his wallet and said, "There, you see, that is a picture of how she really is." Picasso looked at it and said, "She's rather small, isn't she? And flat?" Like Picasso, we must see things for ourselves. In spiritual maturity we find a great sense of autonomy, not as a reaction to authority, but based on a heartfelt recognition that we, too, like the Buddha, can awaken. Mature spirituality has a profoundly

democratic quality in which all individuals are empowered to discover that which is sacred and liberating for themselves.

This questioning combines an open-mindedness, the "don't know" mind of Zen, with a "discriminating wisdom" that can separate what is useful from what is bad, that keeps the eyes open to learn. With an open mind we are always learning.

Our questioning allows us to use the great wisdom of traditions, to learn from teachers and to be part of communities, yet to stay in touch with ourselves, to see the truth and speak the truth with a great respect for our own integrity and our own awakening. This investigation may not bring us to be more sure of ourselves, but it can allow us to be more honest with ourselves, and in this, our spiritual practice becomes filled with interest and aliveness. The Dalai Lama, when asked about his current life in exile, spoke of this when he replied, "Sometimes I think this Dalai Lama is the hardest life of all—but of course it is the most interesting."

7. A seventh quality of spiritual maturity is *flexibility*. Spiritual maturity allows us, like bamboo, to move in the wind, to respond to the world with our understanding and our hearts, to respect the changing circumstances around us. The spiritually mature person has learned the great arts of staying present and letting go. Their flexibility understands that there is not just one way of practice or one fine spiritual tradition, but there are many ways. It understands that spiritual life is not about adopting any one particular philosophy or set of beliefs or teachings, that it is not a cause for taking a stand in opposition to someone else or something else. It is an easiness of heart that understands that all of the spiritual vehicles are rafts to cross the stream to freedom.

In his earliest dialogue, the Buddha cautioned against confusing the raft with the shore and against adopting any rigid opinion or view. He went on, "How could anything in this world bring conflict to a wise person who has not adopted any view?" In place of arrogance, the Buddha recommends freedom, and reminds his followers that those who grasp at philosophies and views simply wander around the world annoying people. The flexibility of heart brings a humor to spiritual practice. It allows us to see that there are a hundred thousand skillful means of awakening, that there are times for formal and systematic ways and times for spur-of-the-moment and unusual and outrageous ones.

A would-be high-school basketball coach named Ron Jones learned this lesson when taking over the San Francisco Center for the Specially Handicapped. He intended to coach his team to great victories, only to discover on the first day that there were just four players who came for training, one of whom was in a wheelchair. This initial impasse was broken when a six-foot-tall black woman came striding out of the men's bathroom demanding to be included on the team as well. The coach describes throwing out his first lesson plan when he found it took forty-five minutes simply to get all five players lined up along one side of the court facing in the same direction. But as he threw his plans away, the basketball team grew. They had practices and cheerleaders and hot dogs, although often they had seven or twelve people on the team instead of five. Sometimes they would stop the game in the middle to play music and invite everyone down to dance. And in the end, they became the only basketball team in history to win a game by over a million points, when one of their members, who was scorekeeper, found joy in pressing the point button on the scoreboard to ring in new baskets.

Easy come, easy go. There is a great freedom that comes in this flexibility. My teacher Achaan Chah spoke of himself as resting like a tree, bearing fruit, giving room for the birds to nest, moving in the wind. The dharma of flexibility is joyful and restful.

8. An eighth quality of spiritual maturity is that of *embracing opposites*, a capacity to hold the contradictions of life in our heart. When we are young children we see our parents as either all good, when they provide us with what we want, or all bad, when they frustrate our desires and do not act as we wish them to. A great development of the consciousness of children eventually lets them see their parents clearly and understand that within the same person there is both good and bad, love and anger, generosity and fear. A similar development occurs as we mature in spiritual practice. We no longer seek perfect parents, perfectly wise teachers or gurus, trying to find that which is all good, as opposed to that which is all bad, separating the victim from the abuser. We begin to understand that each contains its opposite.

One young woman who had been the victim of abuse in her own family spent much of her early spiritual practice healing this pain. As part of her healing, she became a counselor for other victims of abuse and finally began to work with offenders and perpetrators themselves. In the first year of working with this latter group, almost all men, she was clear about what was right and what was wrong, what was unacceptable and who had committed the crimes. However, as her work continued and she listened more deeply to the stories of the perpetrators of abuse, she discovered that almost every one of them had themselves been abused in their own childhood. Here she sat in a room surrounded by men, forty, fifty, sixty years old, yet under the surface was a roomful of abused children. To her shock, she found that many of them had been abused by their mothers and, as she learned their stories further, that their mothers had been abused by the grandfathers and great-uncles in the families, and sorrowful patterns of abuse were revealed that stretched back for generation after generation. What was she to do? Who was she to blame now? All that she had left was to say, "No," with all her strength, "these actions must not continue," and then to hold them all in her heart of compassion, abuser and abused in one person.

As one matures in spiritual life, one becomes more comfortable with paradox, more appreciative of life's ambiguities, its many levels and inherent conflicts. One develops a sense of life's irony, metaphor, and humor and a capacity to embrace the whole, with its beauty and out-rageousness, in the graciousness of the heart.

This paradox of life is always here in front of us. In a well-known story of a Zen master, a disciple asked him, "Please, master, speak to me of enlightenment." As they walked through the pine forest the Zen master responded by pointing to a tree. "See how tall that tree is?" "Yes," answered the student. Then the master pointed to another. "See how short is that other tree?" "Yes," answered the student. "There," said the master, "is enlightenment."

When we embrace life's opposites, we hold our own birth and death, our own joy and suffering, as inseparable. We honor the sacred in both emptiness and form, understanding the Sufi saying, "Praise Allah, but tie your camel to the post." As our spiritual practice matures, we learn to allow the opposites of our practice—the need for a teacher and the need to take responsibility for our own spiritual practice; the transcendent states of consciousness and the necessity to fulfill them in a personal way; the power of our karmic conditioning and the capacity for full human freedom—to be part of the dance of our spirit, to hold it all with ease and humor, to be at peace with it all.

9. The next understanding of mature spiritual life is found in *relationship*. We are always in relationship to something. It is in discovering a wise and compassionate relationship to all things that we find a capacity to honor them all. While we have little control over much of what happens in our life, we *can* choose how we relate to our experiences. Mature spirituality is an acceptance of life in relationship. With a willingness to relate to all things in life, we enter into a gracious spirit of practice that regards all as sacred. Our family life, our sexuality, our community, the earth's ecology, politics, money—our relationship to each being and

action becomes an expression of the Tao, the dharma. Zen master Thich Nhat Hanh is fond of reminding us of how we wash the dishes. "Can we wash each cup or bowl," he asks, "as if we were bathing a newborn baby Buddha?" Each act has meaning, and all our encounters are related to the whole of our spiritual life. In the same way, the care and compassion with which we relate to the difficulties and problems we encounter is the measure of our practice. Spiritual maturity honors our human community and interconnectedness. Nothing can be excluded from our spiritual life.

10. The last quality of spiritual maturity is that of *ordinariness*. In some traditions this is called *post-enlightenment practice*, the ordinariness that arises after the special spiritual states and side effects have faded away. Nisargadatta, the great master of the nondual, was asked how his own consciousness differed from the seekers around him. He smiled and stated that he had stopped identifying with the seeker. Yes, he would sit and wait for his breakfast, wait for his lunch, hungry and perhaps impatient like the others, but underneath and all around was an ocean of peace and understanding. He was not caught up in or identified with any of the changing conditions of his life, and so, unlike those around him, whatever happened, Nisargadatta was at rest.

Ordinariness is a simple presence in this moment that allows the mystery of life to show itself. When Thoreau warns us to "beware of any activity that requires the purchase of new clothes," he reminds us that simplicity is the way we open to everyday wonder. While we can honor the capacity of consciousness to create an infinite variety of forms, ordinariness is interested in what is here and now. This is the ordinary mystery of breathing or of walking, the mystery of trees on our street or of loving someone near to us. It is not based on attaining mystical states or extraordinary power. It does not seek to become something special, but is emptying, listening.

Walt Whitman praises this ordinariness in his poetry:

I believe a leaf of grass is no less than
    the journey-work of the stars. . . .
And the running blackberry would adorn
    the parlors of heaven. . . .
And a mouse is miracle enough to stagger sextillions of infidels.

The ordinariness of spiritual life comes from a heart that has learned trust, from a gratitude for the gift of human life. When we are just ourselves, without pretense or artifice, we are at rest in the universe. In this ordinariness there is no higher or lower, nothing to fix, nothing to desire, simply an opening in love and understanding to the joys and suffering of the world. This ordinary love and understanding brings an ease and peace of heart to every situation. It is the discovery that our salvation lies in the ordinary. Like the water of the Tao, which finds its way between the stones or wears them away a little at a time and gradually lowers itself to return to the ocean, this ordinariness brings us to rest.

There is a great power in ordinariness, a great strength in spiritual maturity. There comes the power to heal ourselves naturally, and just as naturally our sanity and compassion extends to the world around us. The beloved Japanese Zen poet Ryokan filled his life with this spirit of ordinariness and transformed those whom he touched. It is told that Ryokan never preached to or reprimanded anyone. Once his brother asked Ryokan to visit his house and speak to his delinquent son. Ryokan came but did not say a word of admonition to the boy. He stayed overnight and prepared to leave the next morning. As the wayward nephew was lacing Ryokan's straw sandals, he felt a drop of warm water. Glancing up, he saw Ryokan looking down at him, his eyes full of tears. Ryokan then returned home, and the nephew changed for the better.

With spiritual maturity our capacity to open, to forgive, to let go, grows deeper. In this comes a natural untangling of our conflicts, a natural undoing of our struggles, a natural easing of our difficulties, and the capacity to come back to a joyful and easeful rest.

The ancient wisdom of the *Tao te Ching* instructs:

I have just three things to teach:
simplicity, patience, compassion.
These three are your greatest treasures.
Simple in actions and in thoughts,
you return to the source of being.
Patient with both friends and enemies,
you accord with the way things are.
Compassionate toward yourself,
you reconcile all beings in the world.

Thus the wise man residing in the Tao
sets an example for all beings.
Because he doesn't display himself,
people can see his light.

Because he has nothing to prove,
people can trust his words.
Because he doesn't know who he is,
people recognize themselves in him.
Because he has no goal in mind,
everything he does succeeds.

22

THE GREAT SONG

Spiritual practice is revolutionary. It allows us to step outside our personal identity, culture, and religion to experience more directly the great mystery, the great music of life.

Maturing on the spiritual path opens up for us a thousand possibilities. All the magic and enchantment of the ten thousand things that appear before us come alive in a new way. Our thinking and feelings open to an expanded palette. We experience more deeply both the beauty and the sorrow of life; we can see with new eyes and hear the whole great song of life.

When we listen deeply, the great song moves through each of our lives. In Hermann Hesse's story, Siddhartha finally sits by the river and listens.

He was now listening intently, completely absorbed, quite empty, taking in everything. He felt he had now completely learned the art of listening. He had often heard all this before, all the numerous voices in the river, but today they sounded different. He could no longer distinguish the different voices—the merry voice from the weeping voice, the childish voice from the manly voice. They all belonged to each other: the lament of those who yearn, the laughter of the wise, the cry of indignation, and the groan of the dying. They were all interwoven and interlocked, entwined in a thousand ways. And all the voices, all the goals, all the yearnings, all the sorrows, all the pleasures, all the good and evil, all of them together was the world, all of them together were the streams of events and the music of life. When Siddhartha listened attentively to this river, to this song of a thousand voices, when he did not listen only to the sorrow or laughter, did not bind his soul to any one particular voice and absorb it in himself, but heard them all, the whole, the unity—then the great song of a thousand voices consisted of one word: perfection.

When we have not heard this great song we tend to live only in limited possibilities, seeing the world only through the popular myths that have been dispensed to us. The impoverished myths and songs of our culture are sold everywhere: the myth of materialism and possessiveness that says worldly goods lead to happiness; the myth of competition and individualism, which produces so much isolation; the myth of achievement and success, which leads to what Joseph Campbell called "climbing the ladder only to discover it was against the wrong wall"; and the myth of youth, which produces a culture of eternal adolescence and advertising images as our model of reality. These are myths of grasping and separateness. The stories in our culture would have us hold our breath, remain adolescent, grasp our possessions, search for the perfect experience and capture it on film—repeating one small note in the song.

Whenever we try to fix on a particular state, maintain an image, or hold on to an experience, our personal life, our professional life, and our spiritual life will suffer. Suzuki Roshi summed up all of the teachings of Buddhism in three simple words, "Not always so." When we try to repeat what has been in the past, we lose the true sense of life as an opening, a flowering, an unfolding, an adventure. Every molecule of our body is replaced within seven years. Our Milky Way turns like a Ferris wheel every ten million years. The seasons change, our body changes with them. Everything breathes, and in this breathing and movement we are all connected. This interconnection offers us enormous possibilities. Spiritual life can open us to the magnificent music all around us, not just to that music limited by our ideas or plans or by the story that encapsulates us in our culture. In this we can touch the mystery.

A colleague and student who has practiced in Buddhism deeply for years acquired an M.D., Ph.D. in both psychiatry and psychology, studying the nature of mind. He also spent years exploring vision ceremonies with shamans and developed practices in Christian and other mystical traditions. Determined to understand the world's great religions, he began to read the many-volumed *Encyclopedia of World Religions* cover to cover. It detailed the teachings of the major world religions, each a belief system for thousands and millions of people for centuries. It included the ancient religions of the Aztecs, the Australian aborigines, the Zulu, the Siberian shamans, the Hasidim, the Babylonians, Shinto, ten schools of Buddhism, a dozen forms of Christianity, and hundreds of other religions. Each of these systems had powerful teachings about good and evil and about human nature. Each had a compelling story of the creation of the world, and each spoke of gods, spirits, and the divine and how to attain it.

When I asked him what he had learned from his reading, he said with awe that it wasn't the religions that had struck him so strongly, but the light that shines through them. He realized that all the great religions are merely sets of words and concepts, like screens placed over the great mystery of life. They are the ways that groups of us humans have found to interpret, understand, and feel safe in the face of the unnameable, unknowable, the everchanging song of life.

How do we honor this mystery? From an awakened perspective, life is a play of patterns, the patterns of trees, the movement of the stars, the patterns of the seasons and the patterns of human life in every form. Each of these patterns could be called a song or a story. Poet Muriel Rukeyser said, "The universe is made of stories, not atoms." These basic patterns, these stories, the universal archetypes through which all life appears, can be seen and heard when we are still, centered, and awakened.

OUR INDIVIDUAL SONG
WITHIN THE GREAT SONG

As our vision opens we can ask extraordinary questions. What patterns and stories have been given to us in this life? What "individual" form have we taken this time? What are the myths and stories we have inherited, and what stories have we continued to follow in the face of the mystery?

Is our religion materialism or Marxism, is it hopeful or fatalistic, is it isolating or is it communal? Is ours a religion of kindness or of harsh justice? Do we follow a religion of sin and struggle, one of suffering and salvation, one of grace? What is the source of redemption in the story we follow?

We participate in the creation of our story. We can enact the personal myths of warrior, goddess, eternal adolescent, great mother, king or queen, master, slave, or servant of the divine. Is our life a story of riches or poverty, inwardly or outwardly? Are we the victim, the lost soul, the one who suffers, the prodigal son, the workhorse, the conqueror, the mediator, the nurturer, or the sage?

In all these stories we choose and are chosen. The circumstances of our life bring us certain motifs, tasks to fulfill, difficulties we must face, and lessons to learn. We turn these into our story, our song. As we listen deeply we can hear what part we have chosen, how we have created our identity in the face of the mystery. Yet we must ask: Is this who we are?

Spiritual practice is revolutionary. It allows us to step outside the limited view of personal identity, of culture, and of religion and experience more directly the great mystery of life, the great music of life.

The aim of meditation is to open us to this here and now. Alan Watts put it this way:

> We could say that meditation doesn't have a reason or doesn't have a purpose. In this respect it's unlike almost all other things we do except perhaps making music and dancing. When we make music we don't do it in order to reach a certain point, such as the end of the composition. If that were the purpose of music then obviously the fastest players would be the best. Also, when we are dancing we are not aiming to arrive at a particular place on the floor as in taking a journey. When we dance, the journey itself is the point, as when we play music the playing itself is the point. And exactly the same thing is true in meditation. Meditation is the discovery that the point of life is always arrived at in the immediate moment.

Here around us always is the mystery. This great song has joy and sorrow as its warp and woof. Between the mountains and valleys of birth and death, we find every voice and every possibility. Spiritual practice does not ask us to place more beliefs on top of our life. At its heart it asks us to wake up, to face life directly. In this way, our eyes and ears are open. Zen master Seung Sahn, on visiting the site of the Buddha's enlightenment in India, wrote:

> *Once a great man sat beneath the Bodhi tree.*
> *He saw the Eastern star, became enlightened.*
> *He absolutely believed his eyes,*
> *and he believed his ears, his nose, his tongue, body,*
> *and mind.*
> *The sky is blue, the earth is brown,*
> *and so he was awakened to the truth*
> *and attained freedom beyond birth and death.*

Buddhist practice offers us one of the greatest of human possibilities—the possibility of awakening. In this we must listen to the whole song, as Siddhartha did. We will see how difficult this can be. We will encounter all the stories we have held on to to protect ourselves from the suffering of life. We will face the stories of grief and fear, the contracted sense of self that withdraws from the inevitable hardship and sorrow of life. We will sense emptiness and loss in the lack of permanence of ourselves and all things. For a time in practice, all creation may appear to be a limited and painful story, one in which life is impermanent, filled with suffering, and difficult to bear. We may long to remove ourselves from its pains and vicissitudes. But these perspectives are only the first part of our awakening.

The second part of the great story of awakening is not about loss or pain but about finding the harmony of our own song within the great song. We can find peace and freedom in the face of the mystery of life. In awakening to this harmony, we discover a treasure hidden in each difficulty. Hidden in the inevitable impermanence and loss of life, its very instability, is the enormous power of creativity. In the process of change, there arises an abundance of new forms, new births, new possibilities, new expressions of art, music, and life-forms by the millions. It is only because everything is changing that such bountiful and boundless creativity exists.

The hidden treasure in the sufferings, sorrows, and pains of the world is compassion itself. Compassion is the heart's response to sorrow. We share in the beauty of life and in the ocean of tears. The sorrow of life is part of each of our hearts and part of what connects us with one another. It brings with it tenderness, mercy, and an all-embracing kindness that can touch every being.

For the Tibetans there is an ancient practice of becoming the Bodhisattva of Infinite Compassion, of transforming ourselves into a being with
a thousand arms and a merciful heart who reaches out to heal the sorrows
and bring comfort to all who are alive. In the end, it is not the sorrow
of the world alone that matters but our heart's response to it.

In the emptiness of all things—the magical insubstantial way in which
all things arise and vanish, lacking any abiding or fixed self—is hidden
the gift of nonseparateness. One scientist calculated that if we take a
deep breath today, in ninety-nine times out of a hundred it will contain
a molecule from Julius Caesar's dying breath. What is true physically is
true of our hearts and actions as well. Our lives are inseparable from our
environment, our species, our relations with the stream of all that exists.

Spiritual practice offers the possibility of discovering the greatest story
of all—that we are everything and nothing. It is possible to sense everything as connected in creativity and compassion and to rest in the midst
of it as a Buddha. All things are all a part of ourselves, and yet somehow
we are none of them and beyond them.

When T. S. Eliot wrote these simple words of prayer, "Teach us to
care and not to care," he captured the possibility of honoring the preciousness of each moment while knowing that it will soon dissolve in the
great song. We can hold each flowering of life with an open heart without
grasping, we can honor each of the notes of the great song destined to
arise and pass with all things.

The difference between one who is awakened and one who is not is
simply a question of whether or not the person grasps at a limited story.
So the Buddha said, "Those who are unawakened grasp their thoughts
and feelings, their body, their perceptions and consciousness, and take
them as solid, separate from the rest. Those who are awakened have the
same thoughts and feelings, perceptions, body, and consciousness, but
they are not grasped, not held, not taken as oneself."

A HUNDRED THOUSAND FORMS OF AWAKENING

When we do not grasp at the stories of our life, an extraordinary possibility
opens up for us to turn all of our stories, whether inherited or chosen
by us, into the path of a bodhisattva. We have already described the
bodhisattva as a being who takes form in every realm, in every possibility,
and uses each to develop boundless compassion and awaken the interconnected and liberated heart. Out of the mystery of all stories, in a

hundred thousand forms and circumstances, the bodhisattva vows to enter into them and bring awakening to all beings.

One of the greatest Buddhist masters said:

For as long as space endures and for as long as living beings remain, until then may I too abide in every form, bringing my heart to dispel the misery of the world.

This does not mean that we create a grand or inflated vision of ourselves. It is not "we," our "small self" as an individual, who will save the world. Rather it is a letting go of being anywhere else. We are willing to be just where we are, to enter all aspects of life, and to discover there is justice, compassion, patience, and virtue to be found in every realm.

There is no predetermined story for a bodhisattva to follow. To live as a bodhisattva is to touch the spirit of the Buddha within us and to allow that to shine through our own individual life. Buddhist history is filled with a thousand different accounts of how the bodhisattva spirit can manifest in the world. There are bodhisattvas everywhere. One of my teachers lived in a cave for many years, silently radiating compassion to the world. Another was a very wealthy businessman who also taught meditation retreats to tens of thousands of students worldwide. His master was a high-ranking cabinet minister in Burma who got the government officials in his offices to meditate at the start of each day. One of the greatest of modern Buddhist yogis and masters was a woman who lived a simple householder life in Calcutta with her daughter and grandchildren. She taught in her one-room apartment and gave amazing blessings to all who visited her. Another was a nurse who worked with the dying. Another a teacher of young children. Some were stern, some were humorous. Some lived out in the forests, others in monasteries and ashrams, others in the middle of great cities with ordinary jobs and ordinary families.

In all of them a spirit of wisdom and compassion ran through their actions. They acted from their Buddha nature, which connected them with all beings. They did not grasp their own personal stories but lived connected to the whole. Recently some red-robed Tibetan lamas visited New Mexico. A student offered them all hot-air balloon rides. But they arrived in the morning to find that there was room for but one monk to fly. A reporter covering the event asked the others if they were disappointed. "No." They smiled and continued, "He's going for all of us." For a bodhisattva there is joy in the happiness of all beings.

Through the spirit of the bodhisattva our identity shifts away from a small sense of self, from the stories that say: "I'm deficient." "I need that." "I'm angry." "I hope to get this." As these small ideas drop away, there arises a ground of trust that does not seek to control or possess life. Instead, as we become present for the mystery of it all, a great happiness and contentment arises. Our heart becomes more transparent, and the stories around us become clear.

We can acknowledge the stories from our parents, from the society around us, from our schools, from our mentors, from the media. We can see the suffering that arises when we are lost in them, grasping, unskillful, acting out a drama without understanding its lesson. Then we learn to listen as Siddhartha did—without binding ourselves to one particular story, without being only the victim or the conqueror, only spiritual or only materialistic—we can listen and discover how one breath affects the whole dance and how the whole dance around us affects each of our breaths. We can discover the possibility of stepping out of a story or of transforming the myth from one of sorrow to redemption, from one of difficulty to the triumph of compassion and forgiveness.

The awakened heart can answer the key question posed by Buddhagosa, the great Buddhist sage, "Who can untangle the tangle of this world?" We discover a miracle: Every creation of mind and heart can be transformed.

The work of the bodhisattva is to untangle the confusion and sorrows of the world. Discovering our compassionate heart can untangle our sorrow, awakening the eyes of wisdom can untangle our delusion. If you wonder what this transformation can mean for the world, remember Margaret Mead's statement, "Don't think that a small group of awakened individuals cannot change the world. Indeed, it is the only thing that ever has."

When we discover how we create the painful stories of our life, we can then learn to untangle them. In Kurt Vonnegut's novel *Slaughterhouse-Five*, there is a description of what happens when one night a World War II movie is accidentally shown backward.

American planes, full of holes and wounded men and corpses, took off backwards from an airfield in England. Over France, a few German fighter planes flew at them backwards, sucked bullets and shell fragments from some of the planes and crewmen. They did the same for wrecked American bombers on the ground, and those planes flew up backwards to join the formation.

The formation flew backwards over a German city that was in flames. The bombers opened their bomb bay doors, exerted miraculous magnetism which shrunk the fires, gathered them into cylindrical steel containers, and lifted the containers into the bellies of the planes. The containers were stored neatly in racks. . . . There were still a few wounded Americans, though, and some of the bombers were in bad repair. Over France, though, German fighters came up again, made everything and everybody as good as new.

When the bombers got back to the base, the steel cylinders were taken from the racks and shipped back to the United States, where factories were operating day and night, dismantling the cylinders, separating the dangerous contents into minerals. Touchingly, it was mainly women who did the work. The minerals were then shipped to specialists in remote areas. It was their business to put them into the ground, to hide them cleverly, so they would never hurt anybody ever again.

The sorrows created by the mind can be untangled. We can release our sorrows and open to that great song which is beyond all stories, to the dharma that is timeless. We can move through life fulfilling our part, yet somehow free in the midst of it all. When the stories of our life no longer bind us, we discover within them something greater. We discover that within the very limitations of form, of our maleness and femaleness, of our parenthood and our childhood, of gravity on the earth and the changing of the seasons, is the freedom and harmony we have sought for so long. Our individual life is an expression of the whole mystery, and in it we can rest in the center of the movement, the center of all worlds.

MEDITATION ON EQUANIMITY

Equanimity is a wonderful quality, a spaciousness and balance of heart. Although it grows naturally with our meditation practice, equanimity can also be cultivated in the same systematic way that we have used for loving-kindness and compassion. We can feel this possibility of balance in our hearts in the midst of all life when we recognize that life is not in our control. We are a small part of a great dance. Even though we may cultivate a boundless compassion for others and strive to alleviate suffering in the world, there will still be many situations we are unable to affect. The well-known serenity prayer says, "May I have the serenity to accept the things I cannot change, the courage to change the things I can, and the wisdom to know the difference." Wisdom recognizes that all beings are heir to their own karma, that they each act and receive the fruits of their actions. We can deeply love others and offer them assistance, but in the end they must learn for themselves, they must be the source of their own liberation. Equanimity combines an understanding mind together with a compassionate heart.

To cultivate equanimity, sit in a comfortable posture with your eyes closed. Bring a soft attention to your breath until your body and mind are calm. Then begin by reflecting on the benefit of a mind that has balance and equanimity. Sense what a gift it can be to bring a peaceful heart to the world around you. Let yourself feel an inner sense of balance and ease. Then begin repeating such phrases as, *May I be balanced and at peace.* Acknowledge that all created things arise and pass away: joys, sorrows, pleasant events, people, buildings, animals, nations, even whole civilizations. Let yourself rest in the midst of them. *May I learn to see the arising and passing of all nature with equanimity and balance. May I be open and balanced and peaceful.* Acknowledge that all beings are heirs to their own karma, that their lives arise and pass away according to conditions and deeds created by them. *May I bring compassion and equanimity to the events of the world. May I find balance and equanimity and peace.*

23

ENLIGHTENMENT IS INTIMACY WITH ALL THINGS

What a splendid way to move through the world, to bring our blessings to all that we touch. To honor, to bless, to welcome with the heart is never done in grand or monumental ways but in this moment, in the most immediate and intimate way.

Zen master Dogen, the founder of Soto Zen in Japan, declared, "To be enlightened is to be intimate with all things." The air we breathe, the wind that blows around us, the earth that we walk upon, the lives of others around us, the most intimate things of our lives, are the place of our sleep or of our awakening. As one Cambodian teacher of mine put it, "Spiritual practice is about eating, where we eat, what we eat, and how we eat. Often we try to eat other people but do not let them eat us, and the Buddha cries when he sees this suffering." In the end, we can see this either as a world where we all eat and are eaten or as a world where we all have an opportunity to feed one another.

In the beginning of our spiritual journey, we become aware that much of what we do is a way of seeking to love and to be loved. We began this book with an inquiry into the question, "Did I love well?" Perhaps the enlightenment of intimacy is the same as love. Yet love is mysterious. Is it something we can do? An old woman, a patient in the hospice run by the San Francisco Zen Center, had lived her last adult years homeless and on the streets. When she was taken in and cared for, she became curious about the spiritual life of the Zen community around her, and even though dying, she decided to practice the teachings of awakening and compassion. One morning the hospice director came to visit her. Perplexed, she said, "I've been thinking about all this talk of letting go and loving. It seems so important, but I can't figure which to do first. Should I let go or love?" Perhaps they are the same thing.

Love is mysterious. We don't know what it is, but we know when it is present. If we seek love, we must ask where it is to be found. It is here only in this moment. To love in the past is simply a memory. To love in the future is a fantasy. There is only one place where love can be found, where intimacy and awakening can be found, and that is in the present. When we live in our thoughts of the past and future, everything seems distant, hurried, or unfulfilled. The only place we can genuinely love a tree, the sky, a child, or our lover is in the here and now. Emily Dickinson wrote, " 'Til the first friend dies, we think ecstasy impersonal, but then discover that he was the cup from which we drank it, itself as yet unknown." Only in the intimacy of the timeless present can we awaken. This intimacy connects us to one another, allows us to belong, and in this belonging, we experience love. In this we move beyond our separateness, our contraction, our limited sense of ourselves.

If we investigate what keeps us from intimacy, what keeps us from love, we will discover it is always an expectation, a hope, a thought, or a fantasy. It is the same expectation that keeps us from awakening. Awakening is not far away; it is nearer than near. As it says in the Buddhist texts, "Awakening is not something newly discovered; it has always existed. There is no need to seek or follow the advice of others. Learn to listen to that voice within yourself just here and now. Your body and mind will become clear and you will realize the unity of all things. Do not doubt the possibilities because of the simplicity of these teachings. If you can't find the truth right where you are, where else do you think you will find it?"

There are many words for awakening and many expressions of love offered to us in great spiritual teachings. There are expressions of love in action as enlightened activity. There are expressions of enlightenment as silence, and love as heartfelt understanding. There are expressions of awakening as freedom in the realms of form and as that which lies beyond all form. In Buddhism enlightenment is called the unconditioned, that which shines naturally when the heart is not entangled in the forces of grasping, hatred, and ignorance. When the heart is free of these forces, true intimacy and love exist. There is an awakening in the midst of all things, a love that can touch and include all things, a freedom and fearlessness that can enter every realm. In this we do not remove ourselves from life but rest in the very center of it. In this we are able to be intimate with all things.

There is a tribe in east Africa in which the art of true intimacy is fostered even before birth. In this tribe, the birth date of a child is not counted from the day of its physical birth nor even the day of conception, as in other village cultures. For this tribe the birth date comes the first time the child is a thought in its mother's mind. Aware of her intention to conceive a child with a particular father, the mother then goes off to sit alone under a tree. There she sits and listens until she can hear the song of the child that she hopes to conceive. Once she has heard it, she returns to her village and teaches it to the father so that they can sing it together as they make love, inviting the child to join them. After the child is conceived, she sings it to the baby in her womb. Then she teaches it to the old women and midwives of the village, so that throughout the labor and at the miraculous moment of birth itself, the child is greeted with its song. After the birth all the villagers learn the song of their new member and sing it to the child when it falls or hurts itself. It is sung in times of triumph, or in rituals and initiations. This song becomes a part of the marriage ceremony when the child is grown, and at the end of life, his or her loved ones will gather around the deathbed and sing this song for the last time.

Hearing such a story brings a yearning for such intimacy, to be held and listened to so deeply. This listening presence is at the heart of meditation and true spiritual life. To be present with mindful awareness is itself an act of profound intimacy. Each act of our life has this possibility, the mystery of our own breath, the touching of our own body, the movement and voices of those around us. This simple presence is both the beginning and the culmination of spiritual practice.

Our capacity for intimacy is built on deep respect, a presence that allows what is true to express itself, to be discovered. Intimacy can arise in any moment; it is an act of surrender, a gift that excludes nothing. In Buddhist marriage ceremonies, I speak about this quality of intimacy and how it grows as we learn to stay connected with ourselves and respectful of those around us. I teach new couples the mantra of intimacy.

No matter what they hoped to get from one another, how they imagined it should be, what they did not expect to encounter, the mantra has only one teaching, "This too, this too."

To learn intimacy is not an easy thing. Growing up in a divided culture, marked by our wounds and longing, it is hard to be present, hard to be respectful. Like following the breath or walking in meditation step by step, it is learned again and again as we relinquish the fears and conditions that keep us from one another. These barriers and fears, the memories of our past sufferings arise when we come close to one another, when we come close to the mystery of the moment. Many times we will feel our hesitation and tentativeness, a holding back. Yet this, too, can be touched with our intimate attention. And then in a moment we can let go of ourselves, be open and be here, awake and wholly present. Over and over when the world offers itself to us for our awakening, all we have to do is meet it.

As Rumi says:

Today is like every other day, we wake up empty
and frightened. Don't open the door to the study
and begin reading. Take down the dulcimer.

Let the beauty we love be what we do.
There are hundreds of ways to kneel and kiss the ground.

Whenever we stop to kiss the earth, we recognize how unique is each man and woman and each day before us. Never again will we see it in this way. In intimacy we discover a beauty and grace that makes all things worthwhile. Because life is so tentative, it becomes precious. Again Rumi reminds us not to sit with sorrow alone.

When you go to a garden,
do you look at thorns or flowers?
Spend more time with roses and jasmine.

As the capacity for presence grows in us we discover an ease of the heart with all things.

One great teacher in India would remind his students of this with each of the difficulties they would report to him, difficulties in meditation, difficulties in work or relationship. He would listen very kindly and then smile at them and say, "I hope you're enjoying them." In this same spirit, "There are two ways to navigate through this world," wrote E. B. White.

"One is to improve life and the other is to enjoy life." It is a paradox, for both enjoyment and improvement are necessary. Often enjoyment is forgotten in our quest for spiritual awakening. To find true joy we must have passed through our sorrows and come to accept the whole of life into our hearts. Then a deep and genuine joy arises.

André Gide writes of this:

> Know that joy is rarer, more difficult and more
> beautiful than sadness. Once you make this all-
> important discovery, you must embrace joy as a moral
> obligation.

When we become intimate with all things, we discover rest, well-being, and wholeness in this very body. We recognize that we, and all life around us, are supposed to be here, that we belong here as much as the trees and the sun and the turning earth. There comes a healing, an opening, and a grace. The harmony of all things arises for us like the wisdom of Dame Julian of Norwich, who so beautifully declared, "All shall be well and all manner of things shall be well." In intimacy we discover a profound sense of belonging and wholeness that allows us to touch all that we encounter.

When I first practiced as a monk in the forests of Thailand, nearly twenty-five years ago, we were trained to bow three times upon entering and leaving the temple. Bowing was a new experience for me. Then I was instructed to bow when I entered and exited the dining hall, the teachers' quarters, my own hut. Finally I was taught it is proper for a monk to kneel and bow three times when he encounters a monk who is senior to him. Being newly ordained this meant bowing to every monk I met. At first this was difficult. There were monks I respected and honored who were easy to bow to, but at other times I found myself kneeling and bowing to monks I thought ignorant, proud, or unworthy. To bow to some of these fellows simply because they had been ordained a month or two before me rubbed my pride the wrong way. However, I continued to bow in the temple, in my hut, and to all of the monks who presented themselves to me. After some time I felt the pain of my own criticism and how it kept me separate from them. I began to look for something which was beautiful or noble or worthy in each person I met. Then I began to enjoy bowing. I would bow to every monk, to the temples, to all my brothers and sisters, to the trees, and to the rocks. Bowing became a beautiful way of being.

When we have become intimate with ourselves, we are able to bow and to bless all that surrounds us. Yeats as a poet struggled for years with his art, with unrequited love. Then at age fifty, sitting in a coffee shop in London, there came a great illumination in which he found that all that matters is that we can bless and be blessed.

> *My fiftieth year had come and gone,*
> *I sat, a solitary man,*
> *In a crowded London shop,*
> *An open book, an empty cup*
> *On the marble tabletop.*
>
> *While on the shop and street I gazed,*
> *My body of a sudden blazed!*
> *And twenty minutes more or less*
> *It seemed so great, my happiness,*
> *That I was blessed—and could bless.*

To discover the capacity to bless whatever is in front of us, this is the enlightenment that is intimate with all things. It is a freedom and happiness with no cause, a gift we bring to each moment and each encounter.

Once when Kalu Rinpoche, an eighty-year-old Tibetan master, visited in Boston, he was taken to the New England Aquarium, which is filled with colorful sea creatures. Kalu Rinpoche enjoyed seeing all these wonderful forms of life, and before he left each tank, he would tap very softly on the glass because he could not read the sign in English that told him not to. Then he would recite a sacred mantra, *"Om, Mani Padme Hum,"* and peer into the tank for one last time before moving on to the next tank of creatures. After some time a student asked him, "What are you doing, Rinpoche, when you tap on the tanks like that?" and he smiled and said, "I'm trying to get the attention of the beings within, and then I bless them that they, too, may be liberated."

What a splendid way to move through the world, to bring our blessings to all that we touch. To learn how to bless, to honor, to listen with respect, to welcome with the heart, is a great art indeed. It is never done in grand or monumental ways but in this moment, in the most immediate and intimate way.

In the last year of his life another great Tibetan teacher, Karmapa, met with some American guests in a royal receiving room of his palacelike temple in Sikkim. Karmapa was a spiritual guide for a community of hundreds of thousands. He was also ill, yet he graciously made time to receive as many visitors as he could. My friends who visited him found him tremendously warm and receptive. He spoke with them, encouraged them, and blessed them. They felt wonderful. When they left, one remarked, "I felt like I just had a conversation with my closest friend." For Karmapa each visitor was his best friend and in each moment there was nothing else to do but care for and bless that which was in front of him.

It is in the intimacy of each moment that all of spiritual life is fulfilled. Do not seek the Buddha somewhere else. One Hasidic rabbi said, "I did not go to my master to learn his words of wisdom, but to see how he tied and untied his shoes."

My wife, two journalist friends, and I interviewed the Dalai Lama for National Public Radio several years ago. Like Karmapa, he was enormously busy as a spiritual leader and as the head of the Tibetan government in exile, but he greeted us graciously and served us tea himself. He patiently answered all of our questions, especially focusing on the teachings about spirituality and social responsibility. Then he asked if there was anything further he could do for us. "No," we answered. "Don't you want to take my picture?" he inquired. "Yes!" We all remembered. We had brought several cameras with us, but in the excitement of recording our interview, we had forgotten. The Dalai Lama then suggested that we give our cameras to his attendant so that we all could be in the picture together. He stood up and put his arms around us, two on each side. We were all grinning from ear to ear while the pictures were taken. Then when the photography was done, he grasped my hand and turned to me. Since he knows that I am a Buddhist teacher and had visited and lectured at one of our centers in Massachusetts, I expected him to ask how the teaching was going, you know, "How's business?" because, after all, we work for the same company. But he didn't. Instead, he squeezed my hand and looked at me carefully and said, "You're so skinny. You should eat more!" This was the blessing of the Dalai Lama.

To live a path with heart, a life committed to awakening, we, too, must care for whatever we encounter, however difficult or beautiful, and bring to it our presence, our heart, in a great intimacy. We will encounter many marvels in seeking our true way. Then, like the great bodhisattva of Zen who adventured into the forest to find the missing ox and in the process discovered his own true nature, we can return, as it's said, to enter the world with bliss-bestowing hands. "I enter the marketplace with my wine bottle and staff. I enter the shops and crowds, and all whom I look upon become enlightened."

I hope that this book and the practice of wakefulness, compassion, and intimacy in it will bring blessings to your life, that you will have silence as a blessing, understanding as a blessing, forgiveness as a blessing, and that you, too, will bring your heart and your hands to bless all around you.

As Zen poet Basho reminds us,

The temple bell stops
But the sound keeps coming out of the flowers.

APPENDIX

INSIGHT MEDITATION TEACHERS CODE OF ETHICS

Insight Meditation teachers from America and Europe have held regular meetings since 1975. Over the years we have become more aware of the responsibilities held by us as teachers and the care that such a role requires. In Asian Buddhism the conduct of teachers who are monks has been governed by 227 vows and strict Asian custom. Now in the West, there is a large Buddhist community led by lay teachers.

All of us recognize that the foundation of spiritual life rests upon our mindful and caring relationship to the life around us. We acknowledge that without monastic vows and Asian customs, we have a need for clear Western lay guidelines. In keeping with this understanding, and for the long-term benefit of ourselves and the community at large, we, as teachers, agree to continue to uphold the five basic Buddhist training precepts we have taught for so long. Furthermore, in the discussions that led to this agreement, we have refined these precepts to make them appropriate to our role as teachers of the dharma at this particular time in history and in this specific cultural setting. As Insight Meditation teachers in the West, we have established the following guidelines for ourselves.

(1) **We undertake the precept of refraining from killing.**
In undertaking this precept we acknowledge the interconnection of all beings and our respect for all life. We agree to refine our understanding of not killing and nonharming in all our actions. We will seek to understand the implications of this precept in such difficult areas as abortion, euthanasia, and the killing of pests. While some of us recommend vegetarianism and others do not, we all commit ourselves to fulfilling this precept in the spirit of reverence for life.

(2) **We undertake the precept of refraining from stealing.**
We agree to not take that which does not belong to us and to respect the property of others. We agree to bring consciousness to the use of all of the earth's resources in a respectful and ecological way. We agree to be honest in our dealings with money and not to misappropriate money committed to dharma projects. We agree to offer teachings without favoritism in regard to students' financial circumstances.

(3) **We undertake the precept of refraining from false speech.**
We agree to speak that which is true and useful and to refrain from gossip in our community. We agree to cultivate conscious and clear communication, and to cultivate the quality of loving-kindness and honesty as the basis of our speech.

(4) **We undertake the precept of refraining from sexual misconduct.**
We agree to avoid creating harm through sexuality and to avoid sexual exploitation or adultery. Teachers with vows of celibacy will live according to their vows. Married teachers will honor their vows and refrain from adultery. All teachers agree not to use their teaching role to exploit their authority and position in order to assume a sexual relationship with a student.

Because several single teachers in our community have developed partnerships and marriages with former students, we acknowledge that such a healthy relationship can be possible, but that great care and sensitivity are needed. We agree that in this case the following guidelines are crucial:

(a) A sexual relationship is never appropriate between teachers and students.

(b) During retreats or formal teaching, any intimation of future student-teacher romantic or sexual relationship is inappropriate.

(c) If a genuine and committed relationship interest develops over time between an unmarried teacher and a former student, the student must clearly be under the guidance of another teacher. Such a relationship must be approached with restraint and sensitivity—in no case should it occur immediately after retreat. A minimum time period of three months or longer from the last formal teaching between them, and a clear understanding from both parties that the student-teacher relationship has ended must be coupled with a conscious commitment to enter into a relationship that brings no harm to either party.

(5) **We undertake the precept of refraining from intoxicants that cause heedlessness or loss of awareness.**
It is clear that substance abuse is the cause of tremendous suffering. We agree that there should be no use of intoxicants during retreats or while on retreat premises. We agree not to abuse or misuse intoxicants at any time. We agree that if any teacher has a drug or alcohol addiction problem, it should be immediately addressed by the community.

ETHICS COMMITTEE

Over two thousand years ago in the Patimokkha (Code of Discipline), the Buddha established a clear set of procedures to follow when monks and nuns broke their precepts. In minor cases, these included formal apologies, the admission of misconduct, and the retaking of precepts. In more serious cases a meeting was convened of twenty elders who would discuss the misconduct and set periods of suspension and practices for reinstatement. A second meeting would be required to allow the return of suspended members to the community. In the very gravest cases, monks and nuns were suspended from the order for life.

Just as in monastic life, where these groups of elders are established to deal with problems and misconduct, we recognize the need to establish such a council in our own community to deal with such difficulties. We agree to create an ongoing Ethics Committee on each coast, comprised of four members who are widely respected for their integrity:

(1) a teacher (chosen by the teachers)
(2) a board member (chosen by the board)
(3) a staff member (chosen by the staff)
(4) a general community member (chosen by the board).

If a teacher's ethical conduct is questioned, then
(1) Members of the community who are concerned are requested to go directly to that teacher to discuss and try to solve the difficulty.
(2) If this proves unsatisfactory, or if the issue is of major concern,

then the community members are requested to bring the concern to the Ethics Committee, which can be contacted through the Insight Meditation Center offices.

(3) The committee will meet with the teacher and/or the concerned party (parties) either together or separately to address and resolve the problem or to decide, if necessary, any steps toward further resolution.

(4) For matters of major concern that might require the suspension of teaching at our institutions, the Ethics Committee will consult with the general Insight Meditation teachers' body in jointly setting the best course of action.

(5) The Ethics Committee in conjunction with the teachers' body will develop a set of guidelines for responding to ethical problems, based on the monks' rules of order. These guidelines will be made known to the community.

Furthermore, the Ethics Committee, in conjunction with the teachers' body, will also recommend ethical guidelines for staff and board members in the fulfillment of their responsibilities to these organizations.

In creating and further developing these guidelines, we hope to support and include our whole community in a continuing refinement and investigation of ethical living. We do not intend the Ethics Committee to be some kind of moralistic body that seeks out bad teachers or students to punish them. We all jointly hold a responsibility to create an environment of integrity. We invite all students and staff members to help us create this environment and hope that any feelings and concerns can be shared among us all.

We hope that the issues that finally come before the Ethics Committee will be infrequent and easily resolved. By articulating and clarifying the basic Buddhist precepts and our commitment as teachers to follow and refine them, we are honoring a life of virtue and the liberation of all beings. As it is traditionally chanted after the recitation of the precepts:

The five precepts of nonharming
Are a vehicle for our happiness,
A vehicle for our good fortune,
A vehicle for liberation for all.
May our virtue shine forth.

A TREASURY OF BOOKS

The following are a few wonderful and related books that can bring additional light on the topics of each chapter.

Chapter 1—Did I Love Well?
Life After Life, Raymond Moody
Man's Search for Meaning, Viktor E. Frankl
Stories of the Spirit, Stories of the Heart, Christina Feldman and Jack Kornfield

Chapter 2—Stopping the War
In the Footsteps of Gandhi, Catherine Ingram
Peace Is Every Step, Thich Nhat Hanh

Chapter 3—Take the One Seat
The Myth of Freedom, Chogyam Trungpa
A Still Forest Pool, Jack Kornfield and Paul Breiter
Zen Mind, Beginner's Mind, Shunryu Suzuki Roshi

Chapter 4—Necessary Healing
Full Catastrophe Living, John Kabat-Zin
Healing Into Life and Death, Stephen Levine
Legacy of the Heart: The Spiritual Advantages of a Painful Childhood,
  Wayne Muller

Chapter 5—Training the Puppy: Mindfulness of Breathing
The Experience of Insight, Joseph Goldstein
Living Buddhist Masters, Jack Kornfield

Chapter 6—Turning Straw into Gold
Cutting Through Spiritual Materialism, Chogyam Trungpa
A Little Book on the Human Shadow, Robert Bly

Chapter 7—Naming the Demons
Seeking the Heart of Wisdom, Joseph Goldstein and Jack Kornfield
Transformation and Healing, Thich Nhat Hanh

Chapter 8—Difficult Problems and Insistent Visitors
Grace Unfolding, Greg Johanson and Ron Kurtz
The Pearl Beyond Price, A. H. Almaas
The Void, A. H. Almaas

Chapter 9—The Spiritual Roller Coaster: Kundalini and Other Side
  Effects
Spiritual Emergency, Stan and Christina Grof
The Stormy Search for the Self, Stan and Christina Grof
The Tiger's Cave, Trevor Leggett

Chapter 10—Expanding and Dissolving the Self: Dark Night and Rebirth
Beyond the Brain, Stan Grof
The Path of Purification, Buddhagosa (distributed by Wisdom
  Publications)
The Progress of Insight, Mahasi Sayadaw

Chapter 11—Searching for the Buddha: A Lamp Unto Ourselves
Freedom of the Known, J. Krishnamurti
The Zen Teachings of Rinzai, translated by Irmgard Schloegl

Chapter 12—Accepting the Cycles of Spiritual Life
Childhood and Society, Eric Erickson
Seasons of a Man's Life, William Levinson

Chapter 13—No Boundaries to the Sacred
Meeting the Shadow, Connie Zweig and Jeremiah Abrams
The Miracle of Mindfulness, Thich Nhat Hanh

Chapter 14—No Self or True Self?
Chuang Tzu, Thomas Merton
I Am That, Nisargadatta Maharaj
The Teachings of Huang Po, translated by John Blofeld

Chapter 15—Generosity, Codependence, and Fearless Compassion
Codependent No More, Melody Beattie
Compassion in Action, Ram Dass and Mirabai Bush
The Sacred Path of the Warrior, Chogyam Trungpa

Chapter 16—You Can't Do It Alone: Finding and Working with a Teacher
Buddhist America, Don Morreale
Journey of Awakening: A Meditator's Guidebook, Ram Dass

Chapter 17—Psychotherapy and Meditation
Body Centered Therapy, Ron Kurtz
The Only Dance There Is, Ram Dass
Transformations of Consciousness, Jack Engler, Dan Brown, and Ken
    Wilbur

Chapter 18—The Emperor's New Clothes: Problems with Teachers
The Addictive Organization, Anne Wilson Schaef
Power in the Helping Professions, Adolf Guggenbuhl-Craig
The Wrong Way Home, Arthur Deikman

Chapter 19—Karma: The Heart Is Our Garden
Rebirth as Doctrine and Experience, Francis Story (Buddhist Publication
    Society)

Chapter 20—Expanding Our Circle: An Undivided Heart
How Can I Help? Ram Dass and Paul Gorman
The Path of Compassion, Fred P. Eppsteiner

Staying Alive: The Psychology of Human Survival, Roger Walsh
World as Lover, World as Self, Joanna Macy

Chapter 21—Spiritual Maturity
Care of the Soul, Thomas Moore
Toward the Fullness of Life, Arnaud Desjardin

Chapter 22—The Great Song
The Perennial Philosophy, Aldous Huxley
The Power of Myth, Joseph Campbell

Chapter 23—Enlightenment Is Intimacy with All Things
Gratefulness, The Heart of Prayer, Brother David Stendl-Rast
Small Is Beautiful, E. F. Schumacher
Practice of the Wild, Gary Snyder

Poetry of the Awakened Heart
  The Enlightened Heart, Stephen Mitchell
  The Kabir Book, translated by Robert Bly
  One Robe, One Bowl, Ryo Kan, translated by John Stevens
  Open Secret, Rumi, translated by Coleman Barks
  Selected Poems of Rilke, translated by Robert Bly

GLOSSARY

bodhisattva: 1) A being committed to the path of awakening, 2) a Buddha-to-be, 3) an enlightened Buddha figure who serves all beings.

Buddha nature: The luminous pure Buddha-like quality inherent in all beings; our true nature.

chakras: The psycho-spiritual energy centers found in the human body.

deva: An angel or heavenly being.

dharma: 1) Ultimate truth, reality, and universal law, 2) Buddha's teachings revealing these truths, 3) all physical and mental elements, 4) our destiny or spiritual path.

jhana: States of meditative absorption; refined states of consciousness produced by meditative concentration.

karma: The universal law of cause and effect; the volition behind each action, which produces favorable or unfavorable results in the future.

kensho: Satori. A powerful moment of awakening or enlightenment.

koan: In Zen, a contemplative question or puzzle that cannot be solved with the rational mind.

kriyas: Spontaneous movements and sounds that can arise when meditative energy is released in the body.

lama: A Tibetan spiritual teacher, master, or sage.

maha mudra: 1) Universal awakened consciousness, 2) practices that lead to awakening to this universal consciousness.

makyo: Illusion, the unreal visions and images that arise during meditation.

nirvana: The cessation of suffering, the highest peace, the unconditioned.

nondual: The teaching and perception of the fundamental unity or oneness of all things.

pseudo-nirvana: An initial rapturous stage of meditation that can be mistaken for nirvana.

Rinzai school: A school of Zen, founded by Lin Chi, which uses koans and strong determination to attain deep realization and enlightenment.

samadhi: 1) Concentration, 2) states of high concentration, 3) (Hindu) enlightenment.

samsara: The beginningless cycles of birth and death; the cycling of all things in the universe.

sangha: 1) Spiritual community, 2) the ordained community of monks and nuns, 3) a community of all those who have attained some degree of awakening.

sankaras: 1) Conditioned tendencies of mind and body, 2) all created phenomena.

satori: Kensho, a powerful moment of awakening or enlightenment.

satsang: Spiritual community.

shikan-taza: The Zen practice of "just sitting," a meditative presence without any goal.

Soto school: Japanese Zen school that emphasizes "just sitting," no goal; awakening to our true nature just now.

Sufi: The Islamic mystical tradition.

tantra: Buddhist and Hindu tradition of practice that directly transforms the energy of passion and aggression into spiritual awakening.

Tao: The universal law, the force of all life, the way of nature.

Theravada Buddhism: The Buddhist tradition of the "Elders"; the school of Buddhism still practiced in India and Southeast Asia today.

transpersonal: The spiritual dimensions of human experience; beyond the personal.

vipassana: Insight Meditation; the meditative practice of mindful attention.

yoga: Hindu system of meditation; a spiritual practice that can take many forms such as hatha yoga (yoga of the body), raja yoga (yoga of the mind), karma yoga (the yoga of selfless service), etc.

yogi: One who undertakes a spiritual discipline or practice.

PERMISSIONS

ABOUT THE AUTHOR

JACK KORNFIELD was trained as a Buddhist monk in Thailand, Burma, and India and has taught meditation worldwide since 1974. He is one of the key teachers to introduce Theravada Buddhist practice to the West. For many years his work has been focused on integrating and bringing alive the great Eastern spiritual teachings in an accessible way for Western students and Western society. Jack also holds a Ph.D. in clinical psychology. He is a husband, father, psychotherapist, and founding teacher of the Insight Meditation Society and the Spirit Rock Center. His books include *Seeking the Heart of Wisdom, A Still Forest Pool,* and *Stories of the Spirit, Stories of the Heart.*